Dedicated to my

Father, late Gouranga Chandra Paul

Mother, late Surabala Paul

and

Wife, late Banadevi Paul

Bankim Literature

The Sprouting of Western Literary Criticism in Bengal

Krishna Ranjan Paul

ATLANTIC

PUBLISHERS & DISTRIBUTORS (P) LTD

Published by
ATLANTIC
PUBLISHERS & DISTRIBUTORS (P) LTD
7/22, Ansari Road, Darya Ganj, New Delhi-110002
Phones : +91-11-40775252, 40775214, 23273880, 23275880
Fax: +91-11-23285873
Web: www.atlanticbooks.com
E-mail: orders@atlanticbooks.com

Printed & bound in India by Atlantic Print Services

Preface

Bankimchandra entered the field of literature with the publication of his first novel in English, *Rajmohan's Wife* (1864), but he soon turned to writing in Bengali and wrote historical romances, philosophical novels, social and domestic novels of varying length, and miscellaneous essays on diverse topics. He also enriched literary criticism by enunciating literary principles and inspired volumes of criticism by his works. Leaving aside the experimental period in which he set his hands on poems, prose, and drama upto the publication of *Rajmohan's Wife*, Bankimchandra's intensive literary career spread over almost thirty years during which he dominated the literary scene in Bengal. He has been acknowledged by posterity as the greatest literary figure prior to Rabindranath Tagore.

Bankim criticism began in the year 1865 after the publication of *Durgeshnandini,* his first Bengali novel, and it reached its culmination which in its turn contributed to Bankim criticism. Thus, it set modern literary patterns and opened new horizons in Bankim criticism, and the trend has continued unabated. But the seventy-three years of Bankim criticism in the pre-centenary period had distinctive characteristics of its own. There were evolutionary forces at work behind the growth and development of Bankim critics, and much of the archetype of later criticism was formulated during this period. Considering this, the pre-Centenary period needs to be especially investigated for proper appraisal of Bankim criticism. Moreover, this period has also a special significance in the history of Bengali literary criticism because Bankim criticism forms not only the vital but also the major portion of Bengali literary criticism. It was through the criticism of Bankim's works that Bengali literary criticism crossed its infancy and reached the period of youthfulness. But, a comprehensive research is yet to be undertaken on this vital period of Bengali literary criticism, although there is no dearth of piecemeal approaches. In order to fulfill the long-felt need, this noble mission has been undertaken to conduct a thorough investigation into these seventy-three years of Bankim criticism.

The scope of study extends to critical estimates of Bankim's prose works only keeping out of purview all the poetical criticisms since prose is universally considered the most suitable medium of literary flavour. Also, non-literary appraisals have been left out of discussion in order to keep the volume of the book within reasonable limits, though, of course, references have been made wherever necessary to those in order to highlight the evolutionary trend of Bankim criticism. *Rajmohan's Wife,* Bankim's only English novel has been excluded because of its language, while criticism on Bankim's early poems and *Muchiram Gurer Jibancharit* have also been left out. In this limited scope outlined above, the precursors and predecessors in the field of Bankim criticism have been viewed both against the background of their times, as well as from the modern standpoint for a correct assessment of Bankim criticism during the period under study. It needs to be mentioned here that in course of the whole discussion on Bankim criticism I have mainly concentrated on the criticisms of Bankim's literary works and have generally kept out of purview the discussion on the many faceted personality of Bankimchandra, the great man of letters of all times.

The sources of this study are spread over the various periodicals and books published during this period. There is a time gap which separates the pre-centenary period from the present day, and the sources of the study lay scattered over different old libraries at Calcutta and the surrounding areas which I have visited for the collection of materials. It is found that most of the early publications have already become unreadable, and unless proper steps are taken for preservation of these valuable historical documents, these will soon pass into oblivion. I have come across the names of some critics who had contributed to Bankim criticism, but, in spite of my best efforts, I failed to trace the sources. Moreover, time had spoilt some critical essays in such a way that these have become illegible, for which no assessment could be made.

The aim of this study is to throw a flood of light on the evolution of Bankim criticism, the shape that Bankim criticism assumed before the Centenary Year and especially how the different methods of criticism and schools took shape during the period. The findings of the study are intended to benefit all future researchers on Bankim criticism.

For the purpose the investigation has been divided into the following chapters.

The introduction to the investigation forms the subject matter of the first chapter of this volume. Here, an elaborate discussion has been made about the growth and development of Bengali literary criticism with special reference to the evolution of Bankim criticism in historical perspective, keeping in view the formulation of theories and their application, and initiation and furtherance of various methods and schools of criticism. The anonymous criticisms have been given their rightful place here. The role of *Bangadarshan* has been properly evaluated. Bankim's own comments about his works which served as source materials to various critics have also been included in the introduction, while additions and alterations made in subsequent additions of novels, and their impact on the critics have also been adequately highlighted. As the book is being written in English, I have included the general and familiar trends of Bengali literary criticism in the introductions for correct appraisal of the background of each critic.

The second chapter deals with the development of Bankim criticism centering round the novel *Durqeshnandini*. The history of Bankim criticism of *Kapalkundala* forms the subject matter of the third chapter, while the fourth puts in record all the criticism of the major critics on *Mrinalini*. The literary evolution of *Bishabriksha* during the period under study has been embodied in the fifth chapter. The sixth chapter deals with the growth of Bankim criticism on *Indira*, *Jugalanguriya*, *Rajani*, and *Radharani*, which are all novels of short length, and on which only a limited number of discussions has been made by few critics. An elaborate discussion on the development of Bankim criticism around *Chandrashekhar* has been incorporated in the seventh chapter. The series of criticisms on *Krishnakanter Uil* have been placed in the eighth chapter. The next chapter pertains to the evolution of literary criticism of *Rajsingha,* although it drew much less attention of the critics in comparison to other novels. A separate chapter has been devoted to it considering the unique distinctiveness of the evaluation and treatment. The tenth chapter deals with the growth of Bankim criticism centering round *Anandamath*. *Devi Chaudhurani,* and *Sitaram*. These novels have not been extensively discussed like *Bishabriksha* and the number of contributing critics being few. All these criticisms have been put together in this chapter. The eleventh chapter deals with the criticisms on miscellaneous prose and the next chapter partakes the conclusion of the study with the major trends and period divisions. Also, development of several schools along with their characteristic features have been highlighted.

During this period of seventy-three years (1865-1937) of Bankim criticism, various critics belonging to different walks of life have exercised their intellect to evaluate Bankim's works from diverse standpoints. All the major literary critics have been brought under discussion in the aforesaid chapters while a list of minor critics has been included in Appendices.

The methodology followed in the investigation is a combination of inductive, deductive, historical, and comparative methods. The entire discussion of all the major critics has been critically assessed. These critical estimates have been substantiated by quotations from original texts, where ever necessary, with their English renderings. These citations have been given in Roman alphabets.

An assessment of each critic to the development of Bankim criticism has been aesthetically highlighted keeping in view the historical factors. The impact of one critic on another and the similarity and dissimilarity that exists have been discussed and appropriately summed up.

The study is supported by references in the footnotes at the bottom of each page, and an extensive Bibliography has also been incorporated at the end.

In order to collect materials related to Bankimchandra and his works, I have to work in various libraries in and around Kolkata, such as National Library, Joykoshore Library (Uttarapara), Bangiya Sahitya Parishad Library, Vidyabhusan Library (Subashgram), Gauhati University Library (Gauhati), Ramkrishnanagar College Library, besides other libraries. I am grateful to the Librarians of these libraries for giving me scope to work in their libraries. I would also like to put on record my thankfulness to the authorities of the weekly *Desh* to allow me to consult their old files. I am also indebted to the Librarian, British Council, Kolkata, who allowed me to consult English Books in the library. In the present critical assessment, I have drawn freely from various books, and duly acknowledged my indebtedness by mentioning the titles of the books with their authors in the footnotes.

I must acknowledge with gratitude the encouragement and help I have received form many quarters during the long period of my project work. My colleague Dr. Mala Sharma, HoD, English, Ramkrishna Nagar College, deserves special mention for her generous help. My loving daughters, Rituparna Paul (Rudragupta) and Rithika Paul (Dutta) (Gold Medalist), must be mentioned here for their spontaneous support and inspiration. I would be failing in my duty if I do not mention the name of Late Dr. A.K. Duttachowdhury, M.A. (Triple), Ph.D., the former Principal of Ramkrishna Nagar College, who encouraged me from the very beginning to proceed with my work and carry on the investigation in spite of many difficulties that came on the way.

Specifically, I am grateful to Prof. (Dr.) Dipak Sen, retired HoD of Bengali, Gauhati University, and his wife Mrs. Chaitali Sen for their continuous help during the period of my investigation.

Krishna Ranjan Paul

Contents

Abbreviations

B.S.	Bengali Shakabda/Bengali year
B.S.P.	Bangiya Sahitya Parisad
C.F.	Compare
C.U.	Calcutta University
Eg.	As for example
Ibid.	In the same place
i.e.	That is
Op. Cit.	In the work cited

1
Introduction

I

At the outset, a brief discussion on the theoretical backround of Bengali literary criticism is essential in order to understand the role of the critic and the meaning and importance of literary criticism. For the purpose concrete methods and schools of criticism are necessary for study. Otherwise the investigation on the evaluation of Bankim criticism will remain inadequate.

The critic plays the most significant role in the world of literature. "Criticism normally casts a retrospective light on what we have already read."[1] Study of literature leads to criticism and these do not really accumulate as a mass in an appreciative form and structure.[2] As a matter of fact, the critic's first task is to help the readers to read for themselves[3] and he stands like an interpreter between the inspired and uninspired.[4] But the critic acts not only as an estimator, but also as a legislator, i.e. he not only instructs but also dictates.[5]

Although the role of critic is universally acknowledged as an interpreter there are two distinct trends or currents of criticism. Classical versus romantic. There was a time when great debates and controversies centred on the two trends, but in course of time these debates have softened down and the renowned critics have accepted this dichotomy of criticism i.e. classicism and romanticism. They have agreed that although there is no clear cut demarcation between classicism and romantic, and most of the renowned critics have represented both the trends according to their temperaments.[6]

Generally speaking classicism refers to adherence to classical principles and tastes and scholarship in classical literature, as well as an adherence to form, with general effect of regularity, simplicity and restraint.[7] The main features of romanticism are clearly distinguished from classicism.[8] It denotes that kind of criticism that is centred upon the inner[9] rather than upon the outer world and tries to convey the feeling of the writer in a manner uniquely expressive of his experience and personality and not in traditional formal features. A romantic critic does not strive for clarity and restraint of the classicist. He gives predominance to imagination,[10] the mystery and inspiration which sustain works of literature through freedom of expression.[11]

Earlier there was no classical tradition of literary criticism in Bengal. It was a product of modern age under the impact of western culture. There were interpreters of Sanskrit literature who were known as rhetoricians (Alankarik) and commentators (Tikakar).[12]

Thus in Bengali literary criticism the classicist referred to those who adhered to the principles of Sanskrit literature and advocated rigidity in form as laid down by the Sanskrit Alankariks.[13] The romanticist denoted those who went deep into the inner meaning of the work highlighting mysteries and glorifying strangeness and human values.[14] Romanticism in this sense was also imbibed from the West. Both these trends entered into the field of Bankim criticism. The critics of both the trends were found to follow one or more than one of the following methods—Historical Method,[15] Philosophical Method,[16] Subjective Method,[17] Comparative Method[18] and Aesthetic Method.[19]

Corresponding to the above methods of criticism we have Historical criticism, Psychological criticism,[20] Philosophical criticism, Subjective or Impressionistic criticism,[21] Comparative criticism and Aesthetic criticism. The modern realistic criticism is however of recent development.[22]

In the history of Bankim criticism we find that both the classical and romantic trend are simultaneously at work. But we cannot group the critics as classicists or romanticists. This is because in the Bankim and post-Bankim age the society was under the process of socio-cultural transformation, and in the transition phase most of the critics clung to the traditional ideals mainly, and few tried to uphold classical principles and restraint in criticism. We can at best call them conservative or orthodox. Critics with comparatively modern outlook displayed liberal tendencies, and they were occasionally subjective, at times romantic and at other times historical and philosophic. We may call them 'modern critics'. The principles of literary criticism as well as the methods developed in Bengali literature especially through Bankim criticism will be revealed in the following discussion.

II

Before entering into the growth and development of Bankim criticism in the pre-centenary period, we must take into account the social history of the nineteenth century of Bengal since it saw unprecedented social changes, which exerted tremendous influence in shaping the outlook of the critics. It is therefore, essential to discuss in brief the entire spectrum of social life in Bengal from the beginning of the nineteenth century till its end with due emphasis on landmarks, with the changing patterns in response to the varying trends and tendencies of social, political and literary spheres of thought and action. This is required in order to appreciate the forces at work behind the growth and development of Bankim criticism.

Bengali literary criticism like Bengali literature was profoundly influenced by Western thought and culture. The introduction of English education in the beginning of the nineteenth century brought about a great change[23] in the mediaeval outlook of Bengal[24] and a new literature was born in Bengal. It began to flourish with new ideals hitherto unknown. The first half of the nineteenth century witnessed unprecedented and uninterrupted production of creative works. But till then literary criticism worth the name did not make it appearance.

The last three decades of the nineteenth century, labeled as 'Bankim Age' in the history of Bengali literatures synchronized with growth of Neo-Hinduism in Bengal[25] and the period from 1870-1900 has been termed as the period of Hindu Revival.[26] It was a period of decadence of *Brahma Samaj*[27] and this decline of 'Brahma' ideals indirectly helped to strengthen the hold of the Neo-Hindu enthusiasts over the intellectuals of Bengal.[28] It was Bankim who spearheaded the movement for Neo-Hinduism.[29] He tried to strengthen the Hindu faith by explicating the Hindu philosophy and propounding the message of the *Gita*—of selfless service. He tried to give a new life to Hinduism through a synthesis of religion, knowledge and devotion. He evinced new interest in classical legends and tried to establish faith in the *Puranas* (mythology) on logical basis.[30]

Since literature is a reflection of life, we must also take into account various other socio-cultural forces that shaped the literature as well as criticism of the day. As a result of the active role of the *Samajists* in the first half of the nineteenth century, the liberal forces had already struck deep roots in the soils of Bengal, and the *decadents* were at first against Hindu revival. However, the strong current of Neo-Hinduism swept away the decadents, and the noted personalities like Keshab Chandra Sen also fell under its spell.[31] The rise of Sri Ramkrishna in the firmament of Bengal, and the emergence of brilliant star Swami Vivekananda championed the cause that Bankim was striving for.[32]

In the second half of the nineteenth century the adoption of liberal English Education by the Muslims[33] added a new dimension to the socio-cultural life in Bengal, and the growing Muslim consciousness amounting to resurgence became a force to be reckoned with.[34] This growing Muslim sentiment against Neo-Hinduism was sought to be exploited by the British rulers in the beginning of last decade of the last century by sowing seeds of communal discord among the Muslim intellectuals.[35]

But Neo-Hinduism commensurates with national resurgence which soon brought under its fold not only the intellectuals but also the man of literature, and literature was sought to be made a vehicle of spreading nationalist ideas. This resulted in production not only of nationalistic creative works but also nationalistic criticism. As such, few critics could avoid this strong sentiment of nationalism. This has accounted for much orthodoxy and conservatism among Bankim critics.

The Bengali Society thus experienced various currents and cross-currents of social, religious, cultural and political forces, and literature being a reflection of life produced strong reaction. This has again accounted for varying attitudes of different critics, whose outlook was shaped and moulded by the changing social scene of the times. These diverging socio-political forces must be kept in mind while evaluating the critics of the Bankim and post-Bankim Age.

III

The first attempt at modern critical writing began in the second half of the nineteenth century, literary criticism in its rudimentary from could be traced in the *Sambad Prayakar* (1853-55) in which issues editor Iswar Gupta (1812-59) made attempts at writing the biographics of the professional versifiers (*Kabioalas*) while expressing his own satisfaction derived from their poems. It was, however, Rajendralal Mitra (1822-91) who first initiated pure literary criticism in western style in his *Vividhartha Sangraha.*[36] Referring to his contribution to Bengali literary criticism A.K. Bandopadhyay has remarked that Rajendralal's greatest achievement was to lay the foundation of western type of literary criticism in Bengal.[37]

But in acknowledging our indebtedness to Rajendralal, we must not overlook the pioneering work in the field of literary criticism done by Rangalal Bandopadhyay (1827-87) who created a great stir among the elites of Bengal by reading out his literary essay *Bangla Kabita Bishayak Prabandha* on the thirteenth of May, Eighteen Fifty-two in the Boston Society Conference.[38] This essay for the first time introduced realism and research in Bengali literary criticism.[39] Rangalal also employed his modern technique of literary criticism in evaluating Iswarchandra Vidyasagar's *Sanskrits Bhasha O Sanskrita Bishayak Prastab.* At that time, Michel Madhusudan Dutta (1824-26) enriched not only poetry and drama but also critical literature by infusing western thought into it. His critical mind was amply revealed in his letters written to Gaurdas Basak, Rajnarayan Basu and Keshab Chandra Gangulee.

Another man of letters who revealed a great critical insight in that period was, Hemchandra Bondopadhyay (1838-1903). He wrote two prefaces, one after another for Madhusudhan's *Meghnadbadh Kabya,* in which were clearly pronounced his remarkable power of critical analysis and appreciation based on Western value judgements.[40] One of his contemporaries, Rajnarayan Basu (1826-99) made enduring literary judgements on many of the past and present writers, and anticipated modern comparative literary criticism in his assessment of *Meghnadbadh Kabya.*[41]

It was however the periodicals which played the most significant role. These periodicals gave the scope and created the environment for literary appreciation and appraisal of creative works. The role of these periodicals will be evident from the enormity of Bankim criticism and comments published mostly in these periodicals. It is, therefore, essential to put on record some of the most significant anonymous criticism since these are by now going to be virtually extinct and are likely to pass into oblivion.

After the publication of *Durgeshnandini* a criticism appeared *in Sambad Pravakar* appreciating that the novel was free from the contemporary defects of depiction of peculiar and unnatural incidents.[42] In a laudatory letter fourteen unknown youth showered praises on Bankim for writing a novel which had given them the taste of nectar fruit of an immortal tree.[43] Two women wrote two treatises in *Sambad Pravakar* on *Durgeshnandini*, the first characterized that novel as a educative work,[44] the second labeled it is a fine piece of writing.[45] The anonymous attempt at critical appreciation showed marks of great improvement in an essay published of in *Somprakash* which pointed out the defects as well as the merits of *Durgeshnandini.* This unknown writer for the first time pointed out the western influence on the novel. The hero-like attitude of Jagotsingh, the beauty of Ayesha, the intelligence of Bimala appealed to the essayist, while the cowardice of Diggaj frustrated him.[46] He also pointed out the obscenity and rusticity of language.[47]

Next novel which inspired, anonymous criticism was *Kapalkundala*. After its publication an anonymous critic made an interesting discussion on the element of supernatural, artistic creativity, relation between the outward and inward nature, characterization etc. This essay published in *Somprakash* expressed satisfaction regarding the skill in characterization in which Bankim has shown sense of appropriateness, harmony and consistency.[48]

The anonymous debate around *Bishabriksha* marked further advancement in the development in Bankim criticism. After the publication of the novel as serials in *Bangadarshan, Somprakash* reacted seriously charging Bankim not only for faulty language but also for his desertion of the 'eternal principles',[49] and it also pointed out Bankim's immaturity by hinting at the beginning the end result.[50] While criticizing second volume, fourth issue of *Bangadarshan, Somprakash* disparaged *Bishabriksha* and *Chandrashekar* in very strong words. It demeaned *Bishabriksha,*[51] and severely attacked the character of Shaibalini[52] and Foster. Soon an anonymous reader of *Bangadarshan* refuted this charges in a letter to the editor of *Somprakash.*[53] The contents of this letter was challenged by a reader of *Somprakash* in another letter published in *Somprakash.*[54]

Anonymous critics also attempted to evaluate the prose writings of Bankim. One unknown critic pointed out that *Bangadarshan* showed its ass-like intelligence by appreciating the ass in an article "Gardabh" by Bankim,[55] this was published in *Somprakash*. In *Halishahar Patrika*, the faulty language, grammatical defects of Bankimchandra was under criticism of his essay *Uttar Charita,*[56] while in other anonymous writing Sita's character came under scathing criticism.[57] Finally it demanded that Bankim should have been punished for this unlawful work.[58] The same mentality was reflected in the periodical *Madhyastha*[59] in the criticism of Bankim's *Bangadesher Krishak* and *Gardabh*.

In fact, the initial though immature attempt at literary evaluation came from the pens of the anonymous writers who rendered a signal service in building up the critical environment and pressed forward the need for critical evaluation of literary works. The diffidence of the unknown critics can be accounted for three reasons, first, unwillingness for publicity, secondly, doubts about the value of remarks in absence of set pattern, and thirdly, the feeling of insignificance before the towering personality of the literary genius of Bankim.

It must be noted that before the publication of *Bangadarshan*, although a host of periodicals[60] appeared in the literary scene of Bengal, their contribution was mostly confined to social, cultural and religious treatises. Few attempts were made for evaluation of literary works barring those made by the anonvmous critics. It was the publication of *Bangdarshan* that heralded the dawn of a new era in the literary field of Bengal. Referring to this significant role of *Bangadarshan* one critic remarked that what *Bangadarshan* did for Bengal was comparable to what *Edinborough Review* had done for England at one time.[61] Paying glowing tribute to *Bangadarshan*, Rajani Kanta Gupta said that *Bangadarshan* had inspired the readers to study essays.[62] In more elegant language Tagore said that *Bangadarshan* not only conquered the hearts of Bengalees but also broke away the difference between their English education and their souls.[63] Considering this, it is only natural that a critic would say that *Bangadarshan* was the 'Kohinoor' of Bengali literature,[64] and, that the talented contemporary editors of periodicals like *Bangadarshan,*[65] *Bandhab,*[66] etc. would be overpowered with a great shock with the sudden disappearance of *Bangadarshan.* In fact, the essays and discussions published in *Bangadarshan* changed the tastes of the readers, set patterns of criticism, and it was only in the fitness of things that many distinguished personalities came forward to set up new periodicals emulating the example of *Bangadarshan.*

IV

While some English educated men of letters in Bengal were making pioneering efforts in the sphere of literary criticism, Bankimchandra Chattopadhyay was busy in building the solid base of Bengali literary criticism, through his contributions in *Bangadarshan* which he himself edited. He rendered a signal service not only in establishing Iswar Gupta, Pyari Chand Mitra and even Dinabandhu Mitra in their rightful places through impartial value judgements, but also enriched the Bengali tradition of literary criticism by writing such essays as *Uttarcharits, Gitikabya, Bidyapati O Joydev*, Shakuntala-Miranda *abong Desdemona* etc. in *Bangadarshan*. The most distinguishing mark of Bankim as a critic is that he linked up literature with life and this attitude pervaded all through his critical writings.[67] He tried to introduce a moral tone, and bring about a synthesis between art and morality, and between idealisms and realism.[68]

The greatest contribution of Bankim to Bengali literary criticism was to strike a synthesis between the Western and Eastern principles of literary criticism. In fact, Bankim was profoundly influenced by the Western ideals which upheld that the main function of literature was not only creation of beauty but also reflection of life and nature. Referring to these two-fold objectives of literature, he remarked it "Whatever is natural and yet more than natural is to be regarded as excellent poetic creation."[69] Although this reflects his adherence to the western views, he had to compromise with the eastern value of judgements which he could not forsake. Indeed, he found himself at one with the classicist who advocated that literature should be didactic. But, unlike them, he could not consider literature as a only vehicle for moral preachings.[70]

Bankim followed a middle path[71] adopting neither the western nor the eastern principles completely. He synthesized both the opposing tendencies and evolved his own theory that literature should hold up a mirror to nature without sacrificing the moral question. To quote his own words, "The aim of literature is not to give sermons, but literature has the same purpose as morality. The secondary aim of literature is to give joy and purge the soul. Poets are teachers of the world but they do not teach through sermon.... They bring about a catharsis of human soul through the curtain of beauty in excellence. The artistic creation of beauty is the principal aim of literature."[72]

A close study of Bankim's critical writings will confirm this beyond doubt. His criticism of *Uttarcharita* is a marvellous piece of literary criticism. Here he had shown how a literary work is to be evaluated in a balanced manner keeping view both the western and eastern principles.

V

Although Bankim did not write any critical treatise on his own works, he made remarks on his own works regarding their from and nature, and furthermore, in the new editions of his novels he made such improvements as textual changes, additions and alterations etc. which provided good resources to his own critics, particularly in his own age. His remarks are either recorded in the advertisements in writing, or uttered to his close circle of admirers, who however, recorded them in writing.

Even before the publication of *Durgeshnandini* Bankim himself raised the question of grammatical incorrectness to be found in the work,[73] and in the preface to the first edition he labeled it a "Historical Novel". Needless to say, these sources were utilized by the critics after the publication of the first edition of the book. This led to necessary improvements in the language and additions and alterations in the next edition.

There is a great difference between the first and second editions of *Kapal Kundala*. An extensive discussion on fatalism in the first edition (Chapter IV) was abandoned in the later edition, while the Kapalik saved the drowning Nabakumar in the first edition. But not so in the second. It needs be mentioned here that the critics overlooked the subsequent changes and confined their analysis of the novel of the first edition's fatalism. Thus Nabakumar was saved by Kapalik, and with the turn of events changes in the subsequent edition were ignored.

Mrinalini was said to be a 'historical novel' in the first edition, but, in the later edition, the epithet historical was withdrawn, and this happened to be a source of criticism. Incidentally, it may be recorded that Bankim talked about the dramatic qualities of the novel to Shrishchandra Mazumdar.[74]

However, the changes in the different editions of *Bishbriksha* were ignored by the critics, but Bankim remarked to Sureshchandra that *Durgeshnandini's* Tilottama anticipated the simplicity of Kunda and that Kunda's recourse to poison was against the principle of morality[75] which influenced the critics.

Indira was developed into a novel from a tale (Upakatha) by Bankim, and in order to explain Indira's philosophy of life, he quoted a part of the poem of Shelley, but this had no effect on the critics. Likewise, changes and additions of *Jugalangurya* were ignored by them. But Bankim's remarks on *Chandrashekhar* influenced the critics. He remarked, "I have never narrated such scene as swimming in deep waters"[76] "Pratap is wealthy but he is self-restrained."[77] Taking cue from these remarks, the critics of *Chandrashekhar* made elaborate discussion on these points.

Bankim facilitated criticism on *Rajani* by stating in the advertisement that he planned the creation of a blind character after the character of blind flower girl 'Nydia' in Lord Litton's novel, in order to uphold the psychological and moral purposes in the novel.

The character of Rohini and Gobindalal of *Krishnakanter Uil* as appeared in the *Bangadarshan* serials underwent changes when published in book form. The character of Rohini was improved, while Gobindalal's suicide was replaced by his restoration to life. Perhaps Bankim did this with a view to show Gobindalal's expiation for sins, and he wrote to Jyotish Chandra, son of Sanjib Chandra, "the sinner must be punished,"[78] and Gobindalal should be punished for his forsaking of Bharamar.[79] All these opinions of Bankim proved to be a good source of criticism of *Krishnakanter Uil.*

After the first three editions *Rajsingha* made its appearance in the fourth edition in a bigger volume, with a good deal of additions. Bankim's discussion regarding the historical basis of the novel, and the statement that Rajsingha was his first historical novel paved the way for substantial criticism on this core.

The critics of those days were very much influenced by the ideals of the creator of *Anandamath, Devi Chaudhurani* and *Sitaram* and naturally, Bankim's remarks on these works furnished sources for the criticism of these works. Bankim wrote in the advertisement of the first edition of *Anandamath* that a Bengali wife sometimes is of great help to the Bangalees.

Bankim himself threw light on the historical background of *Devi Chaudhurani* and regarding the nature of the novel he remarked. "The substance of religion is culture, the fruit of it is higher life."[80] Besides, Bankim wanted preach the practice of religious culture through *Sitaram* which is evident from some quotation embodied in the beginning of the book. All these served as hints to critics.

Even in *Miscellaneous Essays*, Bankim also made certain comments. Regarding *Krishnacharita* he remarked, "The aim of the work is not to establish the divinity of Krishna. My intention is to discuss the human aspects of the character."[81] Justifying his own stand in interpreting the character of Krishna he remarked in the conclusion that the work of the critic falls into two categories. Firstly, to weed out the age old superstitions, and secondly, to discover the truth, and that in *Krishnacharitra* he had fulfilled the first task.[82]

VI

As a matter of fact, it was Bankim who nurtured the plant of literary criticism to grow into a mighty fully blossomed tree with blossoms and fruits. In order to evaluate Bankim's role as a critic we must carefully consider the role of *Bangadarshan* in the then literary circle of Bengal, since it was through the pages of this periodical edited by Bankim himself that made his critical views accessible to all. He also enunciated his principles of criticism round which two opposing groups of followers and detractors clustered. Some publications made their appearance in the scene only to cry down Bankim's literary creations. Foremost amongst them were *Sompraka, Halishahar Patrika* and *Basantak*. The main target of criticism was Bankim himself, and the invectives against him reached its climax with the publication of *Ayay ghum, Ayay Bangadarshaner Ghum*.[83]

In the pages of *Basantak* Bankim came under scathing criticism both in sarcasm and in cartoon, and in the 'The Bull and the Frog,' Vidyasagar was represented as the 'bull' and the *Bangadarshan* as the 'frog'. This was the most memorable of all such sarcastic designs.[84] *Somprakash* emitted venom against Bankim in such words as. "The study of *Bangadarshan* resulted in perversion of tastes instead of effecting their improvement."[85]

Satires on Bankim were not confined to periodicals alone it soon took to the fields of literary works. *Pyari Monan*

Kabiratna composed some satirical poems on *Bangadarshan.*[86] Kaliprasanna Kabyabisharad published anonymously *Banqiya Samalochak (Kabya).*"[87]

In the later half of the nineteenth century, a section of Bengali Intelligentsia could not accept *Bangadarshan* easily, and this annoyed and irritated section made a desperate bid to resist the circulation and popularity of *Bangadarshan.* Referring to this poet Tagore has remarked, "I remember, when Bankim was the editor of *Bangadarshan.* The number of his mean was not small,[88] hundreds of worthless persons were jealous of him and they did not spare pains to dismiss his greatness."[89] Bankim himself was quite conscious of his harmful satirists and detractors, and he once ventilated his own sentiment to Nabinchandra Sen, saying that there were some writers who even resolved to do away with him for his impartial criticism.[90] Truly speaking Bankim was assaulted four times by the writers belonging to Adi Brahma Samaj.[91]

VII

Bankim dominated the literary scene of Bengal in the second half of the nineteenth century and led the literary movement in Bengal both in the field of creative art as well as literary criticism. And it is therefore only natural that a host of man of letters clustered round him. Indeed, if Bankim is great as writer he is even greater in inspiring a number of writers and leaving behind him a group of followers. The inspired writers and critics were Rajkrishna Mukhapadhyay. Akshay Chandra Sarkar. Haraprasad Shastri.[92] Purnachandra Chattopadhyay. Chandrashekhar Mukhapadhyay. Rajani Kanta Gupta. Chandranath Basu. Purnachandra Basu. Shrishchandra Mazumdar amongst others.

As stated earlier, many new periodicals were published following the footstep of Bankim's *Bangadarshan.* Mention may be made of *Bhramar, Aryadarshan, Bandhab, Nabyabharat, Nabajiban, Prachar, Sahitya, Janhabi,* and *Janmabhumi.* These periodicals carried on the tradition set by Bankim by following his footsteps to enrich Bengali literature in this formative period. These critics generally focused their attention on Bankim's creative literature. Even in the later part of the Bankim age outstanding critic like Girija Prasanna Roychowdhury, Jnyandndralal Roy and Thakurdas Bondopadhyay yielded their masterly pen to evaluate Bankim literature in order to begin with their literary career.

This Bankim Group of critics formed a powerful force in strengthening the roots of Bengali literary criticism. Although they followed Bankim and fell short of him in some respects, they enriched literary criticism in many other ways. Most of them were critics of classical temperament with conservative outlook, and although they were not dogmatic, their opinions and comments emerged from their firm conviction in the way of life they advocated.[93]

Another remarkable contribution of this group was the initiation of scholarly criticism. A close study of their critical works show that they were vastly erudite in various fields, and this scholastic element introduced by them strengthened the base of Bengali literary criticism.[94] Another significant aspect of these critics was that although they followed Bankim they did not follow him blindly. Each of them was a man of strong individuality with his own likes and dislikes, and as such they carried further those principles which were dormant in Bankim. They displayed rare tenacity in discussing the nature, principles and objectives of criticism.

In spite of this, these critics could not show a total approach to literature. They were guided by subjectivism and their personal likes and dislikes stood in the way to the full flowering of their personalities as successful critics.

VIII

As in the nineteenth century, so also in the beginning of the twentieth century, the trend of literary criticism in Bengal underwent a great transformation. This was also observed in the creative works, following the social, political, and economic changes that swept over Bengal during the first half of the twentieth century. It is worthwhile to have a look into the great socio-political transformation of Bengal in order to form a correct estimate of the literary criticism of the period.

Lord Curzon, the then Governor General of India wanted to divide the Hindus and Muslim and rule over them, and with this motive he divided Bengal into two parts in 1905 A.D.[95] Soon the whole of Bengal stood against this malicious imperialist move and the 'Banga Bhanga Andolan' (1905-1911) broke out spread. During this fateful period new developments also took place in the socio-political life of Bengal. This was the growth of terrorism in Bengal.[96] Lord Minto tried to crush the movement by providing for separate representation for the Muslim.[97] The agitationers and extremists become more determined, and the political life in Bengal was very much disturbed.[98] Movement for 'Swaraj' was strengthened. Bankimchandra's *Anandamath* become a source of inspiration, and 'Bandemataram' its patriotic anthem become the song of liberation. Thus, the Swadeshi Movement shook the citadel of British Empire.

The disturbed political state of affairs was further aggravated by the advent of World War I (1914-1919).[99] This period of restlessness had a great impact upon the life and literature of Bengal. Under the pressure of world-wide frustration and uncertainty literature underwent a great transformation. Literary criticism was also not an exception. Objective analysis, logical discussion and argumentative presentation now made their appearance.

The critics who emerged in the context of the changed social-political scene with matured outlook, were Panchkari Bondopadhyay, Rabindranath Tagore, Bipin Chandra Pal, Lalit Kumar Bandopadhyay, Akshay Kumar Duttagupta, Mohitlal Mazumder, Pramatha Chowdhury, Shashanka Mohn Sen and Ramendra Sunder Trivedi.

True to this spirit of the age, Panchkari Bondopadhyay set out to discover the spirit of the nation,[100] in the works of Bankim, which was markedly pronounced in his *Bankimchandrer Trayee.*[101] But altogether in different vein Rabindranath made countless comments on Bankim and his works. It was Rabindranath who affected a revolutionary literary criticism by highlighting the principles of pure literary criticism, assimilating both the western and oriental value judgements. The hallmark of Tagore's criticism of Bankim literature and the creative genius of Bankim is to be found in his three outstanding critical essays[102]—a study of which shows how Tagore had changed the whole approach to Bankim by his versatile genius. This is reflected in elaborate treatises on the aesthetic sense, artistic perception and literary principles embodied in such works as *Prachin Sahitya* (1907), *Sahitya* (1907), *Adhunik Sahitya* (1907) and *Sahityer Pathe* (1936), the publication of which heralded the dawn of a new era in the history of Bengali literary criticism. Tagore's criticism shows a unique blend of impressionist, aesthetic, and philosophical method of criticism.

Tagore was followed by Ramendra Sunder Trivedi whose *Soundarjya Tattba*,[103] enriched the pure literary criticism in Bengal. In this memorable work he tried to bring home to all that the main purpose of beauty was to give joy, it had no relationship with material gain or didacticism.[104] In his discussion of the theory of tragedy he instituted a comparison between *Macbeth* and *Krishnakanter Uil*,[105] and showed the inexorable fate was not responsible for tragedy; it was the interaction between plots, character and fate that lead to tragedy.[106] Ramendra Sundar's greatest contribution lies in emphasizing the aesthetic and comparative method of criticism.

Literary criticism of different taste flowed from the pen of Lalit Kumar Bandopadhyay.[107] A vastly erudite man of letters his attempts at pure literary criticism influenced some of his contemporaries. Foremost amongst whom was Amarendranath Roy.

An upholder of the aesthetic ideals of the truth and beauty in literature, Shashanka Mohan also could not avoid the impact of the growing tide of Nationalism. In his critical works *Bangaban* (1915) and *Banimandir* (1928) he searched for our ancient cultural heritage, and in this nationalistic approach he found that *Rishi Bankim* was more brilliant than *shilpi Bankim.*

In the nationalistic period Bipin Chandra Pal contributed a good deal to Bankim literary criticism. Although predominantly a patriot, he could display close application of this principles of historical method as well as objective method in literary criticism.

But one of his great contemporaries Akshay Kumar Duttagupta could remain free from this all-pervading nationalistic sentiment of the age, and left traces of intelligence, logic analytical power and modernity in his outstanding work *Bankimchandra* (1327).

Another critic Mohitlal Mazumder published two essays on Bankim viz. *Bankimchandra* (1335) and *Ati Adhunik Samalochok O Bankimchandra* (1343) which was later included in his work *Bankim Baran* (1356). Mohitlal remarked that Bankim was greater than his novels. He is not only a creative genius but that he was also the founder of modern Bengali Literature.[108] His contemporary Pramatha Chowdhury the editor of *Sabuj Patra* (1914) advocated the adoption of aesthetic sense in literary criticism. He said that poetry appeals not to moral sense but to spiritual sense.[109] He tried to breathe the spirit of modernism to Bengali literary criticism by entering into elaborate discussion on such topics as 'the good and evil' and 'morality and obscenity' in literature. His artistic sense has been amply manifested in his *Chitrangada* (1334) where he upheld his view that in the sphere of art the question of morality poses an obstacle.[110]

Amongst others who enriched Bengali literary criticism in the closing years before the Bankim Centenary, mention may be made of Atul Chandra Gupta, the leader of *Sabuj Patra* Group. His 'Kavya Jignase' (1928) was a remarkable work which laid down principles of pure criticism of poetry. His contemporary, Sarat Chandra Chattopadhyay raised the question of art versus morality in relation to Bankim literature. His main objection was with respect to the death of Rohini. As he opined, that Bankim had sacrificed art at the altar of morality by bringing about the death of Rohini.[111]

In the closing years before the Bankim Centenary a number of periodicals appeared in the literary scene of Bengal and foremost among them were *Sahitya, Narayan, Bharatbarsh, Banqabani, Bharati Manasi o Marmaoani, Manasi, Prabasi, Bichitra,* etc. After the passing away of Bankim most of the criticism on his works appeared in these periodicals especially in the first four where most of the critics were under the spell of Bankim. And the remaining periodicals most of them were followers of Rabindranath Tagore.[112]

Here in *Shanibarer Chithi and Parichay* deserve special mention as their contributors tried to introduce modern approach to literary criticism. Eminent writers on the eve of the Bankim Centenary such as Sudhindra Nath Dutta, Hirendra Nath Dutta, Abu Saiyad Ayub, etc. contributed learned treatises in *Parichay* (1931) a quarterly published form Calcutta. The publication of *Kavya* by Sudhindra Nath and *Soundarjyer Mulya Ki Swasrayee* by Abu Saiyad Ayub heralded the dawn of a new era in the field of Bengali Literary Criticism. The two celebrated critics in the post-centenary period, viz., Biman Bihari Mazumdar and Subodh Chandra Sengupta also made their first appearance in the pre-centenary period in such essays as *Bankimchandra Nari Jaqaraner Abhash'O Sarat Chandra* (Magh, 1337 B.S).

To conclude we may say that this is a resume of the background of Bankim criticism in the pre-centenary period, against which innumerable Bankim criticism that have been produced for a long period of seventy-three years.

References

1. Lewis, C.S. *An Experiment in Criticism*, p. 104.
2. Eliot, T.S. *The Sacred Wood*, p. 15. Reprinted, Bondopadhyay, Jayanta, *Samalochanar Ruprekha. Bankimk Parba.* First Pub. August 1986, p. 3.
3. Gardner, Helen. *The Business of Criticism*, Oxford, 1959, p. 17.
4. Carlyle. Quoted by Bandopadhyay, Asit Kumar. *Samalochanar Kathe.* 3rd Print. January 1971, p. 8.
5. Ghose, D.N. *Principles of Literary Criticism*, Gwalior, 1970, p. 1.
6. Sengupta, Subodh Chandra, *Bangla Samalochana Parichay,* 1st ed. 1970, p. 25.
7. *Ibid.*, pp. 29-32.
8. (a) Chattopadhyay, Bimal Bhusan, *Sahitya Tattber Ruprekha.* 1st edn. Shraban, 1979, B.S. p. 70.

   (b) Dasgupta, Shanti Kumar. *Sahitya O Alochana.* 1st Pub. Shraban, 1357, B.S. pp. 17-22.
9. Sengupta, Satyaprasad, *Pashchatya Sahityer Samalochanar Dhara,* 2nd print. August 1, 1977, p. 87.
10. *Ibid.*, p. 145.

11. Sengupta, Subodh Chandra. *Bangla Samalochana Parichay*, p. 25.
12. *Ibid.*, p. 21.
13. (a) Bhattacharjee, Bishnupada. *Sahitya Mimansa,* Viswa-Barati: Shraban, 1335, B.S. p. 4.

    (b) Das, Shrish Chandra. *Sahitya Sandarshan*, 5th end., 1966.
14. Das, Shrish Chandra. op. cit., p. 208.
15. (a) Das, Shrish Chandra. op. cit., p. 108.

    (b) Bandopadhyay, Asit Kumar. *Samalochanar Katha,* pp. 26-27.

    (c) Sengupta, Satyaprasad. op. cit., p. 73.

    (d) William, J. Handy & Westbrook, Max. *Twentieth Century Criticism: The Major Statements,* New York, 1974, p. 305.

    (e) Rene, Wellek and Austin Warren said: "The historical scholar will not be satisfied to judge a work of art merely from the point of view of our own time—a privilege of the practicing critic, who will re-evaluate the past in terms of the needs of a present day style or movement." (*Theory of Literature*. London, 1955, p. 34).
16. Das, Shrish Chandra. op. cit., p. 189. (It is a method which is based on psychology dealing with motives that impel the writer to compare the book, and probing into the subconscious not only of the writer but also of his created characters.)
17. Das, Shrish Chandra. *Sahitya Sandarshan*, p. 190. (It is a method which deals with the philosophical basis of the work including religiosity, social awareness, representation of truth, good, and beautiful. It is a method which deals with the philosophical basis of the work including religiosity, social awareness, representation of truth, good, and beautiful.)
18. Bondopadhyay, Jayanta. *Samalochanar Ruprekha, Bankim Parba*, 1st Pub. August. 1986, pp. 26-27. (It is a method expressing in an intensely personal manner the inner convictions, beliefs dreams or ideals of the author. Also, it means impressionistic type, recreating with imagination and feeling the meaning of the author's work.)
19. Bandopadhyay, Asit Kumar. *Samalochanar Katha*, pp. 24-26. (It is a method of criticism based on comparative scholarly study of the works of two critics or writers themselves in order to trace their similarities and dissimilarities. Its popularity is increasing to remove the narrowness of mind.)
20. Bondopadhyay, Jayanta. op. cit., p. 17. (This method is based on 'art for art's sake', and evaluates the work of art from the point of view of aesthetics, i.e., whether the works of literature satisfy the test of creation of beauty and produce unalloyed joy to the reader.)
21. Aber Crombie, Lascelles. *Principles of Literary Criticism*, Vora & Co., 1982, p. 140 ("the sublime and the beautiful are distinct categories in the aesthetic judgement.")

22. Sengupta, Subodh Chandra. *Bangla Samalochana Parichay*, p. 34.
23. Sengupta, Pradyut. *Banglar Samajik Jioan O Natyasahitya*, Oct. 1976, p. 38.
24. Bandopadhyay, Asit Kumar. *Bangla Sahityer Sampurna Itibrittba*, 3rd edition, Agrahayan, 1378, B.S. p. 569.
25. Bhattacharjee, Prabhat Kumar. *Bangla Natake Swadeshikatar Prabhab,* March 13, 1976, pp. 190-91.
26. (a) Mukhapadhyay, Tarapada. *Adhunik Bangla Kabya* (Part I). 5th print. Asharh, 1374 B.S. p. 205.

    (b) Referring to Hindu Revival R.E. Slater remarked in his report that a kind of Hindu Revival was noticed in India. Which indicated both the strength and weakness of Hinduism. There was a resentment among the Hindus. They were eager to accept western lifestyle, but in religious matter they advocated adherence to ancient ideals. (Madras Christian College Magazine, Rept., Basu, Shankari Prasad, *Vivekananda O Samakalin Bhareatbarsha* (Part I). 3rd print, July 1979, p. 160.)
27. (a) Basu, Shankari Prasad. *Vivekananda O Samakalin Bharatbarsha* (Part II), 3rd print, August 26, 1981, p. 183.

    (b) Bandopadhyay, Asit Kumar. *Bangla Sahityer Sampurnna Itibrittba,* pp. 418-19.
28. Shastri, Shibnath. *Ramtanu Lahiri O Tatkalin Bangasamaj*, 4th print, Bhadra, 1390 B.S. p. 272.
29. (a) Mazumdar, Ujjabal Kumar. *Bangla Kabye Pashchatya Prabhab,* 1375 B.S. pp. 25-26.

    (b) Basu, Shankari Prasad. *Vivekananda O Samakalin Bharatbarsha*, (Part I), p. 28.
30. Bandopadhyay, A.K. *Bangla Sanityar Bamournna Itibrittba*, pp. 418-19.
31. Basu, Shankari Prasad. *Vivekananda O Samakalin Bharatbarsha*, (Part II), p. 196.
32. (a) Singha Roy, Jibendra. *Sahitye Rommohan Theke Rabindranath* (Part II), Ashwin, 1368 B.S., pp. 25-26.

    (b) Bandopadhyay, Asit Kumar. *Adhunik Bangla Sahityer Sampurnna Itibrittaba*, 12th end, Ashwin, 1392 B.S., p. 41.

    (c) Bankim's influence pervaded even after his death on Aurobindo Ghose the revolutionary of Bengal. (Roychowdhury. Girija Shankar, *Shri Aurobinda O Banglay Swadeshi Yog*. 1st August 15, 1956, p. 105.
33. Aligarh Muslim University was Established in 1874.
34. Gupta, Sushil Kumar. *Unabingsa Shatabdite Banglar Nabe Jagaran*, 2nd end. Falgun. 1383 B.S. pp. 252-53.

35. (a) Singha Roy. Jibendra. op. cit., pp. 25-26.
    (b) Bandopadhyay, A.K. *Bangla Sahityer Sampurna Itibrittba*, p. 590.
36. Mukhapadhyay, Arun Kumar. *Bangla Samalochanar Itihas, Shraban*. 1372 B.S., p. 15.
37. Bandopadhyay, Asit Kumar. *Bangla Sahityer Sampurna Itibrittba*, p. 569.
38. Sen, Sukumar. *Bangle Sahityer Itihas* (2nd part), 5th edition. 1370 B.S., p. 127.
39. Sengupta, Subodh Chandra. *Bangla Samalochana Parichay*, Magh. 1376 B.S., p. 65.
40. Mukhapadhyay, Arun Kumar. op. cit., p. 30.
41. Basu, Raj Narayan. *Bangla Bhasha O Sahitya Bishayak Baktrita*, Granthan Sanskaran, July 1973, pp. 23-24.
42. *Durgeshnandini;* Sambad Prabhakar, 3rd Baishakh, 1272 B.S., Reprinted, Dasgupta, Jayanta Kumar. *Sambad Prabhakare Banglar Puratan, Bharatbarsha*. 20th Year. Part I, Issue III, p. 453.
43. Editorial, Sambad Prabhakar, Bhadra 27. 1272 B.S. (Sept. 11, 1885), Reprinted Dasgupta, Jayanta Kumar. op. cit., p. 454.
44. *Sambad Prabhakar*, Karitik 18, 1272 B.S., Rept. Dasgupta, Jayanta Kumar. op. cit., p. 454.
45. *Ibid.*
46. *Durgeshnandini, Somprakash,* Issue XXIII, Baishakh 13. 1272 B.S., Reprinted, Ghose, Binay. *Samayik Patre Banglar Samaj Chitra*, Patha Bhawan. July 1966, p. 636.
47. Ghose, Binay. op. cit., pp. 636-37.
48. Kapalkundala, *Somprakash*. Agrahayan 19. 1273 B.S., p. 39.
49. *Bangadarshan, Masik Patra O Samalochana, Somprakash*, Baishakh 1279 B.S., p. 364.
50. *Ibid.*
51. *Bangadarshan, Masik Patra O Samalochana, Somprakash* Sharaban 21. 1280 B.S., p. 607.
52. According to the critic Shaibalini is a bad type of woman and provokes perverted feelings in readers. (Somprakash. Shraban 21 1280 B.S., p. 607.)
53. Chithipatra, Bangadashan Prasanga, *Somprakash. Bhadra* 3. 1280 B.S.
54. *Ibid.*, 11. 1280 B.S.
55. *Bangadarshan: Masikpatra O Samalichans,* Soprakash, Shraban, 1280 B.S.
56. *Bangadarshan O Uttarchariter Smalochana*; H.S.P. Shraban. 1279 B.S.

57. The Critic posed the question—the way in which Bankim had tried to highlight the attitude of site was it worth Site or was it wort a harlot. (*Bangadarshan O Uttarcharita*, Shraban, 1279 B.S., p. 208)
58. *Bangala Sahityer Pancham Khanda O Uttarramchariter Samalochana,* Halishahar Patrika, Bhadra, 1279 B.S., p. 266.
59. *Madhyastha*, Shraban 32, 1280, B.S. & Bhadra 7, 1280 B.S.
60. The most celebrated periodicals were *Sambad Prabhakar Tattbabodhini*. Vivithartha Sangraha, Somprakash.
61. Mukhapadhyay, Thakur Das. *Bankimbabu Sambandhiya Smriti,* Sahitya: Poush, 1319 B.S., pp. 106-07.
62. Gupta, Rajani Kanta. *Pvatibha*, 6th edition, 2319 B.S., p. 57.
63. Tagore, Rabindranath. *Shikshar Herfer*, Poush, 1299 B.S., Shiksha Reprinted: Bankim Prasanga, Viswa-Bharati, 1977, p. 86.
64. Rakshit, Haran Chandra. *Bangasahitya Bankim* : 3rd Edition, Poush, 1317 B.S., p. 36.
65. *Bangadarshan*: *Aryadarshan*: Shraban, 1283 B.S., pp. 191-92.
66. *Bangadarshener Vidayay*: *Bandhab,* Asharh, 1293 B.S., pp. 99-100.
67. Mukhapadhyay, Arun Kumar. op. cit., p. 78.
68. Sengupta, Subodh Chandra. op. cit., p. 82.
69. *Bankim Rachanabali* (Part-II): Sahitya Samsad: 3rd Print, Ashwin, 1371 B.S., p. 184.
70. Bandopadhyay, Jayanta. *Samalochanar Ruprekha*: Bankim Parba, 1st Publication, August, 1986, pp. 45-46.
71. *Ibid.*, p. 46.
72. Chattopadhyay, Bankimchandra. *Bankim Rachanabali* (Part-II). Sahitya Samsad, 3rd Print, Ashwin, 1371 B.S., p. 183.
73. Chattopadhyay, Purnachandra. *Bankimchandra O Dinabandhu*: Bharati, 38th year, Issue-XII, Chaitra, 1321 B.S., pp. 1122-23.
74. Mazumder, Shrish Chandra. *Bankimbabur Prasanga* (Pratham Prastab): Sadhana, 1301 B.S. Reprinted Samajpati, Sureshchandra. *Bankim Prasanga*: 1st Pub. 1922, p. 118.
75. Mazumder, Shrish Chandra. op. cit., pp. 110-17.
76. *Ibid.*, p. 120.
77. *Ibid.*
78. Bhattacharjee, Amitra Soodan. *Bankimchandra O Bangadarshan*: Asharh, 1378 B.S., p. 17.
79. *Ibid.*, p. 17.
80. *Natural Religion* by the author of Ecce Homo, p. 145.
81. *Krishnacharitra*: Revised Advertisement.
82. *Krishnacharitra*: Part-VII, Chapter II.

83. *Halisahar Patrika*: 23rd Kartik, 1280 B.S., Reprinted: Ghose, Manmatha Nath. *Manasi O Marmabani*: Ashwin. 1333 B.S., p. 163.
84. *Basantak*: Issue VIII, Part-I, pp. 124-25.
85. Bangadarshan Haite Bangasamajer Upakar ba Apakar Haibar Sambhabana: *Somprakash*, Bhadra 24, 1280 B.S., p. 678.
86. Kabiratna, Payari Mohan. *Gitabali*: 1307 B.S., pp. 73-76.
87. Babaji, Fakirchand (Kabyabisharad, Kaliprasanna) *Bangiya Samalochak* (Kabya): 1301 B.S.
88. Babaji, Fakirchand. *Bangiya Samalochana* (Kabya), 1287 B.S., pp. 6-8.
89. Tagore, R.N. Bankimchandra: *Sadhana*: Baishakh, 1301 B.S., p. 550.
90. Sen, N.C., *Amar Jiban* (Part-II): *Nabinchandra Rachanabali.*
91. Chattopadhyay, Bankimchandra. Adi Brahma Samaj O Nabya Hindu Sampradayay: *Prachar*, Agrahayan, 1291 B.S., p. 171. Reprinted: *Bankim Rachanabali*, (Pt-II): Sahitya Samad, 1371 B.S., p. 914.
92. According to S.C. Sengupta, although a follower of Bankim, H.P. Shastri was not a man of the Bankim group. (Bangla Samalochana Parichay: p. 112)
93. Bandopadhyay, Jayanta. op. cit., p. 74.
94. *Ibid*., p. 75.
95. The Secretary to the Government of India published the famous newspaper of England *Standard* in the month of may 1905 through which he had declared the division of Bengal : and the Bill relating to the 'Division of Bengal' was made an Act in Simla by the Government in July 1905. (Sengupta, Pradyot, *Banglar Samajik Jiban O Matya Sahitya*: 1st Publication, Oct. 7, 1976, p. 374.
96. (a) Sengupta, Pradyot. op. cit., p. 377.
    (b) Bandopadhyay, Asit. *Bangla Sahityer Sampurna Itibritta*, p. 591.
97. (a) Mazumder, Ujjbal Kumar. *Bangla Kabye Pashchatya Prabhab*: 1st Publication, 1375 B.S., p. 31.
    (b) Mukhapadhyay, Durgashankar. *Mohitlaler Kabya O Kabimanas*: Ashwin, 1379 B.S., p. 52.
98. (a) Bhattacharjee, Prabhat Kumar. *Bangla Natake Swadeshikater Prabhab*: 1st Publication, 1385 B.S., pp. 377-88.
    (b) Mazumder, Ujjal Kumar. op. cit., pp. 29-31.
99. (a) Bandopadhyay, Asit Kumar. *Bangla Sahityer Sampurna Itibritta*, pp. 591-92.
    (b) Mazumder, Ujjal Kumar. op. cit., p. 31.

100. Sengupta, Subodh Chandra. *Bangla Samalochana Parichay*, p. 129.
101. Bondopadhyay, Panchkari. *Bankimchandrere Trayee, Narayan*, 1322 B.S.
102. *Rajsingha* (Chaitra, 1300 B.S.), Bankimchandra (Baishakh, 1301 B.S.) *Krishnacharitra* (Magh-Falgun, 1301 B.S.)
103. Trivedi, Ramendra Sundar. *Soundarjyar Tattba*: Sandhana. 1300 B.S.
104. Sengupta, Subodh Chandra. *Bangla Samalochana Parichay*, p. 127.
105. Trivedi, Ramendra Kumar. *Sahitya Katha*: *Bharati*, Agrahayan, 1302 B.S., pp. 452-62.
106. Sengupta, Subodh Chandra. *Samalochana Sanchayan*: August, 1976, pp. 156-57.
107. *Bankimchandrer Akhyaibabali* (1322 B.S.), *Kabyasudha* (1323 B.S.), *Kapalkundala Tattba* (1325 B.S.), *Premer Katha* (1327 B.S.), *Sakhi* (1326 B.S.), *Ma* (1322 B.S.), etc.
108. Mazumder, Mohitlal. Bankimchandra: Baishakh, 1335 B.S. Reprinted: *Bankim Saran*: 2nd Print, Karitik, 1371 B.S., p. 11.
109. Chowdhury, Pramatha. *Prabandha Sengraha*: Viswa-Bharati, 1974, p. 204.
110. *Ibid*., pp. 203-04.
111. Chattopadhyay, Sarat Chandra. *Sahitya O Niti*: Ashwin 10, 1331 B.S., Reprinted: *Sarat Sahitya Samagra*: Ananda Publication. 1392.
112. Mukhapadhyay, Arun Kumar. *Bangla Samalochanar Itihas*: 1st Publication: Shraban, 1372 B.S., pp. 253-56.

2
Durgeshnandini

RAJENDRALAL MITRA (1824-1891)

As has been observed, that after the publication of *Durgeshnandini*, a number of anonymous critical essays appeared in different magazines. But the first critical work with author's identity was *Durgeshnandini*.[1]

Rajendralal tried to trace out Bankim's originality as a novelist by highlighting his indebtedness to the underlying native tradition and elements behind its outward similarity with the English novels which was obviously apparent to the then readers. He said:

> Those who read the English prose-poetry, they may find the merits of English novel here and there in *Durgeshnandini*, but that does not demean his (writer's) own merits.[2]

In his study the critic pointed out both the merits imbued by western ideology and demerits of *Durgeshnandini* as a novel. According to him, Bankim had used the English manners and concepts in his treatment of the Hindus and Muslims (under the influence of English literature) and this has spoilt the natural flow of his description. For example, he said:

> ...the manner in which Ayesha had nursed the captive Jagotsingh, may be appreciable to the European countries, but it was improbable in case of Muslims in this country.[3]

The critic further opined that

> ...though Ashmani was basically Eastern, her character was also somewhat influenced and moulded by the

> Western tendency and this was the reason as to why her character was irrelevant.[4]

In addition to characterization, and narrative art, the critic also evaluated Bankim's humour and prose style. He appreciated Bankim's art of humour, but at the same time was conscious of its effect on fast growing women readers, and he remarked,

> It is a matter of regret that now-a-day's Bengali novels is being read by the gentle ladies also and that Bankim does not seem to remember it.[5]

Talking about the language and diction, the critic remarked—

> Even if it is generally natural and full of pure literary forces, in places it is prejudicial. In some places he has written words in a long gap which is unlike pure 'Gourhio' style.[6] After pointing out these defects of the book, he finally remarks: "His book is pleasant, inspiring to ideas and is an ideal of new technique."[7]

Rajendralal is the first critic not only of *Durgeshnandini,* but also of Bankim's works. Nevertheless he has shown a taste for literary criticism by his scholarly approach to the novel, as revealed in his evaluation of western influence, emphasis of native element and balancing of the merits and demerits for which his essay drew the appreciation of Manmoth Nath Ghose, who acclaimed it as a piece of impartial criticism.[8]

HARANATH BHANJA

Another critic who has earned reputation as a serve critic on Bankim Literature is Haranath Bhanja's *Suraloke Banger Parichay*[9] is at once a satire on Bankim and an adverse criticism of *Durgeshnandini.* Haranath was proud of his scholarship[10] orthodox in his outlook, jealous of Bankim and failed to appreciate his literary genius and literary style. Satirising Bankim he said that Bankim had to live mainly with the third-class people whose contact had polluted his taste for which his pen gave expression to the thoughts of these third-class people.[11]

According to Haranath *Durgeshnandini* is an obscene book and that Bankim's taste is hateful as Ashmani's pouring of the juice of betel nut into the throat of Bidyadiggaj, etc. are hateful things and reflects perverse taste. He pointed out that the titles of the chapters of the novel were strange and weird, amazing, fanciful. The critic opined that Bankim had quoted from Scott and Lytton where his intelligence did not mingle with his imagination. Haranath criticized Bankim's taste:

> "This writer (Bankim) in order to decorate woman has given 'mekhala' on the thigh, we have seen it used on the breast but never it is used on the thigh."[12] It centres on the taste of the critic.

One thing to be noticed is that despite all such adverse remarks, Haranath admitted that Bankim could represent the story elements in a pleasant manner, which could attract a dunce to sleep.[13]

PURNACHANDRA BASU

Purnachandra Basu made an elaborate discussion on the character of Bimala[14] and set the contemporary trend of character analysis. In initiating the character analysis of novels in Bengali literary criticism, Purnachandra seems to have followed the principle that the critic must play role of a middle man between the writer and reading public.[15] He has presented Bimala in her true colours as a comical, humorous, sweet, brave and clever woman.[16] He in his remark has said that Bimala had not been a victim of atrocities. Her mental strength, determination, patience and heroic spirit would not have found expression.[17] Indeed in his writing Bimala has become a lively woman. It is an example of imaginative recreation of characters.

The editor of *Aryadarshan* has rightly commented that Purnachandra's technique of criticism was new and fine.[18] Because Purnachandra's criticism is neither prejudiced by Hindu ideals nor by too much of emotion. He quite indifferently comments that Bimala is the creation of the then social environment. It was the age in which human intellect, spirit and energy and the spirit of liberty were coming into force, Bankim imagined Bimala with those ideals.[19]

Admitting the novel technique of Purnachandra, it has to be said that he was a little bit traditional in his attitude to life and literature. He raised a mild objection against Bankim and said that Bimala was the ideal of modern English youths only.[20]

Because, according to the critic, physical passions have been so appealing in Bimala that only the scoundrels can desire it. He said:

> Bankimbabu stealthily peeped into Bimala's closet from the doorstep and was so much infatuated by her half-exposed physical beauty that he could not but show it to the readers.[21]

In *Durgeshnandini*, there is a total change in Purnachandra's attitude. It seems, as if with the progress in age Purnachandra's attitude was influenced by traditionalism. His mind was mostly prejudiced by the Hindu superstitions.[22] This prejudice led him to say that meeting of Tilottama and Jagotsingh in the temple of Shaileshwar amounted to spoiling of the sanctity of the temple. Purnachandra's objection against Bankim was that it was the writer who spoilt the sanctity of the holy place by arranging corrupt practice there.[23]

YOGENDRANATH BONDOPADHYAY (VIDYABHUSHAN) (1845-1904)

In the contemporary time Yogendranath Bondopadhyay made some fair remarks about the character of Ayesha in his essay *Bishabriksha*.[24] He said that Ayesha knew from the very beginning that Jagotsingh was Hindu and her life would have to be spent by loving Jagotsingh only. She did not expect any fruit of her love, and therefore, Ayesha's heavenly love never came into any clash with the worldly affairs.[25] It is here that we directly confront a psychological discussion of the character of Ayesha.

DEBENDRA BIJOY BASU

Debendra Bijoy Basu in some of his essays[26] discussed elaborately the aim of the novel along with characterization. He classified the characters of the novel into four groups. The first group consists of the common characters,[27] while the imaginative characters constitute the second group.[28] The third group constitute of characters who represent the basic human qualities and the basic inner truths of life, reflected in their characters as a result of (their study of modern knowledge and science),[29] and the fourth group constitute the poetic and artistic characters where only a singular passion of an individual has been pronounced.[30]

Debendra Bijoy included the characters of *Durgeshnandini* in groups, first and second. According to him, in spite of the influence of some of the English novels in *Durgeshnandini,* the characters like Jagotsingh, Birendra Singh, Osman belong to the first group because through these characters the hopes and desires of the common people have been reflected.[31] Bimala and Ayesha belong to the second group because these characters have been developed through imagination.[32]

This is an example of pure literary approach towards criticism during Bankim's life time. Debendra Bijoy in his short discussion pointed out the influence of English literature on the one side, and, on the other side, he spoke about the application of realism and imagination in this novel.

RAMGATI NYAYARATNA (1238-1301 B.S.)

Ramgati Nyayaratna's *"Banglabhasha O Bangla Sahitya Sishyark Prastab"*[33] shows that the critic's outlook was shaped by strong moral bias and classical erudition.

He raised many objections against Bankim for his defiance of existing social customs. His principal point of attack was that Tilottama and Bimala's nocturnal adventure to the temple of Shaileshwar was against the prevalent social norm. Expressing wonder at such delineation, the critic remarked that obviously Bankim's ideal was English, not Sanskrit literature. Otherwise how could Jagotsingh and Tilottama get attracted to each other at first sight? According to him this is an example of 'animal love'. His second point of objection was that since inter-caste marriage were forbidden in society, how could Jagotsingh and Tilottama fall in love with each other without knowing each other's caste.[34]

The critic reveals classical taste in his estimation of characters. According to him, Birendra Singha is haughty, Jagotsingh is intelligent, spirited, devoted, brave and a lover. His kshatriya-like activities deserving to his heritage. Ramgati discusses their characters in this light.[35] The heroine of the book is Tilottama. The Chieftains daughter is a beautiful, sober, young and a loving one.[36] Ayesha was viewed as a daughter of the Gods. Her beauty, virtue, conscience, piety—all these qualities appeared to be supernatural to the critic, revealed through her activities like nursing of the deceased Jagotsingh. Replying to the queries of Osman, maintaining the secrecy of attraction for Jagotsingh, giving ornaments during the marriage of Tilottama and Jagotsingh etc., the critic has searched for the said qualities in Ayesha. It is for these qualities, that the critic has placed her above Rosinara of *Ongurio Binimay*.[37]

In spite of his classical and ethical pre-occupations in some of his discussions, attempts were made to understand the substance and artistic beauty of the novel. For example, in the Chapter XIII of part II of this novel where Tilottama swoons at the words of Jagotsingh—the critic has appreciated it because it was highly natural and extraordinarily pleasant.[38] There was such a force and motion in *Durgeshnandini*, that the readers' curiosity has gradually increased during the study of this novel. Ramgati has attracted our attention towards this side of the novel.[39] Besides this Ramgati has also commented on the strength of the language used in the book: "The language of this book is modern, but not totally 'Alali'—it is better and sweeter than this."[40]

CHANDRANATH BASU (1251-1313 B.S.)

Chandranath Basu has laid emphasis on the influence of English romance on *Durgeshnandini* in his *Novel ba Kathagranther Uddeshya*.[41] According to him, romance is not profitable, in it only imagination which finds a fine ground of free movement which ultimately affects conscience and sense of consideration, and therefore, study of it yields harmful result which he mentioned of *Durgeshnandini* as an example.[42] Indeed such conservatism made the practice of literary criticism perverse in those days,[43] and, in fact, Chandranath has been held responsible, in no mean measure for deterioration of literary discussion after Bankim Age.[44]

HARIDAS BONDOPADHYAY

In his essay "Banglar Upanyas Lekhak,"[45] Haridas Bondopadhyay has illustrated the qualities of a real critic such as strong imaginative power, sympathetic outlook, liberal attitude and insight.[46] *Durgeshnandini* was the first novel of Bankim in the pattern of English romance, and in its creation, Bankim's strong imaginative power is reflected. Haridas has discussed this point sincerely. According to him, *Durgeshnandini* is the best of Bengali novels,[47] because of fineness of language, blend of wit and humour, careful plot construction and dramatic actions.[48] He opined that Bankimchandra by virtue of his strong imaginative power developed a minor historical event into a fine novel. But he categorically pointed out that the novel had no objective. Since there was no touch of social customs and conventions.[49] Criticism of different characters of this novel has also showed his intellectual sincerity. In his estimation Jagotsingh and Tilottama were the hero and heroine of this novel. While Osman and Ayesha were co-hero and co-heroine respectively.[50] He further emphasized that Tilottama was the daughter of a brave man, but she herself was not brave. Ayesha actually formed the backbone of *Durgeshnandini*, and without her *Durgeshnandini* could not be a novel.[51]

The next important point in this essay is that the critic tried to establish similarities between the incidents and characters of this novel with those of Scott's *Ivanhoe's* Rebeka. Both Ivanhoe and Jagotsingh are brave and lovers, as Ivanhoe incidentally becomes wounded and Rebeka cures him by nursing. So also is the case with Jagotsingh who being wounded is nursed and cured by Ayesha. Ivanhoe is a Saxon and Rebeka a Jew, Jagotsingh is Hindu while Ayesha is a Muslim, etc.[52] Admitting the imitation of *Ivanhoe* in *Durgeshnandini* Haridas did not look down upon Bankim's genius rather he has highly appreciated it.

Haridas was free from the preponderance of conservatism and didacticism which had marred the literary value of the most of earlier criticisms on *Durgeshnandini*. Indeed, his criticism on Durgeshnandini heralded the dawn of impressionistic criticism so far as his criticism shows a fine blending of realism and imagination in the background of his self-realization.

GIRIJA PRASANNA ROYCHOWDHURY (1862-1899)

Girija Prasanna Roychowdhury's *Bankimchandra—(Durgeshnandini)*[53] is the only extensive criticism of *Durgeshnandini* in Bankim Age. His essay marks a break with the past tradition and it ushers in the dawn of a new era in Bankim criticism which again anticipates Rabindranath Tagore. Girija Prasanna attempts to evaluate the principal characters in the novel, and his approach is characterised by deep insight, sensitiveness, delicacy and imagination. He characterised Bimala as a sharp, intelligent, ever-gay and good humoured woman, sometimes heroic and sometimes revengeful.[54] According to him Ayesha is kind, wise and grave, a very sweet and fine woman—but a disappointed lover. Tilottama is as soft as flower, full of love.[55]

Girija Prasanna examined the three characters on the basis of their nature of love. Indeed, he judged the characters of Bimala, Ayesha and Tilottama as expression of varying moods of love. He commented:

> That the basis of this three characters is love. That which is the guiding passion of human character, the very passion which in its gradual development keeps human knowledge in a constant unrest till death—Bimala, Ayesha and Tilottama are the three idols of the first sight of those youths—three pictures where love is manifested with all its sweetness—Bimala, represents the serene lovely picture of it; it is full of exuberance and sweetness in Ayesha; and both these qualities have been epitomized in Tilottama.[56]

Not only had that but also made a psychological probe into the motives of these characters. The critic said that Ayesha's pleasant manner toward Osman is the result of her disappointed love. Osman had been suffering a lot by loving Ayesha, Ayesha could understand it therefore, she loved Osman. Discussing the character of Abhirama-Swami, he said that Abhiram was half-familyman and half-saint and in a gradual evolutionary process Abhiramswami would become a complete ascetic in future novels of Bankim.[57]

Not only in characterization but also in evaluation of other aspects of the novel, Girija Prasanna has displayed the skill of a critic. Influence of English literature, the humour, the prose style, and narrative art—all came under the purview of criticism. His remark about humour in *Durgeshnandini* is worth mentioning. He said, although Bankim tried to create humour through the character of Bidyadiggaj, he failed to create real humour, and it bordered on farcicality.[58]

Although pure literary criticism showed signs of maturity in the hands of Girija Prasanna, he could not wholly get rid of the emotional trend of the age. As for example, seeing Ayesha in the service of the deseased Jagotsingh, the critic said:

> Oh! What a lovely kind lady! What an image of affection in the house of the savage Katlu Khan! What a beautiful lotus on the thorny-stem.[59]

RABINDRANATH TAGORE (1861-1941)

Rabindranath's observations on *Durgeshnandini* are scattered in many of his essays of which mention may be made of two remarkable essays—*Panchabhut*[60] and *Saratchandra*.[61] Here the critic has simultaneously drawn our attention towards the character of Bimala and the real nature of the novel *Durgeshnandini*. Of all the characters of *Durgeshnandini* Bimala is the most active. About this feature of Bimala Tagore said:

> The character of Bimala is indispensable to all the actions of Durgeshnandini. How many of the characters of this novel have shown such skill, such action, such diligence.[62]

The first three novels of Bankimchandra are so highly romantic, that it is difficult to locate the real man there. In these novels, reality is presented as subordinate to imagination. According to Rabindranath, there is in *Durgeshnandini* a phantasmagoria of beauty, even if it is written in colourful fancy, it has a beauty of its own. These are to be accepted without argument, because these are not the things of today—but of the past in which they are hovering over moreover that past should not be cross examined in the light of historical ideals, not even from the side of our common experiences. There, Bimala,

Ayesha, Jagotsingh, etc. have the liberty to do anything except that which creates the readers' displeasure.[63]

RAMESH CHANDRA DUTTA (1847-1909)

In the post-Bankim period Ramesh Chandra Dutta was the first critic of Bankim's *Durgeshnandini.* His criticism: *Bankimchandra o Adhunik Bangiya Sahitya*[64] shows not only his observation on the subject matter and characters but also his literary tastes. Ramesh Chandra laid much emphasis upon the novelty of *Durgeshnandini* and upon its imaginary forces. He said:

> In the Bengali prose-literature, no book like *Durgeshnandini* was found earlier. Such originality, such lovely imaginative fervor, such beauty and attraction, such sweet style and such cleverly-woven plot had never been seen in Bengali prose.[65]

He further said that the spirit and bravery of Birendra Singh, Jagotsingh and Osman, Bimala's cleverness and astonishing sweetness, the calm and quiet Ayesha's silent inner-feeling, *Garhmandaran,* temple of Goddess, festivity in Katlu Khan's house—these pictures were superb and immortal. The great Bankim had brought in this nectar in the Bengali literature by ransacking the sea of imagination.[66]

HEMENDRA PRASAD GHOSE (1876-1963)

Hemendra Prasad Ghose wrote criticism on *Durgeshnandini* in his essay *Bankimchandra.*[67] He primarily dealt with the characters of Bimala, Tilottama and Ayesha. Hemendra Prasad's critical approach is to some extent aesthetic, for he upholds both the inward and outward beauty of these three characters. The critic said:

> The first, Bimala was intelligent, ever-gay, and serious, the second, Tilottama was a fresh as a bud of 'Juthi' after being washed out by rain; the third Ayesha was like the full moon, serious as well as light, love-sick but unselfish.[68]

Hemendra Prasad discussed the beauty of the characters in this light. But he was attracted mostly by Ayesha, because

Bankimchandra through this Muslim lady had left a stamp of his liberal sense of nationalism.[69]

BIRESWAR PANDE (1842-1911)

In the post-Bankim period Bireswar Pande still carried on the trends of the Bankim Age by upholding the Hindu ideals and judged Bankim's genius in that light. In his essay *Bankimchandra O Hindur Adarsha,*[70] Bireswar observed that Bankim had taken the Hindu ideals and ethics as his base. He said that all the female characters of Bankim were based on of Hindu ideals. Despite Western influence on Bimala, her marriage was not performed violating the Hindu norms and conventions; and even if Birendra Singh had attraction for Bimala, he did not marry her on the ground of her racial inferiority.[71]

HARAN CHANDRA RAKSHIT

Haran Chandra Rakshit's criticism of *Durgeshnandini* is found in his book *Banga Sahitye Bankim.*[72] He believed that *Durgeshnandini* was based upon a solid literary foundation; creation of beauty was its chief purpose. Free thinking, fine humour, poetic fervor and nationalism in prose-literature could be found for the first time in *Durgeshnandini.*[73] Haran Chandra in his book tried to make a probe into the development of the mind and art of Bankim's genius. Although his discussion on *Durgeshnandini* is brief, he made a unique contribution to Bankim criticism by throwing light on the poetic elements in the novel. Indeed, Haran Chandra was primarily attracted by the aesthetic elements in *Durgeshnandini.* For the first time he attempted to evaluate the significance of the last chapter where Ayesha's ring is dropped in the water. The description and environment created by Bankim produced supreme poetry. Haran Chandra remarked Bankim had presented here very poetically the relation of human mind with nature.[74]

SHRIMAT UTTAMANANDA SWAMI

Uttamananda Swami's criticism of *Durgeshnandini* is found in his essay *Bankimchandra.*[75] Like Bireswar Pandey Uttamananda Swami also interpreted *Durgeshnandini* on the basis of Hindu ideals; but unlike Bireswar he found *Durgeshnandini's* moral implications were a complete break up with the ancient Hindu ideals. He considered the novel as an imitation of Scott's *Ivanhoe*. The character of Bimala was not only an exception. Uttamananda here raised the objections to this original creation of Bankim and pointed out that the character of Bimala was unrealistic and not a natural portrayal of Hindu woman. He alleged Bankim for doing considerable harm to the country by writing *Durgeshnandini*, etc. in imitation of the English novels. His angry rebuff is that Bankimchandra by describing the indifferent solitary love of Ayesha has led astray many Hindu damsels. This sort of love may be successful in England, but it is sure to lead to the moral degradation of Hindu society, he believed.[76]

SHIBNATH SHASTRI (1847-1919)

Shibnath Shastri discussed Bengali society's reaction to *Durgeshnandini,* and he sought to assess its literary values and determine its rightful place in Bengali literature in historical perspective in his book *Ramtanu Lahiri O Tatkalin Bangasamaj.*[77] He said that *Durgeshnandini* was superior to *Vijoy Basanta, Kamini Kumar* and *Alaler Gharer Dulal,* and that the narrative skill, freshness of language and picturesque description were nowhere to be found in the earlier period.[78]

YOGNESHWAR BONDOPADHYAY (1859-1925)

Yogneshwar Bondopadhyay in his essay "Bangla Sukumar Sahitya"[79] attempted at the critical assessment of *Durgeshnandini* in historical and comparative methods. He was well conversant with both Western and Eastern literature. Discussing the evolution of Bengali literature in the pre-Bankim period, he assessed the contribution of Bankim to the development of literature, not losing sight of Western influence, on the life and literature of Bengal at that time.

He has discussed *Durgeshnandini* in the background of the then social conditions. The critic had very carefully shown that in *Durgeshnandini* the changes in the social conditions under western influence as well as influence of traditional Indian culture have been reflected. As he has said, Shakespeare and Scott had taken characters which are foreign like Miranda,

Juliet, Portia, Rowena, Ophelia, Rebeka, etc. and had adopted them in English literature, so also has Bankimchandra.

He has taken materials from the western literature and had written novels like *Durgeshnandini,* etc. and grounded Bengali literature on a solid foundation.[80] According to Yogneshwar, in Ayesha both eastern and western culture have been merged. In her selfless love she is oriental, but in her freedom in love she is western. He has said that Ayesha's spraying foreign essence on the body poured the doctrine of free love into the ears of Bengali woman and this has entered into their closet. Different ornaments in the body—all from Bengal were fashionable, but inwardly there was flowing the current of free love as initiated by Rebeka and Juliet—the free air of the western culture flowing little by little in her mind.[81]

Yogneshwar had literary tastes along with an ability to write but he could not get himself free from the attraction of old ideals. Mentally he was an orthodox Hindu and therefore taking into consideration the place of *Durgeshnandini* in Bengali novelistic literature and its special characteristics, he said that in *Durgeshnandini* novelistic beauty, literary excellence and dramatic art—everything were there, but it would do no good—because in western society can the original Hindu society which has traditions, remained unaffected in the midst of calamities?"[82] One can hear the distant echo of Chandranath Basu in such remarks of Yogneshwar.

NIRMAL KUMAR CHANDA

In the post-Bankim Age after Yogneshwar Bondopadhyay, Nirmal Kumar Chanda had written quite an elaborate criticism of *Durgeshnandini* in his essay *Durgeshnandini Bankimchandra.*[83] The body of the essay is fraught with excess of emotion and description of the characters in the novel. But a materialistic strain is there all along in the essay. For example, discussing the characters of Bimala and Tilottama, the critic said, "Bimala's case is exceptional, because she is the daughter of 'Shudra' and is know as a 'dasi' (servant). But Tilottama's courtship appears to be unnatural."[84] He left a warning note—if you happen to marry a woman like Tilottama, you will be in serious troubles and Bimala's very sight would burn you.[85] Nirmal Kumar thought that only Ayesha in this novel could be given the status of a Goddess, and in this case, if she was made the heroine, the charm of novel would be spoilt. Therefore, Bankim had made Tilottama the heroine.[86]

But the critic has repeatedly mentioned that Bankim's poetic genius is in his *Durgeshnandini*. He has said that Tilottama's courtship though unnatural, was poetic.[87] But he did not elaborate his discussion on the poetic elements in the novel. And he did not realize that mere finding out of merits and demerits did not make good criticism.

JATINDRA NATH BONDOPADHYAY

Jatindra Nath Bondopadhyay's *Bankimchandra Diggaj Charitra*[88] is an example of how literary criticism is marred by conservative outlook. According to him portrayal of the character of Diggaj was insulting to the Brahmin society. He pointed out that Bankim had committed a serious offence by making Diggaj eat the remains of Ashmani's dish. He also accused Bankim for loosing the tie of Hindu society[89]—making a Hindu young man an object of love of a Muslim woman. Even if Jatindra Nath blamed Bankim, he expressed his anger more against the Western teaching and civilisation. However, Jatindra Nath's limited vision did not allow him to appreciate Bankim as he had made. Ayesha utter "This captive is my life and soul"[90] with the intention of upholding the spirit of universality and secularism in human love.

SURESH CHANDRA SEN

Suresh Chandra Sen in his book *Kabyakatha*[91] refuted the charges of communalism brought against Bankim by many critics of his day. According to him

Durgeshnandini provides the best example of communal harmony. He has shown that in magnanimity and liberal attitude, Osman is as good as Jagotsingh,[92] Suresh Chandra laid much emphasis upon the character of Ayesha and he had tried his utmost to find out the beauty of this character. He had shown that in knowledge, love, joy and action, Ayesha was a vivid portrait of the novel. But for this character, *Durgeshnandini* could not have achieved greatness as a novel, and she was the real heroine of this book.[93] In the eye of the critic, Ayesha as an example of 'Nishkam Karma' was even brighter than Prafulla of *Devichowdharani* so far as the application of Nishkam Tattba is concerned.[94] The critic concluded, "The man who has drawn such a Muslim character as a repository of 'jnan', 'bhakti & karma'. It would be a great sin to think that he was anti-muslim in sentiment."[95]

Through such criticism of Suresh Chandra, his progressive attitude was found, and it brings us back to the literary art. The attitude, in which he has discussed the characters like Ayesha, Osman, etc., is the attitude of a litterateur and the sentiment which he has applied is a free sentiment.

LALIT KUMAR BANDOPADHYAY (1275-1336 B.S.)

Lalit Kumar Bandopadhyay heralds the dawn of a new trend in *Durgeshnandini* criticism after Suresh Chandra in some of his essays[96] and books of essays.[97]

No critic, prior to Lalit Kumar, has made an attempt to justify the title of *Durgeshnandini*. Making a comparative estimate of the qualities in the character like Bimala, Ayesha, Jagotsingh, etc., he said that Tilottama was the main attraction of the readers in the book, particularly the period of fight between the Rajput and the Muslims in the fort of Garhmandaran was the most critical period in Tilottama's life with these words he tried to justify that the book is named after the daughter of the ruler of the fort and not after her.[98]

In some of the essays, Lalit Kumar upheld the family pictures in Bankim literature and in reference he had brought in the characters of same nature from Sanskrit and contemporary literature as well as English literature. Making a comparative estimate the critic had found out the unique qualities of Bankim creativity. But his comparative study is lacking in its aim to explicate the inner truth of the characters. His studies are mainly descriptive. But about the literary utility of the characters Lalit Kumar's discussion is invaluable.

To introduce the heroine Tilottama 'in the new land', mother's death became inevitable after the birth of the daughter.[99]

His thoughtful analysis is that like the English novels. *Durgeshnandini* depicted love, union and separation an reunion after much of troubles, and there and brother's wife.[100] Evaluating the nature of sister in this novel, Lalit Kumar said that Tilottama's mother and Bimala were not born of the same mother, but they were sisters. Had Tilottama's mother remained alive, she could have to live with her co-sister. Therefore, without inviting rivalry in the love for the same husband the writer had taken Tillotama's mother of this world.[101]

Many critics raised objections to the fact that Bankim Chandra had reacted against the Hindu law by initiating love between Tilottama and Jagotsingh in the temple. But Lalit Kumar, with factual representation from Sanskrit literature said that Bankim had followed the foot-steps of Sanskrit literature as for example, he had cited the love affairs between Jimutabahan and Malayabati in *Nagananda*.[102] This Bimala was again taken by the critic as an example of universal friendship. According to him, a friendship between Bimala and Tilottama was like that of Radhika, Lalita and Brindadyuti of Vaishnaba literature.[103]

CHANDI CHARAN BANDOPADHYAY (1264-1323 B.S.)

Chandi Charan Bandopadhyay has written criticism of *Durgeshnandini* in his essay *Bangla Sahityer Kramaunnati O Bankimchandra* Bimala is the subject of his discussion. He has viewed Bimala from the standpoint of his Hindu consciousness. The critic's sentiment for his own community appears to be very strong here. He lamented that Bengali readers were satisfied by giving highest position to Ayesha, which shows that the Bengalees had lost their originality.[105] According to him Bimala is the greatest example of Hindu woman. Chandi Charan discussed the character of Bimala in the light of this ideal.[106]

SHASHANKA MOHAN SEN (1872-1928)

Shashanka Mohan in his book *Bangabani*[107] has expressed opinion contrary to Chandi Charan. According to Shashanka Mohan, this novel is a 'last art' of Bankim's genius. Bankim followed 'art for arts sake' without any motive in this novel. Fact is that, Shashanka Mohan gave priority to the artistic side of the novel, but it seemed that he expected a great idea in literature than mere art and therefore, he hesitated in giving proper weightage to Durgeshnandini's artistic beauty: "Till then his genius was concentrated upon art for art's sake."[108]

BIJOYRATNA MAZUMDER

Bijoyratna's *Bankimer Upanyase Hasya Ras*[109] is a catalogue type essay. The motive here is to provide a systematic analysis of humour in the novels of Bankim. But it shows marks of literary criticism also. As for example, he said Bidyadiggaj of *Durgeshnandini* even if highly comical, his humour was not all pervasive, not even unnatural; everyday Bimala's humour was a certain stage of 'tears and ideas', her good will for Tilottama was there in her sarcastic humour even.[110]

Bijoyratna is the first critic to give special attention to Bankim's humour and has written a separate essay on it for which he deserves credit.

GNANENDRALAL ROY

Gnanendralal's criticism of *Durgeshnandini* is found in his essay *Upanyase Dharma Prachar.*[111] According to him, Bankimchandra had repeatedly propagated in his novels that 'restraint and peace' is the way to 'dharma and swarga', and the contrary is the way to 'O-dharma and Narak'.[112] The critic searched for Bankim's religious mind in *Durgeshnandini* in this light. He believed that through Ayesha, Bankim had propagated the lesson of restraint. But he could not support Bankim unreservedly for his creation of Ayesha. Considering the activities and the relative incidents, the critic came to the conclusion that Ayesha was chaste in helping others and restraint in love, but she had violated the social ethic by nursing the captive Jagotsingh and going to him at night alone.[113]

AMARENDRANATH ROY (1888-1957)

Amarendranath in his essay *Sahitya Prasanga*[114] opposed the views of Gnanendralal. According to him, Gnanendralal's essay *Upanyase Bharne Prachar* is a bad example.[115] He said that Bankimchandra did not write *Durgeshnandini* as an example of restraint. He referred to the meeting of Tilottama and Jagotsingh in the temple of Shaileshwar and said that this meeting was a glaring example of unrestrained passion.[116] The echo of Purnachandra Basu's criticism is heard in the writing of Amarendranath.

Amarendranath's other essay *Binkimer Upanyase Matrichabi*,[117] where he has searched for motherliness in *Durgeshnandini* is also merely narrative in nature. For example, he says that the main thing with Bimala, Ayesha and Tilottama is love and there is no trace of motherliness in them.[118]

JITENDRALAL BASU

Jitendralal Basu's "Adhunik Bangasahitye Ma"[119] is an example of orthodox criticism where *Durgeshnandini* has been examined in terms of traditional motherliness. Jitendralal viewed this novel as 'handicap' because there was no motherliness in it.[120] However, he tried to find out in *Durgeshnandini* the influence of both the western and Indian ideals. He pointed out that Ayesha and Tilottama would remind one of Shakespeare's heroines since these characters pulsate with love and passion like their counterparts in Shakespeare, while the artistic beauty of Bankim's novel would remind one of Kalidas.[121]

KAZI ABDUL ODUD

Kazi Abdul Odud's short but factual criticism of *Durgeshnandini* is there in his essay "Bankimchandra."[122] He tries to present a literary solution to the issue where the Muslim critics condemns Bankim for the creation of Ayesha because Jagotsingh and Ayesha's love is an impossible one at least in the days when rigorous women seclusion was prevailing amongst the Pathans. Odud said that from the literary standpoint Bankim could not be blamed. Because this unnatural feminine regard for a man in danger, that picture of union had crossed the barriers of family society and community. And revealed herself gloriously, that super creation of Bankimchandra could not be ignored by any man having taste for literature.[123]

Thus, Abdul Odud has highlighted the secularism expressed through Ayesha and Jagotsingh's love, and had his paved the way for a happy solution of the charge brought against Bankim.

BIRENDRA KUMAR DUTTAGUPTA

Birendra Kumar Duttagupta has discussed Bankim literature in his essay entitled *Upanyas.*[124] A summary of his discussion reveals that the critic wanted to show that Bankim had ignored the contemporary social life. According to him, the equality and liberalism which Rammohan and Keshabchandra has propagated, Bankim could not have grasp it fully to use in his novels; nothing was said of woman-emancipation in his novels, and these were gradually losing their impact. But when the critic said that the novel was mainly imaginative and therefore it was impossible to fit the imaginative character with reality.[125] We cannot but admit that Birendra Kumar has the eye of a literary critic because it is almost an universally agreed fact that *Durgeshnandini* is a romantic novel which has been pointed out by Birendra Kumar in his brief discussion on it.

TARAKNATH BISWAS (1264-1344 B.S.)

Taraknath Biswas's criticism on *Durgeshnandini* is found in *Taraknath Granthabali,*[126] where it is a mixture of the old and new trends.

Taraknath has mainly discussed the characters in *Durgeshnandini*, Bankim's taste and language. From a study or the characters of Jagotsingh, Tilottama, Ayesha and Bimala, he concluded that the historical characters of this novel were not of high standard. According to him, Jagotsingh was a stern man, and as the daughter of Nawab, Ayesha's nursing at night alone was very odd from the standpoint of the society of Muslim women seclusion.[127]

Discussing Bankim's taste, the moralistic critic Taraknath said that Ashmani's throwing of Betelnut-juice in the mouth of the Brahmin Bidyadiggaj was odd, slang and unpardonable.[128] And he commented on the language of the book that it was nothing more than the Vidyasagria language written in imitation of Sanskrit.[129]

Taraknath could approve nothing of Bankim's language, characterization and taste. But he admitted that Ayesha was a very charming creation of imagination and it was she who contributed largely towards the liveliness of this novel.

He argued that if Hamlet was left out nothing remained of *Hamlet* so also if Ayesha was left out, nothing would remain of *Durgeshnandini*.[130]

AKSHAY KUMAR DUTTAGUPTA

Akshay Kumar Duttagupta, in the contemporary age, has written a considerably detailed criticism of *Durgeshnandini* in his book *Bankimchandra*.[131]

He found out the creations of Bankim from Charles Stewarts *History of Bengal* and has shown the characters created from imagination[132] along with the incidents which had crossed the limits of probability and he found an artistic solution to this. As for example, he said Ayesha's nursing of Jagotsingh: Jagotsingh's entrance into Katlu Khan's closet and such incidents had crossed the limits of probability but considering from the poetic truth in romantic novels these were not offensive.[133]

After the publication of *Durgeshnandini*, many critics had a low idea about Bankim-genius. When they established its near resemblances with *Ivanhoe*, some again found out Bankim's originality in spite of imitation. But Akshay Kumar is the first critic to attempt a comparative study of *Ivanhoe* and *Durgeshnandini* and thereby he has established that *Durgeshnandini* was not an imitation of *Ivanhoe*—it was the original output of Bankim-genius—all the characters were individuals shaped by the genius of Bankim. Substantiating his opinion, Akshay Kumar says that Brain de Bois-Guilbert and Osman did not belong to the same class. Guilbert was proud, arrogant, unmannerly, wanton, devoid of religious sense while Osman was the high priest of the Pathans—a God amongst men.[134] Tilottama was soft and coward while Rowena was strong, spirited and conscious of her own position.[135] Rebeka was a complete character while Ayesha is incomplete. Rebeka's love for Invanhoe was secret up to the last moment, Ayesha has publicly declared her love for Jagotsingh.[136]

Akshay Kumar's comparative criticism is not descriptive in nature, it is analytic. He has tried to explicate the inner realities of the characters by an analysis. As for example, making a comparative study of Ayesha and Rebeka he said that selfless love was the notability as well as magnanimity of both Ayesha and Rebeka. But Rebeka, true to the feminine dignity had kept it secret, while Ayesha had wounded this dignity by exposing it publicity. The critic, finding artistic fault with the naked love of Jagotsingh and Ayesha, said: "Thus, Ayesha has made herself guilty and punishable from the artistic point of view by making a clean confession to Jagotsingh."[137] Besides, he has discussed the language and plot-structure of *Durgeshnandini* ingeniously. According to him, *Durgeshnandini* is the best of Bankim's novels so far as plot and construction are concerned—its plot is simultaneously simple and well-woven.[138]

Akshay Kumar's criticism is a valuable contribution to the history of Durgeshnandini analysis; because it is the most comprehensive criticism where he has covered almost all sides of possible observations to it. He has evaluated the artistic side as well as the novelistic utility of the book in relation to life.

BIPINCHANDRA PAL (1858-1932)

Bipinchandra Pal's criticism of *Durgeshnandini* can be traced in his three different essays.[139] He has been a distinguished critic of post-Bankim period. His psychological thought, subtle sense of taste and imaginative force deserve appreciation. These qualities have been well-exemplified in his criticism of *Durgeshnandini*.

According to him, *Durgeshnandini* is an example of how characters of the standard of Rebeka and Desdemona can be created out of the women born and brought up in the customs and tradition of Bengali.[140] Romance is pleasure created of the inter-play of all-pervasive human elements—here native or foreign, Western or Oriental makes no difference. Bankim raises himself to that romantic realm and creates the characters like Bimala, Jagotsingh and Osman.[141] Chiefly on the basis of this, Bipinchandra has written his criticism of *Durgeshnandini*.

Bipinchandra's attitude is modern; his method of criticism is also based upon matter and life. *Durgeshnandini*, even if a romantic novel, is full of warmth of life. Bipinchandra has tried to find it out. He has beautifully brought out to the notice of the readers that in spite of the limitations set by social customs, a Bengal woman is capable of enjoying liberty and satisfy her nature and pure elemental passions, and that truth has been manifested by Bankim in *Durgeshnandini.*[142]

Taking the main feature of the novel into consideration Bipinchandra has said that in the language of modern European theory of evaluation, *Durgeshnandini* could be termed as a 'thesis' paper so far as the expression of self-satisfaction and self-assertion of human beings is a world of pleasure were concerned.[143]

Another outstanding feature of Bipinchandra as a Bankim critic is that he came forward to refute the charge of communalism against Bankim on logical grounds. He said that communalism was a modern uprising; Bankim was above this. He did not propagate hatred rather he aimed at communal harmony. He was not a hater of the Muslims, in his novels he had represented the Muslims as a symbol of a force opposite to national liberation movement.[144] According to Bipinchandra, by making Bimala stab Katlu Khan, showing Jagotsingh superior to Osman, and picturing Tilottama as sweeter than Ayesha, he inspired the spirit of Hindu nationalism.[145]

Himself a great orator Bipinchandra could write in a unique manner to drive home his arguments to others. He tried to assess Bankim and his work *Durgeshnandini* against the backdrop of the Age, keeping in view the Western influence. He did not lose sight of the historical background of the novel and gave a romantic evaluation of *Durgeshnandini* in true spirit.

GOPAL CHANDRA BHATTACHARJEE

Gopal Chandra Bhattacharjee had attempted a real evaluation of *Durgeshnandini* after Bipinchandra Pal in his essay *Bankimchandra O Rabindranath.*[146] Like Bipinchandra, Gopal Chandra has also considered *Durgeshnandini* against the background of the age. He categorically pointed out that as the romantic movement had a great impact in the European thought, to seek a relationship between external nature and human soul, the romantic movement had gradually crept into Bengal and that Bankim was the high-priest of that romanticism and *Durgeshnandini* was the first fruit of it.[147]

SHIBA PRASAD ROY

After Gopal Chandra, Shiba Prasad Roy has written a life-based criticism of *Durgeshnandini* in his *Bankimchandra O Rabindranath (Upanyase Art)*.[148] Shiba Prasad's discussion is based upon the belief that life and its ups and downs form the basis of literature, and with this belief he has said: "Whatsoever, we enjoy reading the failure of Osman and Ayesha. We do not hear the echo of our heart there."[149] But he does not say that life does not have any warmth. He says that in Ayesha, Tilottama, Osman, etc. there is expression of life, but they are so much static that they seem to be works of a sculptor.[150] A few critics before Shiba Prasad, had searched for life in *Durgeshnandini*, but these were flashy, and here lies the importance of Shiba Prasad as he is the first critic to think of *Durgeshnandini* in that light and thus opens a new window of thought & introspection.

KUMUDNATH DAS

Kumudnath Das's criticism of *Durgeshnandini* in his *Bankimchandra*[151] is brief but substantial. His search for truth going deep into the inner realities of the book is praise-worthy. He admitted the influence of scott's *Ivanhoe* and said:

> The idea, idea of language and characterisation of the book specially the picture of the Royal Court during the Mughals and the Pathans depicted in it, has in it such a novelty, romance coupled with imagination and truth that the book is made even pleasing.[152]

In the history of the evolution of Bengali novels *Durgeshnandini* has its own place, but Kumudnath goes further to say that, not only historically, but also, artistically *Durgeshnandini* stands apart by its own merit as a novel.

RAMSAHAYAY VEDANTASHASTRI

Ramsahayay Vedantashastri's criticism of *Durgeshnandini* is embodied in his two essays, *Bankimchander Bimal*[153] and *Tilottama O Ayesha*.[154] As the titles indicate both the essays deal with principal female characters of *Durgeshnandini*. When a compilation of the author's essays on Bankim works was brought out, Bipinchandra Pal wrote an introduction to it in which he remarked that Ramsahayay mostly weighed Bankim's female characters in the principles enunciated in *Sahitya Darpan* although an erudite Brahmin scholar Ramsahayay could not shake off modern literary trends in Bengal and as such his language is not archaic but modern.[155]

In fact, in Ramsahayay's essays we find the reappearance of classical trend of criticism in the post-Bankim period when principles of modern criticism had a dominating tendency. The critic followed the classical norms in his assessment of evident from his following analysis.

Analysing the characters of Bimala, Ayesha and Tilottama, he concluded that according to the principles of rhetoric, Bimala was fickle (pragalbha), Tilottama was sensible (Mugdha) and Ayesha fall in between the two.[156] He further said that Bimala was the combination of 'Padmini', 'Sankhini', 'Chitrani' and 'Hastini', she is sensible like 'Padmini' and desirous like 'Hastini'.[157] Ramsahaya identified Tilottama's love as 'Rupaja' and terms it as 'Chakshurag' or 'Taramaitrak'.[158]

His aesthetic sense is amply manifested in the analysis of the character of Tilottama. He could create beauty in poetic prose as well be seen from his following remark:

> This creation of the poet reminds one of Apsara of heaven. As if the heavenly image of beauty has come down to this earth. She has brought with her the sweet fragrance of Parijat, the beauty of Eden in her eyes, in her words sweet melody of 'tritantri', and in her love the sweet touch of Amrita.[159]

But the critic's imaginative flights and emotional excess sometimes stand against proper appreciation of his viewpoints overpowered by an interplay of rhetoric and stylistics. Making a comparative study of Tilottama and Ayesha the critic said:

> Tilottama has a mild-current like that of Saraswati, while Ayesha has a strong current like that of Jamuna. Tilottama is a imperial beauty whereas Ayesha is a rural-beauty. The first is a budding Mallika, the second is a full bloomed Lotus.... One is a dream-flower; the

other is the fruit of devotion. One is possession, the other is happiness.[160]

Vedantashastri's facile prose style, and his language, diction, and the use of simile still attract readers. His classical approach to Bankim is characterized by individualistic[161] type of criticism. His aesthetic sense is amply revealed in his treatment of characters. There is also modern touch in him when he analysed the character of Bimala. He says that this motherliness girl being brought up by the father, could not get the chance to come in touch with women in early youth, and therefore, she is not bashful, and it was the lack of training and companion, and this isolation made her nature free and determined.[162] But in his final estimate of Bimala he fails to rise above his classical learning and conservative out-look and comments that Bimala is as shameless as a harlot.[163] Ramsahayay's criticism is a blend of classical and modern trends.

KAMAL KRISHNA GHOSE

The first successful piece of comparative criticism is Kamal Krishna Ghose's *Ayesha O Rebeka.*[164] Making a comparative study of these characters, the critic has pointed out the merits and demerits of the two along with the similarities and dissimilarities existing between them and in his attempt to search for the critical mysteries of the characters, and has tried to show Bankim's originality in the making of Ayesha. This discussion shows Kamal Krishna's matured views. Ayesha, in spite of being an imaginative character, is not entirely indifferent of life—this sensitiveness has raised Kamal Krishna's writing to the level of real literary criticism.

Discussing the two characters the critic concluded that gravity was the base of Ayesha's character while Rebeka's strength was her fickleness and more captive life. Human characters were exposed in the ups and downs of their actions, but Bankim had made Ayesha a little shadowy and for this her character was not developed through the strains and trials of her actions.[165] On the other hand, there was unbound life in Rebeka's fickleness.[166] He adds that the writer did not take the opportunity to picture Ayesha more vividly through ups and downs and a pathos which existed in Rebeka's silent love is not there to that extent in Ayesha's expressed love.[167]

Like his predecessor Akshay Kumar Duttagupta, Kamal Krishna found artistic defect in Ayesha's confession of love for Jagotsingh. According to him, the mysterious history of Ayesha's heart which Bankim was hinting at: *by making a hasty exposition of this mystery, he has killed art itself.*[168] He further adds that by doing so, Bankim has degenerated Ayesha's love. Thus, Kamal Krishna has pointed out the differences of love between these two characters.

BATUKNATH BHATTACHARJEE

As Lalit Kumar Bandopadhyay had tried to find out the homely characters in Bankim literature, so also Batuknath Bhattacharjee has searched for determining the nature of the 'sannyasis' in his essay *Bankim Sahitye Sannyas.*[169] Explaining the character of Abhiram Swami (Shashi Shekhar Bhattacharjee) of *Durgeshnandini,* the critic said that he was a sannyasi of the lowest standard. He placed him in the class of *Kapat Sannyas* or *Bidhur Sannyas* i.e., one renouncing family life being penitent of misconduct or for self-protection. Batuknath noticed this trend in the life of Abhiramswami.[170]

ADHYAPAK HERAMBA CHANDRA CHAKRABORTY

Heramba Chandra in his *Upanyasik Bankimchandra*[171] remarked that Bankim created literature not only with a purpose but also with the aim of giving pleasure, and realisation of his aims and purposes he never lost sight of the relation between individual and society, and blended skillfully imagination and reality in his literature. He further pointed out that Bankim might have tried to propagate lessons of patriotism in *Durgeshnandini* by taking the historical facts, but he did his best to make the story pleasant by infusing wonder and excellence into it.[172] The critic upheld that what mattered with Bankim's novels was pleasure which the readers derive from them and not the problems he had hinted at or the moral or ethical teaching implied in them.[173]

Heramba Chandra's criticism is thus free from traditionalism, emotionalism and moral or ethical preponderance. Indeed, he leads us to the door of modern criticism of Bankim's works.

INDRADEB BASU

Indradeb Basu, in his essay *Banga Sahitye Pashchatya Prabhab*,[174] has discussed the Western influence in different characters of Bankim. As for example, he said that the liberty allowed Jagotsingh and Bimala of *Durgeshnandini* was the direct result of Western influence.[175]

DHIREN PAUL

Dhiren Paul, in his *Bankim Sahitye Pashchatya Prabhab*,[176] has strongly opposed Indradeb Basu. As for example, he says that Jagotsingh's liberty in the matters of love and Bimala's individual freedom are not the result of Western influence, such examples are there in our native literature. As for example, he has mentioned of Arjuna's polygamy without the consent of the guardian.[177]

Although, Dhiren Paul has opposed his predecessor, in fact, he has searched for oriental influence in Bankim literature.

SUMMING UP

Bankim criticism began with the evaluation of the first of Bankim's novels *Durgeshnandini*. The classicist and orthodox critics failed to appreciate the significance of *Durgeshnandini* in proper perspective because of their classical bias and conservatism, while the romantic critics regarded it as a work of imagination. The modern critics had both the contrary approaches in view, and in their assessment, they also considered the novel as reflection of life. The main topics of discussion were the characters, incidents, social and religious questions, humour, structure and contemporary environment. Of the female characters, Bimala and Ayesha created controversy, while Tilottama's meeting Jagotsingh in the temple of Shaileshwar was viewed with different light by different critics. Likewise Ayesha's nursing of the sick Jagotsingh was debated on the question of poetic beauty. Bankim was charged for hating Muslims and insulting Brahmins. Only few could appreciate the artistic beauty of *Durgeshnandini* in novelistic art form.

References

1. Ghose, Monmuth Nath, *Durgeshnandini,* (*Udhrita Samalochana*), Archana, Ashwin, 1329 B.S., p. 28.

2. *Ibid.*, p. 283.
3. *Ibid.*
4. Ghose, Monmuth Nath, *Durgeshnandini, (Udhhrita Samalochana)*, op. cit., p. 282.
5. *Ibid.*, p. 283.
6. *Ibid.*, p. 284.
7. Ghose, Monmuth Nath, *Durgeshnandini, (Udhrita Samalochana)*, Introduction, Archana, Ashwin, 1329 B.S., p. 279.
8. Bhanja, Haranath, *Suroloke Banger Parichay*, 1877.
9. Roy, Alok, *Unish Shatake Bankim Birodhita*, *Rabindra Bharati Patrika*, Magh-Asharh, 1389 B.S., p. 42.
10. Bhanja, Haranath, *Suraloke Banger Parichay*, 2nd Edition, 1882, p. 22.
11. *Ibid.*, p. 25.
12. *Ibid.*, p. 22.
13. Basu, Purnachandra, *Bimala*: *Aryadarshan*, Bhadra, 1285 B.S., pp. 193-99.
14. "The critic become a middle man…of the public". --- Wellek, Rene, *Concepts of Criticism,* 2nd print, Yele University. January 1964, p. 3.
15. Basu, Purnachandra, *Bimala,* p. 198.
16. *Ibid.*, p. 198.
17. Editor. Aryadarshan, *Kabyadarshan (Purnachandra Basur Kaby) Sundari Granther Samalochana), Aryadarshan*, Shraban, 1287, p. 171.
18. Basu, Purnachandra, *Bimala*, pp. 193-94.
19. *Ibid.*, p. 194.
20. *Ibid.*, p. 195.
21. Basu, Purnachandra, *Falashruti*, 1314 B.S.
22. Basu, Purnachandra, *Falashruti,* op. cit., pp. 38-39.
23. Bondopadhyay, Yogendranath, *Bishabriksha, Aryadarshan*, 1284 B.S., pp. 238-61.
24. *Ibid.*, p. 244.
25. (a) Basu, Debendra Bijoy, *Upanyas Sambandha Koyekti Katha, Nabyabharat*, 2nd part, Issue IX , Poush, 1291 B.S., pp. 407-16.
    (b) Basu, D.B., *Upanyaser Charitra Chitra, Nabyabharat*, Part II, Issue XI, Falgun, 1291 B.S., pp. 526-29.
    (c) Basu, D.B., *Upanyaser Charitra (Dwitiya Prastab), Nabyabharat*, Part II, Issue XII, Chaitra, 1291 B.S., pp. 555-64.
26. Basu, D.B., *Upanyas Sambandha Koyekti Katha*, p. 412.

27. *Ibid.*, p. 413.
28. Basu, Debendra Bijoy, *Upanyaser Charitra Chitra*, pp. 526-27.
29. Basu, Debendra Bijoy, *Upanyaser Charitra Chitra, (Dwitiya Prastab)*, pp. 556-57
30. *Ibid.*, pp. 558-59.
31. *Ibid.*, p. 559.
32. Nyayaratna, Ramgati, *Banglabhasha O Bangla Sahitya Bishayak Prastab*, 1873.
33. Nyayaratna, Ramgati, *Banglabhasha o Bangla Sangla Sahitys Bishayak Prastab*, 2nd edition, 1294 B.S., pp. 274-75.
34. *Ibid.*, pp. 272-73.
35. *Ibid.*, pp. 273-74.
36. *Ibid.*, pp. 275-76.
37. *Ibid.*, p. 274.
38. *Ibid.*, pp. 277-78.
39. *Ibid.*, p. 278.
40. Basu, Chandranath, *Novel be Kathgranther Uddeshya, Bangadarshan*, Baishakh, 1387 B.S.
41. Basu, Chandranath, *Novel ba Kathagranther Uddeshta, Bangadarshan*, Part VII, Reflect publication, Sept. I. 1982, pp. 18-19.
42. Sengupta, Subodhchandra, *Bangali Samalochana Parichay, Bangadarshan.* 1st Pub., Magh, 1375 B.S., p. 103.
43. *Ibid.*, p. 153.
44. Bondopadhyay, Haridas, *Banglar Upanyas Lekhak, Kalpana* 6th year. Baishakh, 1296 B.S., pp. 77-88.
45. According to shrish Chandra Das, a real critic must have strong imaginative power coupled with insight and his attitude must be liberal and sympathetic. (*Sahitya Sandarshan,* 5th edn., 1966, p. 187)
46. Bondopadhyay, Haridas, *Banglar Upanyas Lekhak*, p. 77.
47. *Ibid.*, pp. 77-78.
48. *Ibid.*, p. 78.
49. *Ibid.*
50. Bondopadhyay, Haridas, op. cit., p. 78.
51. *Ibid.*, p. 80.
52. *Ibid.*, pp. 79-80.
53. Roychowdhury, Girija Prasanna, *Bankimchandra—Durgeshnandini,* 1297 B.S.
54. Roychowdhury, Girija Prasanna, op. cit., pp. 3-12.

55. *Ibid.*, pp. 13-12.
56. *Ibid.*, p. 3.
57. *Ibid.*, pp. 16-17.
58. Roychowdhury, Girija Prasanna, op. cit., p. 23.
59. *Ibid.*, p. 11.
60. Tagore, Rabindranath, *Panchabhut,* Chaitra, 1299 B.S., Reprinted, *Bankimchandra,* Viswa-Bharati, 1977.
61. Tagore, Rabindranath. *Saratchandra, Prabasi*, Ashwin, 1338 B.S. Reprinted, *Bankimchandra.* Viswa-Bharati, 1977.
62. *Bankimchandra*, p. 88.
63. *Ibid.*, pp. 102-03.
64. Dutta, Ramesh Chandra, *Bankimchandra O Adhunik Bangiya Sahitya, Sahitya Parisat Patrika,* Part-I, Issue-I, Shraban, 1301 B.S., pp. 1-6.
65. *Ibid.*, p. 4.
66. *Ibid.*
67. Ghose, Hemendra Prasad, *Bankimchandra: Dasi*, July, 1895, pp. 388-94.
68. *Ibid.*, pp. 388-89.
69. *Ibid.*, p. 390.
70. Pande, Sireswar, *Bankimchandra O Hindur Adarsha, Sahitya Parisat Patrika*, 1302 B.S., Reprinted: Bondopadhyay, Dr. Shrikumar & Pal, Dr. Prafulla Chandra (edited), op. cit., pp. 298-319.
71. Bondopadhyay, Dr. Shrikumar & Pal, Dr. Prafulla Chandra (ed). *Samalochana Sahitya*, pp. 300-01.
72. Rakshit, Haran Chandra, *Banga Sahitye Bankim*, 1306 B.S.
73. Rakshit, Haran Chandra, *Banga Sahitye Bankim, 3rd edition*, 1317, p. 51.
74. *Ibid.*, pp. 76-78.
75. Swami, Shrimat Uttamananda, *Bankimchandra, Nabaprabha,* Part II, Issue II, Chaitra, 1308 B.S., pp. 75-91.
76. Swami, Shrimat Uttamananda, *Bankimchandra*, op. cit., p. 86.
77. Shastri, Shibnath, *Ramtanu Lahiri O Tatkalin Bangasamaj*, 1903.
78. *Ibid.*, pp. 207-71.
79. Bondopadhyay, Yogneshwar, *Bangala Sukumar Sahitya, Bangiya Sammilan—Karyabibarin O Pathita Prabandha,* Year II, 1315 B.S.
80. Bondopadhyay, Yogneshwar, *Bangla Sukumar Sahitya*, op. cit., pp. 18-19.
81. *Ibid.*, p. 18.
82. *Ibid.*

83. Chanda, Nirmal Kumar, *Durgeshnandinir Bankimchandra, Nabyabharat,* Part XXVII, Issue III, Asharh, 1316 B.S., pp. 137-44 & *Nabyabharat,* Part XXVII, Issue IV, Shraban, 1316 B.S., pp. 209-13.
84. Chanda, Nirmal Kumar, *Durgeshnandinir Bankimchandra*, op. cit., p. 139.
85. *Ibid.*, Shraban, p. 209.
86. *Ibid.*
87. *Ibid.*, p. 210.
88. Bondopadhyay, Jatindranath, *Bankimchandrer Diggaj Charitra, Janmabhumi*, 17th Years, Issue VII, Kartik, 1316 B.S., pp. 235-45.
89. *Ibid.*, pp. 242-43.
90. *Durgeshnandini*, Bangiya Sahitya Parisad 3rd print, 1370 B.S., p. 118.
91. Sen, Suresh Chandra, *Kabyakatha (Bankimchandra O Musliman Sampreday)*, S.K. Lahiri & Co., 1909.
92. *Ibid.*, pp. 47-48.
93. *Ibid.*, p. 48.
94. *Ibid.*, pp. 48-51.
95. *Ibid.*, p. 51.
96. (a) Bandopadhyay, Lalit Kumar, *Bankimchandrer Akhyaikabali, Bharatbarsha*, Asharh, 1322 B.S., pp. 6-11.

    (b) Bandopadhyay, Lalit Kumar, *Ma*, *Bharatbarsha*, 3rd year, Part I, Issue II, Shraban, 1322 B.S., pp. 264-82.

    (c) Bandopadhyay, Lalit Kumar, *Dui Bhagini, Bharatbarhsa*, Year IV. Part I, Issue III, Shraban, 323 B.S., pp. 391-407.
97. (a) Bandopadhyay, Lalit Kumar, *Kebyasudha*, Kartik, 1322 B.S.

    (b) Bandopadhyay, Lalit Kumar, *Premer Katha,* Jaishtha, 1327 B.S.

    (c) Bandopadhyay, Lalit Kumar, *Sakhi,* 1328 B.S.
98. Bandopadhyay, Lalit Kumar, *Bankimchandrer Akhyaikabali,*
99. Bandopadhyay, Lalit Kumar, *Ma*, p. 266.
100. Bandopadhyay, Lalit Kumar, *Kabyasudha*, p. 10.
101. Bandopadhyay, Lalit Kumar, *Dui Shagini*, p. 394.
102. Bandopadhyay, Lalit Kumar, *Premer Katha*, pp. 44-49.
103. Bandopadhyay, Lalit Kumar, *Sakhi*, pp. 18-19.
104. Bandopadhyay, Lalit Kumar, *Banglasahityer Kramaunnati O Bankim Chandra, Manasi,* Year VI, Pt.-II, Issue-III, Kartik, 1321, pp. 417-39.
105. *Ibid.*, p. 434.
106. Bandopadhyay, Chandicharan, *Bangla Sahityer Karmounnati O Bankimchandra*, op. cit., p. 434.

107. Sen, Shashanka Mohan, *Bangabani*, Dhaka Albert Library, 1915.
108. *Ibid*., p. 59.
109. Mazumder, Bijoyratna, *Bankimer Upanyase Hasya Ras, Harmabani*, Bhadra, 1322 B.S., pp. 125-29.
110. *Ibid*., p. 125.
111. Roy, Gnanendralal, *Upanyase Bharma Prachar, Nobyabhnrat*, Shraban, 1323 B.S. pp. 248-53.
112. *Ibid*., p. 248.
113. *Ibid*., pp. 249-53.
114. Roy, Amarendranath, *Sehitya Prasanga, Bharatbarsha*. 4th year, Part I, Issue V. Kartik, 1323, B.S., pp. 793-94.
115. *Ibid*., p. 793.
116. *Ibid*., p. 794.
117. Roy, Amarendranath, *Bankimer Upanayase Matrichaoi, Argna*. 7th Kalpa, Part XII Chaitra, 323 B.S., pp. 391-97.
118. *Ibid*., p. 393.
119. Basu, Jitendralal, *Adhunik Bangasahitye Ma, Manasi O Marnabani*, 8th year, Issue IV, Jaistha, 1323 B.S., pp. 249-55.
120. *Ibid*., p. 451.
121. *Ibid*.
122. Odud, Kazi Abdul, *Bankim Chandra Praoasi*, 1325 B.S. Reprinted, Karim Rejaul *Bankimchandra O Musalman Samaj*, 1944, pp. 128-30.
123. *Ibid*., p. 12.
124. Duttagupta, Birendra Kumar, *Upanyas, Saurabh*, 7th year, Issue-IV, Magh, 1325 B.S., pp. 77-78.
125. *Ibid*.
126. Taraknath Granthabali, (a compilation of Taraknath's series of essays on Bankim, *Bankim Prasanga: Dhaka Review O Sammilan*, Kartik-Chaitra, 1325 B.S.) Hitabati Karyalaya, 326 B.S.
127. *Ibid*., p. 335.
128. *Ibid*., p. 337.
129. *Taraknath Granthabali*, op. cit., p. 335.
130. *Ibid*., p. 336.
131. Duttagupta, Akshay Kumar, *Bankimchandra,* 1st Pub., 1327 B.S.
132. Duttagupta, Akshay Kumar, *Bankimchandra,* 2nd edn., Jignasa, May, 1975, pp. 46-48.
133. *Ibid*., p. 52.
134. Duttagupta, Akshay Kumar, *Bankimchandra*, op. cit., p. 50.
135. *Ibid*., p. 49.

136. *Ibid.*, pp. 51-52.
137. *Ibid.*, p. 54.
138. *Ibid.*, pp. 60-62.
139. (a) Pal, Bipinchandra, *Banglar Nabajugar Katha (Ekadash Katha-Bankim Sahitya), Bengalbai,* 2nd year, Part-I, Issue-I, Falgun, 1329 B.S. Reprinted: Bashi, Pramathanath & Dutta, Bijit Kumar (Ed.), *Sahitya Samput, Viswa-Bharati,* 1965, pp. 98-106.

    (b) Pal, Bipinchandra, *Banglar Nabajuger Katha (Trayodash Katha), Bangabani,* 2nd year, Part-I, Issue-III, Baishakh, 1330 B.S., pp. 375-87.

    (c) Pal, Bipinchandra, *Nabajuger Bangla Sahitye Bankimchandra, Nabyabharat*, Bhadra, 1330 B.S., pp. 235-49.
140. Pal, Bankimchandra, *Nabajuger Bangla Sahitya Bankimchandra*, pp. 240-41.
141. Bishi, Pramathanath & Dutta, Bijit Kumar (edited) op. cit., p. 101.
142. *Ibid.*, p. 100.
143. Bishi, Pramathananth & Dutta, Bijit Kumar (ed.) op. cit., p. 102.
144. Pal, Bipinchandra, *Banglar Nabajuger Katha*, op. cit., pp. 385-86.
145. *Ibid.*, pp. 386-87.
146. Bhattacharjee, Gopalchandra, *Bankimchandra O Rabindranath, Praba,* Pt. XXIII, Issue-III, Poush, 1330 B.S., pp. 293-302.
147. *Ibid.*, pp. 295-98.
148. Roy, Shiba Prasad, *Bankimchandra O Rabindranath,* Upanyase Art, Jamuna, 13th year, Issue-X, Magh, 1330 B.S., pp. 533-40.
149. Roy, Shiba Prasad, *Bankimchandra O Rabindranath,* Upanyase Art, Jamuna, 13th year, Issue-XI, Falgun, 1330, pp. 576-83.
150. Roy, Shiba Prasad, *Bankimchandra O Rabindranath,* Upanyase Art, Jamuna, 13th year, Issue-XII, Falgun, 1330, pp. 536.
151. Das, Kumudnath, *Bankimchandra, Archana,* 21st Part, Issue-X, Agahan, 1331 B.S., pp. 36-67.
152. *Ibid.*, p. 364.
153. Vedantashastri, Ramsahaya, *Bankimchandrer Bimala, Archana,* 23rd part, Issue-I, Falgun, 1332 B.S., pp. 36-39 & Archana, 23rd Pt. Issue-II, Chaitra, 1332 B.S., pp. 51-52.
154. Vedantashastri, Ramsahaya, *Tilottama O Ayesha, Bankimchandra, Bankim Chatushpath,* 1334 B.S., pp. 13-34.
155. *Ibid.,* (Introduction).
156. Vedantashastri, R.S., *Bankimchandrer Bimala, Archana*, Falgun, 1332 B.S., pp. 37-38.
157. *Ibid.*, p. 37.
158. Vedantashastri, R.S., *Bankimchandra*, 1334 B.S., p. 13.

159. Vedantashastri, Ramsahaya, *Bankimchandra, Bankim Chatushpath*, 1334 B.S., p. 13.
160. *Ibid.*
161. Commenting on individualistic criticism Asit Kumar Bandopadhyay says: "The feelings that occur in the mind of the critic after reading of the book, proper representation of those feelings forms the basis of individualistic criticism". *(Samalochanar Katha*, 3rd Print, January, 1971, pp. 14-15)
162. Vedantashastri, Ramsahayay, *Bankimchandrer Bimala*, Falgun, 1332 B.S., p. 37.
163. *Ibid.*
164. Ghose, Kamal Krishna, *Ayesha O Rebeka, Sachitra Shishir*, 2nd year, 36th week, Shraban 2, 1332 B.S., pp. 1105-10.
165. *Ibid.*, p. 1106.
166. *Ibid.*
167. Ghose, Kamal Krishna, *Ayesha O Rebeka, Sachitra Shishir*, 2nd year, 37th week, Shraban 9, 1332 B.S., p. 1124.
168. Ghose, Kamal Krishna, *Ayesha O Rebeka, Sachitra Shishir*, 2nd year, 36th week, Shraban 2, 1332 B.S., pp. 1307-08.
169. Bhattacharjee, Batuknath, *Bankim Sahitye Sannyas, Bangabani*, 5th year, Issue-VI, Shraban, 1333 B.S., pp. 640-51.
170. *Ibid.*, pp. 640-41.
171. Chakraborty, Adhyapak Heramba Chandra, *Upanyasik Bankimchandra, Udayan*, 2nd year, 12th issue, Chaitra, 1341 B.S., pp. 1544-46.
172. *Ibid.*, p. 1546.
173. *Ibid.*, pp. 1545-46.
174. Basu, Indradeb, *Bankimsahitye Pashchatya Prabhab, Desh*, 1st year, 39th issue, Bhadra-1, Saturday, 1341 B.S., pp. 23-24.
175. *Ibid.*, p. 23.
176. Paul, Dhiren, *Bankim Sahitye Pashchatya Prabhab, Desh,* Issue-2nd, Saturday, Bhadra 22, 1341 B.S., pp. 23-24.
177. *Ibid.*, p. 24.

3
Kapalkundala

PURNACHANDRA BASU

Purnachandra Basu wrote the first elaborate criticism of *Kapalkundala* in his essay of the same title.[1] The essay discusses the diction, characterization and inner significance of the novel. The critic attempted at upholding the beauty and solemnity of the massive background of the novel.[2]

Purnachandra pointed out that the tragic pattern incorporated in the novel was borrowed from the western literature, and raised objection regarding the tragic inclination for the classical literature.[3]

He was an admirer of Sanskrit literature. Because of this classical prejudice he stated that the gravity of *Kapalkundala* was intensified by imitating the Greek tragic technique, but it should have been avoided[4] considering that the outcome was evil. Analysing the character of Kapalkundala, he opined that Kapalkundala was so dear to us—a jewel of our heart because of her sufferings.[5] This remarks however appears to be paradoxical.

Purnachandra tried to recreate the characters of the novel giving imagination and emotional touches, and in such emotional recreation of characters, he ran the risk of distorting the very reality of the novel. For example, comparing Kapalkundala with Lutfunnesa, Purnachandra said, "Kapalkundala is a rising full-moon, Lutfunnesa is a setting-sun with the rays in decline."[6] We are also sometime inspired by the deep literary taste and judgement of the critic's remarks. As for instance, finding out the opposite nature of Kapalkundala and Matibibi, Purnachandra said:

> Matibibi's character is clear and bright while Kapalkundala's is vague variety in other...one is earthly, while the other is imaginative. One is real, the other is an idea.[7]

Purnachandra Basu said that although *Kapalkundal*a is short in length, it did not appear to be a small novel because of its depth and width resulting from dimensional greatness of characters, their inherent contradictions and the interactions of characters and incidents which revealed Bankim's fertile imagination and dexterity in plot construction.[8] In fact, Purnachandra is the first critic of *Kapalkundala,* and he deserves appreciation for artistic evaluation of the novel. He also initiated the comparative method of criticism by instituting comparison of Kapalkundala with Shakuntala of Kalidas and Miranda of Shakespeare.

CHANDRASEKHAR MUKHAPADHYAY (1849-1822)

Chandrasekhar Mukhapadhyay wrote in defence of the tragic note of Kapalkundala when Damodar Mukhapadhyay brought out a sequel on *Kapalkundala* under the title Mrinmoyee with a happy ending. Chandrasekhar made a comparative study of Kapalkundala and Mrinmoyee in his essay *Mrinmoyee*[9] to establish his point of view,

> Chandrasekhar was not a true moralistic critic. He characterised Bankim as the mouthpiece of ethics and high ideals of Hindu religion. Even if such an attitude was the force behind this criticism, he laid more emphasis upon the tragic ending rather than happy ending. So, he was more attracted by the miserable Juliet than by Shakespeare, and for this the tragic end of Kapalkundala appeared to be more artistic to him. He said there was no artistic necessity of writing the conclusion of *Kapalkundala.*[10]

It is evident form the above discussion that Chandrasekhar was influenced by the greek English tragedies and he tried to evaluate *Kapalkundala* as a tragic novel on the touchstone of western value judgement.

DEBENDRA BIJOY BASU

Debendra Bijoy Basu's comments on *Kapalkundala* found in the essay *Upanyase Charitrachitra* is brief but penetrating analysis of Bankim's *Kapalkundala.*[11]

Debendra Bijoy grouped the novelistic characters into four types.[12] According to him, Kapalkundala and Padmabati belong to the third group which reveals inner mysteries of nature learned through study of social sciences and gathering of knowledge. He also gave reason why he classed them in the third group. This is because, Bankim had very skillfully blended the motive forces of these characters through his scientific reasoning power.[13]

Debendra Bijoy had drawn our attention towards Bankim's power of characterization, and it is evidently clear from his discussion that Kapalkundala and Padmabati are active characters.

RAMGATI NYAYRATNA (1238-1301 B.S.)

In Ramgati Nyayratna's *Bangla Bhase o Bangla Sahitya Bishyak Prastab,*[14] there was a sudden fall in the standard of criticism of *Kapalkundala* from the standard set by the earlier two critics.

According to Ramgati Nyayratna's *Kapalkundala* is a wonderful creation of Bankimchandra. There is something uncommon in her; she is a living image of nature. But about this *Kapalkundala.* The critic said:

> The poet might have created the character of Kapalkundala to relate the character of a woman who was deprived of worldly happiness by a sad true of fortune.[15]

Matibibi shows Bankim's power of understanding of the nature of woman; but Ramgati made slang remarks[16] about this character.

The critic opined that only the attractive characters are fit for heroes and heroines in novels. Judged from this point of view he assessed Kapalkundala's character and found her to be lacking in devotion as a woman, and, therefore, he raised the question can anybody desire a woman like Kapalkundala as his life partner?[17]

In fact, Ramgati failed to understand that *Kapalkundala* is a romantic novel and that the world of Kapalkundala is bright with romantic and free imagination. Therefore he raised a voice of protest against the finality of Kapalkundala's life and said that the woman who had to be made miserable, there must be a clear display of the fact that she was well-up in her earlier stages—the turn of fortune in her would give rise to pity. Bankim had not given any understanding of the early stages of Kapalkundala; hence the readers are not under any moral obligation to feel pity for her.[18] Of course, this attitude fairly well exemplifies the classical idea of tragic hero.

HARIDAS BONDOPADHYAY

Haridas Bondopadhyay's essay *Banglar Upanyas Lekhak* was a considerably matured criticism of *Kapalkundala*—The critic made a comparative study of Miranda (Shakespeare), Shakuntala (Kalidas) and Kapalkundala, and showing the similarities amongst them tried to show the originality of Kapalkundala. Miranda and Shakuntala also lived in wood, but they were not inexperienced like Kapalkundala. Kapalkundala did not fall in love with Nabakumar at the first sight, but Miranda and Shakuntala did. Haridas tried to explain Kapalkundala's originality in this light.[20]

Explaining the reasons of Kapalkundala's figure in worldly life the critic said that Kapalkundala was an ideal character[21] of Bankim, her wild nature and love of freedom had romanticism in their basis and this inexperience since childhood has made her wild nature so deep-rooted in her that Nabakumar's love could not bind her.[22] Analysing the artistic beauty of the book, the critic opined that *Kapalkundala* was an wonderful creation of Bankim's artistic genius—its incidents and situations and the descriptions of these—reflect the writer's great artistic sense.[23]

The historical value of Haridas's criticism is great both in respect of its comparative criticism and as an ideal of pure literary criticism.

GIRIJA PRASANNA ROYCHOWDHURY (1862-1899)

Girija Prasanna Roychowdhury's essay *Bankimchandra-Durgeshnandini, Kapalkundala O Mrinalini*[24] marks him out as a critic with rare literary taste in Bankim age.

Girija Prasanna deserves much credit for his analytical power of judgement which is found in his analysis of Kapalkundala's love of liberty, benevolence, motherliness, and the working of fate in her. Girija Prasanna explained the reasons behind Kapalkundala had learnt her miserable past from Abhikari. The burden of sorrows, and the atrocities of the kapalik had vehemently reacted in her which are responsible for her extra-ordinary softness of mind; and, therefore, the worldly pleasure and Nabakumar's love would not perturb her.[25]

Kapalkundala's fate was shaped by her love of liberty. Giving a psycho-analysis of this, Girija Prasanna said that living in wilderness she could not remain under the social obligations to depend upon her husband absolutely: "The future of Kapalkundala was built by the interplay of that devotion and fate and force."[26]

Bankimchandra had placed his heroine Kapalkundala in the face of a free unveiled nature as a mysterious image. Girija Prasanna observed it very ingeniously. He said:

> Readers, have you ever seen in picture gallery, a picture of combined colours? A 'lump', colour is here, a 'lump' colour is there, drawn in meticulous care, but looks like one being draw carelessly. Have you seen such a picture? Kapalkundala is such a picture.[27]

And therefore, he said—"One has to go beyond this earth to understand Kapalkundala."[28] Such an impressionistic criticism of Kapalkundala has not been seen earlier.

According to the critic, *Kapalkundala* is not merely a novel. It is more than that. It is a poem, a play and a song—all in one. Here Girija Prasanna makes observation from total impression, and he deserves praise for this.

Girija Prasanna's second criticism of credit was his analysis of the character of Matibibi. This analysis shows his deep understanding and experience of human nature. In explaining the reasons why Padmabati was gradually getting rid of the tendency of sin. Girija Prasanna said that Padmabati did not give it up with the realization that there is sin in sinning, but she had to give it up because there was no peace and happiness in sin, because search for happiness is the primary passion of human beings.

At last, the critic came to the conclusion: "Padma would love her own happiness very much and for this selfishness her aspiration was not bound up permanently in a particular place."[29] The essay is full of such analysis.

Despite merits of Girija Prasanna's criticism it could be said with certainty that he was not entirely free from influence of the age. Much of his criticism is marred by emotionalism. For example, pointing to Kapalkundala's presence in the lonely wood in order to help Nabakumar, the critic says: "Oh! What a beautiful Picture! What a source of kindness in that fiery desert, oh, What a sweet sound."[30]

SUDHINDRANATH THAKUR (1869-1929)

Sudhindranath Thakur's *Kapalkundala O Miranda*[31] is the next example of comparative criticism. But he is an emotional critic. Narrating Kapalkundala's life emotionally, the critic said: "Kapalkundala is no more in this world, but our tears are still dropping on her grave."[32]

However, it is in the comparative study of Kapalkundala and Miranda that the critic's genius is well marked. Sudhindranath gave a reasonable explanation of why Kapalkundala was not surprised to see Nabakumar or did not feel any attraction for him. According to him, to Kapalkundala human figure was not an object of wonder as it was to Miranda, and therefore, Nabakumar's features could not make any impression upon her.[33] Making a comparative study of both the characters, the critic further said: "In Miranda, we find the simple appeal of love upon an wood-lander; while in Kapalkundala, we find a fruitless worldly attraction upon an wood lander."[34]

Such comparative studies not only reveal the basic differences between characters but also help in understanding and appreciation of the characters. Moreover, all this throw light on the critic's power of penetration and introspection.

BIRESWAR PANDE (1842-1911)

Bireswar Pande in his essay *Bnkimchandra o Hindur Adarsha,*[35] attempted to discuss the extent of Hindu ideas and moral teachings reflected in *Kapalkundala*. The very title of the essay indicated this. The critic thought that the pre-marriage formalities in case of Nabakumar such as taking of an account of his ancestry by Adhikari, determining the moment (Logno) by the help of almanac, etc. showed Bankim's carefulness about casteism in the matter of Hindu marriage.[36]

According to Sanskrit rhetoric, both Kapalkundala and Nabakumar were 'virtuous and yet they met a tragic fate. Bireswar gave three points in favour of this argument-first, even if Kapalkundala was Brahmin by caste, her real identity was unkown. So, Bankim did not want to establish the children of an unidentified character in society. Secondly, Bankim did not like a happy life with Padmabati when a seeker of shelter was forsaken, and lastly, Bankim did not want to say the directions of 'Hindu Shastra' either as false or without power. The prayer of kapalik was based on Hindu Shastra. In order to establish the truth Bankim showed that smiting grief, mesmerism and such tantric ways were not false. Therefore, he said that the death of Nabakumar and Kapalkundala was inevitable.[37]

Such analysis of the critic is not wholly baseless. Yet, the critical side in this essay is secondary while search for Hindu ideals is primary.

HEMENDRA PRASAD GHOSH (1876-1963)

The next considerably pure criticism of *Kapalkundala* was written by Hemendra Prasad Ghosh in his essay *Bankimchandra.*[38] He referred to his novel in his essay *Rishi Bankimchandra.*[39] Hemendra Prasad attempted a sympathetic treatment of Kapalkundala. He observed Bankim in *Kapalkundala* as a novelist and a poet.[40] According to him, *Kapalkundala* was a wonderful creation of poet Bankim. He rightly said that slip of trifoliate (Bail-leaf) from Bhabani's feet and dream sequence etc. had added mysteries to the narrative.[41]

As regards worldly experience, Kapalkundala was different from Shakuntala and Miranda; so, glorifying the character of Kapalkundala, Matibibi-episode was non-tempted against Kapalkundala. Such things are intelligently dealt with in the essay.[42]

HARAN CHANDRA RAKSHIT

Haran Chandra Rakshit's *Banga Sahitye Bankim*[43] shows sparks of pure criticism. Haran Chandra claimed that the European tragic appeal appeared in a new perspective in *Kapalkundala*. He sought to determine the poetic and dramatic elements along with the Greek concept of fate in *Kapalkundala*. He concluded that poetically *Kapalkundala* is the best of Bankim's novel. Because, the main objectives of poetry is—creation of beauty,—'a fantasy born of liberal, eternal and superb imagination.'[44] This had been reflected in the innocent beauty living in nature, and that beauty had been flourished in the presence of the Kapalik also. Haran Chandra thought that not only poetically but dramatically also, *Kapalkundala* was best of Bankim's creation.[45]

Haran Chandra thought that dramatic situations depend upon fatalism, and that fatalism combined with the dramatic situations had been reflected in *Kapalkundala* like Shakespeare's *Hamlet*. Because, the working of fate is imaginative and various, and *Kapalkundala's* mysterious origin is also dreamy, imaginative and various.[46]

GOLAK BEHARI MUKHOPADHYAY

Golak Behari's *Kapalkundala*[47] shows that Bankimchandra took a significant turn towards pure literary criticism. The essay is based on argument; it is not only objective but romantic in vein.

Golak Behari tried to assess the greatness of the novel *Kapalkundala* in its varied aspects—its artistic beauty, psychoanalysis, dramatic situation, etc. Turning to the total impression of the novel, the critic points out that the portrayal of beautiful pictures and creation of fair Kapalkundala was not meaningless and aimless since the aim of the book was to highlight the conflict that has developed between nature and man drunk with freedom.[48] This conflict of man with Nature began only after the evil force in the novel had broken its hand after fall from the bank of river. This fall is significant since Kapalik was neither pious nor devoted to God, rather himself claiming to be God.[49]

The speciality with this novel was that here there was easy play of love, no pleasure of union, no repentance of the fatalism, or there were no critical situations, and yet, all these things had added to the beauty of a strong imagination force had made everything lively and forceful. This was the view of Golok Behari and he said: "...but it is silent—it is lost in its own greatness.... There is no dearth of personality and force, all are in the marrow and bone of Nabakumar. Social elements such as Kapalik's malicious designs, Matibibi's revenge, disguise, etc. are there. But all are written with great originality.[50]

Like his predecessors Golak Behari also brought references of Miranda, Shakuntala. He showed that Kapalkundala was more attached to nature than any other. But the notable feature of Golak Behari was that he had drawn our attention to the elemental passions of Kapalkundala: "The gift of precious jewels to a scoundrel on the way shows Kapalkundala's elemental sense of pity."[51]

JITENDRA LAL BASU

In his essay *Bankimchandra,* Jitendra Lal Basu attempted an aesthetic appreciation of *Kapalkundala*. He categorically pointed out that there was no philosophical or spiritual approach in the novel, the only aim of Bankim was creation of beauty. Despite her similarity with Miranda, Kapalkundala was free from inconsistencies. Jitendra Lal upheld that *Kapalkundala* was a wonderful creation of Bankim; she was wholly inexperienced in the ways of the world, she was indifferent to worldly temptation; and she was full of simplicity.[52] When the lonely Nabakumar was miserable on the seashore, nature did not become grave. There was no lack of concentration on the part of Nabakumar to enjoy the scenery of the ocean. This, according to Jitendra Lal, is a wonderful creation of beauty which can be compared with *Kumar Sambhab*, (Part-III).[53]

KUMUD NATH LAHIRI

The next critical essay to be discussed is *Kapalkundala Upanyaser Uddeshaya*[54] by Kumud Nath Lahiri. Critics like Girija Prasanna admitted that creation of beauty was one of the main features of this novel. He strongly opposed Girija Prasanna and said that Bankim had a special purpose to serve in this novel. Narrating the incidents of the novel in details, the critic gave a psychological interpretation of this novel.

Kumud Nath said that Bankim wanted to reveal the subtle truth of the universe through the union between artificial and original, non-fulfilment, anxiety, and eternal conflict of the natural to be united with unnatural, difference between the limited artificiality and the unlimited nature, and also through the sudden union of Kapalkundala with Nabakumar and its consequences.

Nabakumar had an intense anxiety for not getting Kapalkundala wholly. Kumud Nath commented on it: "*Science will forever different from human creation. Kapalkundala's motto* is to express it."[55]

Kumud Nath attempted to make an analysis of the motives of Bankim behind his plan of characterization. Morever, he also tried to explain giving psychological reasons to such questions as why Kapalkundala rescued Nabakumar from the hand of Kapalik and why she was surprised to see the beggar running away. The critic explained Kapalkundala's surprise as the apparent expression of wonder for the natural when confronted with the unnatural. Regarding the rescue of Nabakumar he gave the explanation that Kapalkundala's violent reaction to the Kapalik's atrocities had been expressed through her attempt to rescue Nabakumar from Kapalik's grasp. The critic specially pointed out that in order to crystalize the character of Kapalkundala, Bankim has pitted her against such opposing characters like the Tantrik Kapalik, luxurious Matibibi and Shyamasundari who was deprived of union with her husband.[56]

JOGESH CHANDRA BASU

Jogesh Chandra Basu searched for the source and inspiration of Kapalkundala in some of his essays.[57] About the source and characters, Jogesh Chandra said that Kapalkundala's incidents were not wholly imaginative; Bankim's real experience was reflected in it. The natural beauty of Doulatpur and Dariyapur the beauty of the sea there, the wonderful Sandbank, temple of Knathi, the ancient temple of Dariyapur,[58] the place of Kapalik's was Hijli,[59] Bankim's meeting with Kapalik , all these were the primary sources of *Kapalkundala*.

Jogesh Chandra said that Bankim had taken two contradictory pictures—Kapalkundala and Kapalik in order to exemplify the dualism of beauty and ugliness existing in the world of nature.[60] This kind of observation struck a note of novelty which at the same time contributed to the beauty of literary creation by the critic's awareness of the conflicting nature and its representation in *Kapalkundala*.

Jogesh Chandra's essays as examples of Historical method of criticism have immense value to the future generation of critics.

BHABESH CHANDRA BONDOPADHYAY

Bhabesh Chandra, in his book *Kapalkundala Charitra Somalochana*,[61] discussed the characters of Nabakumar, Kapalkundala and Matibibi. He chose certain elements from each character and discussed the characters in the light of these elements and also analysed the process of growth and development. This criticism showed simultaneously the modern liberal attitude and the ancient trend marked by ethical approach with passion and emotion.

The critic analysed the character of Nabakumar in the light of the characteristic features of his nature like—his calmness in danger, duty-boundedness, helping of others, manliness, gratitude, purity of heart, devotion to God, fatalism, etc.[62] Explaining the character of Matibibi, he said that she was on the one hand jocular, skilled speaker, sharply intelligent, clever, brave, affectionate, proud and on the other hand, lusty, crafty and shamless.[63] In the same manner, he observed in the character of Kapalkundala her deep devotion to God, worldly inexperience, simplicity, love for liberty and belief in fate etc.[64]

In his search for the Hindu ideals, Bhabesh Chandra found that Nabakumar is a fatalistic Hindu Bengalee, the Bengalee Bankim had painted him as an ideal Bengalee.[65] In the eye of the critic, Kapalkundala was not an ideal of Hindu woman since her devotion to God was not combined with her devotion to her husband. This lack of devotion to husband had brought about her disastrous consequences and this was how according to Bhabesh Chandra, Bankim had pin-pointed the ethical question.[66]

It has been mentioned earlier that spark of modern criticism is there in Bhabesh Chandra's approach. The critic said that the incidents which led to the ruin of Nabakumar and Mrinmoyee, is Mrinmoyee's nightly adventure which had added fuel to it. Nabakumar's reading of the letter of disguised Brahmin is the fire and Nabakumar's view of the conversation between Mrinmoyee and the disguised Brahmin had added wind in it. The critic's subtle observation and outspoken attitudes were evident when he said: "Injecting the qualities of man in that co-heroine Matibibi and the qualities of woman in the hero Nabakumar, Bankimchandra has created varieties of characters in that novel in discussion."[67] The most distinctive feature of this essay is Bhabesh Chandra's psychological analysis of the transformation of Matibibi's character. He very subtly observed that long-standing enjoyment of lust, Selim's love for Meherunnesa, despair for her failure to become the principal queen of the Badshah of Delhi, and fruitless efforts to make Khasru the Badshah. Matibibi has been suffering from such despair; she was overwhelmed with sorrow for penance of sin. These things had been pointed out by Bhabesh Chandra as the reasons behind Mati's union with her husband.[68]

However, Bhabesh Chandra's criticism is not entirely free from emotion. One of such emotional expression is—"Alas! when in every Bengalee family a Nabakumar will born."[69]

LALIT KUMAR BANDOPADHYAY (1275-1336 B.S.)

Lalit Kumar Bandopadhyay wrote the most exhaustive criticism of Kapalkundala before Bankim centenary in many of his essays[70] and particulary in his research type book *Kapalkundala Tettba.*[71]

Justifying the title *Kapalkundala*, Lalit Kumar argued that although the novel reflected brightly the heroism, self-restraint and love of Nabakumar, the complex mystery of Padmabati and the sweet friendship of Syama. It was through the character of Kapalkundala that the novelists' aim and purpose had been adequately manifested.[72]

The critic observed the lack of motherliness in the female characters of this book and gave arguments of this lapse. He said that motherliness in *Kapalkundala* would have been a bar to reproduce her wild nature.[73] But the critic's mental dualism is found when he says *Is not her universal sense of pity reflection of her motherliness.*

Even if Lalit Kumar characterised Peshman of *Kapalkundala* as friend of third grade, he drew our attention to the necessity of this character in the novel. He argued that in spite of being Matibibi's waiting woman, Peshman sometimes appeared as her friend and through their conversation the character of Matibibi was exposed.[74] He pointed out the fact that Lutfaunnesa in spite of being a friend of Khasru's mother was in fact her rival.[75] Explaining the friendship between Lutfaunnesa and Meherunnesa, the critic assumed that once they were very closely attached to each other like Shakespeare's Harmia and Helena,[76] but later on, in the contest of love their friendship was pouted like that of Harmia and Helena. Hence it was not an example of genuine friendship. Matibibi pretended friendship in order to know the mind of Mehorunnesa.[77]

Lalit Kumar attempted to deep study of the character of Kapalkundala. His analysis of this character was the result of his deep study and research of both western and oriental literatures. At the very outset Lalit Kumar laid the foundation of his analysis citing examples of the characters of same nature from the world creature. He made mention of Milton's Eve, Kalidas's Shakuntala, Uma, Homer's Nosikeys, Shakespeare's Miranda, Byron's Hydi, Babbhuti's Kapalkundala (Malati Madhad), etc.[78] But the merits and demerits of the characters of the similar nature are not there in his analysis. But it is evident from his discussion that *Kapalkundala* is poetically superior to her counterparts.

Lalit Kumar's philosophical interpretation of Kapalkundala's character is a great contribution to Bankim criticism. He pointed that what elements would constitute a female character when she was forlorn and made to grow by herself away from human civilization, the philosophical question should be considered in understanding the character of Kapalkundala. Then giving psychological analysis of Kapalkundala's character the critic said that the elemental divine passions like love of liberty, curiosity, simplicity, allegiance, bravery, fear, mental purity, sense of pity, etc.[79] had been there with Kapalkundala from the beginning and these were developed through her actions.[80]

Bankimchandra had given an imaginative shape to a philosophical idea and had given a poetic flavor to this philosophical idea and Kapalkundala is the image of this idea. Drawing the attention to this artistic beauty Lalit Kumar said that he did not care for moral teaching or ethical significance in character but paid much attention to poetic beauty, artistic skill imaginative zeal and: "...those who are the followers of art for art's sake, they will be pleased to see the picture and taste the poet her."[81]

Perhaps Lalit Kumar's most significant contribution is the attempt at total evaluation of the novel. He discussed all the interrelated aspects of the novel, e.g., the necessity of the different characters, symbolism, omens,[82] unity of time, place and action,[83] heroine's physical beauty,[84] and characterization and plot construction.

The critic obviously was influenced by the western principle of literary criticism. And this influence is very much pronounced in his critical analysis of the sub-plot in the novel. The critic said that Padmabati episode had introduced as contract to Kapalkundala story. Nabakumar served as mediator between the two, because the fate of both the heroines depends on him, he is the 'protagonist' or co-hero, since the influence of his opposing force is there in the fate of the heroine. Nabakumar was the 'protagonist' of the subordinate episode also and Selim is the 'antagonist'. If both the episodes are viewed simultaneously, Kapalkundala and Padmabati were the heroine and the co-heroine.[85]

As stated earlier, Lalit Kumar gave equal emphasis upon the primary and secondary incidents and characters of the book. He had even left a considerable space for Kapalkundala's husband's sister Shyamasundari. Lalit Kumar observed that though a great bulk of this novel is being occupied by the super-natural power of a Bengalee woman—Shyamasundari at the same time, he had realized the necessity of this character in this novel, and said that in order to incline Kapalkundala towards family life, an affectionate mate was required, and that Shyamasundari had served that purpose.[86]

The characteristic feature of Lalit Kumar's criticism is to cite examples in the context and analyse them. However, a lot of things has made his findings confusing, and it seems as if sometimes he has failed to come out of the maze he has created. But his essays are not doubt rich in literary elements and these are free from moral or ethical implications.

CHANDI CHARAN BONDOPADHYAY (1264-1323 B.S.)

Literature is a 'matter of the mind', [87] but the influence and impact of contemporary time, place and action in it cannot be denied, Chandi Charan Bondopadhyay has searched of this influence in *Kapalkundala* in his *Bangasahityer Kramonnati o Bankimchandra.*[88] *Kapalkundala* is a novel of different taste, upholding of Hindu-ideal is not the chief purpose of this novel but Chandi Charan has concentrated himself in search of this ideal. He says that social picture has not been presented in this novel; but the then historical events and consequences have been hinted there in the book and from those events, Hindu idealism has been reflected.[89] These are only cursory remarks and not based upon arguments.

SHASHANKA MOHAN SEN (1872-1928)

Shashanka Mohan's was a genuine attempt at evaluation of Kapalkundala in his book *Bangabani.*[90] Shashanka Mohan believed that literature cannot be evaluated by hard and fast rules or ideals lay down by 'Shastra'. So, his is an impartial and objective attempt. He wanted to show *Kapalkundala* as a remarkable creation of Bankim's genius. Successful criticism made a bridge between the minds of the writer and the reader with the truth depicted in the book.[91] Shashanka Mohan made such an attempt in his criticism of *Kapalkundala*. According to him:

> Kapalkundala is a joyous product of genius. The poet had known himself, found the spark of his genius, but it is still wild, unsocial and marine.[92]

This shows that the feature with which the poet adorned Kapalkundala, was fully manifested in her and that was her fault. So, Kapalkundala's poetic supremacy had been admitted by the critic. He said:

> The poet has recognized the wild and open nature of man under social garb. In the portrayal of Kapalkundala, there is not so much of Bankim's artistic skill, but the impression is poetic.[93]

Even though impressed by the beauty of Kapalkundala, Shashanka Mohan hesitated to pay tribute for its imaginative romantic passions. He said that Kapalkundala like Nabinchandra's *Palashir Yudhha* was meaningless, purposeless, still it was beautiful, beauty which has not ever been seen.[94] He has deeply impressed and surprised by the beauty of Kapalkundala but was indifferent because of its not having any reality behind it. The insight and understanding of Shashanka Mohan are evident when he says: "*Kapalkundala is not a tale—not a novel, it is a prose-poem—a Greek drama*",[95] this observation is justified. Because there is credit in the plot construction, but no skill of a real novel is there, incidents are romantic, small in volume like Greek drama. Speed is maintained through briefing which ultimately led to the disastrous consequences with inevitable speed. So even though it is novel, it is also a prose-poem. Besides, Shashanka Mohan has drawn our attention to the working of fate following the Greek ideal of fate in it.[96]

AMARENDRA NATH ROY (1888-1957)

Amarendra Nath's *Bankim Upanyase Matrichabi*[97] shows classical approach to Bankim criticism. He raised objection as to the sexuality and inconsistencies in *Kapalkundala* and classified it as 'Rasha-Sahitya'. As the very title indicates, the critic searched for motherliness in Bankim novels, but he was disappointed in not finding 'Batsalya Rasa' (affection for children) in *Kapalkundala*. He also complained that Bankim did not take the opportunity to express 'Batsalya Rasa' through Nabakumar's mother because he thought that the beauty of the novel might be spoilt by this.[98]

JNANENDRA LAL ROY

Jnanendra Lal Roy discussed *Kapalkundala* in his *Upanyase Dharmaprachar-Bankimbabu*.[99] According to him, preaching, of 'Dharma' was the principal aim of Bankim's novels. He even advised to compile all the writings of Bankim in a volume with the title 'Bankim Sahitya' and gave word notes and explanations. The ethical critic said that Kapalkundala violated the social norms by going alone at dead of night with medicine for Shyamasundari. And this was why she had met the fatal consequence and this was the moral lesson of this novel.[100] Jnanendra Lal failed to understand that the real beauty of Kapalkundala was not based upon dry ethic, but upon a pure impression, and that is why he has given a contrary opinion of it.

GOPAL CHANDRA BHATTACHARJEE

Gopal Chandra Bhattacharjee's *Kapalkundalar Kabya Soundarjya*[101] was contemporary criticism with a new taste. The critic was more attracted by the inner beauty of the novel than by the subject-matter in it. Gopal Chandra presented the beauty born of the situations, description of nature and characterization in this novel with a fine touch of his impression. Describing the physical beauty of Kapalkundala, he said that by manifesting in Kapalkundala a bunch of dense long-hair the writer had unfolded a great source of beauty: "...this exceptional hair served as a mysterious limitation separating her from the generalities of person."[102]

In a sense, Gopal Chandra's criticism can be classified as aesthetic, though not purely aesthetic. Regarding aesthetic criticism, Bendetto Croce is of the view that: "True criticism of art is certainly aesthetic criticism but not because it disdains philosophy...."[103] Gopal Chandra's search for beauty in *Kapalkundala* is free from any philosophical implication.

Another feature of Gopal Chandra's essay is that he has tried to explain the writer's attempt to commune the external nature with the inner nature in this book. Bankimchandra had said:

> In poetry, inner feelings are changed by the impact of external nature and the external nature depends upon mental conditions—one is inherently related to the other.[104]

Gopal Chandra explained this feature of *Kapalkundala*. As for example—when Nabakumar deserted in the deep forest, was shivering with the shadow of death, a ray of light coming from a distance relieved him from this thought. Again, in the midst of extreme danger he was cheered up by the beauty of the ocean. Numberless wavelets of the blue ocean created music in Nabakumar's mind. Explaining this mental change of Nabakumar, Gopal Chandra said: "What a unification of tune between within and outside. This external and internal consistency is also a characteristic of this book."[105] He has rightly said that because of the unity of time, place, action, Kapalik is a successful portrayal.[106]

Gopal Chandra was successful in his attempt to analyse the beauty of the novel but his attempt to discuss the subject matter created confusion. Pointing to the marriage of Nabakumar and Kapalkundala, the critic said: "Nabakumar's discussion was like that of a young man, mad after beauty and pleasure."[107]

It cannot be denied that Nabakumar was infatuated by the beauty of Kapalkundala, but his passion for helping the distressed is the motive behind his marriage. Nabakumar says: "If any service can be done to her (Kapalkundala) at the cost of my life, I am ready for it."[108]

In spite of his merits, Gopal Chandra cannot get himself free from the emotional trend of the last century. Explaining the end of Kapalkundala's life, Gopal Chandra has said: "Kapalkundala floated towards eternity like the holy flowers used in worship of God."[109]

KSHIRODE BEHARI CHATTOPADHYAY

The title of Kshirode Behari's essay *Kapalkundala O Miranda*[110] itself shows his intention to make a comparative study of the two characters. But, in fact, it was not so much of a comparative study as it is a plain narrative about the two characters. But he has remarked that Bankimchandra had surpassed Shakespeare by writing *Kapalkundala* as a commentary on *Tempest*.[111]

The next critical work of Kshirode Behari on *Kapalkundala* is his essay *Matibibi*.[112] Here again he narrated the life history of Matibibi. But his observations on some of the actions of Matibibi were quite note-worthy. Nodding of head by Matibibi when she met Nabakumar on her way to Midnapur to represent herself as a servant (Dasi), etc., according to Kshirode Behari indicated Matibibi's genuine love for him. The critic further observed that the dying of the lamp light as soon as Nabakumar told his name, was related to the change of Mati's mind as well as her body.[113]

AKSHAY KUMAR DUTTAGUPTA

Akshay Kumar Duttagupta's *Bankimchandra*[114] shows the predominance of modern trend in Bankim criticism. He laid emphasis upon the fundamental genius of Bankimchandra. He said: "Bankim has found a poetic justice to the scientific and philosophical questions in Kapalkundala."[115]

In the very beginning of his essay, he explained very carefully and scientifically the attitude of the writer, environment, source, the opinions of western biologists about biology and finally, he had given a description and analysis of the various beauties in *Kapalkundala*.

About the source of *Kapalkundala*, Akshay Kumar says that Bankim's attempt here was to solve a very critical question involving sociology as well as psychology. His intention was to show how far human character was shaped and moulded either by nature or by society.[116] But Akshay Kumar was a believer of the principle: "Nature made women, society made them feminine."[117] Referring to the comments of scientists like A.R. Wallace,[118] Akshay Kumar has tried to establish that Kapalkundala is not wholly a child of nature, from the spiritual standpoint she is the daughter of the 'Tantric'. He clearly says that Kapalik and Adhikari have consciously or unconsciously helped developing the spiritual side of her nature.[119]

Simplicity, purity, austerity and pity—all these qualities are mixed in Kapalkundala's character. But the element of love is very dim in her nature. Now the question arises why it is so? Akshay Kumar has searched for the reply to this question in Henry Drummond's novel *Ascent of Man*.[120] In this book, Drummond has tried to show that love is not the instinctive quality of women. It is a family-quality. It is there as a result of the union of husband and wife, as well as a strong affection for the off-spring. Akshay Kumar believed that love did not find expression in Kapalkundala because of her inexperience of the very thing which helps expressing it. Explaining the novelistic necessity of her loveliness, Akshay Kumar said:

> If Kapalkundala was made a loving wife and a happy mother, the writer would have been guilty to science, psychology as well as art.[121]

Besides, Akshay Kumar has left the stamp of his remarkable originality in his findings of the inner mysterious of the character of Nabakumar, Matibibi and Kapalik. He made his judgement through his study and understanding of the western and oriental literature as well as of the writings of his predecessors. As for example: Nabakumar is a literate man, free from superstition, a lover of beauty, unselfish, liberal, helping to others. His attitude and behavior is a tune to the modern age. But soon after his marriage to Kapalkundala, these basic qualities began to suffer a set-back. And towards the end a through transformation is noticed, and unfortunately, he becomes a doll in the hands of fate. This incidental transformation has been explained very ingeniously by Akshay Kumar.[122] He said that Hamlet being adorned with rare qualities was found continuously thinking of self-slaughter, so also Nabakumar once thought of suicide. He said:

> Nabakumar does not think too much like Hamlet. By a strange irony of fate, he becomes a victim.... What Nabakumar has to do in the very important moment of his life, he does not do it.[123]

This penetrating analysis which distinguishes the eminent modern critics of the Post-Centenary period is also noticeable here and there in the criticism of Akshay Kumar. He makes a subtle analysis of the law and impulse in Kapalkundala which sustains her as a social being. His following remark will bear legitimacy to this. He said that Kapalkundala knew the vanity of chastity: "Come and see whether I am faithless or not."[124] In this remark of Kapalkundala, the critic found her guiding law and the vanity of chastity. He asked: "Has not the dominance of law been shown in such womanliness?"[125]

Another feature of Akshay Kumar's criticism was that he has thrown light upon the criticism of his predecessors and tried to establish a distinct opinion. For example, Lalit Kumar Bandopadhyay identified Nabakumar as the hero[126] of this novel, but Akshay Kumar, considering both the western and oriental theories, tried to establish that Nabakumar is not hero of this novel.[127] Instead, all the characters of this novel including Nabakumar had been designed for growth of the character of Kapalkundala. He said: "The glory of the novel Kapalkundala and the characteristic feature of the character of Kapalkundala is that it is devoid of any hero."[128]

Akshay Kumar Duttagupta displays erudition, psychological insight, analytical skill and argumentative power which generally go together in the making of a good critic.[129]

BIPIN CHANDRA PAL (1858-1932)

Bipin Chandra Pal's criticism of *Kapalkundala* can be found in fragments in his three essays.[130] He commented that Bankim had shown in *Kapalkundala* that 'Rasa Sahitya' could be created in Bengali language with Bengali social background.[131] Besides this, all other remarks of Bipin Chandra relating to *Kapalkundala* appear to literary assessment of the novel in social perspective.

He observed that Bankimchandra in his book had tried to get the Bengalees free from the external bindings and turn towards themselves in order to establish the right of enjoyment of the natural human passions, he had shown here that the Bengalee women, inspite of the limitations imposed upon her by the society, enjoys certain liberties; she could establish herself a little in order to satisfy her nature and instinct.[132] Referring to Bankimchandra and the Muslim, Bipin Chandra said—Muslim have not been looked down upon in this novel, Muslim was the symbol of an idea here, the opposite force of the liberation movement was expressed through the muslims.[133]

NARESH CHANDRA SENGUPTA

Naresh Chandra Sengupta searched for the source of *Kapalkundala* in his *Banglar Katha*.[134] According to him, the issue raised by Shakespeare through Miranda and Ferdinand had been solved through Nabakumar and Kapalkundala by Bankimchandra like his predecessor, Jogesh Chandra Basu. Naresh Chandra thought that the sand dune of Knathi, the temple of Kapalik, etc. standing vis-a-vis Bankim's imagination had inspired him in writing *Kapalkundala*.[135] Such remarks show Naresh Chandra's insight. Had it been mixed up with reasonable explanation, his criticism would have been more valuable.

RAMSAHAYA VEDANTASASTRI

The next critical work on *Kapalkundala* was Ramsahaya Vedantasastri's *Kapalkundala Somalochana*.[136] He had scholarship and taste in Sanskrit literature. Stamp of both the qualities were there in his essay. He judged the novel in the light of rhetoric and prosody in Sanskrit literature. And he recreated the character of Kapalkundala according to his taste. Judged from this angle, his criticism shows both classical and aesthetic trends.

Explaining the character of Kapalkundala in the light of his understanding of Sanskrit rhetoric, Ramsahaya said that *Kapalkundala*:

> ...is a word, a story, a poem or a novel. It is heroine based. Kapalkundala is the heroine of the book...she can be termed as an infatuated (mugdha) heroine...an infatuated heroine of a superb taste.[137]

Explaining the heroic elements in the nature of Kapalkundala, he said:

Running away with the sword, without the knowledge of Kapalik, without caring for her life, she sets Nabakumar free, which is an act of her kindness coupled with her heroism. 'Beer-ras' has been categorically explained in Sanskrit literature as 'Doyabir', 'danabir', 'Dharmbir' and 'Yuddhabir', Beer-ras is evident in her entering in to the jungle in utter darkness of the new moon.... This attitude is not a momentary or a perverse attitude.[138]

Explaining the beauty in the character of Kapalkundala, he said:

> The naked and loose and scattered haired Kapalkundala in the seashore is not that Kapalkundala. With the touch of the touchstone the ascetic has become homely. That black cascade of hair has become a big rope. The face does not remain half-hidden by the careless hair. Gold ornaments are there in the ears, in the neck her white dress looks like the white cloud in the firmament brightened by semi-circular moon.[139]

KUMUDNATH DAS

Kumudnath's discussion of *Kapalkundala* in his *Bankimchandra*[140] was brief but it marked the depth of the critic's mind. The critic said:

> Its keynote in the domain of literature is new, and as a literature of power, the book is worthy to be placed amongst the best novels of the world in its inter-action of poetic fancy, spiritual mysticism and objective realism.[141]

According to him *Kapalkundala* is fine piece of pure literature. The lonely forest, seashore, unknown country, difficult path, glory of aristocracy, the 'tantric' Kapalik and his activities, the creation of divinely situation and characters, fate etc. have created a poetic environment in this novel, the natural environment in which the incident starts it ends in the same environment. Objective realism is also not absent in this book. Matibibi and Shyamasundari are the examples. Kumudnath's is a real literary criticism so far as he has concentrated himself to the probable literary forces of this book *Kapalkundala*.

ROMA PRASAD CHANDA (1873-1942)

Roma Prasad Chanda's *Kapalkundala*[142] was a callous, superficial criticism of the book. Some of his observations were confusing. Such observations: Adhikari had taught Kapalkundala a little[143] are based upon lamentable ignorance of the novel. Explaining the character of Nabakumar, Roma Prasad said if Nabakumar could have been infatuated and could infatuate Kapalkundala then their conjugal life would have been different.[144]

Roma Prasad's criticism carries a little weight when he says that Kapalkundala had a strong religious sense, the Bel-leaf slipped from Bhabani's feet, listening to Kapalik's dream,—all these things combined together created such a strongly religious force in Kapalkundala that she could not make an adjustment with Nabakumar in conjugal life.[145] But in the next moment he asked: "Had it been unprofitable to try to make the husband happy?"[146] The critic thinks that Kapalkundala by doing otherwise has insulted the principle of conjugal life.

BATUKNATH BHATTACHARJEE

"*Bankim Sahitye Sannyas*"[147] by Batuknath Bhattacharjee seeks to trace the ascetic tradition in India in the character of Kapalik in *Kapalkundala*. Indeed, he remarked that Bankim's intention was to show what would be the possible change in the ancient Indian Sannyasis in the context of the new age in Bengal. According to him, although an imperfect manifestation of an ascetic, Kapalik is a real representation of the tradition of the 'tantric cult' in Bengal. Bankim had given an artistic portrayal of this tantric order in Bengal. Batuknath, thus tried to uphold to realism in the character sketch of Kapalik which outwardly appears to be an imaginative creation.[148] The critic obviously followed the historical method in evaluation of the character of Kapalik.

MAKHAN LAL MUKHOPADHYAY

In the third decade of the present age, Bankim-criticism took a matured shape. Makhan Lal's *Bankim Upanyaser Rupbarnana*[149] is an example of this matured criticism. While discussing the structural beauty of the novel, he explained with sufficient introspection and tried to evaluate the psychological truth. Bankim Chandra was more idealistic than realistic—Makhan Lal does not agree this. He said that the descriptive side of his novel was based upon realistic pictures. Discussing one of the features of Bankim's portraiture, Makhan Lal said that Bankim had indicated the qualities and blemishes of his chief characters through implications. That is, what is likely to be found in the character through his action has been indicated in that introduction. And this is true of Kapalkundala. Making a comparative study of this attitude and Victor Hugo's *Laughing Man,* and Hardy's *Egdon Heath (The Return of the Native),* he says that there may not be any beauty in the mutilated body of *Laughing Man*, but the artist has made him a symbol of the century's atrocities. Hardy has viewed Egdon Heath in such a way that in the pleasant but indifferent beauty of this place lays the seed of all tragedies. Fate serves as a vital force there. Such a force is there in *Kapalkundala* also. According to critic: "such description either of the external nature or of the human nature does not touch us as shadows only, they become absolutely our own and find a permanent place in our heart."[150]

SUMMING UP

Kapalkundala being a very popular and interesting novel, many celebrated personalities used their learned pen to assess the literary quality of this novel, both in the Bankim Age and in the Post-Bankim period. The contemporaries of Bankim were mainly guided by ethical, moral, philosophical and psychological value judgements, although the application of western principles was very much pronounced. Few could attempt at the total evaluation of the book, while the attempts at romantic appreciation of the novel were even fewer. In the post-Bankim period, the same trend continued, but greater emphasis was laid on the realistic appraisal the character or Kapalkundala and Kapalik, and attempts at classical evaluation of the novel began at the hands of some critics. During this long period of critical evaluation the structure, artistic beauty, subject-matter, source, the writer's psychology, as well as philosophical basis of the novel, working of fate, tragedy, dramatic and poetic elements—all these things came within the preview of the discussion. The characters of Kapalkundala, Matibibi and Kapalik were the major issues.

References

1. Basu, Purnachandra, *Kapalkundala*, Aryadarshan, Jaistha-Ashar-Shraban-Bhadra, pp. 68-77, 97-105, 163-74, 207-16, Reprinted, Kabyasundari, 1287 B.S.
2. Basu, Purnachandra, *Kabyasundari*, p. 30.
3. Basu, Purnachandra, *Sathitye Khun, Sahitya*, 1302 B.S., Reprinted, Bondopadhyay, Shrikumar and Pal, Prafulla Chandra (ed.), *Somalochana Sahitya*, 5th edition, 1379 B.S., pp. 88-102.
4. Basu, Purnachandra, *Kabyasundari*, p. 90.
5. *Ibid.*, pp. 54-55.
6. *Ibid.*, p. 57.
7. *Ibid.*, pp. 81-82.
8. *Ibid.*, pp. 35-36
9. Mukhapadhyay, Chandrasekhar, *Mrinmoyee. Jnanangkur*, 1281 B.S., Reprinted, Bondopadhyay, Dr. Shrikumar & Pal, Prafulla Chandra (ed.). *Somalochana Sahitya*, 5th Issue, Poush, 1379 B.S., pp. 231-37.
10. Bondopadhyay, Shrikumar & Pal, Prafulla Chandra (ed.), *Somalochana Sahitya*, pp. 232-23.
11. Basu, Debendra Bijoy, *Upanyase Charitra Chitra*, (Dwitiya Prastab). *Nabyabharat*, 2nd part, 12th issue, Chaitra, 1291 B.S., pp. 555-64.
12. Basu, D.S., U.C.C. (D.P.), 2nd pt., 11th Issue, Falgun, 1291, p. 527. For detailed discussion please refer to the earlier chapter.
13. Basu, D.B., Chaitra, 1291 B.S., p. 559.
14. Nyayratna, Ramgati, *Bangla Bhasa O Sahitya Bishayak Prostabol*, 2nd issue, 1298 B.S.
15. *Ibid.*, p. 282.
16. Ramgati Nyayratna has said that Matibibi is 'batamukhi ek dhumramakha magi' (B.B. O S.A. Prastab, 2nd edn, 1291 B.S., p. 282).
17. Nyayratna, Ramgati, op. cit., pp. 282-83.
18. *Ibid.*, p. 283.
19. Bondopadhyay, Haridas, *Banglar Upanyas Lekhak*, *Kalpana*, 6th year. Baishakh, 1296 B.S., pp. 10-15.
20. *Ibid.*, p. 92.
21. *Ibid.*
22. *Ibid.*, pp. 94-95.
23. *Ibid.*, p. 95.

24. (a) Roychowdhury, Girija Prasanna, *Bankimchandra-Durgeshnandini-Kapalkundala O Mrinalini,* 1297 B.S., pp. 1-64.

    (b) Two essays with the title of Kapalkundala have been published in the Nabajiban of Jaistha Ashok Kumar Kundu, the writer of Bankim Abhidhan has mentioned only of the Jaistha & Asharh issues 1294 B.S. being written by Akshay Kumar Sarkar. (Bankim Abhidhan, 1st publication, May, 1980, p. Appendix, 3). But it is not true. Girija Prasanna Roychowdhury is the writer of the said essay because later on these two essays have got place in the book of Girija Prasanna titled—*Bankimchandra* critic with rare literary taste in Bankim Age.

25. Roychowdhury, Girija Prasanna, *Bankimchandra-Durgeshnandini-Kapalkundala-Mrinalini,* 1297 B.S. pp. 7-8, Reprinted: *Kapalkundala, Nabajiban*, 3rd part, 11th issue, Jaistha, 1294, p. 674.
26. Roychowdhury, Girija Pasanna, *Kapalkundala*, Nabajiban, 3rd part, 11th issue, Jaistha, 1294 B.S, p. 675.
27. *Ibid*., p. 616.
28. Roychowdhury, Girija Prasanna, *Kapalkundala*, p. 669.
29. Roychowdhury, Girija Prasanna, *Bankimchandra-Durgeshnandini-Kapalkundala-Mrinalini,* 1297 B.S., p. 50.
30. *Ibid*., p. 29.
31. Thakur, Sudhindranath, *Kapalkundala O Miranda*, *Sahitya*, 2nd year, 3rd issue, Asharh, 1298 B.S., pp. 109-13.
32. *Ibid*., p. 113.
33. *Ibid*., p. 112.
34. *Ibid.*
35. Pande, Bireswar, *Bankimchandra O Hindur Adarsha, Sahitya Parishad Patrika*, 1302 B.S., Reprinted, Bondopadhyay, Dr. Bhrikumar & Paul, Dr. Prafulla Chandra (ed.) *Somalochana Sahitya*, 5th edn., Poush, 1379 B.S., pp. 298-319.
36. *Ibid*., (*Somalochana Sahitya*), p. 301.
37. *Ibid*., pp. 318-19.
38. Ghose, Hemendra Prasad, *Bankimchandra (1*), Dasi, May 1895, pp. 282-86.
39. Ghose, Hemendra Prasad, *Rishi Bankimchandra, Narayan*, Baishakh, 1322 B.S., pp. 563-71.
40. *Ibid*., p. 565.
41. Ghose, Hemendra Prasad, *Bankimchandra (1),* Dasi, May 1895, p. 394.
42. *Ibid*., pp. 391-93.
43. Rakshit, Haran Chandra, *Banga Sahitye Bankim*, 3rd edition, 24 Pargana, Poush, 1317 B.S., p. 88.

44. *Ibid.*
45. *Ibid.*, p. 89.
46. *Ibid.*
47. Kapalkundala, Golak Benhari, *Kapalkundla:Bangadarshan* (Nabaparjayay). Year, 7th issue, Kartik, 1315 B.S., pp. 375-79.
48. *Ibid.*, p. 375.
49. *Ibid.*, p. 377.
50. *Ibid.*, p. 376.
51. *Ibid.*, p. 377.
52. Basu, Jitendra Lal, *Bankimchandra, Bangadarshan (Nabaparjyay),* 10th year, 3rd issue, Asharh, 1317 B.S., pp. 113-23.
53. *Ibid.*, pp. 120-21.
54. Lahiri, Kumudnath, *Kapalkundala Upanyaser Uddeshya, Nabyabharat*, Jaistha, 1317 B.S., pp. 75-81.
55. *Ibid.*, p. 81.
56. *Ibid.*, pp. 78-79.
57. (a) Basu, Jogesh Chandra, *Knathite Bankimchandra*, *Suravi*, 1st year, 1st Issue, Ashwin, 1318 B.S., pp. 4-6 & 1st year & 2nd issue, Kartik, 1318 B.S., pp. 26-28.
    (b) Basu, Jogesh Chandra, *Hijli Knathir Bkti Prachin Rahni, Bharati*, 35 year, 10th Issue, Magh, 1318 B.S., pp. 1029-31.
    (c) Basu, Jogesh Chandra, *Bankimchandrer Smriti Chinha*: *Kapalkundalar Parikalpana Kshetra*, 1st Falgun, 1332 B.S.
58. Basu, Jogesh Chandra, *Bankimchandrer Smriti Chinha*, pp. 44-69.
59. Basu, Jogesh Chandra, *Hijli Knathir Ekti Prachin Kahini*, p. 1029.
60. Basu, Jogesh Chandra, *Knathite Bankimchandra*, Ashwin, p. 8.
61. Bondopadhyay, Bhabesh Chandra, *Kapalkundala Charitra Somalochana, Chaitra,* 1320 B.S.
62. *Ibid.*, pp. 1-8.
63. *Ibid.*, pp. 17-27.
64. *Ibid.*, pp. 9-16.
65. *Ibid.*, p. 8.
66. *Ibid.*, p. 14.
67. *Ibid.*, p. 20.
68. *Ibid.*, pp. 22-24.
69. *Ibid.*, p. 6.
70. (a) Bandopadhyay, Lalit Kumar, *Bankimchandrer Akshavikabali*, Bharatbarshe, Asharh, 1322 B.S., pp. 6-11.
    (b) Bandopadhyay, Lalit Kumar, *Ma: Bharatbarsha*, 3rd year, 1st part, 2nd issue, Sharban, 1322 B.S., pp. 264-82.

(c) Bandopadhyay, Lalit Kumar, *Kapalkundala, Bharatbarsha*, 3rd year, Poush, 1322 B.S., pp. 133-48. Reprinted with modification *Kapalkundala Tattba*, Falgun, 1322 B.S.

(d) Bandopadhyay, Lalit Kumar, *Kapalkundala (Dwitiya Prastab), Bharatbarsha*, 3rd year, 2nd part, 3rd Issue, Falgun, 1322 B.S., pp. 453-74. Reprinted with modification- *Kapalkundala Tatta*, Falgun, 1322 B.S.

(e) Bandopadhyay, Lalit Kumar, *Kabyasudha*, Kartik, 1323 B.S.

(f) Bandopadhyay, Lalit Kumar, *Premer Katha*, Jaistha, 1327 B.S.

(g) Bandopadhyay, Lalit Kumar, *Sakhi*, Calcutta-Dhaka-Moymansingha, 1328 B.S.

71. Bandopadhyay, Lalit Kumar, *Kapalkundala Tattba*, Falgun, 1322 B.S.
72. Bandopadhyay, Lalit Kumar, *Bankimchandrer Akshyaikabali*, p. 10.
73. Bandopadhyay, Lalit Kumar, *Ma*, pp. 264-82.
74. Bandopadhyay, Lalit Kumar, *Sakhi*, pp. 44-48.
75. *Ibid*., pp. 63-64.
76. Hermia, daughter to Sgeus, Heiena, in love with Demetrius (A *Midsummer-Night's Dream* by William Shakespeare, *The Complete Works of William Shakespeare*, Abbey Library, p. 175).
77. Bandopadhyay, Lalit Kumar, *Sakhi*, pp. 79-82.
78. Bandopadhyay, Lalit Kumar, *Kapalkundala*, pp. 138-48, Poush.
79. *Ibid*., pp. 134-36.
80. Bandopadhyay, Lalit Kumar, *Kapalkundala* (Dwitiya Prastab), pp. 461-74.
81. *Ibid*., pp. 473-74.
82. *Ibid*., pp. 457-59.
83. *Ibid*., pp. 453-57.
84. *Ibid*., pp. 459-62.
85. Bandopadhyay, Lalit Kumar, *Kapalkundala Tattba*, 2nd edition, 1325 B.S., pp. 59-63.
86. Bandopadhyay, Lalit Kumar, *Kabyasudha*, pp. 10-22.
87. Bandopadhyay, Asit Kumar, *Somalochana Katha*, 3rd print, January 1971, p. 27.
88. Bondopadhyay, Chandi Charan, *Bangla Sahityer Kromonnati O Bankimchandra, Manasi*, 6th year, 2nd part, 3rd issue, Kartik, 1321 B.S., pp. 417-39.
89. *Ibid*., p. 435.
90. Sen, Shashanka Mohan, *Bangabani*, Dhaka, 1915.
91. Bagore, R.R., *Adhunik Sahitya* (Juoeyer), Viswa-Bharati, 1365, p. 153.

92. Sen, Shashanka Mohan, *Bangabani*, Dhaka, 1915, p. 154.
93. *Ibid.*, p. 60.
94. *Ibid.*, p. 61.
95. *Ibid.*
96. *Ibid.*, p. 60.
97. Roy, Amarendranath, *Bankim Upanyase Matrichhabi, Argha*, 7th Kalpa, 12th Part, Chaitra, 1323 B.S., pp. 391-97.
98. *Ibid.*, p. 393.
99. Roy, Jnanendra Lal, *Upanyase Dharma Prachar-Bankimbabu*, Nabyabharat, Shraban, 1323 B.S., pp. 248-53.
100. *Ibid.*, pp. 251-52.
101. Bhattacharjee, Gopal Chandra, *Kapalkundalar Kabyasoundarjya*, *Argha*, 8th year, 7th issue, Kartik, 1324 B.S., pp. 367-81.
102. *Ibid.*, p. 373.
103. Cross, Bendetto, *The Essence of Aesthetic*, London, 1921, p. 101.
104. *Bankim Rachanabali*, (Baibidha Prabandha-Bidyapati O Joydev), Sahitya Samsad, 3rd print, Ashwin, 1371 B.S., p. 192.
105. Bhattacharjee, Gopal Chandra, p. 370.
106. *Ibid.*, pp. 370-71.
107. *Ibid.*, p. 378.
108. *Bankim Rachanabali* (Kapalkundala), Sahitya Samsad, 5th print, Chaitra, 1376 B.S., p. 150.
109. Bhattacharjee, Gopal Chandra, op. cit., p. 380.
110. Chattopadhyay, Kshirode Behari, *Kapalkundala O Mirands, Bharatbarsha*, 6th year, 1st part, 6th issue, Agahyan, 1325 B.S., pp. 732-41.
111. *Ibid.*, p. 733.
112. Chattopadhyay, Kshirode Behari, Matibibi, *Manasi O Marmabani*, 11th year, 1st part, 3rd issue, Baishakh, 1326 B.S., pp. 273-81.
113. *Ibid.*, pp. 276-77.
114. Duttagupta, Akshay Kumar, *Bankimchandra*, 1327 B.S.
115. Duttagupta, Akshay Kumar, *Bankimchandra*, 2nd edn., May, Jijnasa 1975, p. 69.
116. *Ibid.*, pp. 66-70.
117. *Ibid.*, p. 69.
118. A.R. Wallace has said, "Not only is each organism necessarily related to and affected by all things, living and dead, that surrounded it, but every detail of form and structure, of colour, food and habits, must it is now held—have been developed in harmony, and to a great extend as a result of the organic environments." (Duttagupta, Akshay Kumar, *Bankimchandra*, 2nd ed. pp. 67-68.

119. Duttagupta, Akshay Kumar, Bankimchandra, 2nd edition, Jijnasa, May 1975, p. 76.

120. "Love then is no necessary ingredient of the sex relation, it is not an outgrowth of passion. Love is love, and has always been love, and has never been anything lower. Whence, then, come it? It neither the husband nor the wife bestowed this gift upon the world, who did? It was a little child. Till this appeared, Man's affection was non-existence, woman's was frozen. The man did not love the woman, the woman did not love the man. But one day from its mother's very heart, from a shrine which her husband never visited nor knew was there, which she herself dared scarce acknowledge, which was not passion...." (Drummond, Hanry, *Ascent of Man*, 1894, Reprinted, Duttagupta, Akshay Kumar, *Bankimchandra*).

121. Duttagupta, Akshay Kumar, *Bankimchandra*, 2nd edition, Jijnasa, May 1975, p. 82.

122. *Ibid*., pp. 87-95.

123. *Ibid*., p. 94.

124. *Bankim Rachanabali* (Kapalkundala), p. 175.

125. Duttagupta, Akshay Kumar, *Bankimchandra*, 2nd Edn. Jijnasa, May 1975, p. 75.

126. Bandopadhyay, Lalit Kumar, Bankimchandrer *Akshayaikabali, Bharatbarsha*, Asharh, 1322 B.S., p. 10.

127. Duttagupta, Akshay Kumar, *Bankimchandra*, 2nd Edn., Jijnasa, May 1975, p. 87.

128. *Ibid*., p. 87.

129. Bandopadhyay, Asit Kumar, *Samalochanar Katha*, 3rd print, January 1971, pp. 78-79.

130. (a) Pal, Bipin Chandra, *Banglar Nabajuger Katha (Ekadash Katha), Bangabani*, 2nd year, 1st issue, Falgun, 1329, pp. 90-98.

    (b) Pal, Bipin Chandra, *Banglar Nabajuger Katha (Troyodash Katha)*.

    (c) Pal, Bipin Chandra, *Nabajuger Bangla Sahitye Bankimchandra, Nabyabharat*, Bhadra, 1330 B.S., pp. 235-47.

131. Pal, B.C., *Nabajuger Bangla Sahitya Bankimchandra*, p. 240.

132. Pal, B.C., *Banglar Nabajuger Katha (Ekabash Katha)*, pp. 92-95.

133. Pal, B.C., *Banglar Nabajuger Katha* (*Trayodash Katha*), p. 387.

134. Sengupta, Naresh Chandra, *Bangalar Katha, Banshari*, 1st year, 22nd Asharh, 1330 B.S.

135. *Ibid*., pp. 4-5.

136. Vedantasastri, Ramsahaya, *Kapalkundala Samalochana, Archana*, 9th issue, 21st Bhag, Kartik, 1331 B.S., pp. 321-28.

137. *Ibid*., p. 321.

138. *Ibid*., pp. 322-23.

139. *Ibid.*, p. 325.
140. Das, Kumudnath, *Bankimchandra, Archana*, 21st Bhag, 10th issue, Agrahayan, 1331 B.S., pp. 362-67.
141. *Ibid.*, p. 364.
142. Chanda, Roma Prasad, *Kapalkundala, Masik Basumati*, 5th year, Shraban, 1333 B.S., pp. 624-30.
143. *Ibid.*, p. 624.
144. *Ibid.*, p. 626.
145. *Ibid.*, pp. 623-30.
146. *Ibid.*, p. 628.
147. Bhattacharjee, Batuknath, *Bankim Sahitye Sannyas*, Bangabani, 5th year, 6th issue, Shraban, 1333 B.S., pp. 640-51.
148. *Ibid.*, pp. 643-44.
149. Mukhopadhyay, Makhanlal, *Bankim Upanyaser Rupbarnana, Bichitra*, 7th year, 1st part. Agrahayan, 1240 B.S., pp. 642-46.
150. *Ibid.*, p. 645.

4
Mrinalini

RAJENDRALAL MITRA (1824-91)

After the publication of *Mrinalini*, the renowned anthropologist[1] Rajendralal Mitra wrote the criticism of this novel *Mrinalini.*[2] This was the first critical writing on this novel. At first, he pointed out its defects and excellences, no doubt the excellences had become dominant. He showed the tendency to come out of the barriers of orthodox criticism which valued only the use of diction and rhetoric. But Rajendralal upheld that Mrinalini's primary attraction lay in its superb appeal and said:

> ...the real charm of imaginary truth was that the reading of one chapter with excited curiosity to go through the next, and the book had become easily readable because of the avoidance of figures of speech and the dexterous adaptation of sentence structure.[3]

Thus did the critic draw our attention to the skillful handling of structure and style in this book.

According to Rajendralal, the female characters in this novel were drawn neatly. The devotion of a devoted wife and the natural characteristic of a heroine had been well-represented in *Mrinalini.* Girijaya was a supremely charming woman—she was like the servant girl of Dickens' *Martin Chusslewit*. Manorama's self-immolation (Sahamaran) was in accordance with the Indian custom, hers was an unspeakable beautiful character. The character of Pashupati marked the writer's ability of characterization. Mrinalini was a historical novel—a line piece of writing.[4]

The critic had found out the defects of the book along with qualities. According to his judgement, Bankim had successfully created the female characters of the book, but he had failed to produce the same impression in the creation of the male characters. He thought that the principal hero of the book was Hemchandra who had patriotism and bravery which had not been implemented in practice. His patriotism was like that of the modern youths of Calcutta—only oral, his gesture to go to war decorated with precious jewels produced laughter, his action to beat Girijaya was cowardly. The character of Digbijoy was inconsistent.[5]

A few findings of Rajendralal deserve appreciation. As for example the character of Hemchandra, whom Bankim wanted to picture as a prototype of the hero. But the weaknesses of his character as revealed in his behavior towards Mrinalini and Girijaya had been mainly displayed in the book. It is for this reason that Hemchandra was led to draw the reader's sympathy or respect. More than a century elapsed since Rajendralal has drawn the reader's attention in this aspect of Hemchandra's character.

Although marked with imperfections in style and presentation of immature criticism, the essay remains invaluable in the context of the dawn of the Bengali criticism. His importance lies in inspiring later critics, and he deserves special mention as the first critic, who initiated the criticism of *Mrinalini*.

RAMGATI NYAYRATNA (1238-1301 B.S.)

Pandit Ramgati Nyayratna attempted a criticism of *Mrinalini* his book "*Bangla Bhasha O Bangala Sahitya Bishoyak Prastab*". His methods of literary judgement and attitude were almost like those Rajendralal Mitra as revealed in his analysis of Bankim's art of characterisation and plot construction.[6]

According to Ramgati, Monorama was a 'Strange thing'. Like many in one, the unnatural blending of the attitude of the little girl and the gravity of a woman in early age in Monorama was shocking to the critic.[7] In fact, Ramgati was lacking in depth of penetration. But the principle which determines the edifice of a literary criticism was not known to Ramgati. He pointed out the mistake of Bankim in stating that there were thorns in the stem of a lotus....[8] However, this remark about Girijaya was more subtle.[9] He said: "The beggar Girijaya is doll of fondness, a little reservation would make her more beautiful."[10]

AKSHAY CHANDRA SARKAR (1846-1917)

The first realistic criticism of *Mrinalini* could be found in Akshay Chandra Sarkar's essay *Pashupati*.[11] Lalit Kumar Bandopadhyay called Akshay Chandra: "The last hero of the age of Bankim."[12] The heroism of Akshay Chandra was easily discerned, as in the essay under discussion. Too much of emotion, Bankim-adoration and making of a gist of the novel were the characteristics of his essay where a life history of Pashupati had been attempted. In spite of emotionalism the critic's intelligent judgement attracts our attention. He was the first critic to make a sound assessment of Pashupati's action. And without being prejudiced by ethics, he had tried to make a psychological assessment of the 'Man' Pashupati. Speaking about the duty of a critic, the famous German critic Goethe says: "It is difficult but reasonable that the critic should transfer himself into the thoughts of his author and read him into her spirits in which he wrote."[13] Akshay Chandra is therefore successful to a great extent in his attempts to read the mind of Bankim.

Akshay Chandra was the first critic to point out the patriotic instinct of Bankim as revealed in the novel, *Mrinalini*, and the sentiment, which was responsible for the creation of *Bharat Kalanka and Banglar Kalanka* culminating in *Bandemataram,* also leading to the creation of Pashupati. Bankim created Pashupati hunting that Bengal was not conquered till seventeen cavalry.[14]

According to the critic, Pashupati was a top-ranking politician. This he had tried to find through Pashupati's actions like his counsel with Mahmed Ali and his prayer at the temples of 'Devi-Ashtabhuja'. He said:

> ...herein lies Pashupati's conflict with hope and goodness. Politicians maintain reservation and hence his uttering is crafty and very much meaningful. Both sides of the heart are nicely shown in the words.[15]

Pashupati had sought penance for his sin through his love for subjects in this novel. Such was Akshay Chandra's thought.

Bankim's creation of Pashupati was a far greater achievement than Shakespeare's creation of *Macbeth* because Pashupati's actions were limited by Hindu conservatism, while Macbeth was free to act in a non-Hindu society.[16]

Bankimchandra propagated ethics through art. And an analysis of Bankim-philosophy would prove this. Moreover, in Bankim ethics had mingled with art. Akshay Chandra had explained Pashupati's life in that light. He said that Pashupati's love for Monorama was born of sin resulting in the dangerous consequence of his life. But Monorama was essential for the development of Pashupati's character. Specially to relieve Pashupati form the charge of faithlessness in the form of his greed for kingdom, the desiring to introduce Monorama's love was justified from the artistic standpoint.[17] Besides, through the end of Pashupati, Akshay Chandra had highlighted Bankim tragic sense in this essay.[18]

But the unnecessary emotional outbursts of the critic have spoiled his criticism which is otherwise good. He cries out: "Readers! now Pashupati is burnt...won't you cry once? Won't you cry to see the fatal end of patriot-Pashupati for a single laps?"[19] This shows that the critic fails to rise above the tendency of his age, although he had made efforts to do so.

GIRIJA PRASANNA ROYCHOWDHURY (1862-99)

Fine, strong and erudite criticism of *Mrinalini* in Bankim's lifetime could be found in Girija Prasanna's essays—*Girijaya*[20] *and Monorama*[21] *and in his compilation of essays Bankimchandra-Durgeshnandini-Kapalkundala-Mrinalini.*[22] As literary criticism, these essays were remarkable. Natural sense of realization and introspection, subtle sense of analysis and proper judgement were the distinctive qualities of Girija Prasanna's essays. Girija Prasanna was the first impressionist critic of *Mrinalini* during the period of Bankim.

Mrinalini's friend Girijaya was a mysterious character of this novel. She was like a fresh spring toppling out of the mountain in the novel *Mrinalini*. Girijaya was lively representation with the distinct characteristics of humour and fickleness; she was over-joyous and lovesick sharp and distinctly free from social prejudices. She was a heroic expression of life. She was most obedient to Mrinalini but never influenced by her. Hers was a dynamic personality which helped her in giving the impression of an individual character. The critic Girija Prasanna had taken much care in finding the innermost qualities of Girijaya. Girija Prasanna had shown that despite all her anger, jocularity and fickleness, she was a fine woman in love not altogether devoid of romance as Mrinalini was. Girija Prasanna said: "Girijaya is a gay and light-hearted woman in the sense exactly the term '...gay & light-hearted' means in English."[23]

Making a psychological analysis of the actions of Girijaya, the critic reasoned Girijaya's intuitive understanding of Mrinalini's waiting maid was inspired by her instinct of love. Because at that time she had been feeling it in her own bosom. The critic opined that the nature of pure love was such that whosoever came under its spell was found to be its devotee, and therefore, Girijaya had became the companion of Mrinalini in her search for Hemchandra.[24] Girija Prasanna made an observation of Bankim's psychology in creating Girijaya and explained that Girijaya is the daughter of a beggar. And hence, her love should not be raised to the level of Mrinalini's and, therefore, Bankim had occasionally shown crude and unsocial manners in Girijaya's love.[25]

The greatest contribution of Girija Prasanna in Bankim criticism is his analysis of the character of Monorama. Monorama was the most critical, mysterious and curious of all the female characters ever created by Bankim. Monorama was simultaneously childlike in her simplicity and grave as a woman in her matured years. Bankim had related her early history briefly, and indicated that her inconsistencies of manners were due to her early life, but he did not explain the reasons behind this quality. He created her as an individual, complete in herself, and without much exposition he left her to the judgement of the readers and critics. Girija Prasanna Roychowdhury had searched out that to unfold the tale of Monorama's life and in her solitary thought and remarked:

> Monorama is an extremely unhappy woman. And the preoccupation of her mind with this thought is the cause of her simplicity. Although sharply intelligent, at the same time, this thought is the cause of her simplicity, And this is again Monorama's be all and ends all. Her two images—one of gay light-hearted woman and the other of sharply intelligent grave and heroic are born of this thought.[27]

Girija Prasanna, who was well versed in English literature, constituted a comparison between Monorama and Shakespeare's *Hamlet*. He said:

> In the intensity of thought, Monorama has beaten Hamlet.... Hamlet's thought is the thought of a man—introspective and dangerous like the limitless clouds of the unlimited shy, while Monorama's is the thought of a woman like a little serpent, full of poison. The high-minded inactive Hamlet is the superb creation of Shakespeare and gravely crazy, Monorama is the superb creation of Bankimchandra.[28]

Girija Prasanna's critical approach and judgement may appear controversial to modern critics, but no one would deny the contribution of his liberalism and the depth of psychological probe to Bankim criticism. In this he has surpassed his contemporary critics and has taken a significant step towards analysis of literary characters even in Bankim's life-time.[29]

HARIDAS BONDOPADHYAY

The next criticism of *Mrinalini* was written by Haridas Bondopadhyay in his essay *Banglar Upanyas Lekhak: Mrinalini O Bishabriksha*.[30] Unlike his predecessor Girija Prasanna,—Haridas Bondopadhyay discussed that characters and incidents only. Such occasional remarks as—*Mrinalini* was a historical novel like *Durgeshnandini*; the incidents of this novel were curious and dramatic. Hemchandra and Mrinalini here are the hero and heroine, Pashupati and Monorama were the deputies, and they were more attractive characters than Hemchandra and Mrinalini. Monorama's love is full of heavenly ideals. Girijaya belongs to low-caste—she is unselfish and ever-ready to help others etc.[31] His essay abounds with occasional straight remarks without any explanation or analysis. The essay is mostly propagandist, and it reminds the first criticism of *Mrinalini.*

PANCHKARI GHOSH

Bankimchandrer Soundarya Sristhi[32] by Panchkari Ghosh written after the death of Bankim set some new trends. In the very beginning of the essay, Panchkari said his intention is to present the beauty of Mrinalini to the readers.[33] He quoted at random from the text in his essay. He tried to show how the total artistic beauty was created by the writer; and to beautify this he discussed the novel under heads—the miserable condition of Hindus, the beauty of the Hindu youth, the beauty of summer twilight in the confluence of the Ganges and the Jumuna, the character-consciousness of Hindu woman, Girijaya's song, flower-made image of the Goddess, Monorama's beauty, etc., and through these, he has described the different characters and incidents and appreciated Bankim for his ingenuity in landscape description and presentation of ideals. He also briefly discussed Girijaya's songs. And said these are impregnated with the words of *Broja* and written in *Brojabuli*[34] Panchkari believed that these songs had a permanent value and these were precious gems of Bengali language.[35]

SIDDHESWAR ROY

Siddheswar Roy wrote two essays on *Mrinalini* immediately after Panchkari. These were *Girijayar Geet*[36] and *Kaha Mrinal Hamari?*[37]

In the essay *Girijayar Geet,* the critic gave a fine description of the impact of Girijaya's songs in forming a relation between Mrinalini and Hemchandra; and in this context, he tried to categorize the real identity of Girijaya. According to him, Girijaya, her very young age, was an expert in the art of love-making, well-versed in understanding human characters, full of ready wit, simple, fearless, well intentioned, humour-some and a fine singer.[38] The critic remarked that Girijaya resembled Brindaduti and Hiranmalini of Radha-Krishna and Bidyasundar respectively.[39]

Kaha Mrinal Hamari? was purely descriptive. The essayist had given a thorough description of Mrinalini from beginning to end.[40]

HEMENDRA PRASAD GHOSE (1876-1963)

Hemendra Prasad in his essay *Bankimchandra* (3)—*Mrinalini*[41] briefly discussed different characters of the novel. The characters had been studied after the novel with a touch of emotion. And here and there he pressed his own remarks about them. Such remarks like—Monorama is the boon-flower of Bankim genius—a well-knit poem. Bankimchandra's love is not polluted by the poison of selfishness, Mrinalini is the amorous ground of love, it is a combination of Ayesha, Tilottama, Monorama and Girijaya[42]—show the essayist's literary erudition and taste; but these are not well-grounded on logic, and the essay is mainly descriptive.

PRAMATHANATH SEN

In the post-Bankim age the characters of Mrinalini and Girijaya had been exclusively dealt with by Pramathanath Sen. *Mrinalini*[43], his first essay, deals with Mrinalini's character. The sentiment of Suryamukhi was absent in Mrinalini and therefore, the latter was a mere magnanimous character. Mrinalini's love was divine in the sense it was devoid of sentiment towards the beloved. There was no devotion of love in Suryamukhi while Mrinalini was full with it. According to critic the idol of Mrinalini was a mixture of wisdom and love. The chief ornaments of her character were patience and faith.[44] These were the basis of Pramathanath's interpretation of the character of Mrinalini. The idealistic critic believed that Mrinalini's devotion to her husband was fully based on ideals of sentimentality and faithfulness, for which it triumphed, while Suryamukhi and Bhramar's love failed because of lack of this devotion.[45] According to him, Mrinalini was a divine lady, because it was she and she alone could say: "I was devoted to Hemchandra yesterday, I am devoted to him even today." Above all, the critic had found Mrinalini as an ideal character to teach ideals: "Mrinalini is an ideal woman.... It is worth social teaching."[46]

But the critic had drawn the attention to some of the inconsistencies in the character of Mrinalini, e.g., self-surrender of a girl of fifteen to a handsome prince, her departure from her home with her waiting woman in search of her beloved were absurd not only in the olden days but also in the present day. The critic took exception to Mrinalini's antagonism with her father in the matter of marriage, and therefore, the critic thought that the character of Mrinalini did not deserve respect and was unpardonable.[47]

Pramathanath, however, showed far greater skill as a critic in his second essay on *Mrinalini: Girijaya*[48] published two years later after the publication of *Mrinalini*. Here he revealed his ability for in depth study of character coupled with a deep understanding of the mind and art of Bankim. In fact, during Bankim's lifetime, Girija Prasanna Roychowdhury who explained very skillfully the implication of the ever-gay nature of Girijaya. Pramathanath, in the like manner, had searched for this free, easy nature of Girijaya. But Girija Prasanna's searching eyes were fixed upon Girijaya's ever-gay nature while Pramathanath's were fixed upon her free-easy nature. To explain the reasons of this attitude of Girijaya, Pramathanath said that Girijaya never had to face any misfortune, the world had never appeared to her with all its gruesome aspects. She did not have the feel the pangs of hopeless love, since her childhood. She had been patient, industrious, deprived of luxury and therefore, she was free and ever-gay.[49]

The critic said:

> In fact, Girijaya was a superb creation of Bankim; it was like a beautiful lyric, easily understandable and touching to the heart. Plain and simple, free from all sorts of ornaments like allegory, similies and metaphors, and still that which to be said has been said nicely.[50]

Girija Prasanna in analyzing the character of Girijaya remarked that generosity was the characteristic beauty of her character, and the hidden beauty of secret love matched well with the role of messenger she played to Mrinalini. Thus, the critic skillfully portrayed the inner mysteries of the character.

In this he also tried to discover the writer comprehension of life and beauty.

In spite of the analytical skill displayed in his essay Pramathanath fails to rise above the contemporary trend and much of the merit of the essay has been spoiled by emotional overtone. He said that Girijaya is the sea-shore of the earth, ray of the Chitra in the vacuum, her intelligence is far-stretching like the ray of the Chitra.[51]

KUMUDNATH LAHIRI

Kumudnath Lahiri's Monorama[52] was another bright example of emotional criticism. Kumudnath narrated the incidents of Monorama's life very emotionally. He said:

> Monorama is steeped in heavenly fragrance. I do not find any fault in her character and probably, I shall not have.[53]

However, he harps on a real critical tone when he says that Monorama is a curious product, a cumulative effect of simplicity, affection and worldly wisdom, which all combined together to produce the exceptional beauty of her character.[54]

JITENDRA LAL BASU

Although Jitendra Lal Basu did not make an in-depth study of the novel in his essay *Bankimchandra*[55] he gave a new dimension to *Mrinalini* criticism by focusing the influence of the 'Vaishnava Verse' in the character of Monorama. He believed that Monorama was mysterious but not unnatural, rather she was like Bidyapati's Radhika[56] in her adolescence—sometimes a child, sometimes a youth, sometimes gay, sometimes reserved and sometimes fickle.[57] It is no mean credit to highlight the Eastern influence in a Bankim character.

HARAN CHANDRA RAKSHIT

The next critical work about *Mrinalini* was written by Haran Chandra Rakshit in his book *Banga Sahitye Bankim*. Despite his idealistic attitude traces of pure criticism could be found there.

According to Haran Chandra, Mrinalini was a Hindu wife, but not of that class Suryamukhi belonged to.[58] This remark is contrary to that of his predecessor Pramathanath. According to him, Pashupati was the creation of Bankim's 'Swadeshi' spirit which inspired him to write *Bharat Kalanka and Banglar Kalanka*. Pashupati was the fruit of this inspiration, Bankimchandra created Pashupati as a protest against the opinion that Bangladesh was captured by seventy cavalry men.[59] A distant echo of Akshay Chandra Sarkar is heard in Haran Chandra's remark.

In the criticism of Girijaya's song, Haran Chandra's originality and sense of taste are evident. He was the first critic to understand Bankim psychology through such songs. He said that the sincerity, passion and emotion which were expressed through every word of these songs reflected the mind of the writer himself, it seemed as if the devoted Bankim with an unfulfilled passion had sung this song.[60]

PRAFULLA KUMAR SARKAR (1884-1944)

Prafulla Kumar wrote the criticism of *Mrinalini* in his essay *Samaj Sanskare Bankimchandra*.[61] The critic has observed Bankim as a social reformer, and the female characters of the novel had been discussed on the background of Hindu ideals. He emphasized that Mrinalini was the only female character free from voluptuousness, and she was an exceptional ideal of 'Nishkam Prem' in Bankim literature. Mrinalini's love was not self-assertive. Her pride and ego were the results of this ideal. Arguing in favour of Mrinalini as a high ideal of Hindu wife, the critic said that Mrinalini was on the one hand, fearless before sin and atrocity, and on the other hand, she was an embodiment of joy in love making.[62] Such a discussion of Prafulla Kumar shows his idealism more than his literary tastes.

EDITOR, *RONGPUR DARPAN*

The Editor, *Rongpur Darpan*, in his essay, *Bangasahitye Bankim: Mrinalinir Alochana*[63] disparaged Bankim. A criticism of such light-hearted vein could neither be found in the contemporary age nor in the pre-Bankim Centenary period. The essayist was so much pre-occupied with the editor's natural hatred for Bankim, his traditional attitude and religious orthodoxy that it could hardly be termed as a literary criticism. He charged Bankim primarily for not following the principles of Sanskrit rhetoric. He further alleged Bankim for insulting the Hindu culture, introduction of harmful education in society, perverse explanation of history, and grammatical mis-use and wrong use.

The editor said that Hemchandra was not an ideal man, illiterate; therefore, he could not be a poetic hero in accordance with the Sanskrit rhetoric. His decision to kill the 'Guru' for the sake of his beloved was a bad example for the society. *Patni* was an untouchable, so the staying with a woman of the royal family at his house at Nabadwip for a long time was a blemish. Byomkesh was not a lover, and he was wild in nature, so his service for Mrinalini was unbelievable. He remarked, Bankim, in his attempt to draw the picture of a monkey, had added a little colour of Shiba. And he warned Bankim:

> Born in Indian culture which is an abode of the God's, racially being a Bramhim, you can not break the ideals, and this sort of an education is quite unexpected. You have forcibly introduced this ill teaching in India and hence, you are unpardonable.[64]

LALIT KUMAR BANDOPADHYAY (1275-1336 B.S.)

The fact-finding and diligent critic Lalit Kumar Bandopadhyay wrote criticism of *Mrinalini* some of his essays[65] and books of essays.[66] He primarily dealt with the title of the book and the family picture therein.

According to him Hemchandra's bravery, his passion for punishing the enemies, progressive mindedness, etc. deserve appreciation. Monorama was a superb mysterious character, Girijaya's friendship was sweet, but Mrinalini a devoted wife, stood in the centre of this book. There might not be in Mrinalini, the glow which was there in the character of Monorama, but still she was the centre of interest for the readers. Hence the title was justified.[67]

How far the motherliness of the different characters had been preserved and in which roles they appeared in the novel formed the subject matter of the essay *Ma*. According to him Mrinalini's aunt exercised greater influence over her[68] than her mother, and hence, a sort of freedom left its impact upon her love-life; and for the growth of this free nature, Mrinalini's mother's death was inevitable.[69]

Lalit Kumar left the stamp of the spirit of investigation in his search for the origin and development of love between Hemchandra and Mrinalini. He referred to examples from the Indian and the foreign literature in the context of Hemchandra's rescuing of the drawing Mrinalini and the subsequent growth of love between them. These were the rescuing of Debjani from the well by Jojati as described in the *Mahabharata*, the rescuing of the princess Kanaklekha from the hands of Kapalik by Mantragupta, and the growth of love thereafter as described in *Dashakumar Charit* and the similar scene of rescue leading to the growth of love in *Venice Preserved*. But the critic pointed out that Bankim could create the right environment for the blossoming of love between Mrinalini and Hemchandra by creating a situation in which Hemchandra had to nurse Mrinalini for three days together, and for this Bankim deserved credit.[70]

Lalit Kumar's last and final venture on this novel could be found in his essay *Sakhi*. He observed that Mrinalini's luck for friends was better than that of Shakuntala and Cleopatra.[71] Girijaya had been characterised by Lalit Kumar as the best of friends belonging to the class of servants and waiting woman.[72] He further said that Girijaya's love for Mrinalini was so deep and genuine that as a friend she could best be up-graded to the level of Nirmal Kumari or even Basantakumari.[73]

In spite of so much the critic has said, his discussion is more descriptive than analytic, though it is primarily based on numerous comparative studies.

SHASHANKA MOHAN SEN (1872-1928)

While Lalit Kumar engaged himself in finding out the family pictures, the great critic[74] Shashanka Mohan Sen concentrated upon exploring the inner facts in order to find out Bankim's philosophy of life in his critical work *Bangabani*.[75] He said that Bankim had turned down the tone of *Durgeshnandini* and *Kapalkundala*. According to him: Mrinalini was the prototype of Tilottoma, Hemchandra was that of Jagatsingha and Nabakumar, Girijaya was that of Bimala, and Monorama was the 'Bengali edition' of Kapalkundala; and Bankim's social consciousness and patriotism had mixed up with it,[76] and like Hemchandra's Birbahu and Nabinchandra's Rongamati. This patriotism had turned towards unintended emotion.[77]

Critics like Akshay Chandra Sarkar, Girija Prasanna, Roy Chowdhury and Promothanath Sen tried to build up the criticism of this book on a literary base. But this trend was discontinued from Prafulla Kumar Sarkar. It was Shashanka Mohan who tried to restore the original trend.

AMARENDRANATH ROY (1888-1957)

Amarendranath's criticism of *Mrinalini,* in his *Bankimer Upanyase Matriechabi*[78] was a stereotyped one. Like Lalit Kumar Bandopadhyay, the present critic believed that Mrinalini's freedom in the matters of love would have been hindered if her mother had been alive. Therefore, the writer caused her death. He said that Mrinalini, Girijaya and Monorama were the prototypes of Tilottama, Bimala and Kapalkundala respectively.[79] Such remarks are not new, these already appeared in the writings of Shashanka Mohan about a year before the publication of this work.

AKSHAY KUMAR DUTTAGUPTA

Akshay Kumar's criticism of *Mrinalini* in his book *Bankimchandra*[80] shows philosophical tendency coupled with progressive attitude. His critical qualities have found expression in his presentation of new ideals in the explanation of the principal characters and in the comparative discussion of *Durgeshnandini* and *Mrinalini* and in the evaluation of Bankim psychology.

Throwing light upon the character of Monorama, Akshay Kumar said: "The complicacy in Monorama is only external and not internal."[81] But he said that going through the ordeals of sorrow, she became a bit riper than her age and gathered more experiences. The critic had laid much emphasis upon the strength of her nature and believes that this strength was the basis of her character.[82]

He pointed out, in some respects, *Mrinalini* resembled *Durgeshnandini*. As Monorama's genius and intelligence, so her nursing of Hemchandra resembled Ayesa's. Abhiram Swami's knowledge of astrology, his political practice had been developed in Madhabacharya. Jagatsingha's suspicion about Tilottoma and overcoming of this suspicion by the words of Katlu Khan, the deserted Tilottama's dream,—such incidents were there in *Mrinalini* also. The critic also traced similarities in other characters too. In bravery, Hemchandra was like Jagatsingha, he was also a lover like Jagatsingha. As Tilottama appeared in a faded glow beside Ayesa, so also, Mrinalini faded beside Monorama. In Girijaya, one could find the shadow of Bimala so far as their joyous mood and jocular tone were concerned, and form the artistic point of view Bimala was the life-blood of *Durgeshnandini*, so also, Girijaya in Mrinalini. Next to *Kapalkundala*, and *Durgeshnandini* was the last of the trio.[83] Such observations were the outcome of his sympathetic and unprejudiced mind. The depth of Akshay Kumar's taste and understanding is evident in his words:

> *Mrinalini* is a superb book in its song and pleasant jokes. Like that of *Durgeshnandini* and *Kapalkundala*, poetic qualities are more than novelistic qualities in *Mrinalini*. Even if it is inferior to *Kapalkundala* in imagination and artistic skill, it is a thing of the realm of imagination—a superb thing.[84]

Akshay Kumar may be regarded as the precursor of the modern critics who have tried to find out the similarities of incidents between *Mrinalini* and some of Shakespeare's plays. He is the first critic to point out that Girijaya's marriage with Digbijoy resembled Gratiano's marriage with Nerissa after the marriage of their master and mistress, Basanio and Portia in *Merchant of Venice*.[85]

Like Akshay Chandra Sarkar and Haran Chandra Rakshit, he also believed that the motive which inspired Bankim to write *Bangalar Itihas* and *Bangalar Kalankau* also prompted him to write *Mrinalini*.[86]

BIPIN CHANDRA PAL (1858-1932)

Bipin Chandra had briefly but substantially discussed *Mrinalini* in his essay *Banglar Nabayuger Katha (Ekadash Katha)*[87] and *Nabayuger Banglasahitye Bankimchandra.*[88] He said that from the standpoint of plot construction and romantic appeal *Mrinalini* could be regarded as a romantic novel. Individualism and the natural expression of mind of the people of the Renaissance Bengal was one of the features of this book. Bipin Chandra, in his brief discussion, threw light upon this feature.[89] He said that in *Mrinalini,* a universal appeal[90] and a natural tendence of worldly enjoyment had been expressed through literary taste.[91] Bipin Chandra's discussion inclined towards historical method of criticism. He found in it a natural reflection of the common people of Bengal during the renaissance, when he considered the novel from historical point of view.

ADHYAPAK PURNACHANDRA BISWAS AND SACHINDRANATH MUKHOPADHYAY

Purnachandra and Sachindranath, wrote in collaboration and published the book *Bangla Bhasha O Sahityer Songkshipta Sar.*[92] Of the three early novels of Bankimchandra, Akshay Kumar Dattagupta and others places *Mrinalini* after *Durgeshnandini* from the standpoint of gradual development, and *Kapalkundala* was regarded as the best. Purnachandra and Sachindranath also accepted *Kapalkundala* as the best, and opined that *Mrinalini* was another remarkable creation of Bankim in keeping with the spirit of *Kapalkundala.* They said that the conjugal love and patriotic zeal hinted at in this novel had achieved finality in *Anandamath.*[93] It is to be noted that about forty years before Purnachandra and Sachindranath, Akshay Chandra Sarkar had given a similar opinion.

MAKHANLAL MUKHOPADHYAY

Makhanlal Mukhopadhyay wrote criticism of *Mrinalini* before Bankim Centenary in his *Bankimchandrar Upanyase Rupbarnana.*[94] Makhanlal attempted to discuss the merit of Bankimchandra as an artist in this novel.

According to him, Bankim was really a great master of narrative art. His narrative technique clearly reflected his thought that even an ordinary thing became extra-ordinary by his magic touch.

According to the critic, Monorama was a unique creation of Bankim. He had blended the childish fickleness with the natural gravity of the age to clothe her in beauty. Here he found Bankim's genius akin to the great painter Rubens who had left behind him the stamp of his singularity in one of his greatest portrait by projecting it from two angles.[95]

SUMMING UP

The study of Mrinalini criticism shows how the tone and temper of the critics vary with the type of the novel. The novel being a historical romance, it vibrates with imaginative treatment of characters against the historical background, but few critics turned their eyes to this vital aspect of the novel. Most of the criticism centred round characters, and little attention was paid to plot construction, the art form of the novel and Bankim's philosophy of life. However, the attempts of critics at romantic recreation of characters are commendable, though, of course, there appears the same orthodoxy and conservativeness of some critics to mar their literary assessment. It is to be noted that the same critics fared much better in *Durgeshnandini* and *Kapalkundala*. However, Girija Prasanna and Akshay Kumar Duttagupta shine at their best as *Mrinalini* critics.

References

1. Ghose, Monmuth Nath, *Mrinalini (Bhumika), Archana*, 22nd part, Issue III. Baishakh, 1333 B.S., p. 105.
2. Mitra, Rajendralal, *Mrinalini, Rahasya Sandarbha*, 1927 Sambat, Reprinted, *Archana*, 22nd part, 3rd issue, Baishakh, 1333 B.S., pp. 105-08.
3. Mitra, Rajendralal, Mrinalini. *Archana*, p. 107.
4. *Ibid.*, pp. 107-08.
5. *Ibid.*, p. 108.
6. Nyayratna, Ramgati, *Bangala Bhasha O Bangala Sahitya Bishoyak Prostab*, First Edition, 1872.
7. *Ibid.*, 2nd Edn., 1944 Sambat, p. 284.

8. *Bangala Bhasha O Bangala Sahitya Bishoyak Prastab.* 2nd Edn., pp. 284-85.
9. *Bankim Rachanabali (Mrinalini), Sahitya Samsad*, 5th Publication, Chaitra, 1376 B.S., p. 196.
10. *Ibid*., p. 284.
11. Sarkar, Akshay Chandra, *Pashupati, Nabajibon*, 12th Issue, Asharh, 1295 B.S., pp. 721-40.
12. Sengupta, Subodh Chandra, *Bangala Somalochana Parichay*, 1st Pub., Magh, 1376 B.S., p. 111.
13. Sengupta, Dr. Satyaprasad, *Pashchayatya Sahitye Somalochanar Dhara*, 2nd Print 1st August, 1977, p. 73.
14. Sarkar, Akshay Chandra, op. cit., p. 738.
15. *Ibid*., p. 724.
16. *Ibid*., pp. 723-25.
17. *Ibid*., pp. 727-28.
18. *Ibid*., p. 736.
19. *Ibid*., p. 737.
20. Roychowdhury, Girija Prasanna, *Girijaya, Prachar*, Poush-Magh, 1295 B.S. pp. 344-63.
21. Roychowdhury, Girija Prasanna, *Monorama, Prachar*, 1295 B.S., Reprinted, *Somalochana Sahitya*, Edited by Dr. Shreekumar Bondopadhyay, Dr. Prafulla Chandra Paul, 5th Edition, Poush, 1379 B.S. pp. 262-85.
22. Roychowdhury, G.P., *Bankimchandra-Durgeshnandini-Kapalkundala-Mrinalini*, 1297 B.S.
23. Roychowdhury, Girija Prasanna, *Girijaya*, p. 346.
24. *Ibid*., p. 350.
25. *Ibid*., p. 359.
26. *Samalochana Sahitya*, pp. 368-74.
27. *Ibid*., p. 271.
28. Roychowdhury, Girija Prasanna, *Bankimchandra (Mrinalini)*, 1297 B.S., pp. 12-13.
29. Sengupta, Subodhchandra, *Bangla Samalochana-Parichay*. 1st Publication, Magh, 1376 B.S., p. 156.
30. Bondopadhyay, Haridas, *Banglar Upanyas Lekhak (Mrinalini O Bishabriksha)* Kalpana, Jaistha, 1296 B.S., 6th Year, pp. 149-58.
31. *Ibid*., pp. 149-51.
32. Ghosh, Panchkari, *Bankimchandrer Soundarjya Sristhi (Mrinalini)*, Anusandhan, Asharh, 15, 1301 B.S., pp. 264-69, & Asharh 22, 1301, pp. 296-97.
33. *Ibid*., p. 264.

34. *Ibid.*, Asharh 22, 1301 B.S., p. 287.
35. *Ibid.*
36. Roy, Siddheswar, *Girijaya Geet*, *Anusandhan*, Bhadra 01, 301 B.S. pp. 468-71.
37. Roy, Siddheswar, *Kaha Mrinal Hamari*, Kartik 09, 1301 B.S. Kartik 16, 1301 B.S., pp. 683-85.
38. Roy, Siddheswar, *Girijaya Geet*, p. 469.
39. *Ibid.*, p. 468.
40. Roy, Siddheswar, *Kaha Mrinal Hamari, Anusandhan*, Kartik, 1301 B.S., pp. 662-66, 683-85.
41. Ghose, Hemendra Prasad, *Bankimchandra (3) Mrinalini*, *Dasi* October, 1895, pp. 549-54.
42. *Ibid.*, pp. 551-54.
43. Sen, Pramathanath, *Mrinalini, Bharati*, Agahan, 1312 B.S., pp. 764-89.
44. *Ibid.*, pp. 764-81.
45. *Ibid.*, p. 781.
46. *Ibid.*
47. Sen, Pramathanath, *Mrinalini*, pp. 787-88.
48. Sen, Pramathanath, *Girijaya, Sahitya*, 18th year, Issue-X, Magh, 1314 B.S., pp. 574-87.
49. *Ibid.*, p. 579.
50. Sen, Pramathanath, *Girijaya*, p. 575.
51. *Ibid.*, p. 774.
52. Lahiri, Kumud Nath, *Manorama, Sahitya*, Kartik, 1313 B.S., pp. 395-405.
53. *Ibid.*, p. 404.
54. *Ibid.*, p. 402.
55. Basu, Jitendralal, *Bankimchandra, Bangadarshan (Nabaparjay)*, Year-X, Issue-III, Asharh, 1317 B.S., pp. 113-23.
56. Bala Shaishaba Tarun Bhet/Lokhaina pariya jaitha konthe/... Shaishaba Joubana Upajala Chand/Koina mania joy abased.
57. Rakshit, Haran Chandra, *Bangasahitye Bankim,* 1306 B.S.
58. Rakshit, Haran Chandra, *Bangasahitye Bankim*, Poush, 1317 B.S., p. 118.
59. *Ibid.*, p. 119.
60. *Ibid.*, pp. 65-66.
61. Sarkar, Prafulla Kumar, *Samaj Sanskare Bankimchandra, Bangadarshan, (Naba Parjay)*, 1317 B.S., Reprinted: Chattopadhyay, Nakul (ed.), *Prafulla Kumar Sarkarer Prabandha Sangraha,* Ananda Pub., 1376 B.S., pp. 9-29.

62. Sarkar, Prafulla Kumar, *Prabandha Sangraha*, p. 19.
63. Editor, Rongpur Darpan, *Bangasahitye Bankim—Mrinalinir Samalochana*, Rongpur Saraswati Press, 1318 B.S.
64. *Ibid.*, p. 5.
65. (a) Bondopadhyay, Lalit Kumar, *Bankimchandrer Akhyaikabali, Bharatbarsha*, Asharh, 1322 B.S., pp. 6-11.
    (b) Bondopadhyay, Lalit Kumar, *Ma, Bharatbarsha*, 3rd year, 1st part, 2nd Issue, Shraban, 1322 B.S., pp. 264-82.
    (c) Bondopadhyay, Lalit Kumar, *Dui Bhagini, Bharatbarsha*, 4th year, 1st part, 3rd Issue, Bhadra, 1323 B.S., pp. 391-407.
66. (a) Bondopadhyay, Lalit Kumar, *Premer Katha,* Jaishtha, 1327 B.S.
    (b) Bondopadhyay, Lalit Kumar, *Sakhi*, 1328 B.S.
67. Bondopadhyay, Lalit Kumar, *Bankimchander Akshvaikabali, Bharatbarsha,* Asharh, 1322 B.S., p. 9.
68. Bondopadhyay, Lalit Kumar, *Dui Bhagini*, p. 394.
69. Bondopadhyay, Lalit Kumar, *Ma*, pp. 267-68.
70. Bondopadhyay, Lalit Kumar, *Premer Katha*, pp. 56-57.
71. Bondopadhyay, Lalit Kumar, *Sakhi*, p. 21.
72. *Ibid.*, p. 53.
73. *Ibid.*, pp. 60-61.
74. Sen, Sukumar, *Bangla Sahityar Itihas, (2nd part),* 5th edn., p. 500.
75. Sen, Sukumar, *Bangabani*, (1st and 2nd part), Dhaka, 1915.
76. *Ibid.*, p. 63.
77. *Ibid.*
78. Roy, Amarendranath, *Bankimer Upanyase Matrichabi, Argha*, Chaitra, 1323 B.S., pp. 391-97.
79. *Ibid.*, pp. 393-94.
80. Duttagupta, Akshay Kumar, *Bankimchandra*, 1327 B.S.
81. Duttagupta, Akshay Kumar, *Bankimchandra*, 2nd Edn., Jignasa, May 1978, p. 113.
82. *Ibid.*
83. *Ibid.*, pp. 113-16.
84. *Ibid.*, p. 119.
85. *Ibid.*, p. 117.
86. *Ibid.*, pp. 119-20.
87. Pal, Bipin Chandra, *Banglar Nabayuger Katha, (Ekadash Katha), Bangabani*, 2nd year, 1st part, 1st Issue, Falgun, 1329 B.S., pp. 90-98.
88. Pal, Bipin Chandra, '*Nabayuger Bangasahitye Bankimchandra*', *Nabyabharat*, Bhadra, 1130 B.S., pp. 235-49.

89. Pal, Bipin Chandra, *Banglar Nabayuger Katha*, pp. 93-95.
90. *Ibid.*, p. 94.
91. Pal, Bipin Chandra, *Nabayuger Bangasahitye Bankimchandra*, p. 240.
92. Biswas, Adhyapak Purnachandra and Mukhopadhyay, Sachindranath, *Bangla Bhasha O Sahityer Sangkshiptasar*, 1332 B.S.
93. *Ibid.*, p. 183.
94. Mukhopadhyay, Makhanlal, *Bankimchandrer Upanyase Rupbarnana*, *Bichitra*, 7th year, 1st Part, Agrahayan, 1340 B.S., pp. 642-64.
95. *Ibid.*, p. 645.

5
Bishabriksha

JOGENDRANATH BIDYABHUSAN (1845-1904)

When *Bishabriksha* was published in serials in *Bangadarshan* discussions on the novel appeared in *Somprokash* through some letters which showed that though the novel evoked sufficient curiosity among the readers, objective criticism was yet to make any headway. It was Jogendranath Bidyabhusan who in his article *Bishabriksha*[1] took a step forward in this regard. First, for common readers, he gave an outline of the novel with his own observations. Then he tried to make a psychological study of Suryamukhi and Kundanandini. He is the first critic of *Bishabriksha* who initiated the synthesis of classical and modern critical trends.

The critic looked upon Bankimchandra as a social and moral reformer, and he considered *Bishabriksha* as a didactic novel exposing the dangers of incestuous life. The critic defended the novel as an attempt to show the possibility of social reformation and spiritual purification through the fire of self-sacrificing love. He also asserted that Bankimchandra's grasp over the inner psychology of his characters was only next to the ancient master-minds like Balmiki, Vyas, Bhababhuti, Kalidas and Banavatta.[2]

Jogendranath tried to recreate the character of Suryamukhi from psychological point of view. He gave a psychological analysis not only of Suryamukhi's desertion of home but also her return. Regarding desertion, the critic specifically pointed out that it was the jealousy for co-wife which prompted her to leave her once dear home because jealousy is a passion hard to conquer. However, she had to take further lesson in the school of life, and learn how to conquer this indomitable vile passion.

Hence, there was her final return, a conquest over jealousy, a rare thing in literature. The critic categorically pointed out: "Jealousy for the co-wife is common and even Suryamukhi's celestial heart fails conquers the melody."[3] The critic observed that Suryamukhi discovered a major blemish in Nagendra mainly because of Nagendra's sudden coldness to her. Her selfish love for herself won over her overwhelming love for Nagendra. She deserted her home.[4]

The critic considered this desertion of home by Suryamukhi as a moral degradation for a Hindu wife. But her return restored her to the citadel of Hindu womanhood. She became a repentant wife—more glorious with the glow of a redeemed angel. Indeed, she had conquered her jealousy for the co-wife by her devotion to husband.

The critic's assessment of the flows of Suryamukhi's character is conditioned by his own idealistic vision of the traditional Hindu wife. Suryamukhi has been put to rigorous test against the rigid code of conduct of an ideal Hindu wife. She has not been looked upon as a woman of flesh and blood. This critical opinion is based on prudish standard of morality. However, the critic shows his grasp over the labyrinth of human psychology in his attempts to analyse the reasons of Suryamukhi's desertion of home. Turning to Kundanandini, the critic said that she was an innocent angelic woman, devoid of all awareness of the confounding complexities of the world. She was a shy-coy-self-effacing woman, almost childlike ignorant about the human nature. The critic aptly perceived Kunda's nature. Her predicament was due to her simplistic belief that as her marriage with Nagendra took place with the Suryamukhi's happy approval there was no reason for Suryamukhi's grief on that account. Otherwise, her self-sacrificing mind would not hesitate to forgo even her long cherished goal for others happiness. The critic said:

> Kunda's love for Nagendra is purely platonic.... She could not understand why she was drawn so inexorably to Nagendra. She could defeat her death wish only at the sight of Nagendra—herein lies the remarkability of

> her love. Without her death, Bishabriksha would not be such an overwhelmingly tragic novel.[5]

Jogendranath could not tower over his age completely—this largely explains the intrusion of the traditional literary critical style in his writing. Quoting ancient classical critical texts, Jogendranath observed that Suryamukhi-Nagendranath's love based on their respect for mutual qualities. Nagendra's love for Kunda's physical beauty (Rupaja), but Bankimchandra had not tried to unravel the mystery of Kundanandini's love for Nagendra. Bhavabhuti, the ancient master, also had failed to understand the reason or the nature of such love and called this "Spontaneous (Okaran) or metaphysical love."[6] Kunda's love for Nagendra is an example of such a concept of love.

In the counter part of the article, under the sub-title: *Suryamukhi and Kundanandini*,[7] using Bankim's own brand of language, Jogendranath had tried to posit the difference between the two women characters. In an emotional hyperbole, he remarked,

> Suryamukhi's love is endless; Kunda's love touches the deepest bottom of the ocean of love. Suryamukhi is fully blossomed. Whereas Kunda is a half-blossomed flower...Suryamukhi's heart is like the full moon of the autumn...pure, bright—visible to the bare eyes. But Kunda's heart is an Autumn Star—pure and bright. Though in itself a huge sun, to the other planets, she is not visible even to the minutest watcher. Suryamukhi heart is beautiful and as aesthetically satisfying as that of then naked body of a fairy—matchless and bewitching. Kunda is a veiled beautiful lady, passionate, charming and exciting.[8]

Further, Jogendranath also observed the fusion of both western and oriental literary forms in Bankim Chandra's delineation of these two-woman characters. In his opinion

> Suryamukhi was a synthesis of Sita and Desdemona, while Kunda combines in her a symmetrical combination of Sakuntala and Miranda.[9]

In spite of the sporadic over-indulgence in emotional hyperbole and occasional exaggerations, the value of Jogendranath's contribution to criticism of this novel can hardly be overestimated. He will be remembered with reverence for his trend-setting literary evaluation of this novel.

PURNA CHANDRA BASU

Purna Chandra Basu's lengthy article *Kundanandini*[10] suffers from the limitations of the age. The critic treads the beaten track. There is the some stereotype method—summary of the novel, use of Bankim's own brand of language, evolution of characters, inner significance of the novel and emotional exuberance.

The main contents of the discussion were Kundanandini's simplicity, her unusual quietude, softness, and her silent love: "Though silence is not a particular trait of her nature, it is a manifestation of her total being."[11]

In this lengthy article Purna Chandra carefully drew our attention to some facts. He felt that through *Bishabriksha* Bankimchandra had drawn our attention to the inner social life of the Bengalee society. Kunda, Suryamukhi and Kamalmani were typical representatives of the Bengalee Hindu women.[12] It needs to be mentioned here that Purna Chandra showed an artistic awareness. And observed:

> Kundanandini is an imaginative culmination of the concept of the coy, simple, soft, sober, inexperienced Bengalee traditional woman. In fact, Kunda is a symbol of the soft-spoken Bengalee house-wife.[13]

But, in spite of all these laudable observations, Purna Chandra's article in its style and content, seems to be near repetition of Jogendranath's article. To defend himself against the criticism Purna Chandra stated that while writing our observations about the novel: "We did not discuss the novel, our articles were in the press at the same time."[14] This attitude of Purna Chandra underwent a remarkable change in his later years as revealed in his book *Falashrut*[15] which was published thirty years after the publication of his first article. Here he evaluated the same novel once again, but his assessment was profoundly influenced by the age and he, like his contemporaries, tried to analyse Kunda in the light of the rigid code of traditional Hindu society, against this prudish moral code.

Nagendra was treacherous man, who married the daughter-like, shelter less child-widow Kunda and thus defiled his home and reduced her to a concubine. This immoral act destroyed the sanctity of the Hindu-home,—the temple of purity. In an emotional outburst he said: "to a Hindu his home is a fortress of purity and his relatives are a part of the integrated morally purposeful life: fie! Fie! in such a holy pace, Nagendra lives with a concubine! What can be more shameful than this!"

DEBENDRA BIJOY BASU

Debendra Bijoy in his articles,[16] discussed the innumerable forces shaping human nature and its complexities. He insisted that to understand the complexity the human nature, one must study characters into four distinct groups—(1) the common man without complexities,[17] (2) the ideal man,[18] (3) the modern man exposed to science[19] and (4) symbolic characters representing some dominant aspects of human behaviour.[20]

The critic found all the four varieties of characters in *Bishabriksha*, and as such, he considered the novel as a treasure house of human psychology.[21] While Shrish and Kamalini represented the first group; Suryamukhi and Kundanandini were in the second; Debendra and Hira, the third, and Nagendra Nath with licentious behavior, the fourth group.[22]

Debendra Bijoy is the first critic to propagate the need for evaluation of the novel *Bishabriksha* from an artistic standpoint rather than the prudish moralistic standpoint. Familiarity with the western literature and literary critical canons, led Debendra Bijoy to believe that 'truth' is the soul of 'art' and 'art' is the lifeblood of the novel. To him, truth is absolute and he looks negatively at the concept of relative truth. He posed the question: "What should we do with the truth that leaves room for both good and evil, honesty and dishonesty?"[23] Reacting from this background of conviction, Debendra Bijoy considered *Bishabriksha* as a remarkable example of a perfect novel and asserted that in the face of *Bishabriksha* and *Kapalkundala* all other Bengali novels faded into insignificance.[24]

In another article, *Kundanandini*,[25] Debendra Bijoy had studied Kunda with deep sympathy and compassion. Though on the whole, the article traced the pathetic life of Kunda, it bore testimony to the critic's romantic imagination, aesthetic delight in beauty and his access to the world of deeper psychological reality. He stated: "There is a world between sleep and reality—the world of dream...Kunda belongs to this world."[26] Debendra Bijoy's aesthetic perception was revealed in the comment that: "Kunda is calm and luminous white flower against the background of the pitch dark night, her life is a reflection of such quiet glow."[27]

He explained Kunda's behavior in the light of psychological analysis. A simple, women, without any complexities, she had agreed to marry Nagendra and did not suffer from any feeling of guilt or self-abnegation, because of her ignorance of the ways of the world. Kunda, in her complete innocence, did not know that a Hindu widow should not fall in love with a man or not even think of love which explained the absence of self-control in her.[28] This interpretation of the Kundanandini's character by Debendra Bijoy, deserves praise because it throws a flood of light on the inner working of human soul.

BALENDRANATH THAKUR (1870-99)

Balendranath Thakur's articles *Kundanandini O Suryamukhi*,[29] and *Swavab O Sahitya*[30] were steeped in traditionalism: character analysis of Kundanandini and Suryamukhi, summary of the novel and liberal use of quotation to substantiate his arguments.

But his criticism has distinctiveness. Without restoring to didacticism, he traced artistic beauty of the novel. He was apparently quite moved by the beauty of the two women characters Kunda and Suryamukhi. Suryamukhi in her homely beauty appeared angelic to him—an incarnation of the 'Lakshmi'[31] (ideal of a Bengalee woman). In knowledge, intelligence, conscience, and love; she was an ideal wife. Her love for husband was like that of Sita. Likewise, Kundanandini was also a heavenly beauty. But she was not an ideal better-self. She was an ordinary wife. The beauty of her character lay in her love for Nagendra and her child-like innocence.

Balendranath displayed liberalism and modernity—when he repeatedly asserted that Suryamukhi's desertion of home did not affect her integrity and beauty. She was superior to Kunda in all respects: love, understanding, conscience, education, and knowledge about the world. Balendranath was deeply impressed by her motherly qualities. Even though childless Suryamukhi was not devoid of motherliness which was her inner strength. And this quality had made her the cynosure in Nagendra's big family.[32]

Balendranath is the first critic to take note of the fact that the essential spirit of the novel is tragic. He observed:

> Suryamukhi's all happiness and peace disappear with Kunda's death.... Her death in its huge jaw swallows all her joy, happiness and peace. Bishabriksha ends as a tragedy.[33]

Indeed, the tragedy was manifested through the death of Kunda although the novel ended in the reunion of Nagendra and Suryamukhi. It was Balendranath who first focused the reader's attention to the essential beauty of the tragic character when he said:

> Bankimchandra has almost always kept Kunda hidden in darkness and shade, her character becomes clearly visible only through occasional flashes of light focused on her face.[34]

Balendranath is the first critic to point out the artistic merit of realism in Bankim novels. He said that literature should follow nature and synthesize light and shade, which increases another and intensities as they do in real life. He thus highlighted a great quality of Bankim overlooked by predecessors and contemporaries. Indeed, Bankim gave a realistic portrayal of the tragic character of Kundanandini, built up in the inter play of light and shade, which lent a tragic undertone.

CHANDRANATH BASU (1844-1910)

A product of Neo-Hinduism, Chandranath weilded his pen to protect, preserve and glorify the ancient ideals, and playing the role of a critic, he expounded his own literary principles in *Novel ba Kathagranther Uddeshya*[35] in such strong orthodox terms that the later critics like Sukumar Sen, Arun Kumar Mukhopadhyay, Subodh Chandra Sengupta besides others had found very solid grounds for strong objections.[36] However, the facts remain that in the social and cultural as well as the religious background of the then Bengal, Chandranath was a force to reckon with, and as such, it would be very much pertinent to have a proper evaluation of his criticism since much of what he said could not stand the test of time. In his *Novel ba Katha-granther Uddeshya,*[37] he asserted that social morality should be the prime occupation of novel. He also pointed out that the Bengali novel should not be only a blind imitation of the English novel—as the two societies are completely different.[38] Basu held a didactic view about the aim of literature and condemned reading stories of romance, and suggested a ban on writing about extra-marital love. Bengali novels, he felt, depicted such things only under the influence of English literature. According to him, this tendency accounted for the popularity and glorification of immoral characters like Kunda.[39]

However, Chandranath showed literary and romantic perceptibility in evaluating Kunda. He said:

> Kunda tried to convince her heart against the incestuous love for Nagendra but failed. She had to be blamed for this failure. But one who blames her for her fall is heartless and cruel, because Kunda was in the grip of irresistible love.[40]

But the conservative-didactic strain in him surpassed again, when he called this love, 'incestuous' and 'abominable'.

Chandranath Basu had given a detailed outline of the character of Suryamukhi in the article *Duiti Hindu Patni*.[41] But the discussion has little literary merit. He discussed Suryamukhi in the touchstone of an ideal Hindu womanhood. He said, "In our everyday life, we see wife like Suryamukhi in every Bengalee household, Suryamukhi, a perfect Hindu wife in our ancient Sanskrit tradition."[42]

Chandranath is a product of his age and it is in him that we notice exuberance of the orthodoxy, narrowness, parochialism, and limited vision. His discouragements of romance, his inability to appreciate the artistic beauty in delineation of human love, and his didactic overtone have marred most of his criticism. In fact, his criticism has hardly any literary value, although none will deny its historical importance.

HARIDAS BONDOPADHYAY

Haridas Bondopadhyay wrote a lengthy criticism on *Bishabriksha,* in his article, *Banglar Upannyas Lekhak Bankimchandra Chattopadhyay (Mrinalini O Bishabriksha).*[43] It is a piece of descriptive criticism. The main topics of discussion were the characters of Nagendra, Debendra, Suryamukhi, Kamalini, Kundanandini and Hira.

Haridas analysed the role of these characters in the novel. His critical temperament is to be found in the remarks he made here and there about these characters. These reveal his orthodox nature. The Judgement he passed on Suryamukhi is one such example. He said that although Suryamukhi was a woman of many qualities and her devotion to her husband was exemplary, she could not be called an 'ideal Hindu wife'[44] since she was not capable of self-sacrifice.

However, his assessment of Kundanandini is a fine example of good criticism. Analysing her character the critic said, that she was a character of endless virtues, and that such a character delineation was only expected of a man of literature on Bengal, not in other places.[45] This reveals his nationalist sentiment peculiar to the latter half of the nineteenth century.

The article is not without sparks of pure literary criticism. The way in which he evaluated the character of Kunda with her sweetness, shyness, loveliness and delicacy speaks of his artistic nature and love of beauty. He remarked, the novelist had created this celestial beauty of Kunda by combining in her simplicity, shyness, timidity, love, sorrow, endurance, sympathy and self-sacrifice.[46]

SUDHINDRANATH THAKUR (1869-1929)

Sudhindranath Thakur's article *Suryamukhi O Kundenandini,*[47] is an example of emotion and exaggeration without any substantial objective stand. But an aesthetic critical standpoint can be noticed in the article. Discerning the gradual development of characters, their fall, their intense repentance, occasional pessimism, flashes of happiness, role of love and struggle for existence, Sudhindranath called *Bishabriksha* a novel of life in its totality.[48]

Attempting a comparison of Suryamukhi and Kundanandini Sudhindranath observed:

> Kunda is the dawn, Suryamukhi is the dusk.... Kunda is half-blossomed, while Suryamukhi is a full-blossomed flower. Kundanandini is a chattering coquettish stream.... Suryamukhi is a deep ocean. Kunda is beautiful; Suryamukhi is the culmination of beauty.[49]

Uses of such supercharged language speak of Sudhindranath's love for the rhetoric.

Sudhindranath, while analyzing the woman character, commented that Kundanandini represented the western woman. Kamalmani was a combination of the East and the West, and Suryamukhi was the epitome of beauty of a Bengalee woman—pride of Bengal.[50] Such an interpretation at once establishes his identification with and difference from the other critics.

He differs sharply with Purna Chandra on the issue that all the women characters of *Bishabriksha* are from the Indian Bengali Society.[51] Sudhindranath assesses that only Suryamukhi is a totally Indian Bengali women. Again, his point of difference from Haridas Bondopadhyay can be observed in his attitude to Suryamukhi. While Haridas condemns Suryamukhi for her failure of self-sacrifice at the altar of her husband's happiness.[52] Sudhindranath believes that Suryamukhi's very being is made of love. And love enables her to sacrifice her own happiness for others.[53]

Balendranath Thakur did not find any resemblance of Kunda and Suryamukhi. To him, her love for Nagendra is the haughty passion of youth.[54] But on the other hand, Sudhindranath has compared Kunda with the dawn, and naturally he could not subscribe to the Balendra's view point. But both of them have agreed that Suryamukhi is superior to Kunda.

Even though Sudhindranath did not pretend to delve deep into criticism, his opinion is free from any parochial and aggressive assertion of the rigid code of morality.

NARENDRA NATH BASU

Narendra Nath Basu's *Tulanay Somalochana (Bishabriksha o Krishnakanter Uil) Kundanandini o Rohini*[55] bears the mark of contemporary trend of criticism. The said article shows the traditional view of morality conduct. In *Bishabriksha* portion, character of Kundanandini is examined in the norm of rigid formal Hindu social code. The critic examines Kunda's love on the touchstone of classical principles.

Discussing the nature of love of Kundanandini he observed that her love to a great extent was 'spiritual'[56] (gunaja), although subsequently this spiritual love was intensified by the physical (Raupaja) elements. Kunda had given her body, not her life. In gratitude to her benefactor. Fearing the reprimand of the society for a Hindu widow's love-making, Kunda desired to marry Nagendra.[57] The didactic critic could not forgive Kunda from what he considered to be her licentiousness, put her on trial and passed cruel judgement against her in following manner. Kunda's first fault was her infatuation with a man as old as her father, her second fault was that she sacrificed the purity of widowhood for the sake of bodily pleasure. Her third fault was that she betrayed the loving and affectionate Suryamukhi by snatching away Nagendra from her.[58] Her 'no' to Nagendra was in fact, 'yes'.[59]

Narendra Nath was so orthodox that he even argued for expelling *Bishabriksha* from the field of Bengali novels, because it depicted the English lifestyle and foreign culture, while a Bengali novel must reflect the Hindu social code.[60]

MAHENDRA NATH MAZUMDER

Mahendra Nath's criticism *Sahitya O Samaj Athaba Bankimbabur Bishabriksha*[61] is another piece of contemporary criticism, in the same orthodox manner. The critic has tried to analyse the novel in the light of Hindu religious scriptures, Hindu code and also against the background of Baishnav Pada Sahitya. In fact, he was frustrated to see that *Bishabriksha* did not reflect any high ideal. Mahendra Nath considered Vababhuti's Sita and Vyas's Suniti as ideals of Hindu womanhood. According to him, Bankim had debased the higher ideals of the Hindu womanhood in the characters of Suryamukhi and Kundanandini.[62] He observed that Kundanandini's suicide was aimed at punishing Nagendra. He further pointed out that Bankim's Kundanandini violated the standard of morality as set by poet Sashisekhar and Krishnakamal in *Vaishnab Sahitya* in the character of Radhika.[63]

Trying to explain the nature of dedication of Suryamukhi and Kundanandini to the husband, he said that Suryamukhi and Kundanandini's love for her husband falls miserably short of the ideal of an ideal wife's love for her husband.[64]

Mahendra Nath sharply criticized the characterization and prose style of the novel. The critic raised stern objection to the comparison of Suryamukhi with the glow of the full moon and her complexion with the melted gold on the ground that this was improper combination of simile and metaphor.[65]

However, some of his observations are not without critical value. He interprets Suryamukhi's desertion as an outward expression of her pride, jealousy and anger resulting from her failure to establish herself with Nagendranath and not due to self-sacrifice as a consequence of self-forgetfulness.[66]

BIRESWAR PANDE (1842-1911)

In his article, *Bankimchandra O Hindur Adarsha*[67] Bireswar Pande seeks to establish that in *Bishabriksha* Bankim in reality upheld the ideals of Hinduism, and his opinions appear to be refutation of the charges leveled against Bankim by Mahendranath.

He analysed this novel along with others and showed that Bankim did not violate the Hindu religious and social code in *Bishabriksha*. He instituted a comparison between Suryamukhi of *Bishabriksha* and Bhramar of *Krishnakanter Uil* in order to establish his point of view. According to him, unlike Bhramar, Suryamukhi was devoted to her husband just a Hindu wife should be, considering herself dedicated to the service of their husband, her lord. Because of this attitude of Suryamukhi the novel struck a different note form *Krishnakanter Uil*.[68]

HEMENDRA PRASAD GHOSE (1876-1963)

Hemendra Prasad's article *Bishabriksha*[69] is a significant contribution to the critical studies on *Bishabriksha*. This article stands on its own merit among the host of critical articles appeared so far. The article to a large extent is free from the usual emotional exuberance, dogmatic Hinduism, aggressive didacticism, typical of Bankim's age, and shows the characteristics of modern critical trend.

Hemendra Prasad sharply criticized Chandra Sekhar Mukhopadhyay, because of the latter's acceptance of *Bishabriksha* as a representative *Hindu Poem*.[70] He based his criticism on his conviction that *Bishabriksha* is a 'picture of the real life'[71] and the issues introduced in the novel are 'real life issues'.[72] He asserted that the artistic achievement of *Bishabriksha* was mainly because of the contrasting sets of characters presented in the novel, Suryamukhi and Kundanandini, Hira and Kamalmani, and Nagendra and Debendra.[73] Hemendra Prasad furnished the psychological reasons of Kunda's suicide. He commented that Kunda committed suicide because she lacked Suryamukhi's qualities of tolerance and self-sacrifice.[74] About Kamalmani he inferred that she was loving, merciful, sympathetic, her greatest quality was her motherly traits.[75] Indeed, she was an ideal and fully devoted wife. Regarding Hira he observed that revenge was the sustaining force behind Hira's life.[76]

Hemendra Prasad pointed out that by introducing the widow remarriage in the novel Bankim had sown the seeds of a new social code in the minds of his readers contrary to the prevailing practice. There was a great risk in going against the current tide. But Bankim's skillful handling of the plot and characters led to such an artistic finish of the fiction of the new principle. That towards the end of the novel, readers are moved to tears forgetting the propriety of widow-remarriage.

Hemendra Prasad branded the dream-element in the novel as a blemish of the novel. To him: "The dreams in the novel have been vested with an incredulously enormous significance."[77] Hemendra Prasad is in sharp contrast with his predecessors in his impartial analysis, objective approach, and artistic appreciation. He has occupied an important place as a critic of *Bishabriksha*.

SHAILENDRA NATH SARKAR

Shailendra Nath's article *Bishabriksha Anushilon*[78] has an emotional undertone, and it tries to discern the Hindu elements present in *Bishabriksha*. But at the same time, the article looks into Bankim's success in elevating the religious outstanding problems because of his ability to look into the complexities of the characters from a humanitarian angle. His article bears an imprint of the ancient and the modern analytical method.

In a deep emotional tone, Shailendra Nath hailed Kunda:

> Kunda we shall adore you as a goddess, even though you are an unfortunate woman. You are heavenly fragrant flower in the mundane world of ours.[79]

His moralistic tone condemned Nagendra's marriage with Kunda. He felt that Nagendra's only saving grace was his marrying Kunda, instead of keeping her like Rohini (*Krishnakanter Uil*). Because of this, he was finally rewarded and allowed to unite with Suryamukhi.[80]

Shailendra Nath also considered Suryamukhi as an ideal of the Hindu woman...i.e., act of her giving away the husband to another woman was 'matchless'.[81] But, unlike his predecessors, Shailendra Nath did not look down upon Suryamukhi's desertion of home as an immoral act violating Hindu ideals. On the other hand, he considered that in her desertion, Bankim had shown the natural reaction of a normal woman in such circumstances which reveals the novelists grasp over married woman's psychology.[82] Regarding Kamalmani, Shailendra Nath asserted that though she was projected as a typical representative of Hindu womanhood, her dominant qualities were love, friendship and affection.[83]

Shailendra Nath is the first critic to emphasise that the dream element in the novel is just a supernatural phenomenon,[84] and that the events in the novel spring from actions and reactions from within the plot and characters and the dream which foretells the future course of Kunda's life is only a matter of coincidence. The dream as such is forgotten by the readers in the spontaneous flow of incidents and it should be dismissed simply as supernatural and the debate regarding its reality or unreality is needless. Substantiating his argument, he remarked that Kunda's bewilderment in confronting Nagendra and Hira often the dream might not be an expression of surprise because of the dream coming true, rather a natural reaction of such a meeting in such circumstances.[85]

He goes ahead and says that Kunda's dream in the novel is not as pivotal as Durbasha's curse to Shakuntala. Whereas in *Shakuntala* the curse is an indispensable part of the plot, in *Bishabriksha*, Kunda's dream is not indispensable.[86]

Shailendra Nath had also treated Nagendra from a humanitarian standpoint. To him, Nagendra was normal man.... A combination of both good and evil. He said: The dogmatic puritans may find fault with Nagendra, but we do not consider this fact as an unpardonable vice. Nagendra only shows the weakness of a human being.[87]

Shailendra Nath's freshness of approach marks a departure from the earlier trend of criticism.

HEMENDRA CHANDRA BASU

In this article, *Bishabriksha,*[88] Hemendra Chandra Basu has drawn the attention of the readers to the novelist's motive of characterization in *Bishabriksha.* According to him, Bankim created pairs of contrasting characters symbolizing virtue and vice, pity and materialism, and selfishness and selflessness with view to educate the people. He pointed out that in *Bishabriksha* Nagendra was juxtaposed with Debendra, Kundanandini with Suryamukhi. Again, he examined Bankim's treatment of love in *Bishabriksha* in the light of classical principles. According to the critic Suryamukhi and Nagendra's love was more purified and lasting, because it was 'Gunaja', and Nagendra's love for Kunda which dwindled faster, because it was 'Rupaja' in character.[89]

BIRESWAR GOSWAMI

Bireswar Goswami's article *Kunda, Suryamukhi O Kamal,*[90] reflects his conservative and emotional tone and resorts to traditional methods of evaluation of the novel. But the article is outstanding, because it looks at *Bishabriksha* as a realistic novel, and compares the women characters with those of the women characters of western literature.

He did not consider Suryamukhi as an incarnation of a goddess like Sita and Sabitri, but a Bengali daughter and housewife, Suryamukhi was the heroine of the novel, and the characters of Kunda and Kamal had been perceived to contribute to Suryamukhi's growth. Kunda's innocence is the cause of her suffering and defeat. Her suicide and Suryamukhi's desertion did not stretch beyond the limit of impossibility. Kamalmani's intelligence, sympathy for others, qualities of human devotion and love for the husband, made her an ideal Hindu wife. Suryamukhi's love for husband shows devotion, while Kamalmani's love had more of the quality of friendship and Kunda's love was vast as the quiet ocean.[91] These observations speak of Bireswar's ability as a critic.

We find a remarkable literary perception in Bireswar when he contradicts with the comments[92] made by his predecessor, Sudhindranath Tagore and points out that Tisa's (George Eliot) simplicity is almost idiotic. Moreover, Tesa is jealous to Romula, the co-wife, whereas Kunda is free from jealously. Bireswar sees more similarity of Kunda with 'Ila' (*Raja O Rani*) of Tagore, than with that of Lytton's Alice.[93]

Bireswar's Goswami's modest attitude is evident in his attitude to Bankim Chandra's art of characterization. The characters are not mere puppets, they are lifelike. Kunda, Kamal, Debendra, Hira, Sreeish even Surendra are all radiant with his or her own individuality.[94]

BINODE LAL MAZUMDER

In his article *Kundanandinir Swapna*,[95] Binode Lal Mazumder discusses the influence of dreams on Kunda and sets the trend of the future evaluation of the novel on literary merit. Binode Lal felt that the dreams did not burden the flow of the novel; they gave a direction to the outline of her life. Kunda's love for Nagendra had been indirectly triggered by her dreams, and ceaseless sufferings led her to long for death—the dreams intensified her desire for suicide. Appearance of the handsome figure of Nagendra[96] in her dream evoked her love for him. When she saw him the next day, she stared dumbfounded at him, and tells Champa, that she had never seen such beauty in man before. This was the beginning of her love for Nagendra. Binode Lal further feels that wonder can very easily lead to admiration, and it can be the foundation of love, and Desdemona's love for Othelo also owes its origin to wonder. He quotes the English author, 'Admiration is the stepping stone of love.'[97]

Through an examination of Kundanandini's strife-torn life, the critic asserted that, the Kunda's destiny was shaped by her vision of the beautiful angelic appearance in dream and her love for Nagendra.[98]

Binode Lal's criticism is marked by impartiality, logical coherence and depth of thought; and his overall discussion is further enlivened by his search for the source of the fountain of love that binds Kunda and Nagendra together.

JATINDRA MOHAN GUPTA

A conservative strain dominates the attitude of Jatindra Mohan's article, *Bankimbabur Stri Charitra*.[99] He charged that, Bankimchandra had caused damage to the society by misrepresenting the traditional motherly character of the Hindu Bengali women. Suryamukhi and Kamalmani had the motherly qualities, but Bankim's westernized approach had reduced them to nothingness.[100]

SOURINDRA MOHAN GUPTA

Sourindra Mohan, in his article *Upanyase Stri Charitra,*[101] contradicted Jatindra Nath's view and defended Bankim's women characters. He asserted that Bankim had aimed at delineating the women Suryamukhi and Kundanandini as Hindu wives and not as mothers and had done the job remarkably well. Bankim could have been blamed for furnishing the Hindu-ideal, if the widow, Kunda would have lived happily, and Suryamukhi, in at spite of her devotion, had not been united with her husband. But at the end the characters, were rather to champion of the cause of Hindu moral vision and belief. The characters taking to the life of lust had to succumb to an internal suffering and finally perished in the fire of retribution, and through the life of the characters the ideal of renunciation is upheld.[102]

Sourindra's article is a search for the Hindu elements in the novel without much substantial literary merit.

JANAKI NATH GUPTA

Janaki Nath's *Suryamukhi O Kundanandini*[103] also shows conservative strain while analyzing Suryamukhi and Kundanandini. According to him, Suryamukhi's defiance and Kunda's marriage were death-bolts to the Hindu moral code.[104] But he demonstrated psychological understanding of the reasons of Suryamukhi's desertion. He believed that Suryamukhi left her home out of pride and ego, consequently Nagendra's well of love for Kunda dried up. Kunda died young because of Nagendra's loss of love for her.[105]

LOKENATH CHAKROBORTY

Lokenath's articles *Bishabriksha,*[106] *Suryamukhi,*[107] *Bishabriksher Coekti Chitra-Kundanandini,*[108] *Kamalmani,*[109] *Nagendranath,*[110] *Bishabriksha-Debendra O Haimabati,*[111] speak of his interest in the novel. He was considerably powerful writer with a literary mind, but was bereft of romantic temperament. He could not tower over the traditional spirit of his age. His writings suffered from emotional exuberance, moral, dogmatism, partiality and Bankim-idolatry, even though his literary talent made sporadic appearance in his realistic and sympathetic attitude to the human errors. His didactic concepts of the purpose of art is evident in his assertion that characters of Nagendra, Suryamukhi, Kamalmani and Debendra act out Bankim's moral vision of society. He upheld that *Bishabriksha's* themes were not the outcome of Bankim's familiarity with European literature. The novel showed Bankim's graduation to maturity.[112] Here, he had adorned the daily Bengali life with literary beauty. Lokenath has analysed in details the plot-structure, diction and the poetic sensibility of Bankim. The criticism leaves a lasting impression on the readers' mind.[113]

To Lokenath, Suryamukhi was a glowing example of a Hindu wife, who surrendered her husband to another woman. By this act, she even went higher than Sita of *Ramayana*.[114] But, surprisingly enough, he showed a deep psychological understanding in his analysis of the reasons of Suryamukhi's desertion and return, Suryamukhi was caught in between the forces of self-sacrifice and love for her husband. Self-sacrifice led her away from her home, but her love for husband brings her back. Her sobriety, patience and tolerance tie her firmly to life.[115] The novelty of approach lies in his assertion that Suryamukhi's desertion contributed to her final emergence as a true Hindu wife.[116]

Kunda was looked upon as an angelic woman sojourning our strife-torn earth,[117] and she committed suicide, to enable Suryamukhi return her real pedestal, and not because she was neglected by Nagendra. But the critic added that Kunda also had human traits and her human qualities helped development of the characters of Nagendra and Suryamukhi.[118] Lokenath also showed originality in his interpretation of Kunda's dreams. He said the dream, evoking the supernatural, performed three purposes, viz., to establish Kunda's innocence, to introduce Hira and Nagendra, and to predict Kunda's future journey with Nagendra.[119]

Lokenath's article 'Kamalmani' to a large extent falls into the category of aesthetic school of criticism. It mainly deals with Kamalmani's natural beauty. "Kamalmani does not need any elaboration. Her simplicity, playfulness, cleanliness, uncomplicated nature are self-evident."[120] Between Suryamukhi and Kamalmani, the most striking difference is mother-hood—Suryamukhi is a wife, whereas Kamalmani is a mother too.[121] Such observations of the critic show his maturity.

According to Lokenath, Bankim used Nagendranath as an instrument for social education. Nagendra fell a victim to the charms of the maiden Kunda, but could not marry her because in those days of arranged marriages, love marriage was considered a social sin, and, therefore, Bankim made him marry his former beloved after she had become a widow, considering the necessity of mass education for widow remarriage.[122]

Moreover, Lokenath thought that Bankim introduced the Evil in the novel through Debendra and Hira to intensify the glory of the Good representation by Nagendra and Suryamukhi.[123] But analyzing the character of Debendra who represented the

Evil, Lokenath showed that Debendra was after all an object of pity in spite of his blemishes.[124] He had also thrown a new light into the character of Hira who supplemented Debendra in the determination of the evil in the novel by emphasizing the sterling quality of her restraint and her immense strength to preserve her chastity.[125] Here Lokenath, strikes a new note by bringing out the latent qualities of the so-called evil characters and drawing sympathy of readers to them.

JITENDRA LAL BASU

Jitendra Lal Basu in his essay *Bankimchandra*[126] believed that in spite of its social overtone *Bishabriksha* was not a realistic novel.[127] It was mainly an allegory trying to exemplify the victory of the virtues of Hinduism and final defeat of the lust. He had tried to explore Bankim's outlook through an analysis of the characters and their role in creating social awareness.

Jitendra Lal also had resorted to the historical method of criticism. The women characters of *Bishabriksha* were not imitation of the west, they showed the moral decline of the women of Bankim's time from the traditional qualities of Aryan womanhood.[128] In interpreting the women characters against the historical background, Jitendra Lal has displayed his originality.

HARAN CHANDRA RAKSHIT

Although Haran Chandra's outlook was limited by the principles of Hindu social code, his book, *Bangla Sahitye Bankim*[129] contained sparks of pure literary criticism. Like his predecessors he also believed that Bankim had let Kunda die because widow-remarriage was not acceptable to the then Hindu society. But, unlike them, he pointed out that Kunda was an imaginative creation a beautiful flower in the garden of poetic love, and a blooming lotus which marked her out distinct from Kapalkundala Tilottama; the other outstanding female characters of Bankim's novels.[130]

Regarding Suryamukhi's desertion of home he opined that she left home not because of sentiment but owing to her natural feminine weakness and lack of foresight and farsight.[131]

SITARAM BANDOPADHYAY

The footsteps of the twentieth century are, however, more distinctly heard in the article *Kundanandini*[132] by Sitaram Bondopadhyay. Here the discussions on Hindu ideals, assessment of characters from the point of view of Hindu social code which dominated the critical writings of Bankim Age are conspicuous by their absence. The critic made an evaluation of *Bishabriksha* from artistic and literary point of view.

He tried to focus Kunda as an epitome of selflessness, simplicity and love, while he sought to establish that the artistic beauty of the novel was embedded in the widowhood of Kunda and fall of Nagendra. His argument was that had she not become a widow, Nagendra's fall would not have taken place, and that much of the beauty of the novel would have been lost without Nagendra's fall.[133] Sitaram's assessment of Bankim's novel, *Bishabriksha* shows that a new era in Bankim criticism, and Bengali literary criticism was near at hand.

PRAFULLA KUMAR SARKAR (1884-1944)

Prafulla Kumar in his articles *Samaj Sanekare Bankimchandra,*[134] and *Niti Shikshay Bankimchandra,*[135] looked at *Bishabriksha* as a synthesis of the Hindu moral and the western social code. Suryamukhi, Kamalmani were the examples of this synthesis. Prafulla Kumar had taken a historical purview in his analysis of *Bishabriksha*. According to him, though, Suryamukhi was an ideal of modern Hindu woman, yet she was fond of songs, painting, etc. like the modern European woman, she was co-worker with her husband in his all affairs and her husband was also a friend, philosopher and guide to her.[136] The critic further opined that Suryamukhi is a human being, not a goddess, and she left her home out of natural weakness of a woman and not out of anger for her husband.[137]

Bankim, in his opinion, played a historical role in protecting Hinduism caught in between the blind imitation of the west, and Hindu dogmatism. In spite of his maturity of understanding, Prafulla Kumar also falls prey to the dogmatic Hindu outlook and looks at *Bishabriksha* as an example preaching the society about the sad destiny and retribution of the sinners.

SHACHIS CHANDRA CHATTOPADHYAY

Although not basically a critic, Shachis Chandra wrote a fine piece of criticism on *Bishabriksha* in work on Bankim, *Swargiya Bankim Chandra Chattopadhyayer Jibon Charit.*[138] It being a biographical work, the writer made a subtle distinction between the poet-Bankim[139] and reformer-Bankim and stated that there was a tug-of-war between the two. In this tug-of-war the poet-Bankim became victorious over the reformer-Bankim in the incident of Kunda's death in *Bishabriksha*. Incidentally he remarked that Kunda's marriage in widowhood, and finally her suicide were against the Hindu code of conduct, and he emphatically stated: "We do not want to see such a wife in a Hindu home."[140] Obviously as a digression is a biography he concentrated on the character of Kunda and analysed her special traits and remarked that Kunda was "paragon of beauty, as soft, as simple as Miranda and as love—as Shakuntala."[141]

Shachis Chandra's prose style is fascinating, and his treatment is marked by brevity, but his criticism of *Bishabriksha* did not develop in a consistent manner perhaps because the book was mainly a biographical work.

HARIHAR BHATTACHARJEE

It is not the aim of the essay to make a comparative estimate as a whole between *Ratnaboli O Bishabriksha*—there are certain points of similarities in certain parts and occasional resemblances are there between characters—the essay aims at pointing to these. This sort of confession of Harihar Bhattacharjee forms the basis of his *Ratnabali O Bishabriksha.*[142] The essayist writes Sagarika's meeting with Batsaraj in *Ratnabali* and Nagendranath's meeting with Kundanandini in *Bishabriksha* both these incidents are due to the working of fate. Both Kunda and Sagarika wanted to die on apprehension of the unfulfillment of love while none could die because of her sweetheart.[143] Batsaraj was beside himself in love for Sagarika like Nagendra. Both Basabadatta and Suryamukhi were selfless. For the happiness of her husband Basabadatta handed Ratnabali over to the king like that of

Suryamukhi.[144] Such resemblances have been pointed out in this long essay. But the merit and demerit which are likely to be found in such comparative estimates are absent in this essay.

LALIT KUMAR BANDOPADHYAY (1275-1336 B.S.)

Lalit Kumar Bandopadhyay, in his realistic approach and intellectual depth, is the most mature critic of his time as reflected in the criticism of *Bishabriksha* in his essays[145] and books of criticism.[146] In course of his analysis of the heartrending love story of Nagendra, Suryamukhi and Kunda, he felt that Bankim in *Bishabriksha* had played the dual role of a moralist and a social thinker.[147] He believed that Bankim's search had revealed to him that the poisonous tree (Bishabriksha) germinated from the seed of blind fury of passion. This was the soul, structure and the message of the novel which justified the tile.[148]

Lalit Kumar felt that to work out this in the Bengali domestic background, Bankim had made Suryamukhi a childless wife, and Kunda's mother was made to die to serve the dramatic purpose of fuller development of Kunda's complex situation in the novel.[149] Kunda's second dream only served to intensify her already tormenting condition.[150]

According to Lalit Kumar, Kamalmani in *Bishabriksha* was the only full-length woman, a good wife, sympathetic friend, sister and ideal sister-in-law and a mother. She was compared with a full-blown rose.[151]

In fact, Lalit Kumar's criticism of *Bishabriksha* confirms that the transition of orthodox criticism into pure literary criticism was complete by the second decade of the twentieth century. This vast erudite critic made the commendable attempt to evaluate *Bishabriksha* from the viewpoint of total impression, and, as such, his credit lay in evaluating *Bishabriksha* as 'a swork of art'. He pointed out that the sorrowful tale of Suryamukhi formed the main plot in the novel, while Kunda-Nagendra episode could be considered as a sub-plot,[152] because it was Suryamukhi who demanded reader's attention most of the time.

It was Lalit Kumar who first brought out the justification of Kunda's suicide from artistic point of view,[153] and he remarked that Kunda's suicide was an example of 'poetic justice' in the ancient oriental rhetorical norm, a catharsis in the ancient oriental rhetorical norm.[154] Indeed, by introducing the suicide, Bankim solved not only the social problem but also raised *Bishabriksha* to a great work of art. Himself against widow-remarriages he made Kunda fall in love with Nagendra before marriage, but he did not give any prominence to that love[155] quite artistically, otherwise Kunda's marriage in widowhood might have appeared as a natural friction of former infatuation. Here, the critic noted, and rightly said that by hinting at that love through Suryamukhi's letter, Bankim had set such an example of irony in literature which equals him with Shakespeare and Sophocles.[156]

Bishabriksha as a work of art stands on its own merit delineating the universal human situation, so the novel deserves attention mainly as a work of art. Lalit Kumar deals with *Bishabriksha* in detail keeping in view the above fact to substantiate his article and to his credit, has done the job remarkably well.

Lalit Kumar's last article titled *Sakhi* discussed the women characters of the novel. The women characters were presented in pairs; Kunda and Chanpa; Hira's Gangajal and Malati; Suryamukhi and Kamalmani; and the critic placed them under distinct groups. In his opinion, Bankim like Bhababhuti and Michael, out of compassion had created Chanpa for Kundanandini.[157] Lalit Kumar is the first critic to draw our attention to the 'Sakhis' (Girl-friends).

Lalit Kumar's proficiency to the Western and Indian literature has enabled him to look at the novel from a wider perspective. This is evident from his appreciable treatment of analysis of the motives of actions of Kunda and Nagendra and the evaluation of the artistic necessity of the Debendra-Hira sub-plot.[158]

Finally, it must be recorded here that Lalit Kumar tried for the first time to introduce artistic significance of symbols in the novel. His study of symbolism in *Bishabriksha* is aptly illustrated by his reference to the symbol of the flies flying to the fire. Here Lalit Kumar tried to read the evil protest of this symbol on Kunda-Nagendra love episode.[159]

CHINTA HARAN DEY

Discussing the impact dream in literature in his article, *Sahitye Swapner Prabhab,*[160] Chinta Haran Dey drew illustration from *Bishabriksha*. In a brief discussion he gave a fine literary interpretation of dream. Referring to the artistic skill of Bankim in handling the element of dream, he remarked that Kunda's dream was the root of the *Bishabriksha* (Poisonous tree) which branched out to impart a unique beauty to *Bishabriksha*. "The enchanting power of the dream drives the reader to move forward to the future in fear."[161]

BIPIN CHANDRA PAL (1858-1932)

Bipin Chandra, in his different articles,[162] evaluated *Bishabriksha* in the background of social awareness and political consciousness of Bengal. Bankim had tried to bring a happy union of idealism and realism in his novel, and the realism of the novel was based on Bankim's own experience of life and his belief that literature should imitate life. Bipin Pal felt that Bankim to some extent had shaped the thoughts of the new Bengali society by portraying social and family picture based on the typical Bengali value-structure. Bishabriksha successfully portrayed the constant conflict between instinct—the passion of men and the social norms.[163] Nagendra, Suryamukhi, Kundanandini, Kamalmani and Hira all were parts of the picture gallery, Hira and Kamalmani were the most successful portraiture in terms of art, though not in terms of the moral code.[164] Bipin Pal's analysis of Hira show his depth of understanding of the motives and nature of this vivacious,[165] but uncultured, uneducated woman of bad taste. Through this minor character of the novel, Bankim displayed his sense of realism. Hira was the eternal sorceress, capable of evoking deadly lust and temptation in man, Bipin Pal observed,

> In Hira, there is a powerful all-devouring instinctive passion. She radiates passion, even when she ignores, and there is a sense of appeal in her grim struggle.[166]

However, Bipin Pal's greatest achievement is in his attempt to study Bankim and his art as a whole, and in his efforts to trace the relationship between the poetic imagination and the social vision of Bankim in the novel. His evaluation of *Bishabriksha* gives a new turn to Bankim criticism. However, Bipin Pal's categorical statements are not fully elaborated for proper comprehension of the readers.

JATINDRA KUMAR LAHA

Like Chinta Haran, Jatindra Kumar Laha also tries to analyse the impact of dream in literature, but Chinta Haran's essay, *Kundanandinir Swapna*[167] deserves more attention since it deals only with Kunda's dream in *Bishabriksha*. According to the critic, Kunda's dream was supernatural, and even though a manifestation of motherly love, it got interwoven with Kunda's life so much so that it ultimately shaped the destiny of Kunda.

In fact, the critic viewed the developments in the life of Kunda in the novel as profoundly influenced by the dreams. He analysed the character of Kunda and found that she was fundamentally lacking in self-confidence, shy and timid, and it was not impossible for a girl of her nature to take such a daring step as suicide. Indeed, it would be unnatural in her part to take such a step without any excitement. It was the dreams which gave her the impulse to put an end to her earthly existence and take rest in her mother lap in the abode of peace. This inspiration promoted her to self-sacrifice.[168]

Doubtless such an analysis of Jatindra Kumar leaves room for debate, but his psychological interpretation is nevertheless praiseworthy.

SHASHANKA MOHAN SEN (1872-1928)

Shashanka Mohan's criticism on *Bishabriksha* in *Bangabani*[169] marks the beginning of literary exercise in pure criticism. The essay speaks of the critic's deep insight, sound reasoning and keen penetration.

According to Shashanka Mohan, there was an evolutionary process at work behind the development of the mind and art of Bankim Chandra, and. As such *Bishabriksha* could not be evaluated in isolation. The critic traced the origin of the concept of *Bishabriksha* in *Kapalkundala*. What he meant to say was that the characters and ideas passed through an evolution in Bankim's novels. According to him Nabakumar and Kapalkundala had first sown the seed of the poisonous tree when they fell into the clutch of cruel circumstances, subsequently the same seed was sown in *Durgeshnandini* and *Mrinalini* by the hands of doubts, but fortunately the seed did not germinate. Later on the same seed of the poisonous tree was planted in the novel of the same name 'Bishabriksha', and now, character and fate joined hands together to make the seed germinate and grow, and consequently. Kapalkundala and Monorama appeared as Kundanandini, and she met her tragic end by eating the fruit of this poisonous tree.[170]

Subsequently, *Bishabriksha's* depth of vision, Kapalkundala's imaginative power and the positive traits of Nabakumar (*Kapalkundala*). Hemchandra (*Mrinalini*) and Nagendranath appeared in Rajani. The quiet Kundanandini gave up resignation, and materialised in the form of beautiful and assertive Shaibalini.[171]

Shashanka Mohan's attempt at evaluating *Bishabriksha* as a part of Bankim's world of fiction has given a new dimension to Bankim criticism which will finally take the shape of literary assessment of the mind and art of the novelist Bankim at the hands of future critics.

HARIPADA BHATTACHARJEE

Haripada Bhattacharjee's assessment of *Bishabriksha* in *Bishabrikher Darshan Tattba*[172] in the middle of the second decade of the present century shows the return of the neo-Hindu approach and a retrograde step to traditionalism.

The critic sought to highlight the philosophic mind of Bankim by giving a pedantic explanation of Haradev Ghosal's letter to Nagendra Nath. In order to impress upon the readers that Nagendra's infatuation for Kunda amounted to lust fraught with dangerous consequences, Bankim introduced this letter as a forewarning to what would follow if a helpless girl was exploited.[173] The critic wanted to show Bankim's didacticism.

BATUKNATH BHATTACHARJEE

Batuknath Bhattacharjee in his articles entitled *Bankim Prativa*[174] and *Bankim Sahitye Sannyas*[175] makes an artistic attempt to analyse the novel and attains a fair level of success. He looks at the characters with sympathy and understanding. Refusing to accept *Bishabriksha* as an example of didactic novel he said:

> Human passion is natural, and it simply does not die at the behest of the scriptures, ... so, we cannot condemn Kunda to a slow and painful death in the husk-fire, only because she falls in love.[176]

Besides, the critic had classed Shibapada Sharma as the so-called 'Sannyasi'[177] commonly found in Bengal, and according to him Bankim had achieved totality of his novel through such character creation.[178]

Batuknath is completely free from the shackles of traditionalism, and he ushers in realism in literature, which is a product of the complexity of the second decade of the twentieth century.

RAMSAHAYA VEDANTASASTRI

Ramsahaya Vedantasastri wrote three scholarly articles[179] which were all published in *Archana* in between 1918 A.D. & 1928 A.D. Ramsahaya is the last stalwart of the oriental classical school of criticism which was almost overpowered by the infiltration of Western principles through the impact of English language and literature in the beginning of the century. A profound scholar in Sanskrit and Bengali, Ramsahaya had a thorough theoretical grasp over the Sanskrit rhetoric, prose style and the narrative art.

In fact, he judged the novel *Bishabriksha* in the set of classical standards. He weighed the pros and cons of Kunda's desertion of home with reference to Sanskrit texts which added extra luster to his criticism. He stated that three reasons can be assigned to Kunda's love for Nagendra. Her instinctive (*Chakkhurag Taramaitrak*) inclination to him, his qualities, and her feeling of gratitude to him.[180]

The critic grouped Suryamukhi as 'Mugdha', and partly 'Madhya' in the Sanskrit tradition and Kamalmani as 'Mugdha' and partly 'pragalva'.[181] Sexually, he classified Suryamukhi as a 'Padmini woman' and Kamalmani as a mixture of 'Sankhini' and 'padmini' woman.[182] He also asserted that in the classical tradition, the characters of the novel justify their names. As for example, the critic said that Suryamukhi is really a 'Suryamukhi flower', she always looks at the sun and her sun is Nagendranath, and Nagendra's love is that sunshine.[183]

Ramsahaya is so devoted to Sanskrit literature that his prose style reveals his classical taste, and occasionally his high flown language and farfetched similes may appear as marks of emotionalism which is evident from his comparison between Suryamukhi and Kamalmani:

> These two women, like two sisters, run parallel to each other towards the same object, just like the two rivers Ganga and Jamuna. One is slow moving river with clear water while the other is fast-moving with black water.[184]

This classical critic, however, displays the touch of imagination also in his analysis of Kunda's character. He gives a literary interpretation to Kunda's death scene where she refused to drink water from Nagendra even when she was dying of thirst.[185] The critic's psycho-analytical penetration was revealed in his analysis of Kunda's reaction of Nagendra's love for her. According to him, as Kunda was at the prime of her youth even after the death of Taracharan. She was able to realise what possibly could satisfy Nagendra. She had understood that Nagendra had seen her widowhood and had been attracted to her, and this was the turning point of Kunda's life. She had felt intuitively that Nagendra was not a moon in the sky beyond human reach; he was a man of flesh and blood just like her. This was a new incentive for her who had been in a state of despair: The pure currant of Kunda's love has been turned red and critical by love and lust and she has lost control over herself.[186]

He displays his literary perception when he comments that Kunda's death will continue to haunt the conjugal life of Nagendra and Suryamukhi. There is an element of tragedy in this play of life and death.[187]

But Ramsahaya runs into imagination excesses, which displays his romantic temperament, the most pronounced such example is when he remarks that the Goddess of joy of Heaven has appeared in the form of Kamalmani forshaking her characteristic fickleness.[188] However, the fact remains that he has an idealistic approach to characterization when he says that the characteristic feature of the characters of the great poet's is that they are unreal even though real, and remain free and independent although confined to time and place,[189] and this saves him from what may called his limited vision and emotionalism.

AKSHAY KUMAR DUTTAGUPTA

Akshay Kumar Duttagupta wrote a dispassionate criticism of *Bishabriksha* in his critical work, *Bankimchandra*.[190] Discussing the novel, he made an analysis of the structure, artistic skill in plot construction and characterization. He pointed out that there was a touch of idealism in the romance of *Bishabriksha*, its beauty was not without glory, and that although the contemporary social life and earthly elements constituted the materials for the novel, the poetic imagination had imparted a glow to the romance of *Bishabriksha*, to lift it to the level of poetic creation.

Akshay Kumar said Kundanandini was a plaything in the hands of fate like Kapalkundala, in the final stage of the life's journey. Kunda heard the call of her dead mother just as Kapalkundala got suggestions in her final stage from the Goddess 'Bhairabi'.[191] According to the critic these were the real poetic excellences of the novel. He had rightly remarked that Kunda became sick seeing the fruitless efforts of the insects on the glass panes of Nagendra's bed chamber, which hinted at her final tragic end.[192]

Akshay Kumar made a very subtle penetration into the character of Suryamukhi. He opined that almost all the idealism in the novel centred round Suryamukhi. Yet Bankim did not make a character without flesh and blood. Indeed, she pulsated with sentiment and love. Because of the endowment of these human qualities by the novelist, she also could become a life-size character.[193]

Akshay Kumar also evaluated the novel from the artistic point of view. In his artistic evaluation he laid emphasis on parallelism. According to him the families of Debendra, Nagendra and Shrishchandra were all pitted against one another, and, likewise, the contrasts and similarities in between the members of the said families had strengthened the artistic beauty of the novel.[194] All these show Akshay Kumar a balanced critic of modern age.

HEMCHANDRA MUKHOPADHYAY

Hemchandra Mukhopadhyay's *Manab Prakriti*[195] is an example of traditional criticism. In the advertisement of the book the writer had said that the principal aim of his book was to uphold the beauty of *Bishabriksha* and to show the gradual growth and development of characters in relation to circumstances. Hemchandra had taken the characters as the basis of his analysis. His ethical pre-occupation had helped his presentation of the growth and development of characters, while his scriptural and philosophical understanding were responsible for the analysis of the inner mysteries of human nature and he had portrayed to characters in imitation of the novel.

Hemchandra said that like Shri Gauranga (Baishnab Sahitya), Suryamukhi's departure was due to the impact of love.[196] Just as the solitary ascetic abandons worldly happiness and moves around holy places in search of God so also Suryamukhi feels that Nagendranath being crazy of worldly love was mean,[197] and therefore, she came out to see around her the image of a husband who had derived his power from the all-powerful God.[198]

But Hemchandra's criticism is not altogether ethical. Nagendranath is a lover of beauty, but he lacks the power of judgement, therefore, he was infatuated by the childlike simplicity of Kunda, her worldly inexperience and fickleness.[199] Such a view of the critic even if debatable is no less psycho-analytical.

KSHITINDRANATH THAKUR (1869-1937)

Kshitindranath Thakur in his book *Art O Sahitya*[200] analysed *Bishabriksha* and found that the novelist had failed to establish the good in the novel. He, however, agreed that Bankim wrote *Bishabriksha* for social welfare. But the critic raised objections to introduction of Kunda's eating the fruit of the poisonous tree, Debendra's disguise as baishnabi, and Nagendra's lust and such other obscenity. All these had robbed the novel of its artistic beauty, Indeed, all these were unnatural, and banished the good from the novel.[201] Kshitindranath has seen literature as an impression of the truth, good and beautiful, and, as such, he belongs to the didactic school of literary criticism.

MURALIDHAR GONGOPADHYAY

Muralidhar Gongopadhyay basically tried to assess the essayist Bankim in his article, *Prabondhe Bankim Prativa*[202] and he had also endeavoured to trace the elements of essay of even in the novel of Bankim. Such an attempt indeed shows a kind of academic interest, and this marks a new trend in Bankim criticism. According to him the scenic description of the boat journey of Nagendranath is a fine descriptive essay[203] in which the novelist has expounded the eternal relation that exists between the Nature and human nature.[204]

JATINDRA NATH DUARA

Jatindra Nath Duara's *Art O Sahitya*[205] is a critical evaluation of Kshitindranath's work. Although he subscribed to Kshitindranath's argument that the purpose of art is to create beauty and goodness in the natural way, he differed from Kshitindranath in his approach to the analysis of the reason of Kunda's suicide and Debendra's obscenity and inferred that these actions were not in artistic and natural. He had tried to discover morality and consistency in the incidents by painting out Debendra's gradual improvement as a man because of the development of his love for Kunda. He also asserted that Kunda's suicide was the most natural act of a deserted, neglected, and lovely woman.[206]

BIMAN BIHARI MAZUMDER

Biman Bihari Mazumder's article *Bankimchandra Nari Jagaraner Abhash*[207] is a reflection of the modern critical temperament. In Suryamukhi's desertion, the author sees the rebellious action of the century-old neglected tortured Bengali woman.[208]

MOHITLAL MAZUMDAR (1888-1952)

Mohitlal Mazumdar's sense of restraint, sharp intellect and power of objective observation have infused modern spirit into his articles.[209] He hailed *Bishabriksha* as a living example of life and its complexities. He upheld that *Bishabriksha* owed its origin to Bankim's vision of the problems of the society, and his idea of the role of individual in shaping the society.[210] The novel also bore the impact of the tumultuous western experience of the contemporary Bengali mind.

To Mohitlal, *Bishabriksha* was outcome of the new western consciousness view for sensuousness. The novel bore a deep imprint of the rejection of the Hindu view of treating the external world as an illusion and showed the human efforts to establish a meaningful relation with the beautiful world of senses. *Bishabriksha* was rooted in the world of overwhelming human passion, and it glorifies the intense desire of the Bengalee mind to break the prison of self-imprisonment and to establish a vital link with Nature.[211]

SUBODH CHANDRA SENGUPTA

Next to Mohitlal, Subodh Chandra Sengupta, a notable literary critic, has a brief but remarkable criticism on Subodh Chandra Sengupta in his article *Bankimchandra O Saratchandra*,[212] which is an out-standing contribution to the critical estimation of Bankim as an artist. Referring to conformed, the eminent critic of "Greek Literature", Subodh Chandra observed that some forces inside us are so powerful and irresistible that they assault us just as strongly as the external forces shaping the human destiny. According to him, *Bishabriksha* is such a tragedy.[213] He strongly feels that Bankim's vision was largely shaped by his faith in the inexorable nature, of destiny, and he had always seen destiny closely linked with human passion.

He explicated his theory by referring to the examples of Nagendra and Kunda. Nagendra understands that he is being drawn to Kunda, it tortures him, but he could not stop the force engulfing him. Kundanandini is shy, coy, and unassertive woman. Although her dreams of happiness centre on Nagendranath, she does not take the leading role in the marriage. She merely submits to Nagendra's wish. She helplessly notices the marriage bringing disaster—leads away Suryamukhi from the house and ruined her happiness. Subodh Chandra observed:

> Bishabriksha is a perfect example of the total helplessness of man, in the hands of the forces of destiny. The all powerful forces of fate, reduces man's dreams of happiness to an absurd exercise, and cruelly destroys all his happiness.[214]

Subodh Chandra's article shows the critical estimation of Bishabriksha from the canon of modern western critical temperament. The article has both literary and historical importance. It speaks in clear terms about of its definite Bengali Social background.

INDRADEB BASU

Indraded Basu in his article *Bankim Sahitye Pashchatya Provab*[215] has levelled a charge against Bankimchandra that he has deviated from his moralistic vision of art due to the influence of western literature and philosophy. This account for Debendra and Nagendra's absence of self-control in spite of their basic decency and the Hindu woman Suryamukhi's desertion of home.[216] Like Subodh Chandra Sengupta he also asserts that all the characters of *Bishabriksha* are pawns in the hands of destiny.

DHIREN PAL

Dhiren Pal, in his article *Bankim Sahitye Pashchatya Provab,*[217] contradicts Indradeb's opinion regarding Suryamukhi's desertion and upholds that in Suryamukhi's coming back to subjugation of Indian woman to man is vindicated. This is not Western in attitude and spirit.[218]

SUMMING UP

Attempts have been made in this chapter to evaluate the critical approaches of about fifty critics from Jogendra Nath Vidyabhusan to Dhiren Pal. Differences of attitude and judgement characterize their essays. Bankim attempted to go deep into the social life of Bengal incorporated in *Bishabriksha*. Naturally some social questions had been posed by many of the critics in the period of Bankim.

During the first two decades of the post-Bankim period two parallel trends continued. The first is the decay of traditionalism. The second is the growth of pure literary criticism. In most of the critics, both the trends were at work. Leaving aside a few exceptions since the beginning of the third decade of post-Bankim period, traditionalism started losing its grip yielding place to the new progressive attitude to see the artistic qualities which *Bishabriksha* had presented.

Besides characterization, Suryamukhi's leaving of the house, Kunda's dream, her marriage as a widow and her suicide—such incidents were the matters of interest with most of the critics. In some of the essays western and oriental influences and the tragic qualities were discussed.

References

1. Bidyabhusan, Jogendranath, *Bishabriksha, Aryadarshan*, 1284 B.S. Reprinted, *Somalochana Mala*, 1284 B.S. & *Somalochana Sahitya*, Edited by Shrikumar Bondopadhyay & Prafulla Chandra Paul, 5th edn., Poush, 1379 B.S., pp. 238-61.
2. *Somalochana Sahitya.* (op. cit.), p. 238.
3. *Ibid.*, p. 244.
4. *Ibid.*, p. 243.
5. *Ibid.*, pp. 248-49.
6. *Ibid.*, p. 249.
7. *Ibid.*, pp. 259-61.
8. *Ibid.*, pp. 260-61.
9. *Ibid.*, p. 260.
10. Basu, Purna Chandra, *Kundanandini*, *Bangadarshan*, 1285 B.S., Reprinted, Kabya Sundari, Shraban, 1287 B.S., pp. 1-28.
11. Basu, Purna Chandra, *Kabyasundari*, Shraban, 1287 B.S., p. 11.
12. *Ibid.*, pp. 1-5.

13. *Ibid.*, p. 4.
14. *Ibid.*, p. 1.
15. Basu, Pruna Chandra, *Falashruti*, 1314 B.S., pp. 38-40.
16. (a) Basu, Debendra Bijoy, *Upanyas Sambandhe Kayekti Katha*, *Nabyabharat*, 2nd part, 9th Issue, Poush, 1291 B.S., pp. 407-16.

    (b) Basu, Debendra Bijoy, *Upanyaser Charitra Chitra*, *Nabyabharat*, Falgun, 1291 B.S., pp. 526-29 & Chaitra, 1291 B.S., pp. 555-64.

    (c) Basu, Debendra Bijoy, *Naveler Shilpa ba Kabittba*, *Nabyabharat*, 1292 B.S., Reprinted, *Somalochana Sahitya*, op. cit., pp. 37-50.
17. Basu, Debendra Bijoy, *Upanyas Sambondhe Kayekti Katha*, op. cit., p. 412.
18. *Ibid.*, p. 412.
19. Basu, Debendra Bijoy, *Upanyaser Charitra Chitra*, op. cit., p. 527 (Falgun).
20. *Ibid.*, p. 556 (Chaitra).
21. *Ibid.*, p. 559 (Chaitra).
22. *Ibid.*, pp. 559-60 (Chaitra).
23. Basu, Debendra Bijoy, *Novela Shilpa O Kabittba*, *Samalochana Shahitya*, op. cit., p. 41.
24. *Ibid.*, p. 47.
25. Basu, Debendra Bijoy, *Kundanandini*, *Bharatbarsha*, Magh, 1325 B.S., pp. 171-79.
26. *Ibid.*, p. 171.
27. *Ibid.*
28. *Ibid.*, pp. 175-77.
29. Thakur, Balendranath, *Kundanandini O Suryamukhi*, *Bharati O Balaka*, Falgun, 1295 B.S., pp. 653-60.
30. Thakur, Balendranath, *Swavab O Sahitya, Bharati O Balak*, Agrahayan, 1296 B.S., Reprinted, *Balendra Granthabali*, B.S. p. III Edn. Shraban '72, pp. 233-77.
31. Thakur, Balendranath, *Kundanandini O Suryamukhi*, op. cit., p. 675.
32. *Ibid.*, p. 658.
33. *Ibid.*, p. 665.
34. *Balendra Granthabali*, B.S., op. cit., p. 237.
35. Basu, Chandranath, *Novel ba Kathagranther Uddyesya*, *Bangadarshan*, 7th year, 1st Issue, Baishakh, 1287 B.S.
36. (a) Sen, Sukumar, *Bangla Sahityer Itihas (Part-II)*, 5th Edition, 1370 B.S., p. 273.

    (b) Mukhapadhyay, Arun Kumar, *Bangla Somalochanar Itihas*, First Publication, Shraban, 1372 B.S., p. 169.

(c) Sen, Subodh Chandra, *Bangla Somalochanar Parichay*, First Publication, Magh, 1376 B.S., p. 153.

37. Basu, Chandranath, *Novel ba Kathasahityer Uddeshya, Bangadarshan,* 7th year, 1st Issue, Baishakh, 1287 B.S.
38. Basu, Chandranath, *Novel ba Kathasahityer Uddeshya, Bangadarshan*, 7th part, Reflect Publication, 1st part, 1982, p. 22.
39. *Ibid*., pp. 23-24.
40. *Ibid*., p. 23.
41. Basu, Chandranath, *Duiti Hindu Patni, Prochar*, Bhadra-Ashwin, 1295 B.S., pp. 212-20.
42. *Ibid*., p. 214.
43. Bondopadhyay, Haridas, *Banglar Upannyas Lekhak Bankimchandra Chattopadhyay*, *(Mrinalini O Bishabriksha)*, *Kalpana,* 6th year, 1296 B.S., pp. 149-58.
44. *Ibid*., p. 155.
45. *Ibid*., p. 157.
46. *Ibid*, p. 147.
47. Thakur, Sudhindranath, *Suryamukhi O Kundanandini, Sahitya*, Second year, Second Issue, Jaishthya, 1298 B.S., pp. 73-80.
48. *Ibid*., p. 74.
49. *Ibid*., pp. 75-79.
50. *Ibid*., p. 75.
51. Basu, Purna Chandra, *Kabya Sundari*, Shraban, 1287 B.S., p. 4.
52. Bondopadhyay, Haridas, op. cit., p. 156.
53. Thakur, Sudhindranath, op. cit., p. 75.
54. Thakur, Balendranath, *Suryamukhi O Kundanandini*, op. cit., p. 658.
55. Basu, Narendra Nath, *Tulanay Somalochana* (*Bishabriksha O Krishnakanter Uil*) *Kundanandini O Rohini, Sahitya Kalpadrum,* 3rd year, 8th issue, 1299 B.S., pp. 217-23.
56. *Ibid*., p. 217.
57. *Ibid*., pp. 217-18.
58. *Ibid*., pp. 219-22.
59. *Ibid*., p. 222.
60. *Ibid*., p. 223.
61. Mazumder, Mahendra Nath, *Sahitya O Samaj Athaba Bankimbabur Bishabriksha*, 1301 B.S.
62. *Ibid*., pp. 24-80.
63. *Ibid*., pp. 28-32.
64. *Ibid*., p. 32.

65. *Ibid*, p. 6.
66. Ibid, p. 18.
67. Pande, Bireswar, *Bankimchandra O Hindur Adarsha, Sahitya Parishad Patrika*, 1302 B.S., Reprinted, *Somalochana Sahitya*, op. cit., pp. 298-319.
68. *Somalochana Sahitya*, op. cit., pp. 212-13.
69. Ghose, Hemendra Prasad, *Bishabriksha, Dasi*, Oct '95 & Dec '95, pp. 656-66.
70. *Ibid.*, October 1895, pp. 665-66.
71. *Ibid.*, December 1895, p. 656.
72. *Ibid.*, October 1895, p. 664.
73. *Ibid.*, December 1895, p. 657.
74. *Ibid.*, p. 659.
75. *Ibid.*, p. 661.
76. *Ibid.*, October 1895, p. 663.
77. *Ibid.*, p. 664.
78. Sarkar, Shailendra Nath, *Bishabriksha Anushilon, Prayas*, 1st year, 1899, pp. 8-20.
79. *Ibid.*, p. 16.
80. *Ibid.*, p. 10.
81. *Ibid.*, p. 17.
82. *Ibid.*, p. 18.
83. *Ibid.*
84. *Ibid.*, p. 19.
85. *Ibid.*, p. 11.
86. *Ibid.*
87. *Ibid.*, p. 12.
88. Basu, Hemendra Chandra, *Bankimchandra*, *Sahitya*, Falgun, 1309, pp. 680-714.
89. *Ibid.*, p. 692.
90. Goswami, Bireswar, *Kunda, Suryamukhi O Kamal, Samalochani*, 1st year, 11th Issue, 1309 B.S., pp. 431-50.
91. *Ibid.*, p. 441.
92. Sudhindranath Thakur has found a little similarity in the character of Kundanandini with that of Tesa of George Eliot in respect of their respective restlessness, simplicity and love. *(Suryamukhi O Kundanandini*, op. cit., pp. 79-80).
93. Goswami, Bireswer, op. cit., p. 448.
94. *Ibid.*, pp. 432-33.

95. Mazumder, Binode Lal, *Kundanandinir Swapna, Pradip*, Agrahayan, 1310, pp. 300-04.
96. *Ibid.*, p. 302.
97. *Ibid.*
98. *Ibid.*
99. Gupta, Jatindra Mohan, *Bankimbabur Stri Charitra, Somalochani*, 2nd year, 1st Issue, 1310 B.S., pp. 9-15.
100. *Ibid.*, p. 302.
101. Gupta, Sourindra Mohan, *Upanyase Stri Charitra, Somalochani*, 2nd year, 1st Issue, 1310 B.S., pp. 129-32.
102. *Ibid.*
103. Gupta, Janaki Nath, *Suryamukhi O Kundanandini, Bani*, Bhadra, 1313 B.S., pp. 628-37.
104. *Ibid.*, p. 613.
105. *Ibid.*, p. 633.
106. Chakraborty, Lokenath, *Bishabriksha, Bangadarshan*, 10th year, 10th Issue, Magh, 1317 B.S., pp. 497-511.
107. Chakraborty, Lokenath, *Suryamukhi, Bangadarshan*, 10th year, 11th Issue, Falgun, 1317 B.S., pp. 565-78.
108. Chakraborty, Lokenath, *Bishabriksher Coekti Charitra, Bangadarshan*, 10th year, 10th Issue, Magh, 1317 B.S., pp. 497-511.
109. Chakraborty, Lokenath, *Kamalmani, Bangadarshan*, 12th year, 2nd Issue, Jaistha, 1319 B.S., pp. 86-89.
110. Chakraborty, Lokenath, *Nagendranath, Bangadarshan*, 12th year, 6th Issue, Aswin, 1319 B.S., pp. 663-67.
111. Chakraborty, Lokenath, *Bishabriksha, Debendra O Haimoti, Bangadarshan*, 12th year, 8th Issue, Agahayan, 1319 B.S., pp. 497-99.
112. Chakraborty, Lokenath, *Bishabriksha*, op. cit., p. 497.
113. *Ibid.*, pp. 498-508.
114. Chakraborty, Lokenath, *Suryamukhi*, op. cit., p. 565.
115. *Ibid.*, p. 576.
116. *Ibid.*, pp. 576-77.
117. Chakraborty, Lokenath, *Bishabriksher Coekti Chitra-Kundanandini*, op. cit., p. 450.
118. *Ibid.*, p. 451.
119. Chakraborty, Lokenath, *Bishabriksha*, op. cit., pp. 501-502.
120. Chakraborty, Lokenath, *Kamalmani*, op. cit., pp. 86-87.
121. Chakraborty, Lokenath, *Bishabriksha*, op. cit., p. 507.
122. Chakraborty, Lokenath, *Bishabriksha*, p. 503.

123. Chakraborty, Lokenath, *Bishabriksha-Debendra O Haimaboti*, p. 497.
124. *Ibid.*, p. 497.
125. *Ibid.*, pp. 497-99.
126. Basu, Jitendralal, *Bankimchandra, Bangadarshan*, 10th year, 4th Issue, Shraban, 1317 B.S., pp. 169-80.
127. *Ibid.*, p. 169.
128. Rakshit, Haren Chandra, *Banga Sahitye Bankim*, 3rd Edition, Poush, 1317 B.S.
129. *Ibid.*, p. 117.
130. *Ibid.*, pp. 116-17.
131. Bandopadhyay, Sitaram, *Kundanandini, Jamuna*, Falgun, 1317 B.S., pp. 395-96.
132. *Ibid.*
133. *Ibid.*, pp. 396-97.
134. Sarkar, Bankimchandra, *Samaj Sanskare Bankimchandra, Bangadarshan*, Ashar, 1318, pp. 129-51. Reprinted, *Prafulla Kumar Sarkerer Probondha Sangraha*, Edited by Nakul Chattopadhyay, Shraban, 1376 B.S., pp. 9-29.
135. Sarkar, Prafulla Kumar, *Niti Shikshay Bankimchandra, Bangadarshan*, Magh-Chaitra, 1318, Reprinted, *Prafulla Kumar Sarkarer Probondha Sangraha*, pp. 30-60.
136. *Ibid.*, p. 16.
137. *Ibid.*, p. 17.
138. Chattopadhyay, Shachis Chandra, *Swargiya B.C. Chattopadhyayer Jibon Charita*, 1318 B.S.
139. Chattopadhyay, S.C., *Swargiya Bankimchandra Chattopadhyayer Jibon Charita*, 2nd Edn., 1322, pp. 300-92.
140. *Ibid.*, p. 476.
141. *Ibid.*
142. Bhattacharjee, Harihar, *Ratnabali O Bishabriksha*, Archana, 9th year, 7-8 Issue, Bhadra, Aswin, Kartik, 1319, pp. 255-59, 289-99, 329-37.
143. Harihar Bhattacharjee says that the incident which distinguished Ratnabali from Bishabriksha is the ultimate death of Kunda by drinking poison. *Ratnabali O Bishabriksha*, p. 250 (Bhadra).
144. *Ibid.*, p. 259.
145. (a) Bandopadhyay, Lalit Kumar, *Bankimchandrer Akshyaikabali, Bharatbarsha*, Asharh, 1322 B.S., pp. 6-11.
     (b) Bandopadhyay, Lalit Kumar, *Bidhaba, Bharatbarsha*, 9th year, 3rd Issue, Bhadra, 1328 B.S., pp. 415-21, 9th year, 1st part, 2nd

Issue, pp. 272-80, 9th year, 1st part, 4th Issue, Ashwin, 1328 B.S., pp. 522-29.

(c) Bandopadhyay, Lalit Kumar, *Bidhaba, Bharatbarsha*, 9th year, 3rd Issue, Bhadra, 1328 B.S., pp. 415-21, 9th year, 1st Part, 2nd Issue, pp. 272-80, 9th year, 1st part, 4th Issue, Ashwin, 1328 B.S., pp. 522-29.

146. (a) Bandopadhyay, Lalit Kumar, *Kabyasudha*, Kartik, 1328 B.S.

(b) Bandopadhyay, Lalit Kumar, *Premerkatha*, Jaistha, 1327 B.S.

(c) Bandopadhyay, Lalit Kumar, *Sakhi*, Calcutta-Dhaka-Moymonsingha, 1328 B.S.

147. Bandopadhyay, Lalit Kumar, *Bankimchander Akshayaikabali*, p. 11.
148. *Ibid.*
149. Bandopadhyay, Lalit Kumar, *Ma*, p. 271.
150. *Ibid.*, p. 272.
151. Bandopadhyay, Lalit Kumar, *Kabyasudha*, p. 28.
152. Bandopadhyay, Lalit Kumar, *Bidhaba*, (Bhadra), p. 416.
153. *Ibid.*
154. *Ibid.*, pp. 416-17.
155. *Ibid.*, p. 420.
156. *Ibid.*, p. 419.
157. Bandopadhyay, Lalit Kumar, *Sakhi*, p. 91.
158. Bandopadhyay, Lalit Kumar, *Bidhaba*, pp. 272-74.
159. Bandopadhyay, Lalit Kumar, *Bidhaba*, p. 524.
160. Dey Chintaharan, *Sahitye Swapner Prabhao*, 5th year, Jaistha, 1322, pp. 52-56.
161. *Ibid.*, p. 56.
162. (a) Pal, Bipin Chandra, *Shirshak-Dharma-Niti-O-Art, Narayan*, 2nd part, 5th Issue, Ashwin, 1322 B.S., pp. 1173-81.

(b) Pal, Bipin Chandra, *Banglar Nabajuger Katha (Skadash Katha), Bangabani*, 2nd year, 1st part, 1st Issue, Falgun, 1329 B.S., pp. 90-98.

(c) Pal, Bipin Chandra, *Nabajuger Bangla Sahitye Bankimchandra, Nabyabharat*, 24th part, 5th Issue, Bhadra, 1330, pp. 235-49.

(d) Pal, Bipin Chandra, *Banglar Nabajuger Katha (Dwadahs Katha), Bangabani*, 2nd year, 1st part, 2nd Issue, Chaitra, 1329, pp. 225-35.

163. Pal, Bipin Chandra, *Banglar Nabajuger Katha (Ekadash Katha)*, pp. 94-95.
164. Pal, Bipin Chandra, *Shirshak, Dharma-Niti O Art*, p. 1179.
165. Pal, Bipin Chandra, *Bangla Nabajuger Katha (Dwadash Katha)*, p. 226.
166. Pal, Bipin Chandra, *Shirshak, Dharma-Niti O Art*, p. 1180.

167. Laha, Jatindra Kumar, *Kundanandinir Swapna*, Archana, 12th Year, 12th Issue, Magh, 1322 B.S., pp. 453-58.
168. *Ibid.*, pp. 554-56.
169. Sen, Shashanka Mohan, *Bangabani (Part-I & II)*, Dhaka Alber Library, 1915.
170. *Ibid.*, p. 65.
171. *Ibid.*, pp. 65-66.
172. Bhattacharjee, Haripada, *Bishabriksher Darshan Tattba, Jamuna*, Shraban, 1323 B.S., pp. 142-46.
173. *Ibid.*, p. 145.
174. Bhattacharjee, Batuknath, *Bankim Prativa, Bharatbarsha*, 4th year, 1st part, Agrahayan, 1323 B.S., pp. 605-09.
175. Bhattacharjee, Batuknath, *Bankim Sahitye Sannyas, Masik Basumati*, 5th Year, 6th Issue, Shraban, 1333 B.S., pp. 640-51.
176. Bhattacharjee, Batuknath, *Bankim Prativa*, p. 908.
177. So-called *Sannyasi*, according to Batuknath, is an incomplete stage.
178. Bhattacharjee, Batuknath, *Bankim Sahitya Sannyas*, pp. 641-42.
179. (a) Vedantasastri, Ramsahaya, *Kundanandini*, Archana, 16th Part, 4th Issue, Agrahayan, 1325 B.S., pp. 120-25.
    (b) Vedantasastri, Ramsahaya, *Bishabriksher Nayak (Somalochana)*, Archana, 24th Part, 1st Issue, Falgun, 1333 B.S., pp. 1-5.
    (c) Vedantasastri, Ramsahaya, *Suryamukhi O Kamalmani- (Tulanay Somalochana)*, Archana, 26th Part, 1st Issue, Falgun, 1335 B.S., pp. 16-24.
180. Vedantasastri, Ramsahaya, *Kundanandini*, p. 120.
181. Vedantasastri, Ramsahaya, *Suryamukhi O Kamalmani*, p. 17.
182. *Ibid.*, p. 18.
183. *Ibid.*, p. 17.
184. Vedantasastri, Ramsahaya, *Suryamukhi O Kamalmani*, (Tulenay Somalochana), p. 16.
185. Vedantasastri, Ramsahaya, *Kun Anandini*, p. 122.
186. *Ibid.*, p. 121.
187. *Ibid.*, p. 125.
188. Vedantasastri, Ramsahaya, *Suryamukhi O Kamalmani*, p. 17.
189. *Ibid.*, p. 16.
190. Duttagupta, Akshay Kumar, *Bankimchandra*, 1327 B.S.
191. Duttagupta, Akshay Kumar, *Bankimchandra*, 2nd Edn. May, 1975, p. 166.
192. *Ibid.*
193. *Ibid.*, p. 167.

194. *Ibid.*, pp. 168-70.
195. Mukhopadhyay, Hemchandra, *Manab Prakriti (Swargiya Bankimchandrer Bishabriksha Abolombone Rachito)*, Chuchurha, 13th Jaistha, 1328 B.S.
196. *Ibid.*, p. 123.
197. *Ibid.*, p. 116.
198. *Ibid.*, p. 124.
199. *Ibid.*, pp. 23-25.
200. Takur, Kshitindra Nath, *Art O Sahitya*, 8th May 1329 B.S.
201. *Ibid.*, pp. 85-89.
202. Gongopadhyay, Muralidhar, *Prabandhe Bankim Prativa, Sahitya*, Bhadra, 1329 B.S., pp. 420-23.
203. *Ibid.*, p. 422.
204. *Ibid.*, p. 423.
205. Duara, Jatindranath, *Art O Sahitya, Archana*, 20th Part, 10th Issue, Agrahayan, 1330 B.S., pp. 383-86.
206. *Ibid.*, p. 385.
207. Mazumdar, Biman Bihari, *Bankimchandra*, Baishakh, 1335 B.S.
208. *Ibid.*, pp. 720-21.
209. (a) Mazumdar, Mohitlal, *Bankimchandra*, Baishakh, 1335 B.S. Reprinted, *Bankimchandra (2nd Print)*, 1371 B.S., pp. 1-11.
    (b) Mazumdar, Mohitlal, *Adhunik Bangla Sahitya*, 1336 B.S. Reprinted, *Sahitya Samput, Biswabharati*, 1965, pp. 289-311.
210. Mazumdar, Mohitlal, *Bankimcharan*, p. 10.
211. Mazumdar, Mohitlal, *Sahitya Samput*, pp. 298-302.
212. Sengupta, Subodh Chandra, *Bankimchandra O Saratchandra*, Bichitra, Magh, 1337 B.S., pp. 164-71.
213. *Ibid.*, p. 166.
214. *Ibid.*
215. Basu, Indradeb, *Bankim Sahitye Pashchatya Provab, Desh*, 1st Year, 39th Issue, 1st Bhadra, Saturday, 1341 B.S., pp. 23-24.
216. *Ibid.*
217. Pal, Dhiren, *Bankim Sahitye Pashchatya Provab? Desh*, 1st year, 42nd Issue, 22nd Bhadra, Saturday, 1341 B.S., pp. 23-24.
218. *Ibid.*, p. 24.

6
Indira, Jugalangurio, Rajani, and *Radharani*

INDIRA

LALIT KUMAR BANDOPADHYAY (1275-1336 B.S.)

Lalit Kumar wrote about motherliness and family life as depicted in *Indira*.[1] His criticisms are found in his two separate essays and separate books.[2]

In *Ma* the critic tried to prove that in the character of Ramanbabu's mother, one can see a reflection of a loving mother in Bengalee domestic life. The critic thought that although Subhasini was created mainly to serve the purpose of a friend, this character created interest both in respect of mother and conjugal love.[3] He said that Subhasini seemed to be the younger sister of Kamalmani in respect of sympathy and motherly love as well as exercising influence over husband.[4] In *sakhi*, the critic said that as a friend (Sakhi) she was not only superior to Kamalmani, but also one of the greatest in Bankim literature.[5]

In the essay *Dui Bhagini*, Lalit Kumar tried to establish that Indira and Kamini form a picture of happiness in the novel.[6] In *Kabyasudha*; he said that the family portrayals, the episode of Subhasini's living with her mother-in-low in the enlarged version seemed to be more attractive to Lalit Kumar. He said that Bankim's old age was responsible for the creation of such pictures.[7]

BIJOY RATNA MAZUMDAR (1861-1942)

The next criticism of *Indira* can be found in Bijoy Ratna's *Bankimchandrer Upannyase Hasyaras*.[8] Bankim had resorted to sarcasm in order to lash the social evils, and his humour was true to the real world. Mainly, in this light, Bijoy Ratna discussed the humour of this book. He said that Bamun Thakurani, Harani and Brojasundari of this book were the examples of that idea.[9]

AKSHAY KUMAR DUTTAGUPTA

Akshay Kumar gave a brief discussion of *Indira* in his book *Bankimchandra.*[10] He said that Bankim's largeness of design[11] was applicable only in novel and not in short story, therefore, in such short stories like *Indira*, Bankim, in order to compress his imagination, he made them artistically poor. He has clearly said: "Indira, being enlarged, has not glorified with requisite beauty."[12]

JUGALANGURIO

LALIT KUMAR BANDOPADHYAY (1275-1336 B.S.)

Lalit Kumar Bandopadhyay in his two separate essays,[13] and in one book of essays[14] wrote about *Jugalanurio.*

According to Lalit Kumar, although the story element of the book was based upon the growing love of Purandar and Hiranmoyee, the mystery behind their marriage was based upon the ring, which was further effective in unfolding the mystery (Like the ring in *Abhignan Shakuntala*), hence, the title of the book was justified.[15]

Lalit Kumar marked in this book the circumstances adverse to the growth of motherhood. He believed, the death of Hiranmoyee's mother was demanded by the transformation of plot and growth of the character of the heroine, and therefore, Bankim made Hiranmoyee's mother to accept death willingly following her husband.[16]

According to the critic, although a slave, Amala in this book had acted as a messenger, so, she could be termed as a third-class slave.[17]

NIRODE KRISHNA BONDOPADHYAY

Nirode Krishna, in his "Bankimer Apatya Sneha"[18] discussed about the paternal love of Dhanadas towards Hiranmoyee. Through this paternal affection the critic probed the Bankim psychology. He said that for the happiness and well-being of the daughter he kept her separate and witnessing her distress, he had been suffering from endless pain. The critic said: "It is the reflection of the writer's philosophical bend of mind, when shall we find the final and vivid example of such a refined egoism? John Stewart Mill's theory stands insignificant to it."[19]

RAJANI

PURNA CHANDRA BASU

In Purna Chandra Basu's discussion of *Rajani* in his book *Kabya Sundari*[20] special attention was given to Rajani and Lobongalata and it was been subordinate to by a comparative discussion of some of the characters of *Chandrasekhar* with those of *Rajani*. In this book the trend of criticism of Bankim's time is clearly visible. Purna Chandra's criticism reveals a search for the characters development and achievement along with an analysis of inner significance in the summing up of the novel. Side by side in the discussion of Rajani and Lobongalata, Purna Chandra had left an impression of psycho-analytical tendency and in finding out the basic element of both the characters; he tried to cross the limitations of the trends of Bankim criticism during his life time.

Purna Chandra thought that Rajani's ideal of love is like that of Kalidas's *Shakuntala* but unlike that of Litton's Nydia.[21] Because both Shakuntala and Rajani expressed the natural development of love in its silent satisfaction of loving the beloved.[22] On the other hand, he had shown that the simplicity which had made Nydia brave and free, was there in Rajani also, the mingling of the virtues like intelligence, softness, seriousness, roughness, pride and passions was nicely shown in Rajani also. On the other hand, he discussed the apparent dissimilarities of the characters also. Purna Chandra believed that Nydia's love being unsuccessful, strove the sympathy of the readers permanently and Rajani occupying a place permanently in the heart of Shachis, had been deprived of the sympathy of human hearts. He clearly said that Nydia had nothing worldly except heavenly and she did not belong the blue-blood—and this characteristic placed her above Rajani. Ultimately her (Rajani's) blue-blood stood in the way of her personal qualities.[23]

Purna Chandra brought out the points of dissimilarities between the characters of Nydia and Rajani and had shown that in certain points. Rajani was characteristically different from Nydia. These distinctly characteristic points of differences of Nydia are personal genius, thoughtfulness, solitary nature and quite attitude. Purna Chandra drew the vivid picture of Rajani pointing out that characteristics.[24]

Regarding Labongalata Purna Chandra remarked that she had produced a special aura to this novel as a mother, wife and above all, as a humour-some young girl.[25] He further pointed out the other qualities of Lobongalata like her self-control, pride and spirit.[26] He said that Lobonga was a spirited woman, but she had the capacity to control her spirit, her pride was not of her beauty and youth, but of her honesty and integrity and therefore, she was brave.[27] Besides, the critic thought that Lobonga's spirit was due to her old husband's findings and lack of control over her. She had the potentiality to control others, but since there was none, she controlled herself. She won over nature by virtue of this self-control, won over Amarnath, and therefore, she did not hesitate to go to Amarnath.[28] The critic clearly remarked:

> The strength which was the fortress of Lobongalata's spirit and freedom, treasure of religion, strength of her insatiable passions, Amarnath's blemish as a 'thief' identified this strength.[29]

He has further said that by marking on Amarnath's back, Lobonga did not only punish himself, but, in fact, warned the entire world of sin.[30]

According to Purna Chandra the deficiency in *Chandrasekhar* was fulfilled in *Rajani*. The boldness and strength of mind which were not there in Shaibalini, Rajani was endowed with it. That the manliness of Pratap and could behaving in a woman, Lobongalata was the instance of it. Amarnath was superior to Pratap so far as pure love was concerned. Purna Chandra has made a comparative estimate of Chandrasekhar and Rajani in this light.[31] He says that Pratap is a symbol of human nature, while Amarnath wanted to live on it—"Pratap was worldly and Amarnath was saintly. Pratap was full of actions, Amarnath was full of emotions."[32] Such judgements are everywhere in the discussion.

Purna Chandra's discussion is based upon literary judgements. He has carefully restrained the occasional emotional tendencies. In fact, his discussion is free from vagueness. A liberal attitude is reflected throughout the discussion. And it needs mention that Purna Chandra is the first critic of *Rajani.*

HARIDAS BONDOPADHYAY

Haridas Bondopadhyay's *Bangalar Upannyas Lekhak-Chandrashekhar O Rajani,*[33] appeared after a decade of Purna Chandra's critical treatise. But the surprising thing is that the factors and elements used by Purna Chandra were also used by Haridas in his criticism. He said almost in the same fashion of the writer of *Kabya Sundari*—"Rajani is a transcription of Shaibalini of Chandrasekhar."[34] Shaibalini's shortcomings were fulfilled in Rajani. What Pratap had done as a man, Lobongalata being a woman, did the same. Pratap life was full of struggle, while that of Amarnath was peaceful.[35]

Besides, like Purna Chandra, he also opined that while Nydia captured the hearts of readers by her inner beauty, Rajani failed to do so in spite of her internal qualities because of her high growth.[36] This echo of Purna Chandra robs much of his originality.

HEMENDRA PRASAD GHOSE (1876-1963)

Hemendra Prasad, in his essay *Rajani,*[37] attracted the attention of the readers towards the artistic beauty of the book. He also discussed the characters of Rajani, Lobongalata, Amarnath and Shachish. In spite of the lack of reflective insight, Hemendra Prasad's discussion is based upon a literary criticism of lighter vein.[38]

The critic pointed out that Rajani bore structural resemblance to Collin's novels—*Women in White* and *Moonstone*—and the character of Rajani was an original creation of Bankim.[39] Hemendra Prasad primarily discussed the inordinate firmness and sharp intelligence of the character of Rajani and the consciousness of feminine virtues in the character of Lobonglata.[40] The part, covered by the comparative discussion of both the characters in the whole body of criticism is the best as for example: "Rajani is an imaginary ideal of beauty; Lobongalata is a realistic picture of beauty—a worldly representation of beauty."[41]

In the analysis of Amarnath, Hemendra Prasad supported his predecessor Purna Chandra Basu. Like Purna Chandra, the present critic is also satisfied with the saintliness of Amarnath.[42]

M O

After Hemendra Prasad, a critic, having the pen-name MO, wrote the essay *Lobongalata.*[43] Purna Chandra's influence is noticed in his long essay also. Like Purna Chandra, the present critic had also given emphasis upon the points that Lobongalata was primarily a wife, a mother and humorous woman and these virtues made her character brighter.[44]

But the present critic's originality is marked in his psycho-analytical discussion of Amarnath's punishment by Lobongalata. He said that through this act of inflicting Amarnath with punishment, Lobongalata's love and her deep regards for human nature had been reflected. Lobongalata let Amarnath know his own nature by showing that it was better to punish the object of her love by herself than allowing others to punish him.[45]

JITENDRA LAL BASU

Jitendra Lal Basu, in his essay *Bankimchandra*[46] passed nice and ingenious remarks about the character of Rajani. He viewed the writer of Rajani as a philosopher-novelist. In fact, through the character of Rajani Bankim had shown that[47] the body and mind of a woman, whose physical features were build up in a niggardly manner by nature, became restless to dedicate her love to the beloved.

Jitendra Lal had pointed out this inner truth of the character of Rajani. He had clearly said that Rajani was a loving image of certain critical psychological problems coupled with certain philosophical ideas. Whether love could grow in the mind of a blind woman—the character of Rajani was the solution of this problem.[48]

KSHETRA LAL SAHA

In the contemporary age, the character of Lobongalata had been psychologically treated by Kshetra Lal Saha in his essay *Lobongalata.*[49] Lobonga's self-control and the cause of this self-control cover the entire discussion where a psycho-analytical treatment based upon proper reasoning is clearly evident. The critic had emphatically said that Lobongalata had whole-heartedly loved Amarnath. But in her personal life, the concealment of this love made for her tragic strain and this was the final truth of Lobongalata's life. Lobonga adorned her old husband with flowers, perfumed him with scents, if he snored, she tried to awake him by moving her anklets and produced sounds. This was an indication of her joy, but it was only an attempt to forget and thwart grief. Lobonga tried to cool down her burning mind with the cold water of devotion to her husband.[50]

The idea that Bankim did not write novels to teach morals, but the principal aim of his novels was to give a pen-picture of life had made Kshetra Lal's discussion lively. This idea led him to say that Lobonga could have punished Amarnath, because she loved him deeply and again, she could not approve of his stealthy entrance into the house of somebody else because of the same reason.[51] Kshetra Lal, here, had searched for the deep truth of human life.

An additional contribution of this essay along with the psychological analysis of the character of Lobongalata is the explication of Bankim consensus. Drawing proper facts, Kshetra Lal said that Lobonga, even if, had not got Amarnath in her earthly life—the thirsty heart of the unfortunate woman was looking for the other world to live with him. The critic thought—"It is here that Bankim has maintained a balance between ideal love and ideal moral character."[52]

SARACHANDRA GHOSAL

Sarachandra Ghosal pointed out the modifications done by Bankimchandra in *Rajani* when it was published in book form, the original of which was published in *Bangadarshan.* In his *Rajanir Kromobikash,*[53] it needs to be mentioned here that the critic does not make any attempt to evaluate the qualitative distinction or artistic significance of this modification. But Sarachandra could not support Rajani's action of attacking Haralal by throwing stick in darkness in the modified version on the ground of its impropriety. He believed that Rajani's action, as appeared in the original published in *Bangadarshan*, deserved approval, because it was in conformity to the situations.[54] He had further pointed out that the Amarnath of *Bangadarshan* was shrewd and revengeful, but in revised edition he is a selfless and ideal character.[55]

(SHRI) JNANANJAN PAUL

Rajani (Somalochana)[56] of Jnananjan Paul is the first emotional criticism of the novel *Rajani*. The chief characteristic of his essay is not literary evaluation, but an emotional approach to the life of Rajani. Besides, this essay is full of irrelevant discussion. The critic said: "The poetic beauty, created by the poet, is so superb that in that ocean of beauty, I lose my entity and enjoy this beauty."[57] But this attempt ends in expression only. Emotionally he says: "At last we have seen Rajani as mother and satisfied our eyes."[58]

AKSHAY KUMAR DUTTAGUPTA

Akshay Kumar Duttagupta wrote a pretty long criticism of Rajani in his book *Bankimchanda*.[59] In this essay, the critic made an attempt to evaluate the structure, artistic skill, characterization, etc. of this novel.

Akshay Kumar Duttagupta found fault with the story telling method adopted by Bankim in *Rajani*, since the narration of the incidents by the characters was, in fact, the narration of the novelist himself which had spoiled the charm of the novel. He said, "The three characters (Rajani, Amarnath, Shachindra) are writing dictation from Bankim."[60]

Akshay Kumar Duttagupta pointed out the similarities existing between some of the characters of *Rajani* had some characters of other novels of Bankimchandra. He said that Ramananda (*Chandra Sekhar*) and sannyasi of *Rajani* were the element of same nature, the technique responsible for arousing love in the mind of Shaibalini for Chandra Sekhar. The same technique is responsible to arouse love in Shachindra for Rajani, Lobongalata was a new edition of Bimala of *Durgeshnandini.* Like Bimala, Lobonga was clever, jocular, adorned with rare intelligence and mental strength. As Bimala was an object of reader's sympathy, so also was Lobongalata. Both loved towards the children of their co-sister (Satin), although, Lobonga went to step further to feel proud of being a mother of her co-sister's son.[61]

Regarding the miraculous cure of Rajani's blindness Akshay Kumar as if, sarcastically said:

> All the elegant and good impulses of Rajani have been made complete. Can such a woman be left incomplete? Whatever may be the law of nature, poetry is not the slave of nature.... So her blindness is removed by charms and spells.[62] By pointing out this improbability he has displayed modern out-look.

RAMSAHAYA VEDANTASASTRI

Ramsahaya Vedantasastri looked at the characters through excess of emotion and excess of devotion in his essay *Lobongalata.*[63] He mainly viewed Lobongalata through her controlled manner, duty-boundness, and self-control in practical life. Those elements of the natura of Lobongalata made her character beautiful and magnanimous. Pointing to Lobongalata, the emotional critic said: "In whatever direction her impulses may flow after death, we can at least forecast that she will have her place in the sanctified abode of heaven."[64]

RADHARANI

SARACCHANDRA GHOSAL

The first criticism on *Radharani* is Saracchandra Ghosal's *Bankimchandrer Radharani.*[65] Saracchandra's main criticism was based upon the transformation of Radharani in the fourth edition. According to him, Radharani was first painted as extremely fickle, but in the revised edition, she had been transformed into a sober one—and thus, Bankim had presented to the readers a woman—just normal and beautiful. He rightly observed that Radharani had shown extreme shamelessness by ordering the maid-servant to play on 'shankha', while she had been garlanding Rukmini Kumar, but in the revised edition, Bankim changed it and thus had shown his artistic skill and his understanding of human nature.[66]

LALIT KUMAR BANDOPADHYAY (1275-1336 B.S.)

Lalit Kumar Bandopadhyay wrote the next comparatively pure criticism of Radharani in his essay *Ma*[67] and in his book of essay *Sakhi*.[68] Lalit Kumar pointed out that the unset relation of Radharani and her mother, despite their poverty, as depicted in the story of this book, was almost of the same type as found in first section of *Devi Chaudhurani*, and he further marked the influence of Greek myth in Radharani's mother's character. He believed that Radharani was as good as *Niobe* of the Greek mythology with regard to her motherly affection.[69] Besides he thought that Radharani's mother's death was a dramatic necessity so far as the growth of the character of the heroine and transformation of story element were concerned.[70]

Lalit Kumar pointed out the influence of "Dutitattaba" in Sanskrit Literature on the character of Basanta Kumari, friend of Radharani. Explaining the artistic necessity of the character of Basanta Kumari, the critic said that in the days of anxiety due to disunion of the heroine, she needed a friend, who would supplement her to the attainment of her goal—Basanta Kumari had fulfilled this need.[71]

AKSHAY KUMAR DUTTAGUPTA

Akshay Kumar's literary taste is evident in his discussion of Radharani in his *Bankimchandra*.[72] He had drawn the attention of the readers towards the artistic side of the story. He said that despite Radharani's love episode 'too sweet and touching'[73] Bankim, by making her fickle and humorous like *Indira* towards the end, had mocked her sweet love. And he further found lack of art in Rukmini Kumar's confession of love.[74] It needs be mentioned here that Akshay Kumar criticized Radharani which was published in *Bangadarshan*.[75]

SUMMING UP

Attempts have been made in this chapter to assess the literary value of Bankim criticism on *Indira*, *Yugalangurio*, *Rajani* and

Radharani. These works of Bankim drew the attraction of few critics. Of these, *Rajani* was more widely discussed. Except Purna Chandra Basu, all the critics belong to the post Bankim period, and in their criticism traditional, moral, and ethical tendencies are found to be absent. These are marked with artistic tastes and temperaments of the critics. The most widely discussed topics of these works are the characters of Rajani, Lobongalata and Amarnath. None discussed these works from the point of view of total impression.

References

1. (a) Bandopadhyay, Lalit Kumar, *Ma, Bharatbarsha*, 3rd year, 1st part, Issue III, Bhadra, 1322 B.S. pp. 501-22.
   (b) Bandopadhyay, Lalit Kumar, *Dui Bhagini, Bharatbarsha*, 4th year, 1st part, Issue III, Bhadra, 1322 B.S. pp. 391-407.
2. (a) Bandopadhyay, Lalit Kumar, *Kabyasudha*, Kartik, 1323 B.S.
   (b) Bandopadhyay, Lalit Kumar, *Sakhi*, Cal-Dhaka-Moymensing, 1328 B.S.
3. Bandopadhyay, Lalit Kumar, *Ma,* p. 505.
4. *Ibid.*, p. 505.
5. Bandopadhyay, Lalit Kumar, *Sakhi*, p. 111.
6. Bandopadhyay, Lalit Kumar, *Dui Bhagini*, p. 396.
7. Bandopadhyay, Lalit Kumar, *Kabyasudha*, Kartik, 1323 B.S. pp. 90-99.
8. Mazumder, Bijoy Ratna, *Bankimchandrer Upannyase Hasyaras*, *Mormobani*, Bhadra, 1322, B.S. pp. 123-25.
9. *Ibid.*, pp. 127-28.
10. Duttagupta, Akshay Kumar, *Bankimchandra*, 1327 B.S.
11. Duttagupta, Akshay Kumar, *Bankimchandra*, 2nd Edn. Jingnsa, May, 1975, pp. 171-72.
12. *Ibid.*, p. 171.
13. (a) Bandopadhyay, Lalit Kumar, *Bankimchandrer Akshyaikabali, Bharatbarsha*, Asharh, 1322 B.S., pp. 264-82.
    (b) Bandopadhyay, Lalit Kumar, *Ma*, op. cit., pp. 264-82.
14. Bandopadhyay, Lalit Kumar, *Sakhi*, op. cit., 1328 B.S.
15. Bandopadhyay, Lalit Kumar, *Bankimchandrer Akshayaikabali*, op. cit., p. 10.
16. Bandopadhyay, Lalit Kumar, *Ma*, op. cit., p. 279.
17. Bandopadhyay, Lalit Kumar, *Sakhi*, op. cit., pp. 31-41.
18. Bandopadhyay, Nirode Krishna, *Bankimer Apatya Sneha*, Archana, 20th part, 9th issue, Kartik, 1330 B.S., pp. 330-32.

19. *Ibid.*, p. 332.
20. Basu, Purna Chandra, *Kabya Sundari*, G.C. Basu, & Co. Shraban, 1267 B.S., pp. 123-56.
21. Bankimchandra writes that the character of Rajani is written in imitation of the character of the blind flower girl Nydia of *Last Days of Pompeii* by Lord Litton. (Advertisement on Rajani)
22. Basu, Purna Chandra, op. cit., pp. 130-32.
23. *Ibid.*, p. 134.
24. *Ibid.*, pp. 136-48.
25. *Ibid.*, p. 153.
26. *Ibid.*, pp. 154-55.
27. *Ibid.*, p. 154.
28. *Ibid.*, p. 155.
29. *Ibid.*, p. 156.
30. *Ibid.*
31. *Ibid.*, pp. 123-30.
32. Ibid, p. 129.
33. Bondopadhyay, Haridas, *Bangalar Upannyas Lekhak; Chandrasekhar O Rajani, Kalpana*, 6th year, Asharh, 1296 B.S., pp. 213-20.
34. *Ibid.*, p. 219.
35. *Ibid.*, p. 220.
36. *Ibid.*
37. Ghose, Hemendra Prasad, *Rajani, Dasi*, March 1896, pp. 139-47.
38. Bankimchandra has said that expression of the part of a novel in first person is a rare thing in existing style. This style was first introduced in Collin's book "Women in white", Rajani is written following this style, (Advertisement on Rajani).
39. Ghose, Hemendra Prasad, op. cit., p. 144.
40. *Ibid.*, pp. 143-45.
41. *Ibid.*, p. 144.
42. *Ibid.*, p. 146.
43. MO, *Lobongalata (Charitra Somalochana), Bamabodhini Patrika*, 35th year, 339th issue, Chaitra, 1304 B.S., pp. 460-65.
44. *Ibid.*, pp. 461-62.
45. *Ibid.*, p. 462.
46. Basu, Jitendra Lal, *Bankimchandra, Bangadarshan*, 10th year, 4th issue, Shraban, 1317 B.S., pp. 169-80.
47. Bankimchandra has written that the psychological and ethical questions this book aims at will be expressed clearly through the blind girl and therefore, the character of Rajani has been drawn upon such basis. (Advertisement on *Rajani*)

48. Basu, Jitendralal, op. cit., p. 172.
49. Saha, Kshetralal, *Lobongalata, Suprabhat*, 8th year, Magh, 1321 B.S., pp. 296-302.
50. *Ibid.*, pp. 297-301.
51. *Ibid.*, p. 302.
52. *Ibid.*
53. Ghosal, Sarachandra, *Rajanir Kromobikash, Sankalpa*, 1st year, 1st Pt. 5th issue, Poush, 1321, pp. 623-29, Magh, 1321 B.S., pp. 645-65.
54. *Ibid.*, Poush, 1321 B.S., pp. 624-25.
55. *Ibid.*, p. 626.
56. Paul, Jnananjan, *Rajani (Somalochana), Narayan*, 1322 B.S., pp. 572-87.
57. *Ibid.*, p. 572.
58. *Ibid.*, p. 587.
59. Duttagupta, Akshay Kumar, *Bankimchandra*, 1327 B.S.
60. Duttagupta, Akshay Kumar, *Bankimchandra*, 2nd edition, *Jingasya*, May 1975, p. 178.
61. *Ibid.*, pp. 177-79.
62. *Ibid.*, p. 182.
63. Vedantasastri, Ramsahaya, *Lobongalata, Archana*, 27th part, 8th issue, Ashwin, 1337 B.S., pp. 264-68.
64. *Ibid.*, p. 266.
65. Ghosal, Sarachandra, *Bankimchandrer Radharani, Sankalpa*, Bhadra, 1321 B.S. pp. 35-38.
66. *Ibid.*, p. 37.
67. Bandopadhyay, Lalit Kumar, *Ma*, op. cit.
68. Bandopadhyay, Lalit Kumar, *Sakhi*, op. cit.
69. Bandopadhyay, Lalit Kumar, *Ma*, op. cit., p. 281.
70. *Ibid.*, p. 282.
71. Bandopadhyay, Lalit Kumar, *Sakhi*, op. cit., pp. 99-100.
72. Duttagupta, Akshay Kumar, *Bankimchandra*, 1327 B.S.
73. Duttagupta, Akshay Kumar, *Bankimchandra*, 2nd Ed., May 1975, p. 183.
74. *Ibid.*, p. 183.
75. In the advertisement of the fourth edition of *Radharani*, Bankim has written that the rectify the defects of this small novel, it has to be expanded in volume. (*Bankim Rachanabali*, Sahitya Samsad, 5th Publication, 1333 B.S., p. 521.

7
Chandrashekhar

PURNA CHANDRA BASU

Purna Chandra Basu's *Shaibalini,*[1] a criticism of *Chandrashekhar*, was published in 1284 B.S. In this treatise, an analytical study of the character of Shaibalini forms the central point of discussion.

According to critic, love instills enthusiasm and bravery and thus gets itself strengthened in turn.[2] Purna Chandra showed that Shaibalini lived for love, it was love which imparted distinctiveness, desperateness, and dignity to her character. Of course, he was not blind to the influence of nature in Shaibalini. In his modified version of the character of Shaibalini in *Kabya-Sundari* he thought Shaibalini to be a symbol of nature with her unspeakable speed indomitable energy, love of freedom and simplicity.[3] Purna Chandra has also shown a skill in character study. In the criticism, we find that he had distinguished between the two contradictory traits of Shaibalini's character. In her one aspect Shaibalini was a chaste, loving, very courageous and devoted wife after her expiation of sin. In her other aspects, Shaibalini went against the social norm and there she might be called an unchaste woman.[4] According to Purna Chandra it was a grievous fault on the part of Shaibalini not to forget Pratap after marriage and leave her husband's home with Fostar. Because of this, Shaibalini character had been spoiled and her innocence lost. According to the critic, it was the spot in the character of Shaibalini.[5] Here we notice Purna Chandra judging the character of Shaibalini from social point of view.

In fact, Purna Chandra was influenced by his age. He said that the good characters and bad characters i.e., characters of the good men and the characters of sinners should be separated, one should not be mixed with another. He clearly pointed out that Shaibalini was unchaste and sinner: and, as such, she should be condemned. But the novelist had presented her to the readers in such a way that she draws sympathy. Purna Chandra could not accept this, since it is against the natural justice.[6]

Comparing the intensity and fervor of love of Shaibalini with Dalani and Pratap, Purna Chandra writes in a rhetorical way Shaibalini's love force is like the flow of waters during rains towards the sea, mad after union with the beloved, while Dalani's love though directed towards the sea is averse to union. Shaibalini's love is an example of that real love sold against gold coins inside the interior of a cottage while Dalani's love is an example of that real love which is rare inside the pleasure grove of affluence. In the love of one there is devotion to earlier beloved, in case of another (Dalani) the tragic mood of love pronounced.[7] Comparing Shaibalini's love with Pratap's love the critic writes "In Shaibalini's heart, there is the strength and restlessness of love, while in Pratap's heart there is control and sobriety of love."[8] Although the central theme of Purna Chandra's criticism of *Chandrashekhar* was the character of Shaibalini, he did not loose sight of the other major aspects of the novel, and he displayed almost near classical taste in attempting at evaluating the novel in the total artistic effect.[9] He pointed out that the artistic excellence reached by the novelist as revealed through literary and philosophical representation of nature in the scene of Shaibalini's expiation.[10] Herein lies the greatest contribution of Purna Chandra to the criticism of Bankimchandra.[11]

Purna Chandra's views regarding the ending of the novel are not striking. According to him the ending of the novel would have been more artistic if the novelist had drawn it to a close by leaving a meaningful hint through Chandrashekar's consent to accept Shaibalini as his wife. The addition of one full chapter after Shaibalini expiation reminded one of the ordeals of Sita (*Ramayana*). This was most irritating to the readers. Moreover, he could not at all accept the introduction of spiritualism at the end. His argument was what the modern man had forgotten spiritualism, and as such, the appearance of ghost, at the end was really shocking.[12]

Although admitting that the introduction of Dalani had brightened and glorified the character of Shaibalini, Purna Chandra objected that the Dalani-Mirkashem episode of *Chandrashekhar*, had not been woven into the main plot of Shaibalini-Pratap-Chandrashekhar, and the links between the two stories were so thin and flimsy that Dalani-Mirkashem story could have been shaped into a separate novel without damaging the main plot.[13] In his criticism of plot construction, Purna Chandra anticipates modern critics.

The publication of *Shaibalini* gave rise to a controversy. One critic Srilo Lakshinarayan supported Purna Chandra, while Lokenath Chakraborty contradicted him.

SRILO LAKSHINARAYAN

Although Srilo Lakshinarayan wrote *Chandrashekhar-Shaibalini*[14] supporting Purna Chandra Basu, his essay deserves special mention because of originality in the treatment of *Chandrashekhar*. He emphasized the physical love[15] of Shaibalini more than Purna Chandra. Like Purna Chandra he also considered Shaibalini a social rebel fit to be despised, and not a character whom the readers could forgive, and in case of such a character expiation had no value since she was lacking in repentance.

But Lakshinarayan finds a literary justification in the creation of such a character of Shaibalini. He said that the purpose of introduction of Shaibalini in the novel was to glorify Chandrashekhar just as Iago was essential to brighten the image of Othelo.

However, he displayed his critical mind when he remarked that Shaibalini could not put an end to her life because in her desire for satisfaction of physical love had remained unsatisfied.[16] Perhaps, Lakshinarayan was the first critic to this psychological aspect of Shaibalini's character, which came to be elaborately dealt with by some later critics.

LOKENATH CHAKRABORTY

Another of Purnachandra's contemporary critic Lokenath Chakraborty contradicted Purna Chandra's *Shaibalini*,[17] in *Anusengik Patra*.[18] Refuting the arguments of Purna Chandra regarding the lack of chastity in Shaibalini, Lokenath had remarked that Shaibalinis expiation taught the necessity of observance of social norms, it did not give encouragement to break them.[19]

The novelist tried to depict the glory and significance of eternal love as manifested in Shaibalini-Pratap, and when he found that the universal principles of love had come in conflict with the society in which Shaibalini-Pratap lived, he introduced expitation to satisfy the prevailing social taste.[20] He said:

The faults of Shaibalini spring from the great and deep love which is the jewel of a women's heart.[21]

Lokenath was conscious of the role of the man of letter to hold up mirror to nature and had condemned in strong words the moralizing tendency of writers.[22]

The critic appreciated Bankim saying, Bankim knew that Pratap had dedicated his heart to Shaibalini: and Shaibalini would never attain happiness without Pratap. It was with this idea that he had planned the Pratap-Shaibalini plot; he did not weave a story keeping his eyes fixed on the Bengali Society. Here one notices of the rudiments of literary appreciation on a higher plane. Lokenath also gave a five artistic explanation[23] of Shaibalini sliding into the path of sin when he said that the novelist thought it necessary to make Shaibalini leave her home to impart greatness to the character of Pratap.[24]

Lokenath's contribution to literary criticism of Bankim was perhaps even greater. It was who first brought to focus that the question of Shaibalini's chastity or unchastity must not come within the purview of literary criticism. In fact, Lokenath followed the Aristotalian principle: "It is not the function of the poet to relate what has happened but what may happen. What is possible, according to the law of probability,"[25] and pointed out that Shaibalini represented what was possible in human nature. Lokenath also argued that literature must not be confined within the limits set by moral and social principles; and Bankim by rising above time's religion and society was successful in creating literature with eternal meaning.

The other essay of Lokenath Chakraborty on *Chandrashekhar*, is *Chandrasekhar (Somalochana)*.[26] The first part of the essay deals with Chandrashekhar's life history,[27] when he has been described as one free from pride and egotism, polite, lover of learning self-less sober in love and God-like man.[28] In the second part the religious ideals and ethical awareness have been discussed.[29]

Literary awareness and taste of Lokenath Chakraborty found in his criticism of Shaibalini are absent in the essay in discussion. Commenting on Chandrashekhar, Lokenath said that the character which gave rise to devotion leading to worship, lightness turned to gravity, ignorance turned into wisdom, man became God and is the dead-darkness of a new moon night becomes graceful be the touch of moon beam so was the character of Chandrashekhar.[30] The critic observed that Chandrashekhar was created to teach the lesson of selflessness, and the great teacher of this 'Mahabharata', Ramananda Swami, was an incarnation of selfless God on earth, and the same had been shown with direct example by God-like Pratap. The critic's typical Hindu-feelings are expressed when he said that a Pratap could be created in European society but a Chandrashekhar and Ramananda Swami were only possible creations of Hindu brain. Pratap, even if materialistic, was devoid of the evils of materialism. Humanism and moral progress were fully developed in these characters. According to Lokenath, Chandrashekhar's dispassionate approach to materialism marked the temporal finality of Hindu civilization while Ramananda Swami's philanthropic approach in spite of his total avoidance of materialism mark the final and the heavenly stage of the Hindu civilization.[31]

YOGENDRANATH VIDYABHUSAN (1845-1904)

Dalani Begum[32] and *Pratap*[33]—these two essays mark Yogendranath's criticism of *Chandrashekhar*. The first essay deals with the through life-history of Dalani Begum where Dalani's love life has been discussed in details along with a comparative estimate of the love of Dalani with that of Shaibalini and finally Dalani's love is made more glorious than Shaibalini's love. The conjugal life of Dalani has been discussed and analysed in the light of the following points—Dalani's heart is the reservoir of unlimited love, it is the ocean of deep love, that she has created a heaven of love in the luxurious abode of the Nawab. In the second essay following the same principles he has discussed the character of Pratap. The basic strength of Yogendranath's criticism is his highly impassioned expression, imaginative fervor coupled with moralistic strain. Yogendranath's expression of grief for Dalani is one of his many hyperbolic expressions—"We shall have to weep for Dalani throughout the life—she shall never be forgotten in life."[34] At the same time such remarks sufficiently expresses his romantic attitude coupled with love of beauty, for example: "Shaibalini's love is like a deep river—too much forceful to be merged with the ocean."[35] and Dalani's love is "like a lake with its banks beautified with fragrant flowers, its deep water with a little fickleness on the surface—a sight captivating to the eyes of the spectators."[36]

In his analysis of the character of Pratap, the critic characterized Bankim as a social teacher. Hence, he concluded his essay with conviction that Bankim's motive to show the cowardly, timid, passionate Bengali society through Pratap might be successful there be Pratap's in every Bengali family.[37]

Yogendranath, though maintains conformity to the contemporary trend so far as excess of emotion, Bankim worship and moral probing area concerned, has gone beyond it in his analytic and argumentative skill. Analysing Shaibalini's inability to drown herself in the Ganges and Rupasi's marriage with Pratap the critic said: the love which teaches self-sacrifice with Rupasi became inevitable in order to prepare the ground to forget Shaibalini.[39] This shows a direction of criticism which gives the impression of psycho-analytic method.

AKSHAY CHANDRA SARKAR (1846-1917)

Akshay Chandra Sarkar in his essay *British O Bangiya Chitrabali*[40] makes a comparative study of Chandrashekhar,

Shaibalini and Pratap with Arthur, Suyenibiesy and Lancelot of Alfred Tennyson's *Idylls of the King*.[41]

In this long essay, the critic has drawn our attention not only towards the attitude of Bankim but also towards the characteristics features of the characters. As for example he said that Chandrashekhar was born of the spiritual inspiration of the Aryan poet. While Arthur showed Western materialistic tendency; Chandrashekhar had a thirst for knowledge, he was a lover of peace, devoted to God and a critic of himself: and he believed that God as the absolute authority of everything. On the other hand, Arthur was active, spirited, and patriotic; to do away with the enemies and to punish the wrong doers was his religion and he did not depend upon God's judgement. Despite this difference of understanding the critic thought—"Both the conceptions are great, but the polarization is due to place and education."[42] The comparative estimate of Chandrashekhar and Arthur has been made in this light.

Making a comparative study of Shaibalini and Guinebier the critic said that the sin which the British poet Tennyson had found in Guinebier, the Aryan poet Bankim Chandra found the same in Shaibalini. But one inspired by materialism while the other by spiritualism. And it was due to this difference that Shaibalini's sin of mind was purified by her penance, but Guinebier's penance had its different consequence. Chandrashekhar accepted Shaibalani but Guinebier remained unaccepted in this life. The Aryan poet showed that love was the accomplishment of devotion while the British poet showed that love got perverse due to the fault of the individual.[43] Pratap and Lancelot, both were devoted to Masters, Pratap's love was pure but Lancelot's love was filthy on the basis of this point these two characters had been discussed.

He thought that the character of Pratap was created to develop the character of Shaibalini, and the character of Pratap was originally being thought of as a secondary character. But finally, Pratap is a principal one in the end.

In this long essay Akshay Chandra has made a dispassionate criticism of the characters of Chandrashekhar. He has followed the comparative method of criticism. This method has gained popularity in recent times.[44] Considering this Akshay Chandra may be given the status of one of precursors of moderns criticism. This method best brings out the merits and demerits of literary work.[45] But in the rudimentary stages of the comparative method of criticism, one must not expect the excellence of modern critics, from the hands critic of the Bankim age. However, Akshay Chandra deserves praise for just and accurate selection of parallel lines of both the texts under his comparative study.

HARIDAS BONDOPADHYAY

The next critical work on the novel *Chandrashekhar*, is Haridas Bondopadhyay's *Chandrashekhar O Rajani*.[46] In the beginning of this essay the structure of the book is discussed along with an overall introduction. He said that *Chandrashekhar*, despite being a historical novel was dominated by domestic characters and its plot had been designed with two different incidents. In the next section, the characters of Chandrashekhar, Pratap, Shaibalini and Doloni, etc. have been discussed. And, there, by making much comments as Bankim has expressing qualities,[47] and 'the writer has shown skill'[48] etc. he has tried to show the greatness of the writer.

But he very carefully discussed the reasons for readers' sympathy for Shaibalini. He said that Pratap and Shaibalini's childhood love was developed very firmly but it could not achieve finality due to social limitations. Chandrashekhar did not behave well with Shaibalini after marriage, and lastly, she was scolded by Pratap even though she left the house for him. The critic analysed these reasons for Shaibalini's popularity with readers. But he could not overcome the Neo-Hindu sentiment. According to him Chandrashekhar was an image of a country which have produced Buddha and Chaitanya, and that Shaibalini could not be said to be a Hindu wife in terms of Hindu ethics and codes.[49]

So, Haridas's critical attitude reveals a touch of Modernism over traditionalism, and it is for adherence to traditionalism that he could not accept Shaibalini as a Hindu woman in spite of his full sympathy for her.

RABINDRANATH TAGORE (1861-1941)

Rabindranath's critical remarks on the novel *Chandrashekhar*, are found in his essays *Shikshar Herfer*[50] and *Sahityarup*.[51] Rabindranath considered Chandrashekhar and Pratap as epitome of Bengali gentlemen.[52] Tagore attempted to trace the warmth of individual's life through the historical characters. He said that Chandrashekhar was a pandit, but in the novel this was not a point, what really mattered was how his personality had been reflected through language style incidents and the rhythm produced by the expressed and the unexpressed.[53] So he said that Bankimchandra had very ingeniously expressed the personality of Chandrashekhar. So, here, Rabindranath had pointed out the right approach towards Chadrashekhar evaluation, at the same time he had appreciated artist Bankim.

HEMENDRA PRASAD GHOSE (1876-1963)

The next dependable criticism of *Chandrashekhar*, was written by Hemendra Prasad Ghose in his essay *Bankimchandra*.[54] He had analysed the characters of the novel *Chandrashekhar*. Chandrashekhar, he said, was a spiritual hero with insatiable thirst for knowledge, softness of heart, and love. Pratap was self-restrained, dispassionate, heroic and magnanimous, Shaibalini was sharply intelligent, spirited, and passionate; Dalani was full of strength and sanctity of heart, Ramananda Swami was a philosopher, philanthropist and helping to others. These are the points on which the analysis of the characters rested.

Hemendra Prasad had the realization that probing of only ethic and ideal did not form the basis of literary criticism. He had treated the characters as normal human beings with usual merits and demerits. He said that despite all the superhuman qualities was nothing more than a human being. Our sympathy and emotion touched him because of the human weakness in him. That he was not a God but a human being was proved by his attempt to test Shaibalini.[55] The expression of life in Chandrashekhar which was told by Rabindranath Tagore had found a gradual development in Hemendra Prasad.

HARAN CHANDRA RAKSHIT

Certain modern critic has commented that even if Haran Chandra's attitude was guided by idealistic principles, seeds of pure criticism are scattered all over his critical work[56] *Bangasahitye Bankim.*[57] The statement bears some truth. Haran Chandra was an idealistic and ethical critic in the real sense of the term, but he was conscious of the fact that too much preponderance of ideals would make the creation laudatory. He said that the Hindu poet Bankim had created ideal characters like Sita and Sabitri, and at the same time he had created such doubtful characters like Shaibalini.[58] But whenever he had gone to give excuse to the readers his poetry became less aesthetic down and the ideal also degenerated. The critic rightly remarked that the writer had brought in entire irrelevant matters dream like Yoga, philosophy, and after life existence to show whether Shaibalini was polluted—her womanhood was demolished by Foster.[59] This remark show marks of literary criticism, but it is nothing new; even two decades before Hemchandra, Purnachandra Basu, the first critic of *Chandrashekhar*, drew our attention to those irrelevant points.

SHAILENDRANATH SARKAR

The next critical work to be reckoned with is Shailendranath Sarkar's *Chandrashekar Anushilan.*[60] According to the critic *Chandrashekhar*, is a romantic novel because under the shadow of historical characters the writer finds an opportunity to stress his imagination and above all, both uncanny and exaggeration are grounded in this book.[61] Shailendranath in the present essay tried to establish this supra-naturalism. Besides, he analysed the characters from the standpoint of morality and idealism.

According to Shailendranath the most unusual things in the book are the lonely night adventure of a Bengali woman with a Sahib and Sundari's going in to the Sahib's boat in disguise to rescue Shaibalini.[62] The ethical critic characterized Shaibalini as the greatest sinner, greatest harlot in the world. Attempting union with a paramour she had grossly violated the justice and ethics of Hindu religion. Pratap, violating the ethical norms wronged his wife at the cost of self-sacrifice.[63]

PRAMATHANATH SEN

Pramathanath Sen's *Chandrashekhar Charitra*[64] shows an excess of emotion and hero-worshiping attitude, but at the same time it is characterised by distinctive mark of literary assessment.

Pointing out the qualities of Chandrashekhar he said that Bankimchandra like Vyas and Balmiki had rendered immense service to the Hindu society by creating characters like Chandrashekhar. He had emotionally remarked: "The purification and pleasure of the mind derived from listening to the names of the holy place like Haridwar, Badrinath, Kedarnath, etc. the same can be have from listening to the name of Chandrashekhar."[65]

Pramathanath's critical approach is a combination of both the traditional and the modern trends. He said that burning of the books which were as good as his blood expressed his severe inner strife, the fire which was burning in his distressed heart for his beloved was symbolically expressed through the burning of books.[66] Doubtless the psycho-analytical discussion of the character of Chandrashekar and the symbolic meaning attributed to the burning of the books are new addition to *Chandrashekhar* criticism.

SURESHCHANDRA SEN

Chandrashekhar has been critically dealt with by Sureshchandra Sen in his *Kabyakatha*.[67] He tried to show Bankim's credit and originality in creating the historical character like Mirkashim and Taki Khan. He has very substantially analysed that Mirkashim, the Nawab of Bengal was a historical character. Like the Nawab of history he was active, just and patriotic but from the considerations of sense of humanity Mirkashim was a superb creation.[68] Sureshchandra's speciality is that he has brought out the man Mirkashim out of historical smoke, and he is the first man to probe into historical elements of this book.

KALIKUMAR SINGHA

Kalikumar Singha in his eulogistic essay *Shaibalini*[69] has sought to elaborate and explain the shortcomings and flaws in the character of Shaibalini as depicted by Bankim. The cause of Shaibalini's sufferings being rooted in herself, the critic poses the question, why she did not try to forget Pratap after having so nice a husband?[70] But the critic is so much possessed by the novel that he falls in love with Shaibalini and Pratap, and runs into emotional excess when he remarks, "We satisfied our lives by touching the feet of Pratap first and then Shaibalini."[71]

JITENDRALAL BASU

Jitendralal Basu, while discussing *Chandrashekhar* in his essay *Bankimchandra*[72] tried to explicate the sensitivity of the writer. He said that Bankim had created character like Pratap and Shaibalini to show the consequences of lack of self-restrain in family life. According to him, Bankim expressed his full regards to Indian philosophy through the expiation of Shaibalini.[73]

PRAFULLA KUAMR SARKAR

Critical discussions on *Chandrashekhar*, are there in Prafulla Kumar Sarkar's essay *Nitishikshay Bankimchandra.*[74] As the title itself suggests, Prafulla Kumar has seen Bankim as a moral teacher. He characterized Pratap as a 'human-God'[75] (Naradewata) and placed him above Dadhichi and said that Bankim inspired people in moral teaching by creating Pratap.

Prafulla Kumar's idea of literary aim seems to be traditional. According to him literature seeks to establish the eternal truths about humanity. He found that Bankim was successful in achieving this aim in *Chandrashekhar*. Pratap was burning example of this. Even if Prafulla Kumar has patronized the traditional approach of literary criticism, marks of progressive outlook are also there. For example, he said that Pratap had been suffering unbearable mental torture for Shaibalini's love—he was neither devil nor a God, he was just a human being. And therefore he has mitigated his mental torture by self-sacrifice.[76] Besides, explaining the vain attempt of Shaibalini's self-scrifice by drowning in the Ganga the critic said that Shaibalini failed because of her self-love and weak heart.[77] This sort of a solution is nothing more than an echo of his predecessors.

LALIT KUMAR BANDOPADHYAY (1275-1336)

Lalit Kumar's critical views on *Chandrashekhar*, are scattered in some of the contemporary essays[78] and books of essays.[79] In *Bankimchandrer Akshaikabali*, Lalit Kumar seeks to justify the title of the novel *Chandrashekhar*. He said that Shaibalini's hectic love, moral degradation and severe penance, Dalani's steady devotion to her husband, Sundari's friendship were all attractive lively and forceful things in the novel. Nevertheless, the liberal minded pure and self-restrained Brahmin Chandrashekhar formed the backbone of the novel. Hence the title is justified.[80] In the essay *Ma,* Lalit Kumar brings out the literary significance of lack of motherliness of the female characters in *Chandrashekhar*. Here he had discussed also the artistic necessity of the deaths of the mother's of Shaibalini and Chandrashekhar and also of Shaibalini's barrenness. He said that Shaibalini was not reluctant to have a child, she had all the urge for having a child which is indicated in her conversation with the disguised she-barber Sundari.[81] She was left baren because of her illicit and impassioned love, which was the main theme of the novel and that would have been barred by the arrival of a child, therefore, Bankim had kept her childless like Tennyson's Guinevier.[82] Explaining the reasons of the death of the mother's of Shaibalini and Chandrashakhar the critic said that intensity of the married Shaibalini's love for Pratap had made this death inevitable.[83] Lalit Kumar said that the English proverb 'Handsome is that handsome does' was highly applicable in case of Sundari.

In *Kabyasudha,* the critic has shown that Sundari's sacrifice for Shaibalini and her hard labour although indicated her genuine love, were nothing romantic adventure.[84] In the essay *Sakhi,* Lalit Kumar explained the nature of friendship with the female characters and the novelistic significance of these friendships. According to him Kulsam and Asmani are the developed from the Pesman. He said that in poetic drama there was no scope for love-making amongst the Sakhi's (friends), the heroine's action was the main thing, but Kulsam had violated it. The critic thought that this device was a necessity in order to make Dalani's actions of life more tragic. He believed that

Kulsam's boldness, steadiness, truthfulness and sympathy were equal to those of Shakespeare's Emilia.[85]

Lalit Kumar has delt with the various aspects of characterization in the novel Chandrashekhar hitherto ignored by other critics, and thus, drawn the attention of the readers to the art-form of the novel. Had he set his hands to other issues in the novel, Bankim criticism would have been more enriched.

BIPIN CHANDRA PAL (1858-1932)

Bipin Chandra Pal in some of his scattered essays[86] has critically discussed *Chandrashekhar*. He has initiated his discussion basing upon classical trend. Bipin Chandra pointed out that *Chandrashekhar* was a novel of amatory sentiment and in the background of the ancient Indian rhetoric (alankar shastra) Pratap was the 'dhiradatta' and Chandrashekhar, 'Dhiroprasanta' of the amatory sentiment.[87]

The time gap has led him to take stock of to the then Bengali society. As a believer of materialism in literature, Bipin Chandra said that Bankim has supplemented the objectives of Bengal Renaissance by giving the total picture of the Bengali character in the perspective of Bengali society in addition to his creation of beauty.[88] He further said that by transmuting the epicurism of the then educated Bongalees into romance Bankim had attempted to develop and beautify it by co-ordinating epicurism and Asceticism.[89]

It is to be noticed that Bipin Chandra started the discussion in the classical method of criticism and ended in the historical method. Moreover, an important point is that Bipin Chandra is the first critic to make an important probing of the influence of contemporary life and the creation of beauty there upon.

SHASHANKA MOHAN SEN (1872-1928)

The next criticism on *Chandrashekhar*, is found in Shashanka Mohan Sen's *Bangabai*.[90] He is perhaps the first critic of Bankim to evaluate his individual work in relation to his other works.[91] He did not consider Chandrashekhar in isolation, he viewed it as a part of Bankim's world of fiction. According to him *Bishabriksha* might be the first domestic novel of Bankim but *Chandrashekhar*, was a better and greater artistic creation. He said that *Chandrashekhar*, combined together the imaginative force of *Kapalkundala* with the ingenuinity of *Bishabriksha*, and the qualities of Nabakumar, Hemchandra and Nagendranath combining together had been manifested in Pratap and Kundanandini except her silent grace appeared here as the glamorous Shaibalini.[92]

Another characteristic of Shashanka Mohan's criticism was a probing of Bankim-psychology. He clearly brought out the evolution in Bankim's treatment of conjugal love. He opined that in the Indian ideals of conjugal love there was not merely a contract, it was more that in the sense that once marriage was solemnized, it could not be undone. Bankim realized this ancient truth that adultery must not have any place in the ideals of conjugal love. Hence, he made Shaibalini undergo ordeals.[93] Shashanka Mohan remarked that the creation of the adulterous character of Shaibalini left Bankim dissatisfied which prompted him to set his hands on *Krishnakanter Uil*.[94]

Shashanka Mohan is the first critic to trace fatalism in Chandrashekhar. He said—"Is it less working of fate for the glamorous Shaibalini to have the book-worm Chandrashekhar?"[95]; and sought the answer to the question of Shaibalini to Chandrashekhar—"We (Pratap and Shaibalini) two flowers blossomed in the same tree—why did you tear?"[96] Shashanka Mohan thus introduced a new dimension to Chandrashekhar criticism.

AKSHAY KUMAR DUTTAGUPTA

Akshay Kumar Duttagupta in *Bankimchandra*[97] viewed *Chandrashekhar*, from a wider perspective. His criticism includes analysis of artistic beauty of the novel, artistic significance of the characters, construction of plot and comparative studies with similar works in English literature.

He remarked that Bankimchandra believed in psychic force, but the motive with which it was introduced in Chandrashekhar had spoiled the art. He had further pointed out that the Dalani captured the writar's sympathy so much that after her death the rest of the story suffered a setback due to the writer's negligence.[98] About the narrative art he said that Pratap-Saibalini's swimming into the deep water, the description of landscape following Shaibalini's mountaineering expedition, the feelings of the infinite in the Ganges and on its banks in moonlit night, description of Shaibalini's dream in Foster's boat and her visions of hell etc. were very strongly poetic. "Discussing the plot-structure the critic said that in *Chandrashekhar*, the method of parallelism used in English literature had been followed. Two separate love stories ran parallel to each other and therefore, the grace of one and the blemish of the other were presented vividly."[99] He remarked that the character of Dalani might not have anything extra-ordinary from the artistic point of view, but it was successful from the standpoint of parallelism.

Shaibalini in spite of being a sinner in personal life draws the sympathy of the critic. And that leads him to ask—"what care did Chandrashekhar take to attract her towards him after he married her?"[100] He gave reasons for his sympathy. He said: "The wound created by fruitless passion of love in a very soft and silent corner of her mind which bleeds."[101] This draws our sympathy for her.

Akshay Kumar gave a poetic implication of Shaibalini's penance which according to Shashanka Mohan was introduced as the directive of Shastra. He said that Shaibalini's penance "Is right and meaningful from the standpoint of both shastra and poetry."[102] But he did not explain the poetic justification of 'Shaibalini's penance. Akshay Kumar's *Chandrashekhar* seeks to make a literary and artistic appraisal of *Chandrashekhar*, and in it social prejudices, religious bias and contemporary outlook do not interfere in correct appraisal of the novel.

KSHITINDRANATH THAKUR (1869-1932)

Kshitindranath Thakur's criticism of *Chandrashekhar* can be traced in his book *Art O Sahitya*.[103] His main points of discussion are the artistic significance of the two scenes of the Shaibalini's swimming in the Ganges. Kshitindranath believed that the artistic motto of literature was to maintain naturalness and establish the truth. Shaibalini's swimming scenes had been discussed from this standpoint. It showed the critic's spirit of literary nationalism. He was pleased by Bankim's creation of artistic beauty, but he could not agree to the western concept of 'art for arts sake'. He said that the second scene of swimming where Shaibalini jumped into the river rescuing Pratap from the British boat was as natural as beautiful. So, artistically it was successful,[104] but about first scene of swimming he took exception to, it was highly unnatural on the part of a girl of below twelve to attempt suicide for the pangs of love and then her retreat,[105] but this impropriety was compensated to a great extent by the description of external beauty especially in the embracing scene. But the critic contradicts his own statement when he considers Shaibalini-Pratap love episode from social and ethical point of view. He could not support this from Bramanistic standpoint and condemn this because of its "Western odour" (Bilaiti Gandha).[106] Here the conservative Kshitindranath overpowers the artistic Kshitindranath, and he slashes the swimming scene as unnatural and heinous.

Such duality of mind of Kshitindranath revealed in the essay has spilled much of his great arguments.

HARAPRASAD SHASTRI (1853-1931)

Haraprasad Shastri in his brief discussion of Chandrashekhar in the essay *Bankimchandra*[107] pointed out the thematic defects as well as Bankim's imaginative force. He said that Mirkashim-Dalani episode seems to be inconsistent with the main plot, it could have been shaped as a separate novel.[108] He further said "There is no greater thing than the dream of Shaibalini in Bengali.[109]

In fact, the strongest human-ambition and its fruitless consequence depicted in *Chandrashekhar* glorify the inherent romanticism in Bankim, and Haraprasad indicated this in his essay.

SARAT CHANDRA CHATTOPADHYAY (1876-1938)

Sarat Chandra Chattopadhyay draws a line between the attitudes of the ancients and the moderns in Chandrashekhar criticism, in his casual discussion of the same in *Adhunik Sahityer Kaifiat.*[110] He raised a new question in *Chandrashekhar*—criticism and indirectly created a consciousness about the new critical ideals. He observed that beginning from Shaibalini's attempt to drown herself to her leaving of her husband's house everything depended upon her adolescent love. But the then readers where happy with the penance of Shaibalini because of her wrong doing, and they appreciated the self-sacrifice of Pratap. But the modern readers viewed it in a different way, they liked to see it Shaibalini's love was strong enough for such an injustice. They would say, even if manliness was there in Pratap's self-sacrifice on the plea of war, it could not be supported since by this he had done injustice to his family members and relatives.[111]

HEMENDRA KUMAR ROY (1888-1963)

Hemendra Kumar's criticism of *Chandrashekhar* in *Sekele Bankim*[112] resembles the attitudes of Sarat Chandra. He said that Shaibalini loved Pratap since infancy and it strongly developed with age and "the force of this love is a sufficient incentive for her to do this wrong."[113] According to Hemendra Kumar, Shaibalini's action is not only natural but also based on the 'science of human mind'.[114] It is to be noticed that this question of the science of human mind was first raised by Hemendra Kumar.

SATYA RANJAN SENGUPTA

Satya Ranjan has discussed *Chandrashekhar* in his essay *Bangla Sahitya Bankimchandra*.[115] In spite of his dominant Hindu attitude Satya Ranjan's discussion shows modern tendencies. He did not approve of a married woman's leaving the husband's house from the standpoint of Hindu ideals, but he accepted it as natural because Shaibalini had no other alternative.[116] So, his traditionalism was mixed up with modern liberalism. He said that human heart was not confined to ethical restrictions. The aforesaid remark shows a modern approach to life.

Satya Ranjan goes a step further to trace the influence of Vaishnab Sahitya[117] in Shaibalini's love, he finds in the impassioned love of Shaibalini, a story impact of *Baranarir Abhisar*[118] described by the Vaishnab poet.

RAMSAHAYA VEDANTASASTRI

The next critical work to be discussed in Ramsahaya's *Shaibalini O Pratap*.[119] The body of this essay built upon the life history of Pratap and Shaibalini. The elements found in Bankim criticism in the initial stage like excess of emotion, highly poetic language, are present in this essay. Ramsahaya, recreating the character according to his own feeling described in a highly poetic language how they had either supplemented the ethical norms or violated it. Making a comparison of the nature of love of Pratap and Shaibalini he said:

Pratap's love is the heavenly ambrosia, of sacrifice, so its makes him heavenly, Shaibalini's love is the earthly drink, the adulterated oil of enjoyment, so it had led her to suffer the pranks of hell in her lifetime.[120]

About Pratap he further commented:

> Pratap is a Brahmin in self-discipline, a kshatriya in bravely, a baishaya in diligence, a shudra in service.... He is as grave as the Himalayan as patient as the earth, as deep as the sea.[121]

Vedantasastri viewed very severely the immoral side of the character of Shaibalini. Described Shaibalini's leaving of the house as an act of a harlot, and Shaibalini after her penance had been described by him as the ornament of the Godly Chandrasekhar's head.

ANUBHUTI BHATTACHARJEE

Anubhuti Bhattacharjee, a contemporary of Ramsahaya Vedantasastri was an orthodox as Vedatasastri. Discussing Pratap and Shaibalini's love in the essay *Bankimbabur Upanyase Premer Naitik Chitra*[122] the critic comes to the conclusion that Shaibalini's love for Pratap is luscious and unsanctified in the eye of Shastra, and so leading her through the ordeals of penance the writer has rendered some service to the society.[123]

RAMESH CHANDRA BASU

Ramesh Chandra Basu has written a brief criticism of *Chandrashekhar* in his book *Bankim Sahitye Manabatar Adarsha*.[124] He upheld the view that Bankimchandra in his literary works had tried to focus human values.[125] The critic heard the great proclamation of modern literature, when Bankim made Pratap say: "What will you understand, you are a saint."[126]

MANJUGOPAL BHATTACHARJEE

Rationalistic, factual and a subtle observer of characters Manjugopal Bhattacharjee has written criticism of *Chandrashekhar* in his essay—*Arter Dik Diya Bankimer Kono Chitra Ki Asangata.*[127] Manjugopal's attention was directed towards the analysis of the characters of Pratap, Shaibalini and Chandrashekhar and particularly how far these characters were appropriate from artistic point of view. He further tried to investigate the psychological realm of the writer's mind.

As a believer of Bankim literary ideals Manjugopal said about the psychological change in Shaibalini, that the artistic skill in Shaibalini's change was due to the society. But a sudden change might give a semblance of disbelief. So, the writer created the conflict in Shaibalini's mind by a blow of being deserted by Pratap, and a doubt whether Chandrashekhar would accept her or not. And thus, by affecting her balance of mind the novelist prepared ground for her being attracted by Chandrashekhar. Shaibalini's final gesture to place Chandrashekhar in the elevated position of God and to think of Pratap far below him was also "a reaction of her imbalanced mind".[128]

Explaining the psychic force described in the book Manjugopal also like his predecessors found it artistically substandard. But defending Bankim he said that as *Chandrashekhar* is not a realistic novel like *Krishnakanter Uil*, especially when all its incidents are touched with a semblance of unnaturalness. So according to him introduction of psychic force was not unreasonable.[129]

SUBODH CHANDRA SENGUPTA

Subodh Chandra Sengupta in the context of *Chandrashekhar* criticism in his essay *Bankimchandra O Saratchandra*[130] mainly discussed about the difference of understanding of the value of life of the two writers. Thus, he said that Bankimchandra had given priority to ethical restraints through his portrayal of

Pratap while Saratchandra through Debdas had given greatest value to the feelings of heart—Pratap loved Shaibalini but because he had not given this right by *Shastra,* he deserted on the plea of it being lust, on the other hand Debdas thought it to be a great sin not to marry the woman he loved.

Subodh Chandra's attitude is modern, and his critical ideals are also based upon the modern trend. And he has searched for the multifarious facets of this life through Pratap. He remarked that Pratap's self-sacrifice was an outward defeat and through it appeared brightly the glorious victory of his mind.[131] Analysing the significance of the characters of Pratap and Debdas Subodh Chandra said that Pratap symbolizes the human strength where Debdas symbol of the limitless weakness of man.[132]

RADHARAMAN CHAKRABORTY & SATYAKINKAR MUKHAPADHYAY

Radharaman Chakraborty and Satyakinkar Mukhapadhyay are the co-author of the critical work *Chandrashekhar Tattba*[133] which is an exhaustive discussion on *Chandrashekhar* in its various aspects.

It is very interesting to note their justification of the title of the novel, which clearly brings out their traditional outlook. According to them the novel could have been better named as Shaibalini since the chief purpose of the book was the solution of a critical social question following Shaibalini's love. Again, as the believer of ethics they thought that Shaibalini being a sinner it has been wiser to name the book after the holy *Chandrashekhar*.[134]

Another remarkable feature of their criticism which deserves special mention is their explanation of the naming of the characters. Explaining the significance of the names of characters they said Chandrashekhar was another name of Mahadev and the Chandrashekhar of the novel was depicted in that ideal. Shaibalini meant a river and she was as impassioned as a river, and Dalani had floated everything by virtue of the power of her chastity, etc.[135] The critic however had not tried to analyse the inner conflicts of the characters. The occasional reference of a conflict had been solved ethically. The example, the critic said that Shaibalini has committed serious offence hence her penance in accordance with the severe *Hindu Shastra* and Pratap had been thrown into death in order to uphold the conjugal ideals.[136]

Following modern western literature, they initiated the discussion regarding the introduction of the sub-plot in the novel. The critic said in the chapter *Bankimchandrer Upar Pashchayatya Prabhab*[137] that the tangle of the Dalani-Mirkashim sub-plot with the main plot is an imitation of the English complex plot. They found the influence of Milton and Dante in the gruesome pictures of hell given in the book.[138] This sort of an approach however is a new addition in *Chandrashekhar* criticism.

The next vital characteristic of this critical work is to compare through evaluation the attitudes and literary ideals of two pillars of Bengali literature—Bankimchandra and Saratchandra. They said that Bankimchandra was a believer of Hindu Shastra and therefore, love between Shaibalini and Pratap could not become successful, and that Saratchandra was a believer of the appeal of heart, Debdas is the example of it.[139] This opinion is an echo of Subodh Chandra, but the critics originality is found when they said that how dangerous and disastrous can be the position of woman for not having the desired union. Bankimchandra holds this question in *Chandrashekhar* and his attempted a solution but Saratchandra in Debdas has showed the extent of degradation on the part of a man, but no attempt is made towards solution.

Besides, the justification of title and the naming of characters, analysis of the sub-plot and the comparative study between Bankim and Saratchandra they also sought to justify the headlines of the chapters. They pointed out the defects in the presentation of historical characters, development and achievement of characters; and the motive forces which guided them. They were also not blind to the western influence and what is most striking in their joint endeavor is all comprehensive view of the novel. Their book *Chandrashekhar Tattba* shows their adherence both to the traditional and as well modern approach to the study of *Chandrashekhar.*

HEMENDRANATH DASGUPTA

Hemendranath Dasgupta in his essay *Bankimchandrer Naricharitra,*[140] analysed the events of Shaibalini's life. He said that Shaibalini was not only a brave and dauntless woman, womanliness was the source of all her activities and women-emancipation was voiced by her. He clearly said: "We like to see the womanliness of Shaibalini as a whole without being prejudiced by this flaw or that defect or that sin of her mind."[141]

Hemendranath in his elaborate discussion of Shaibalini has laid emphasis upon her human feelings and here he has found her womanliness and the woman-emancipation championed by her. He is the first critic to find the tone of woman-emancipation in *Chandrashekhar.*

PRAFULLA KUMAR MANDAL

Prafulla Kumar Mandal is another critic of sound judgement and modern attitude. The critic in his essay *Shaibalini' O Kiranmoyee*[142] tried to point-out a fundamental difference between Bankimchandra and Saratchandra and further making a comparative estimate of Shaibalini and Kiranmoyee had tried to show their similarities and dissimilarities along with an artistic evaluation of the characters.

He said that Bankim literature was the creation of his Age, while Sarat literature was created in a modern environment. Therefore, realism was faded before idealism in Bankim literature, while it had dominated Sarat-literature. The critic said that Shaibalini of Bankim was reborn as Kiranmoyee of Saratchandra. But he believed that realism was not totally absent in Bankim literature. This realism was indicated when Shaibalini told Pratap even after her penance that she could not find happiness so long he was alive, so he must meet her in his life.[143] That Shaibalini's love was not destroyed even in stern asceticism her love for Pratap knew no death.[144] This was indicated by this remark. It is a good step towards *Chandrashekhar* evaluation, because the critic here makes for the permanent appeal of *Chandrashekhar*

Through a comparative study of Shaibalini and Kiranmoyee the critic discovered the influence of Age. He said both Shaibalini and Kiranmoyee had revolted against the circumstances; both even if socially degraded were not degraded in respect of self-sacrifice. But from the consideration of the Age Shaibalini's penance was a necessity, because her restoration in her husband's house was the main trouble with Bankim. Shaibalini was an uneducated woman of village while Kiranmoyee was a highly educated woman of town. Education was at the root of Kiranmoyee's revolt and hence she was more critical, whereas Shaibalini was free from complexities because of her lack of education, and this was the cause of her being diverted for the love of Pratap.

But the artistic evaluation in this essay is the most striking thing. According to the critic, Shaibalini and Kiranmoyee may be sinners to the society but from the standpoint of literature both the characters are fine and wonderful. Whatsoever blemish might be there in Shaibalini's leaving her husband's house, the artistic beauty of the book absolutely depend upon these blemishes. Shaibalini left her husband's house with Foster but she did not to arms against Foster to depend herself and she saved her honour but putting this weapon on Foster's breast.[145]

Literature is the artistic representation of life. Prafulla Kumar in his has tried to view it in this light. His essay is a valuable edition in *Chandrashekhar* criticism with all its simplicity of language, analytic skill, psychological insight and argumentative skill.

CHAPALAKANTA BHATTACHARJEE

Chapalakanta Bhattacharjee is the last critic of Chandrashekhar before Bankim-Centenary. In his essay *Debdas-Gobindalal-Pratap-Tulanay O Prabhede,*[146] Chapalakanta has shown the similarities and dissimilarities of the three characters. Debdas. Gobindalal, Pratap all are dejected lovers, but none have transformed their dejection into malice, rather they have compromised in a spirit of self-sacrifice. The critic said, Pratap and Shaibalini, even if tempted by circumstances, have kept it under control, on the other had, Debdas and Gobindalal surrendered to circumstances and are compelled to accept the failure of life.[147]

SUMMING UP

Criticisms of diverse tastes by thirty-six critics on *Chandrashekhar* form the subject matter of this chapter. In many of the critical writings there were conflicts between traditional ideals and modern value judgements. Controversies centred round the character of Shaibalini and introduction of Yogic cult in the novel. The critics of Bankim and post Bankim Age discussed the mainly the characters, Bankim's psychology and artistic merits of the novel. The vision of the critics of the Bankim Age in most cases was limited by the Age while modern note was struck by the critics of the post Bankim period. Of the characters, Shaibalini, Dalani, Chandrashekhar and Pratap were widely discussed.

References

1. Basu, Purna Chandra, *Shaibalini, Aryadarshan*, Baishakh, 1284 B.S. pp. 33-43 & Asharh, 1284 B.S., pp. 128-35. Reprinted: *Kabyasundari,* Shraban, 1287 B.S., pp. 82-110.
2. Basu, Purna Chandra, *Shaibalini, Aryadarshan*, Baishakh, 1284 B.S., pp. 37-38.
3. Basu, Purna Chandra, *Kabyasundari,* Shraban, 1287 B.S., pp. 119-21.
4. Basu, Purna Chandra, *Shaibalini, Aryaderahan*, p. 134.
5. *Ibid.*
6. *Ibid.*, p. 34.
7. *Ibid.*, p. 41.
8. *Ibid.*, (Asharh), pp. 129-33.
9. *Ibid.*, Kabya-Sundari, Shraban, 1287 B.S., pp. 117-18.
10. Mukhapadhyay, Arunkumar, *Bangla Samalochanar Itihas*, Shraban, 1372 B.S., p. 103.
11. Basu, Purna Chandra, *Shaibalini,* Asharh, 1284 B.S. Aryadarshan, p. 132.
12. *Ibid.*, Baishak, p. 33.
13. Srilo, Lakshinarayan, *Chandrashekhar-Shaibalini, Aryadarshan*, Poush, 1284 B.S., pp. 408-14.
14. *Ibid.*, p. 409.
15. Srilo, Lakshinarayan, op. cit., p. 410.
16. Chakraborty, Lokenath, *Shaibalini Charitra Samalochana, Aryadarshan,* Bhadra, 1284 B.S., pp. 241-55.

17. Chakraborty, Lokenath, *Anusangik Patra (Chandrashekhar-Shaibalini), Aryadarshan*, Poush, 1284 B.S., pp. 414-22.
18. Chakraborty, Lokenath, *Shaibalini Charitra Samalochana: Aryadarshan,* Bhadra, 1284 B.S., pp. 244-55.
19. Chakraborty, Lokenath, *Anushilon Patra (Chandrashekhar-Shaibalini), Aryadarshan*, Poush, 1284 B.S., pp. 419-20.
20. Chakraborty, Lokenath, op. cit., p. 417.
21. *Ibid.*, p. 416.
22. Chakraborty, Lokenath, op. cit., p. 420.
23. Chakraborty, Lokenath, op. cit., Bhadra, 1284 B.S., p. 253.
24. Sannyal, Bhabani Gopal, *Aristotoler Poetics O Shahitya Tattba,* 1st publication, Shraban, 1375 B.S., p. 54.
25. Chakraborty, Lokenath, *Chandrashekhar (Samalochana),* Nabyabharat. 1st part, 6th issue, Agrahayan, 1290 B.S., pp. 297-313.
26. *Ibid.*, p. 308.
27. *Ibid.*, pp. 297-307.
28. *Ibid.*, pp. 307-13.
29. *Ibid.*, p. 298.
30. *Ibid.*, pp. 312-13.
31. Vidyabhusan, Yogendranath, *Dalani Begum, Aryadarshan*, Asharh, 1285 B.S., pp. 1-12.
32. Vidyabhusan, Yogendranath, *Pratap, Kalpana*, 2nd year, Ashwin, 1288, Bhadra, 1289 B.S., pp. 47-50, 92-94, 123-27, 162-67.
33. Vidyabhusan, Yogendranath, *Dalani Begum*, p. 12.
34. *Ibid.*, p. 2.
35. *Ibid.*
36. Vidyabhusan, Yogendranath, *Pratap*, p. 167.
37. *Ibid.*, p. 168.
38. *Ibid.*, p. 94.
39. Sarkar, Akshay Kumar, *British O Bangiya Chitrabali, Nabajiban*, 2nd Voume, 6th issue, Poush, 1292 B.S., pp. 321-35 & 2nd Vol. 8th issue, Falgun, 1292 B.S., pp. 478-93.
40. *Ibid.* (Introduction).
41. *Ibid.*, p. 331 (Poush, 1292 B.S.).
42. *Ibid.*, pp. 473-93.
43. Bandopadhyay, Asit Kumar, *Somalochanar Katha,* 3rd Print, January, 1971, pp. 24-26.
44. Das, Shrish Chandra, *Sahitya Sandarshan*, 5th Edition, 1966, pp. 190-91.

45. Bondopadhyay, Haridas, *Chandrashekhar O Rajani, Kalpana*, 6th year, Asharh, 1296 B.S., pp. 213-20.
46. *Ibid.*, p. 215.
47. *Ibid.*, p. 216.
48. *Ibid.*, p. 214.
49. Tagore, Rabindranath, *Sankalap*, (Shikshar Herpher, 1299 B.S.), Viswa-Bharati, 1973, p. 15.
50. Tagore, Rabindranath, *Sahityarup*, 1335 B.S.
51. Tagore, Rabindranath, *Sankalan*, p. 15.
52. Tagore, Rabindranath, *Bankimchandra, Viswa-Bharati*, 1973, p. 100.
53. Ghose, Hemendra Prasad, *Bankimchandra, Dasi*, January, 1396, pp. 6-18.
54. *Ibid.*, pp. 6-7.
55. Sengupta, Subodh Chandra, *Bangla Somalochanar Parichay*, 1st Pub. Magh, 1376 B.S., p. 157.
56. Rakshit, H.C., *Banga Sahitye Bankim*, 1st Pub., 1899.
57. Rakshit, H.C., *Banga Sahitye Bankim,* 3rd edn., 24 Pargana, Poush 1317 B.S., p. 73.
58. *Ibid.*, p. 70.
59. Sarkar, S.N., *Chandrashekhar Anushilan, Prayas*, Jan., 1900, pp. 18-31.
60. *Ibid.*, p. 18.
61. *Ibid.*, pp. 20-28.
62. *Ibid.*, pp. 28-31.
63. Sen, Pramathanath, *Chandrashekhar Charitra, Sahitya*, 18th year, 2nd Issue, Jaishtha, 1314 B.S., pp. 92-105.
64. *Ibid.*, p. 93.
65. *Ibid.*, p. 99.
66. Sen, Suresh Chandra, *Kabyakatha, (Bankimchandra O Musalman Sampraday)*, 1909, pp. 39-59.
67. *Ibid.*, pp. 51-55.
68. Singha, Kalikumar, *Shaibalini, Jamuna*, Magh. 1316 B.S., pp. 317-20.
69. *Ibid.*, p. 318.
70. *Ibid.*, p. 320.
71. Basu, Jitendralal, *Bankimchandra, Bangadarshan*, 10th year, 4th issue, Shraban, 1317 B.S., pp. 169-80.
72. *Ibid.*, pp. 171-72.

73. Sarkar, Prafulla Kumar, *Niti Shikshay Bankimchandra, Bangadarshan*, 1318, Repd. Chattopadhyay, Nakul (ed). *P.K. Sarkarer Prabandha Sangraha*, 1st Publication, Shraban, 1376 B.S.
74. *Prafulla Kumar Sarkarer Prabandha Sangraha*, p. 51.
75. *Ibid.*, pp. 57-58.
76. *Ibid.*, p. 51.
77. (a) Bandopadhyay, Lalit Kumar, *Bankimchandrer Akshyaikabali, Bharatbarsha*, Asharh, 1322 B.S., pp. 6-11.
    (b) Bandopadhyay, L.K. *Ma, Bharatbarsha*, Shraban, 1322, pp. 264-82.
    (c) Bandopadhyay, L.K., *Dui Bhagini, Bharatbarsha*, Bhadra, 1323 B.S., pp. 391-407.
78. (a) Bandopadhyay, L.K., *Kabyasudha*, Kartik, 1323 B.S.
    (b) Bandopadhyay, L.K., *Sakhi,* 1328 B.S.
    (c) Bandopadhyay, L.K., *Premer Katha*, Jaishtha, 1327 B.S.
79. Bandopadhyay, L.K., *Bankimchandrer Akshyaikabali*, p. 10.
80. Bandopadhyay, Lalit Kumar, *Ma*, p. 277.
81. *Ibid.*
82. *Ibid.*, pp. 275-76.
83. Bandopadhyay, Lalit Kumar, *Kabyadudha*, p. 25.
84. Bandopadhyay, Lalit Kumar, *Sakhi*, pp. 49-52.
85. (a) Pal, Bipin Chandra, *Shirshak-Dharma-Niti O Art, Narayan*, 2nd part, 5th issue, Ashwin, 1322 B.S., pp. 1173-74.
    (b) Pal, Bipin Chandra, *Banglar Nabajuger Katha (Ekadash Katha), Bangabani*, 2nd year, 1st part, 1st issue, Falgun, 1329, pp. 90-98.
    (c) Pal, Bipin Chandra, *Banglar Nabajuger Katha (Dwadash Katha), Bangabani*, 2nd year, 1st part, 2nd issue, Chaitra, 1329 B.S.
    (d) Pal, Bipin Chandra, *Nabajuger Bangla Sahitye Bankimchandra, Nabyabharat*, Bhadra, 1330 B.S., pp. 235-49.
86. Pal, Bipin Chandra, *Shirshak-Dharma-Niti O Art*, pp. 1173-74.
87. Pal, Bipin Chandra, *Banglar Nabajuger Katha (Ekadash Katha)*, p. 94.
88. Pal, Bipin Chandra, *Banglar Nabajuger Katha (Dwadash Katha)*, p. 226.
89. Sen, Shashanka Mohan, *Bangabani* (1st & 2nd part), Dhaka Albert Library, 1915.
90. Ramnarayan, *Bankimchandra O Shashanka Mohan, Desh*, 2nd year, 26th issue, 4th Jaishtha, 1342 B.S., p. 47.
91. Sen, Shashanka Mohan, *Bangabani,* pp. 65-66.
92. *Ibid.*

93. *Ibid.*, pp. 67-70.
94. *Ibid.*, p. 66.
95. *Bankim Rachanabali, (Chandrashekar) Part-I*, Sahitya Samsad, 5th Pub. 1376 B.S., p. 468.
96. Duttagupta, Akshay Kumar, *Bankimchandra*, 1327.
97. Duttagupta, Akshay Kumar, *Bankimchandra,* 2nd edn, Jaishtha, 1382, p. 172.
98. *Ibid.*, p. 147.
99. *Ibid.*, p. 174.
100. *Ibid.*, p. 175.
101. *Ibid.*, p. 147.
102. Thakur, Kshitindranath, *Art of Sahitya*, Magh, 8, 1329 B.S.
103. *Ibid.*, pp. 104-07.
104. *Ibid.*, p. 148.
105. *Ibid.*
106. Shastri, H.P., *Bankimchandra, Masik Basumati*, 1329, pp. 417-22, 604-08.
107. *Haraprasad Rachanabali, Pt. II,* 1st Pub. Poush, 1366 B.S., p. 53.
108. *Ibid.*, p. 53.
109. Chattopadhyay, S.C., *Adhunik Sahityer Kaifiat, Sangabani*, 2nd year, 1st part, 6th issue, Shraban, 1330 B.S., pp. 681-85.
110. *Ibid.*, p. 684.
111. Roy, Hemendra Kumar, *Sekele Bankim, Jamuna*, 13th year, 7th issue, Kartik, 1330 B.S., pp. 387-94.
112. *Ibid.*, p. 392.
113. *Ibid.*
114. Sengupta, Satya Ranjan, *Bangla Sahitye Bankim, Archana*, Vol. 21, 6th issue, Shraban, 1331 B.S., pp. 215-22.
115. *Ibid.*, p. 220.
116. *Rupalagi anakhi jure gune man bhor Prati anga lagi kande prati anga mor.*
117. Sengupta, Satya Ranjan, op. cit., p. 219.
118. Vedantasastri, Ramsahaya, *Shaibalini O Pratap, Archana*, Vol. 22, 10th issue, Agrahayan, 1332 B.S., pp. 372-378 & Poush, 1332 B.S., pp. 394-98.
119. *Ibid.*, p. 374.
120. *Ibid.*, p. 375.
121. Bhattacharjee, A.J. *Bankimbabur Upanyase Premer Naitik Chitra, Manasi O Marmabani,* Year-18, Part-I, Issue-IV, 1333 B.S., pp. 328-33.

122. *Ibid.*, p. 332.
123. Basu, R.C., *Bankim Sahitye Manabatar Adarsha, Sabuj Patra*, 1334 B.S.
124. *Ibid.*, p. 636.
125. *Bankim Rachanabali, Sahitya Samsad.*
126. Bhattacharjee, M.G., *Arter dik diya Bankimer kona charitra ki asangata, Panchapushpa*, Chaitra, 1336 B.S., pp. 1675-1701.
127. Bhattacharjee, Manjugopal, op. cit., p. 1700.
128. *Ibid.*, pp. 1700-01.
129. Sengupta, Subodh Chandra, *Bankimchandra O Saratchandra, Bichitra*, Magh, 1337 B.S., pp. 164-71.
130. *Ibid.*, pp. 168-69.
131. *Ibid.*, p. 169.
132. Chakraborty, Radharaman & Mukhopadhyay, Satyakinkar, *Chandrashekhar Tattba,* Baishak Purnima, 1339 B.S.
133. *Ibid.*, p. 11.
134. *Ibid.*, p. 12.
135. *Ibid.*, pp. 53-54.
136. *Ibid.*, pp. 70-72.
137. *Ibid.*, pp. 71-72.
138. Chakraborty, Radharaman & Mukhapadhyay, Satyakinkar, op. cit., pp. 53-54.
139. Dasgupta, Hemendranath, *Bankimchandrer Naricharitra, Panchapushpa*, Agrahayan, 1339 B.S., pp. 841-71.
140. *Ibid.*, p. 815.
141. Mandal, Prafulla Kumar, *Shaibalini O Kiranmoyee, Archana*, 32 years, 3rd Issue, Baishak, 1342 B.S., pp. 77-81.
142. *Bankim Rachanabali, Sahitya Samsad*, 5th Pub., Chaitra, 1376 B.S., p. 474.
143. Mandal, Prafulla Kumar, *Shaibalini O Kiranmoyee*, p. 81.
144. Mandal, Prafulla Kumar, op. cit., p. 79.
145. Bhattacharjee, Chapalakanta, *Debdas-Gobindalal-Pratap-Tulanay O Prabhede, Desh*, 2nd year, 34th Issue, Asharh 28, Saturday, 1342 B.S., pp. 30-32.
146. Bhattacharjee, Chapalakanta, op. cit., p. 32.
147. *Ibid.*, op. cit., p. 32.

8
Krishnakanter Uil

GIRIJA PRASANNA ROY CHOWDHURY (1862-1899)

Bankimchandra-Krishnakanter Uil O Chandrashekhar[1] by Girija Prasanna Roy Chowdhury was the first original work of criticism on *Krishnakanter Uil*. Girija Prasanna had dealt not only with the characters of Gobindalal, Bhramar, and Rohini in the chapters on *Krishnakanter Uil*,[2] but also with the artistic and stylistic aspects of the novel. He also did not lose sight of the wonderful interaction of the characters and action in the great novel.

Girija Prasanna traced the gradual development and denouncement of the character of Gobindalal in three chapters. In the first chapter he pointed out that Gobindalal was saintly eclectic and kind in whom there was no difference between theory and practice, his love for Bhramar was not characterized by lust but by idealism.[3] The second chapter dealt with gradual development of Rohini's attachment to Gobindalal till her drowning,[4] while the third chapter centered on events beginning from Rohini's regaining consciousness to the end of Gobindalal's eventful career.[5] In spite of his profound mental strength, Gobindalal fell a victim to the charms of Rohini and thus lost the courage to fight against odds. Girija Prasanna showed that Gobindalal's attachment to Rohini was the result of his deep sympathy and kindness for her, hinting at the eternal truth that submission to sensual pleasures finally leads to physical, moral, and spiritual degeneration.[6]

Turning to Bhramar, Girija Prasanna found her a fickle, happy-go-lucky, polite, sober and blushful Aryan woman. Although born to the great tradition of Savitri, the western education made her different. The critic raised the objection that Bhramar, by her temporary impiety to her husband, had fallen from the magnificent Aryan cult.[7] Even then Girija Prasanna believed that the character of Bhramar was built upon two lofty ideals-devotion to husband coupled with her religious sanctity and inherent abhorrence to sin. Girija Prasanna's analysis revealed Bhramar as a unique combination of these high ideals.

Girija Prasanna found the character of Bhramar so designed as to assist the fullest development of Gobindalal's character. Her sorrows and sufferings, piety to her husband her death—all these were necessary for unfolding Gobindalal's character in true colours. Finally, Girija Prasanna emphasized the inevitability of Bharmar's death for intensification of the punishment of Gobindalal.[8]

In dealing with the character of Rohini, Girija Prasanna pointed out that the dominant force which guided and directed all her actions was her sensuality. Her better self-guided by virtuousness and uncontrolled by proper education had been led astray by lasciviousness. Girija Prasanna searched for these misguiding passions of Rohini's life. Rohini was an active force in bringing about degeneration of Gobindalal. Obviously, this was the motive behind her creation by the novelist. But degeneration in a character like Gobindalal could not have been brought about by a sheer whore—hence she could not be made altogether devoid of virtues.[9] Girija Prasanna further side that Rohini's character was really depicted with a poetic skill, but he avoided to analyses the character from artistic point of view simply because she treaded the path of sin.[10]

Analysing the theme, action, and environment in *Krishnakanter Uil* the critic remarked that these bore close resemblance to the novels of George Eliot.

However, Brahmananda's reflections on Haralal's wealth. Rohini's attempt to commit suicide, stealing of Krishnakanta's Uil, scandal about Gobindalal, Rohini's drawing, Bhramar's death and finally Gobindalal's death showed Bankim's highly imaginative poetic skill and philosophic insight on the one hand, and his strong realistic attitude on the other.[11]

This pretty long essay has been regarded as the first piece of critical study on *Krishnakanter Uil*, and it has a great significance. First, moralizing or idealism is not the tone of this essay—its tone is one of psychological analysis of the characters. Secondly, Girija Prasanna has attempted to highlight the total impression of the novel through a sympathetic critical judgement. He has rightly said that Bankim had successfully represented: "...those subtle principles of life which more subtly govern our actions."[12] He has pointed out that Gobindalal and Bhramar are more than more creations of imagination they pulsated with the urge and tension of modern man and modern woman.[13] Such critical insight is seen in abundance in the essay. Thirdly, the language of the essay and its artistic treatment bear the stamp of genius. Last, but not the least, Girija Prasanna has been successful in no small measure in interpreting the mind and art of Bankimchandra.

Even then, Girija Prasanna is not free from such blemishes as emotional outbursts leading to digressions as is evident when he writes: "Her (Bhramar) heart is a mine of kindness a spring of softness, a haven of love, is the paradise of happiness the palace of sweetness, and is the image of beauty."[14]

CHANDRANATH BASU (1844-1910)

Chandranath Basu's criticism on *Krishnakanter Uil* in his two essays, *Ananta Muhurta*[15] *in 'Duiti Hindu Patni'*[16] had been compiled in *Tridhara*.[17] In *Ananta Muhurta*, the last moments of Bhramar's life had been described, and an idealistic impression left by her had been explained, while a comparative study of Bhramar and Suryamukhi had been made in the background of Hindu creed in *Duiti Hindu Patni*.

Chandranath Basu in his attempt to analyze the scene prior to Bhramar's death said that although Bhramar had wished for the blessings of her husband, her insolence and sternness were not subdued. The reason according to Chandranath Basu was that her spirit and sternness where not born of her pride and dauntlessness—it was an outcome of her sentiment of love. Even in her deathbed she could not forgive her object of love to Gobindalal because she was a sinner.[18] And the critic here went to the extent to remark that the moment of Bhramar's death was not momentary but eternal-God's purpose was evidently reflected in the last scene of Bharamar's life.[19]

In his comparative estimate of Bhramar and Suryamukhi, Chandranath remarked that both the characters were basically Hindu, but circumstances had brought about the differences in their hehaviour and attitude. The anger and sentiment of Suryamukhi were subdued by her deep-rooted regards for her husband in spite of being misbehaved by him, while in, Bhramar these remained hidden under her devotion to her husband who had wronged her.[20] It needs mention here that Chandranath had very clearly brought out the internal conflicts in these two characters in his analysis.

These two essays of Chandranath Basu are more important from historical rather than literacy point of view. As because, an examination of the character of Bhramar in the religious standards of Hinduism has detracted much of his criticism from its pure literary value. However, marks of enduring literary judgement are still visible as is evident from his attempt to analyse the inner mysteries of characters mentioned in the last paragraph.[21]

SARACHHANDRA SARKAR

Sarachhandra Sarkar was the first critic to bring under literary preview the ethical and artistic aspects of their subsequent modifications incorporated in the later edition of *Krishnakanter Uil*, published in *Bangadarshan*. In his essay *Krishnakanter Uil Samparke Kayekti Katha*[22] Sarachhandra's discussion centred round rejuvenation of Gobindalal in the fourth edition who was actually shown dead in the second edition. The dead Gobindalal's rejuvenation and his subsequent renunciation served no other purpose but to hint at the new phase of Bankim's philosophic thought found in *Sitaram* and *Devi Chaudhurani*. And he questioned, if Gobindalal's devotion indicated his total surrender to the path of God, then why he has been brought back to Haridragram to see the image of Bhramar? And, when so much was done, why had not Bhramar been rejuvineted?[23]

According to Sarachhandra, the writer could have avoided making Bhramar so stern particularly when Gobindalal wanted to fall flat on her foot after having reverting himself from the extreme end of the world of sin following Rohini's death. And it would have served the dual purpose—Gobindalal would have come back to Haridragram and Bhramar too would not have died, particularly when Haridragram and Bhramar's death was not the inevitable end. And thus, the natural beauty of the book would have remained uncontaminated.[24] This sort of explication indicates the critic's depth of artistic sense and value judgement which anticipates twentieth century critics.

RAMENDRA SUNDAR TRIVEDI (1864-1919)

A more dependable and beautiful contemporary criticism of *Krishnakanter Uil* could be found in Ramendra Sundar's *Sahitya Katha.*[25] The main intention of Ramendra Sundar was to consider the tragic intensity of the character of Gobindalal instituting a comparison with Shakespeare's *Macbeth*. The evil instincts of Macbeth were so sharpened after being instigated by the wired sisters that these led him to abysmal sin which proved to him a point of no return, in spite of the fact that Macbeth was not so had a man.[26]

Likewise, Gobindalal as a man was little more than the average. But in the cruel sequence of dramatic actions[27] "the hero of *Krishnakanter Uil* appeared to be a living image of sin in the last chapter.[28] His kindness and his propensity to do good to others were the weaknesses that lead him to ruin. Incidentally the cooing of cuckoo on the bank of Baruni, stealing of the 'Uil', Rohini's attempt to commit suicide, scandal against himself, Bhramar's sentiment, Krishnakanta's last 'Uil', etc.—all these made Gobindalal like "a ship on that is sinking and sinking to such depths that there was no hope of rescue."[29] This is the brief the point of Ramendra Sundar's discussion.

Ramendra Sundar's principle of judgement appears to be based on Aristotle's theory. His discussion is reasonable and logical. Following Aristotle, Ramendra Sundar's literary ideas are neither limited nor corrupted by moral preponderance. Indeed, his approach is in perfect conformity with Aristotle's theory which makes fate responsible for human tragedy. Character has a limited responsibility in the tragic catastrophe as Ramendra Sundar has hinted at. His tragic vision as revealed in establishing similarities with the apparently dissimilar characters of Macbeth and Gobindalal shows the profundity and depth of his criticism. He highlights that the plot, character, and fate combine together to make a tragedy. Subodh Chandra Gupta, an eminent modern critic has paid glowing tribute to Ramendra Sundar's critical genius revealed in this treatise and remarks that Ramendra Sundar's approach may be regarded as a supplement to Aristotle's *Poetics* in consideration of its simplicity, clarity and introspective tendency.[30]

BIRESHWAR PANDE (1842-1911)

Bireshwar Pande's *Bankimchandra O Hindur Adarsha* was the next critical work on the *Krishnakanter Uil.*[31] His approach is characterized by emphasis upon the Hindu ideals highlighted in *Bishabriksha* and *Krishnakanter Uil.* The arguments which he put forward in support of Gobindalal's degeneration and the consequent tragedy deserve attention. The critic, after a through analysis of the actions of Gobindalal's life concluded that despite Gobindalal's utmost endeavour to defend himself he became a victim of circumstances beyond his control, and these adverse circumstances contaminated the character of Gobindalal. Bireshwar's criticism resembles Ramendra Sunder's in many points, but with a difference. In fact, what had been implicit in Ramendra Sundar become explicit in Bireshwar. Substantiating his argument with materials Bireshwar concluded that: "Circumstances so speedily worked upon Gobindalal that he had slipped before he realized how much slippery was the path of sin."[32] Bireshwar's argument gives expression of his genuine literary taste and insight. The argument which he has put forward in support of the tragic consequence of *Krishnakanter Uil* is solid but based upon ethical and idealistic grounds. For example, he has said: "Gobindalal was a hero having vices of his character and Bhramar was not a woman having the virtues of a wife—hence the tragedy of *Krishnakanter Uil.*[33] This remark is the glaring example of how the critical attitude of the critics of those days was vitiated by ethical bias.

SAILENDRA NATH SARKAR

Sailendra Nath Sarkar's essay *Krishnakanter Uil Anushilon*,[34] may be divided into two parts—first, ethical and second, literary. According to Sailendra Nath, Bhramar stood poles apart from the ideal Hindu woman. Gobindalal's acceptance of Rohini beyond the Hindu socio-religious creed (Shastra), and the ultimate consequence of Gobindalal were due to the violation of this creed. In like manner, Bhramar's impiety to her husband being contradictory to the Hindu creed, death became inevitable for her.[35] Such a tone is indeed ethical.

However, the essay contains a good deal of pure literary criticism. According to Sailendra Nath Gobindalal and Rohini were not wholly responsible for their tragic end, fate and primitive human instinct were also responsible to a great extent. Bhramar's stern attitude was only a helping factor of this tragic end. Further, he said that the best part of the novel was that concerning the incident of Baruni pond, in fact, it was the most critical thread in the whole action. It was the Baruni incident which marked the turning point in the lives of Rohini, Gobinda and indirectly of Bhramar and led them to face the painful consequence.[36] About Gobindalal's rejuvenation in the new edition of *Krishnakanter Uil*. Sailendra Nath said that Gobindalal's suicide in the old edition was more natural. He had opined that the novel moved to the catastrophe through the curse of beauty, delusion and sentimentality, the interaction of which had led to the inevitable and of the criminal husand.[37] The problem of locating the heroine in this novel put the readers into dilemma because Bhramar twinkled with a faint light beside Rohini who shone like the Moon. According to Sailendra Nath, Rohini was the real heroine because she was the central female character involved in all the major incidents in the novel.[38] All the actions of Haralal were nothing more than what might be called "Prologue of English plays".[39]

Sailendra Nath's criticism marked a transition in the history of Bengali criticism. There were two contrary forces directly affecting the critical mind—one was the existing but gradually weakening orthodox critical trend and the other was the irresistible current of Western ideas of literary criticism, and Sailendra Nath's criticism was caught up in this phase of transition.

HARAN CHANDRA RAKSHIT

Krishnakanter Uil in *Bangashahitye Bankim*[40] by Haran Chandra Rakshit shows that the spite of being overshadowed by the old standards, it made a shift towards modern realistic criticism. Haran Chandra contradicted Chandra Nath Basu's interpretation of Bhramar's character and pointed out what Bhramar could never be a Hindu woman since her behavior was markedly European, which could not be expected[41] of women born in the tradition of Sita and Savitri. This novel, he said, could not be considered the best work of fiction by Bankimchandra when judged from strictly literary standards. It had however its distinctiveness so far as presentation, the art of narration, characterization, and subtlety of logic were concerned. He appreciated the novelists beautiful analysis of human nature even in minor perspectives.[42] This new approach to characterization as wells as dramatic situations marks a departure from the orthodox trend.

NITYA KRISHNA BASU

Sahitya Seboker Diar[43] was the compilation of Nitya Krishna Basu's diary. In the 23rd Baisak,[44] chapter of this compilation, Nitya Krishna mentioned of Sarachhandra Sarkar's *Krishnakanter Uil Samparke Kayekti Katha* published in the *Purahit,* Falgun, 1300 B.S., and said that Sarachhandra's demand of Bhramar's rejuvenation along with Gobindalal's was not reasonable because it could not fulfil the poetic demand. But he subscribed to Sarachhandra view that Gobindalal's restoration had, to some extent, spoilt the poetic beauty, because Gobindalal's early actions leading to his self-exposition roused not only awe and wonder but also sympathy. The reaction in reader was aversion to sensuousness and appreciation for the punishment of the sinner of course; Gobindalal's death intensified that ethic. But he believed Gobindalal's restoration gave a tremendous blow to everything.[45]

Evidently, Nitya Krishna is a follower of Aristotle in his judgement of tragedy. According to Aristotle, if life is beautifully expressed, it gives pleasure even if the events are painful. "Though the object themselves may be painful to see, we delight to view the most realistic representation of them in art."[46] Nitya Krishna found that poetic beauty in the sequel of the novel. The real value of this essay lies in the application of Western principles of criticism to Bankim literature.

GOLAK BEHARI MUKHAPADHYAY

The first attempt to view *Krishnakanter Uil* both from the romantic and the realistic standpoints was Golak Behari Mukhapadhyay's essay, *Krishnakanter Uil.*[47] Although, this essay primarily aimed at psycho-analysis of the characters of Gobindalal, Rohini and Bhramar, it also death fairly well with the ideology of the novelist, the dramatic sequences of incidents, the structure and other relevant matters.

At the very outset he explained that the primary motive in the novel was to establish that a mall seed could manifest itself into a huge tree. Golak Behari cited an example. The 'Uil' spoke itself of the consequence: "...a family is ruined, a beautiful life sacrificed, a sinful life ruined, a pure-man's downfall and his continuous penance of the sin."[48]

He had further told that a small silent sensitiveness of Bhramar was the root of her separation from Gobindalal, and further that the glorious exposition of those little thins impregnated with great consequences contributed to the development of dramatic situation in this novel.[49]

Credit goes to Golak Behari for his analysis of the protagonists in the book. He delves deep into the heart of the characters and attempts to make a threadbare analysis against the background of the silent working of the mysterious fate.

Analysing the characters of Rohini and Gobindalal, Golak Behari said that both the characters suffer from the same flaw of carelessness and unbridled passion. Gobindalal knew the religious commandment but he did not have devotion, he was lover, but he did not have lover's patience and forgiveness. His self-reliance amounting to inaction was the rest cause of his degeneration. He made wise arguments with himself prior to his help to Rohini, but did not enter into the inner recesses of his mind to consider his ability to relieve her.[50]

According to Golak Behari, Rohini's fetching of water is a major factor in helping a psycho-analysis of her character "Subtle analysis of the complexities of psychology, has been brilliantly displayed with positive beauty."[51] When Rohini began to weep floating her earthen jar over the current less clear water of Baruni, the deep desire of her heart, the blow of hopelessness, the limitless emptiness of her mind—all these passions were symbolically expressed through her tears and the floating vessel. Golak Behari had gone to that extent to pose a comparison between the Baruni of *Krishnakanter Uil* and the Eden of *Paradise Lost* because it was there that Gobindalal was unconsciously being tempted by the Satan:

> Perhaps it is here that Gobindalal is caught in the golden chain of temptation. Again, the lone adventure to fetch water from the Baruni, the glorious beauty of blooming flowers of this lonesome tract, and Gobindala's unblemished youthful beauty are collectively responsible for Rohini's fall.[52]

Referring to Rohini's death, Golak Behari said that it was the inevitable end because had she not got her penance at the cost of death, Gobindalal's salvation would have been prolonged particularly when Rohini reached a point of no return. So, any difference idea would have been unnatural amounting to a blemish of the book.[53]

Now, coming to Bhramar, Golak Behari said "ever growing adolescent love, faith, mutual adjustment, and religion"[54] these are her main qualities of her character. Her sensitiveness was born of these ingredients. According to the critic, if Gobindalal could have told freely and frankly, when he was asked of his indifference by Bhramar, then the matter would not have been so grievous. Gobindalal could not say so because his pure heart had been touched by sin. In the same fashion, Adam and Eve were suspicious and shrinking from appearing before God when they committed the sin.[55] Golak Behari further pointed out that since then Bhramar had been suspicious and gradually the seed of suspicion grew to be a huge tree, and the feminine fickleness of Bhramar added fuel to the fire of the friction of Bharamar's sentimentality with Gobindalal's audacity.[56] Bhramar could not realize that her blind love impregnated with too much of faith was loading Gobindalal towards the path of sin, and Gobindalal too, could not realize his own lapse.[57]

According to Golak Behari, Bhramar left her husband's house lest she would fail to give her husband his due honour and accept him as deeply as she did earlier. Golak Behari found a parallel of this incident in 'Delicia's Murder' of Mary Corelle where Delicia left for the seashore to safeguard her husband's prestige.[58]

Golak Behari has presented very skillfully the main them of *Krishnakanter Uil* which according to him is a literary version of uncontrolled passions.[59] Such judgements are there everywhere in the essay. Every sentence of his criticism bears the stamp of his genius. Liberal attitude of the critic, depth of explication, all clear statement and explanation mark those qualities which are evident in Golak Behari's criticism of *Krishnakanter Uil.*

LOKENATH CHAKRABORTY

Lokenath Chakraborty's criticism of *Krishnakanter Uil* is spread over in three different essays—*Krishnakanter Uil Samalochana,*[60] *Bhramar (Krishnakanter Uil)*,[61] and *Bhramar Prosonga.*[62] In the first essay, the critic dealt with *Krishnakanter Uil* and all other incidents relating to it, ups and downs of the characters in relation to the 'Uil', justification of the title, the motive and the moral behind, and the main characters particularly Rohini. The character of Bhramar with the problems relating to her was dealt with in the second essay (Bhramar), and the third and the last essay of the series (*Bhramarer Probondha*) reflected the life history of Gobindalal, Lokenath Chakraborty's essays in question revealed the divided attitude of a critic like these of Sailendranath Sarkar. On the one hand, there was an analysis of Bhramar, Rohini and Gobindalal in the light of the ethics, on the other hand, Rohini had been analysed with a more liberal romantic temperament. Lokenath had seen the Bankim *Krishnakanter Uil* primarily as a moral teacher as well as a critical judge of good and evil. But sometimes, certain attempts were there to find out the genius of Bankim as a poet and artist. Lokenath said that the motive force of the tragedy of this novel was not Krishnakanta Roy, the person but his 'Will'. Hence, according to him the title was justified.[63]

While explaining the aim and objective of the novel the critic pointed out that in *Krishnakanter Uil* Bankimchandra had roamed about in the grass-roots level and had shown that happiness achieved through unbridled passions could not last. Bankim assumed this ethical implication in *Bishabriksha* to be fulfilled in *Krishnakanter Uil*.[64]

Analysing the character of Rohini, Lokenath said that Rohini was a Hindu woman, her education, culture and intuition to good and evil—all directed and governed by the Hindu tradition but the excess of epicureanism in her over-powered everything.[65] Lokenath pointed out the mysterious working of circumstances upon Rohini's lust. He said that the song of cuckoo amidst the pleasant atmosphere of the Baruni Pond was an allegorical presentation of Rohini's fickle mindedness. Rohini's nature and attitude, her heart, the possibilities and promise of her character—all these were typified in the description of the Baruni. According to Lokenath, "The future actions of Rohini's life are only further developments of this picture."[66]

According to Lokenath, the cause of Rohini's self-slaughter was to be found in her luscious nature. She had an impassioned carnal desire to be united with Gobindalal and that desire rose to such an extreme height that she could not bear the burden of it any more and sought relief in suicide. This was further intensified by her jealousy for Bhramar's happiness and grievance against Gobindalal and the despondency born of hopelessness to win him.[67]

The early critics of Bankimchandra thought that the mainstream of Bankim literature was directed towards moral and ethical teaching. Lokenath followed the same tradition in analyzing the character of Bhramar and searched for Hindu ideals in her. It is no wonder that he found Bhramar as good as Sabitri in her determination and the power of chastity. What an outburst of emotion is where in his remark:

Bhramar's appearance in this earth was pre-ordained to enshrine with heavenly bliss the everyday life of the great, the saintly Gobindalal. On her return to heaven after her success in earth, she was welcoming Gobindalal there too.[68]

Lokenath's analysis of Bhramar's character of is orthodox devoid of literary flavor.[69] Lokenath fails to catch the main point that the sentimentalism of an unlettered woman is the vital force behind the character of Bhramar.[70]

According to the critic, Gobindalal is the 'image of reality',[71] a burning example of how disastrous can be the consequence of a slip in real life. Lokenath further said that the gradual deterioration of self-restraint in the ancient Hindu society had been highlighted by Bankim in the character of Gobindalal.

In this light Lokenath has discussed the character of Gobindalal. It has been mentioned earlier that Lokenath criticism is the combination of the attitudes of both old and new trends. He is both a classic and a romantic. The classic Lokenath is the stern supporter of Hindu social cult, and the romantic Lokenath has the realization of the working of the human heart in emotional plane.

JATISH CHANDRA BASU

Jatish Chandra Basu discussed the character of Bhramar in his essay of the same title by citing quotations from the novel.[72] And he made casual remarks here and there to establish that in spite of being a Hindu woman, her ideals were shaped by western ideas. Nothing more could be found in this essay. Jatish Chandra said that western education was at the root of Bhramar's catastrophe—"The western education had a very bad impact into her eastern mind, Bhramar died."[73] As a matter of fact, Jatish Chandra Basu investigated the western influence in the character of Bhramar.[74]

JATENDRALAL BASU

Form the idealistic point of view, Jitendralal Basu's Bhramar as appeared in his *Bankimchandra* the western influence had a very serious impact upon the Aryan woman leading her to frustrating calamities. But he probed into the psychological realm also. He said that with Bhramar the religious force was greater than the force of conjugal love—"She thought that she had a separate existence beyond her husband."[75] And this remark adds a new element in the discussion on the character of Bhramar.

SACHIS CHANDRA CHATTOPADHYAY

Sachis Chandra Chattopadhyay the biographer of Bankimchandra in his book *Swargiya Bankimchandra Chattapadyayer or Jibon Charit*,[76] he said that as Milton's *Paradise Lost* was superior to *Paradise Regained* so also *Krishnakanter Uil* was superior to *Chandrasekhar.* In *Chandrashekhar,* the man Pratap in the beginning was developed to be a God in the end, but in *Krishnakanter Uil*, Gobindalal had three stages of life which marked an anti-climax-first he was a God, then a man and finally an animal.[77] Sachis Chandra proved that Gobindalal's ruin was caused by his kindness for Rohini, blame put to his character by Bhramar and, the last, "Will" of Krishnakanta.[78] Analysing the reason of Bhramar's pre-mature death, Sachis Chandra said that Bhramar failed to be an ideal life, her westernized relation with her husband caused her death.[79] Although such remarks of Sachis Chandra are orthodox, his criticism is not unmixed with romantic attitude specially when he remarked that Gobindalal was not merely a 'God' but a 'Man' also.

SARACHHANDRA GHOSAL

Krishnakanter Uil was first published in *Bangadarshan* serially. When Bankim published it in the form of a book he did some modification in the characters of Rohini and Gobindalal. Sarachhandra Ghosal discussed about the qualitative side of this modification in his essay, *Krishnakanter Uil.*[80]

According to Sarachhandra, the Rohini of *Bangadarshan* was a greedy, mean, shameless scoundrel who aroused our hatred only. And the modified Rohini exacted sympathy from us. This modification added to the merit of the book. This was because a disrepute character aroused both hatred and sympathy simultaneously, but was in reality a reputed literary character. Of the other merits of this modification, Sarachhandra said that Rohini wanted to steal the 'Will' not being greedy for money but for her gratitude to Haralal coupled with her inclination to marry him. This modification had transformed the greedy scoundrel Rohini to a lascivious one, eager to be united with Gobindalal.[81] This sort of analysis is indicative of reflective tendency. Speaking of the modification brought in the character of Gobindalal the critic said that suicide, even if recognized in western literature was forbidden in that of the east. Gobindalal's suicide was not a penance for his sin; it was further the addition of a new crime with the old. Penance of sin could be done through repentance. Therefore, the writer, without presenting Gobindalal committing suicide had delineated one who had to purify himself through repentance and unconditional surrender to God.[82]

Sarachhandra's view shows a combination of the old and new approaches. His critical approach to Gobindalal marks his classical tendency while his critical approach to Rohini spells him out as modern.

RAMSAHAYA VEDANTASASTRI

Ramsahaya Vedantasastri's criticism of *Krishnakanter Uil* was embodied in his three distinct essays—*Bhramar (Samalochana),*[83] *Gobindalal Charitra,*[84] and *Bhramar O Rohini.*[85] Even though written at different times, these essays are not detached papers in so far as technique and critical approach are concerned.

The first essay (Bhramar Somalochana) on Bhramar's life contained an analysis and evaluation of her actions. Here there is evidence of the application of different critical theories. Such comment of Ramsahaya: Gobindalal's playmate and companion of heart, Shrimati Bhramar stands around him like a large black bee,[86] show his aesthetic sense. With a classic moralizing tone Vedantasastri said that sentimentalism coupled with jealousy was the more dominant force in Bhramar than her regard for her husband and that was completely against the ideal of Indian womanhood. He concluded that the excess of momentary excitement in Bhramar marked her out as a bad example of a sentimental woman whereas Radha of the *Vaishab Padabali* had set a good example of a sentimental woman by her moving piety. To Radha, attraction for Krishna was the most vital force; but it is altogether absent in Bhramar in relation to her beloved. Judged from the ideals left by Sita, Sabitri, Damayanti, one could not but find fault with Bhramar, but considering her as an innocent girl and a domestic woman, she could be pleaded not guilty.[87] This attitude of Vedantasastri strikes a note of freedom from custom, and indicates a charge in the trend criticism on *Krishnakanter Uil.*

In the second essay (Gobindalal Charitra) attempts had been made to explain the significance of the title, and analyse the character of Gobindalal from the spiritual standpoint.

According to Vedantasastri, 'Gobindalal' meant self-surrender to the feet of God, and the word 'Lal' was from rural dialect, and the incorporation of 'Lal' was responsible for the lasciviousness of Gobindalal in the middle part of his life 'Rajagoon' and 'Lal', sentiment, anger and luxury and such other qualities were reflected in Gobindalal's middle age.[88] The character of Gobindalal had been explained on the basis of these principles. Vedantasastri said that in the beginning Gobindalal's character was adorned with godly human virtues, and the illusion was produced just to make him surrender to the feet of God.[89] In such arguments as these, one is sure to find the painstaking imagination rather than genuine literary criticism. However, the sparks of value judgement are not unnoticeable, especially in comments regarding the final estimate of Gobindalal's character. He said, the real truth regarding Gobindalal's character was not to be found in his unethical acts; he was a victim of circumstances, and external forces were responsible for his fall.[90] He added, Gobindalal's fall and resurrection had a very close relationship with Rohini's murder and the creation of the golden image of Bhramar.[91] Like the first one, this essay also contains much that is orthodox or puritan. But it also anticipates in many points the new liberalism which is bound to carry the day in near future.

Bhramar O Rohini was written about a decade later, but there was no distinct change in Vedantasastri's attitude, except clarity and simplicity. The characters of Bhramar and Rohini were discussed from idealistic standpoints. Rohini was considered as considered as selfish lascivious prostitute and Bhramar as godly and chaste but sentimental and jealous.

According to Ramsahaya "Bhramar is a tub of water while Rohini a spark of fire, Bhramar a double jasmine of love, Rohini—a blood storm of lust, one dazzles the eye, the other softens the mind, one is inspiration the other is excitement, one is the celestial Ganges (Mandakini), the other is what spoils the work (Karmanasa), one is the Goddess, the lotus of chastity, the other is a she-demon, a tree with haphazard leaves Saptachad of unchastity."[92] It is an admitted fact that Ramsahaya is more subtle in drawing a comparative estimate of Rohini and Bhramar, and he deserves appreciation on this score.

CHANDI CHARAN BONDOPADHYAY (1858-1916)

Chandi Charan Bondopadhyay, in his essay "Bangla Sahiter Kromonnoti O Bankim Chandra"[93] remarked that: *Krishnakanter Uil was not a realistic portrayal of Bengali* social life. Bankim Chandra depicted the impact of Western culture on Hindu Social life and its terrible reaction. Bhramar was the product of that western influence.[94] And this is the main point with Chandi Charan's criticism of *Krishnakanter Uil.* While evaluating a social novel, the social background of which the novel is a product needs to be essentially discussed. Here in his the credit of Chandi Charan. He has criticized *Krishnakanter Uil* in the light of the social background and has opened a new horizon in Bengali literary criticism.

ADHYAPAK LALIT KUMAR BANDOPADHYAY (1275-1336 B.S.)

Bankim Chandrer Akhyayikabali,[95] *Ma,*[96] *Dui Bhagini,*[97] *Kabya Sudha,*[98] *Sakhi,*[99] contained Lalit Kumar's criticism of *Krishnakanter Uil.*

In the first essay attempt was made to justify the title, the second essay showed a search for finding out the motherhood in the female characters, the third, determination of Yamini's contribution to the bad days of Bhramar, the fourth *Shwashuri Bou* under *Kabyasudha*, the features of mother-in-law and daughter-in-law relationship; and the last essay *Sakhi,* the role played by Kshiri.

Lalit Kumar found a justification of the title since the 'Will' of Krishnakanta Roy was the focal point of all the dramatic situations in the novel.[100]

After a study of the mothers in the book, Lalit Kumar pointed out that Gobindalal's mother was a silent witness to her son's neglect and indifference to Bhramar and finally his fall. Had she tried rectification, a very favourable atmosphere could have been created with love and regard centering mother and son which the writer had missed. On the other hand, Bhramar's mother was more active and elaborate than Gobindalal's Lalit Kumar thought that Bhramar's mother had represented the image of that Bengalee woman who can exercise and exert a great influence within the limitation of her intelligence and capacity.[101] Exploring the motherliness of Bhramar, he said that there was no dearth of motherliness in Bhramar even if she had lost her son in her confinement. In the days of her misfortune, the overwhelming grief for her son filled her life with enormous sorrow adding to the beauty of the novel itself.[102]

To justify the introduction of Yamini, the critic said that during her unendurable sufferings and torture, Bhramar required someone who could nurse her, console her and look after her with all kindness and sympathy. This was fulfilled fairly well by Yamini. Doubtless it showed the superb artistic sense of the novelist.[103]

Exploring the nature of the relation between mother-in-law and daughter-in-law in *Krishnakanter Uil*, Lalit Kumar said that even in her extreme misfortune, Bhramar did not lose sense of duty towards her mother-in-law, the tittle disobedience she had shown was the result of her child-like fickleness and uncompromising sentiment towards her husband. On the other hand, the mother-in-law's behavior towards Bhramar was marked by impropriety which imparts blemish to her character.[104]

Regarding the role played by the maid-servant Kshiri, Lalit Kumar said that this realistic picture was devoid of any romantic aura, and the role was of a very moderate type.[105]

In conclusion it can be said that Lalit Kumar has discussed in details the family portraits in *Krishnakanter Uil* and did not venture into the study of complex, mysterious relationship between man and woman.

SHASHANKA MOHAN SEN (1872-1929)

Shashanka Mohan Sen's essays in his *Bangabani*[106] and *Banimandir*[107] marked a comparatively better contemporary criticism on *Krishnakanter Uil* Shashanka Mohan had erudition in European literature and philosophy, but, the Indian literature and philosophy attracted him much.[108] In his criticism of *Krishnakanter Uil* Shashanka Mohan made use of this experience. His aim was to determine how far Bankimchandra was influenced by the ideals of ancient Indian literature in writing this book and its resemblance to English books. He said, in *Krishnakanter Uil*, "The saint of the East has found out the subtle ideals of conjugal love."[109] He sought to establish the artistic and literary superiority of *Krishnakanter Uil* over the novels of *Rita* and the *Heavenly Twins* of such grand scale to which it had idealistic resemblance.[110]

Analysing the idealistic basis of this book in relation to the gradual development of Bankimchandra's thought, Shashanka Mohan said in so far as the duty and ideals in conjugal life were concerned, man and woman were equal—any deviation from this norm must bring in equal punishment for both man and woman—*Krishnakanter Uil* was the result of this ethical thought. Therefore, with the murderer Govindalal, Bhramar's permanent separation was wrought. According to Shashanka Mohan—"Gobindalal's punishment was natural and it was ethically right."[111] Even if Gobindalal was rejuvenated in the fourth edition, the critic thought that he remained the same 'dead' in family life. According to Shashanka Mohan, Kundanandini and Shaibalini appeared in the shape of a lascivious whore—the widow Rohini, Nagendra Nath in the shape of Gobindalal, and Suryamukhi in the shape of the dark lady Bhramar—all these appeared in *Krishnakanter Uil* in order to exemplify the penance both the husband and the wife had to undergo if they slip from the conjugal ideal.[112]

Shashanka Mohan's literary thought was ideally presented in the *Banimandir.* He drew attention to the origin of creativity in literature with reference to Bhima Pond.[113] Then classifying the novel as a 'tragedy of fate', he said Rohini drowned herself in the Bhima, and by a strange irony of fate Gobindalal had to rejuvenate her through a sweet touch to the lotus-like mouth of Rohini. And he has enjoyed the pleasure of this sweet touch even against his will. The consequence of this was the fatal tragedy of Gobindalal leading to his death.[114] Here he found the inner significance of art coupled with artistic skill.[115] Shashanka Mohan went on to compare this scene with that scene of the longest death-kiss in Shakespeare's Romeo-Juliet and remarked—In the one hand, the grand combination of ideal with reality, and on the other hand, there is the fine blend of life and death.[116] Shashanka Mohan's interpretation of the Bhima Pond incident revealed the understanding of the inner realities of life. Despite the artistic fault in the murder of Rohini, Shashanka Mohan rejected any possible objection from the point of view of ethics.[117]

KALIPADA BONDOPADHYAY

Kalipada Bondopadhyay in his essay *Pranaye Amulak Sandeha*[118] has written that Bhramar suspecting Gobindalal even when there was no traces of his attachment towards Rohini and it was the cause of the fatal consequence of the novel.[119] Secondly, he thought that Rohini's murder was not connected with the main plot of the book. Gobindalal murdered Rohini out of suspicion, just as Bhramar left her paternal home with a suspicious mind.[120] Kalipada's love in *Krishnakanter Uil* is a new contribution to Bankim criticism.

AKSHAY KUMAR DUTTAGUPTA

In Akshay Kumar Duttagupta's Bankimchanda[121] attempts were made to evaluate the material, story, literary taste and characters etc. Akshay Kumar attempted to prove logically that realism is the very basis of this novel. He pointed out that in the main plot of this novel there was no excess of imagination. A balance was maintained in characterization all along, and there was no dearth of feeling and taste.[122] Besides, the intensity of the book rather than idealism attracted him ore. He said that like "Rajsingha" the emotional intensity in *Krishnakanter*

Uil was not the outcome of external forces rather sprang from within the characters. He was also profoundly impressed by the exceptional speed in the movement of action especially after the incident of theft of the will.[123]

The critic opined that Rohini was inferior to Matibibi of Kapalkundala, she was deceitful, highly willful, and badly passionate and lascivious.[124] Interpreting the controversial incident of Rohini's death, Akshay Kumar remarked that had Rohini not been killed by Gobindalal, the burden of sorrow with Bhramar would have been light and weak. The critic was very clear in his opinion that it was Rohini's death and not Gobindalal's desertion of home which constituted the crisis in the novel.[125]

In the analysis of the character of Bhramar Akshay Kumar was mainly concerned with her devotion towards her husband and her sentiment. He opined that Bhramar was neither and ideal nor an 'Westernised'[126] lady, she was a Bengalee woman intensified: "Bankim has combined together devotion of a universal Bengalee woman and her sentiment leaving aside the idealism."[127]

The freedom of thought revealed in the judgement of *Krishnakanter Uil* attracts our attention. Akshay Kumar's critical judgement is characteristically modern so far as the sincerity of his arguments, dexterity in analysis, depth of taste and understanding of Bankim's literary principle are concerned.

NARESH CHANDRA SENGUPTA (1882-1964)

Naresh Chandra's criticism on *Krishnakanter Uil* is embodied in two separate essays entitled *Sahitye Swadhinata*[128] and *Banglar Katha*.[129]

In the *Sahitye Swadhinata*, Naresh Chandra pointed out the futility of the orthodox approach to *Krishnakanter Uil*, and remarked that the main point of consideration was whether Bhramar's words and actions were in conformity with her character and situation.[130] Surprisingly enough in *Banglar Katha* written a year after, he himself could not get rid of this conservatism. He said that Bhramar's ego, her spirit were akin to religion like those of Draupadi of the *Mahabharata*, and that through this book the author made an attempt to put old wine into the new bottle.[131] However, there are occasional spark of pure literary criticism which has imparted some value to these essays.[132]

SARATCHANDRA CHATTOPADHYAY (1876-1938)

Saratchandra's criticism on *Krishnakanter Uil* could be traced in two essays *Adhunik Sahityer Kaifiat*[133] and in *Sahitya O Niti.*[134]

In both the essays, Saratchandra's point of discussion was Rohini's death and the artistic blemish thereon. According to him, Bankim's Rohini was altogether inconsistent. He pointed out that Bankim started narrating the love episode of Rohini with such sympathy as if her inclination for love was the outcome of the natural desire and just claim of a love-sick wisdom deprived of love since birth. Subsequently, when he found that she had started drawing sympathy of the readers towards her then, suddenly he was disturbed by the ethical consequence of this development. Rohini's attachment to another was a social crime. So, Bankim made her undergo penance. Being oblivious of the duties of an artist he pushed Rohini to death and thus, emphasized the dangerous ethical consequence of illicit love thereby indicating his strong ethical sense. Here Saratchandra did not agree with him. He clearly said—"The poetic sense in Bankim, is sacrificed at the cost of his social and ethical sense."[135] By Rohini's death the so-called social and ethical codes were preserved at the cost of her death. This was also the death of art itself.[136] As a modern writer Saratchandra would not agree with this.[137]

Saratchandra's objection to the ethics is moderate, but he mainly reacts to the way Rohini dies. It cannot be denied that even if Rohini's sudden death is pre-planned by the writer, it is 'bad art.'[138] Because, the writer does not prepare his readers sufficiently for such a consequence. Finally, Saratchandra's viewpoint strikes the modern critical tendency indicating a matured approach of *Krishnakanter Uil.*

HEMENDRA KUMAR ROY (1888-1963)

Hemendra Kumar in his essay entitled *Sekele Bankim*[139] had vehemently opposed Saratchandra's view and pleaded in favour of Bankim to justify Rohini's death. According to him, Rohini was never in love with Gobindalal; 'lust' was the basis of her character. So, her murder did not indicate the victory of purity against sin. Any man under the same pressure would have acted like Gobindalal. It was all natural with Bankim.[140] It seems that by 'natural' Hemendra Kumar means 'real'. And here he differs with Saratchandra. Hemendra Kumar believes in 'the poet of relation to what has happened.'[141] While Saratchandra pleads 'art for art's sake'.

ADHYAPAK BIMAN BEHARI MAZUMDER

Considering that Bankimchandra treated Rohini in accordance with the ideals of Renaissance Hindu woman, Biman Behari discussed the character of Bhramar in his "Bankimchandra Nari Jagarener Abhas."[142] Bankimchandra had created Bhramar as a rebel against the seclusion and injustice and ill-treatment of woman. But Bankim was above all a Hindu and therefore, his creation of a woman was unlike Nora of Ibsen, she did not leave her husband for good, being penitent she came back to him.[143] It can be noticed that Biman Behari is the first critic to give a judgement of the psychology of Bhramar's creator in the background of the Renaissance Bengal.

JATINDRA MOHAN SINGHA

Jatindra Mohan's criticism in *Arter Anushasan*[144] was based upon Saratchandra's remark. According to him Bankimchandra had neither sacrificed art at the alter of morality nor he was influenced by the social codes. He believed that even if Gobindalal sought shelter in his later life, Bhramar refused him. That proved that Bankim Chandra's art has overlooked social codes and religious restraints.[145]

Jatindra Mohan's second point of argument was that Bhramar's attachment to Gobindalal was nothing short of lasciviousness. In her attempt at self-sacrifice, her relentless passion was revealed, and it was very like the attempt at suicide of a patient suffering long from a dangerous and incurable disease. According to him Rohini's love was very like 'flirtation, conquettry',[146] and her game with Nishakar was nothing but a 'sharp technique of art.[147] Analysing the tragic elements of the book, Jatindra Mohan said that Rohini's murder was inevitable for the sake of art. But for this murder Bhramar Gobindalal tragedy would not have been so intense.[148]

Jatindra Mohan seeks to establish that ethics had become a part and parcel of the art of Bankim just as it is so in real life. And here he comes closer to the French critic Jean Baudrillard when the later says: "The children utopianism of the school of art for art's sake, in ruling out morals...was doomed to sterility."[149] However, Jatindra Mohan, in his attempt to oppose Saratchandra, has ultimately accepted much of the view of Saratchandra. Finally, he comes to the conclusion that life is governed by the principles of moral law and that Rohini's murder is not an exception to this.[150]

BHUPENDRA KISHORE ROYRAKSHIT

In his *Rohini Charitra*,[151] Bhupendra Kishore's discussion was without prejudice and he incorporated much of the human element's there. His grievance against Bankim was that Bankim had done positive injustice to this character.

From the idealistic point of view, Rohini was contemptible and deserved punishment, but the society which governed her was itself responsible for her fall. People liked Haralal, etc. had instigated her into commit wrong. She had been the victim of stern social neglect since her early childhood. Her love for Gobindalal was the spontaneous expression of her latent youthful passions. In short, this was the criteria of Bhupendra Kishore's psycho-analysis of Rohini's character; Bhupendra Kishore laid stress upon the human element in Rohini and explained that in spite of all the faults in her, one must consider that her actions were not unnatural since she was after all a woman and not a goddess. When the ill-treated Rohini found that the villagers are playing with her chastity, her last refuse, then she had no other alternative but to act as she had acted.[152]

Bhupendra Kishore found fault with the writer when the later had shown Rohini attracted towards Nishakar in a moment's acquaintance and again in the tune of death he made Rohini to cry "Don't kill me, don't kill me, I am young in age."[153] These are according to the critic nothing but natural development. He remarked—"The writer has done injustice to Rohini—such serious woman-disparity is beyond all tastes."[154]

Bhupendra Kishore is the probably the first critic to consider Rohini as woman of flesh and blood, and evaluate her actions form all possible human considerations. And here is the triumph of Bhupendra Kishore's judgement since he links life with literature.

ADHYAPAK MANJU GOPAL BHATTACHARJEE

Manju Gopal in his essays—"*Arter dik dia Bankimer kno charitra ki asanggata*,"[155] and "*Art O Bankimchandra*,"[156] contradicted contemporary criticism on Rohini. Unlike Bhupendra Kishore, Adhyapak Bhattacharjee believed that Rohini's death was not an isolated sudden accident. He explained the psychology behind Rohini's actions. Haralal provoked her sexuality and when she missed Haralal she liked to apply it to Gobindalal. In fact, her attachment towards Gobindalal was the result of her sexual impulses and not of love. Therefore, when she found Gobindalal completely in her grip, she was conscious of the fact that she had not conquered him by love. And this consciousness had inspired her to turn towards Nishakar. Therefore, the charges that Rohini's development was unnatural, and Bankim had done injustice to Rohini were not based upon facts.[157]

The consequence of Gobindalal and Rohini, according to Adhyapak Bhattacharjee, was not an artistic failure but an artistic success. He said: "To Bankimchandra was punishment of the sinners and nullification of their evil designs is the art."[158] Adhyapak Bhattacharjee's explication of Rohini's character, no doubt evokes controversy but his attitude to art reverberates the ancients.[159]

AMARENDRA NATH BASU

Amarendra Nath Basu, in his essay *Krishnakanter Uiller pradhan charitraguli byartha hailo keno?*, discussed in details the three principal characters—Gobindalal, Bhramar and Rohini, and tried to find out the causes of their failure.

He explained that the incidents as well as the characters in this book were governed by fate, and hence, it was fate which was responsible for the failure of the characters. According to Amarendra Nath, the entire book was covered by the history of Gobindalal's failure.

His finding was that Gobindalal has to fight against unseen oddities and ultimately had to admit defeat.[160]

Amarendra Nath said that the end of Rohini was not a sudden accident, it was rather a natural and usual development, and he went a step further to explain that the author had prepared the ground for this final catastrophe thus—when Rohini was lost in musical outbursts, in the Prosadpur, Gobindalal was found deeply absorbed in a novel in the other end which was bound to lead to the final separation, and here Nishakar was only a means to an end.[161]

Amarendra Nath's essay is significant in the sense that it poses towards and explanation based upon literary theory completely free from social implications and prejudices. "Fatalism" which was hinted at by Shashanka Mohan has been elucidated by Amarendra Nath.

BALAI DEBSHARMA

Balai Debsharma in his *Krishnakanter Uil Biyoganta Kina?*[162] explained the tragic implications of this book and the same tone was found in the discussion in *Bankim Protiva.*[163]

Analysing the tragic situations of the book he said that as from the western point of view the *Ramayana* and the *Mahabharata* were tragedies, so was *Krishnakanter Uil.* But as from the oriental point of view the said epics were not tragedies. The critic took into consideration the oriental attitude and explained that the moralistic ideals posed in the *Ramayana* and the *Mahabharata* had been posed by Bankim here too. To avoid nihilistic idea Gobindalal was rectified and revived after Rohini's death.[164] Balai Debsharma believed this revival of Gobindalal to be the result of Bankimchandra's belief in Indian cult of transmigration,[165] and Gobindalal's rectification through revival was psychological.[166]

SUBODH CHANDRA SENGUPTA

Subodh Chandra Sengupta was the last critic of *Krishnakanter Uil* before Bankim Centenary. In the essay entitled *Bankimchandra O Saratchandra,*[167] Subodh Chandra Sengupta pointed out that Bankimchandra's unmitigated regards towards the Hindu religion was the main spring of his blue-print of the character of Bhramar. Subodh Chandra found Bhramar a woman of inordinate inner spirit, self-confidence and strong sense of chastity. According to him, Bhramar's death was not the last word of her misfortune—"It is surprised by a strong spark of chastity and inordinate self-respect in her."[168] Needless to say Subodh Chandra has searched for Bankim's philosophy of life through Bhramar.

SUMMING UP

The main trend of discussion in about fifty essays of thirty-two critics dealt with in the chapter is whether the characters of this novel are sustained by the Hindu ideals or not. However, there are few critics who have attempted to evaluate Bankim's artistic genius. As a result, the opinion that 'Baruni Pond' is the best example of artistic beauty in this novel has been voiced even in the age of Bankim.

During the first three decades after the death of Bankim the trend of Bankim age prevailed, and side by side an awareness of pure literary criticism gained around. In most of the critical works a blending of the old and modern trends are marked. Conflicting attitudes of the critics are also noticed. Some critics, in spite of being influenced by the western trends, have remained faithful to the oriental ideas. Even in some of the critical works it has been indicated that Bankimchandra wrote this novel against the background of the social changes flowering in Bengal Renaissance.

After the first three decades of the post-Bankim period Saratchandra raised the question of art regarding Rohini's death. This initiates a lively debate that is to continue till the Bankim Centenary.

In short, most of the discussions are based on the following issues—Bhramar's sentiment, her leaving of her husband's house, her death, Gobindalal's moral degredating his subsequent rejuvenation to life, Rohini's lustiviousness and her death, whether Bhramar—is an ideal of Hindu woman or western woman, Baruni Pond and the incidents relating to it.

References

1. Roy Chowdhury, Girija Prasanna, *Bankimchandra-Krishnakanter Uil O Chandrashekhar*, Bhadra 1293 B.S.
2. *Ibid.*, pp. 1-106.
3. *Ibid.*, pp. 4-6.
4. *Ibid.*, pp. 6-8.
5. *Ibid.*, pp. 9-13.
6. *Ibid.*, pp. 10-11.
7. *Ibid.*, p. 72.
8. *Ibid.*, p. 73.
9. *Ibid.*, p. 91.
10. *Ibid.*, p. 92.
11. *Ibid.*, pp. 95-102.
12. *Ibid.*, p. 106.
13. *Ibid.*
14. *Ibid.*, p. 43.
15. Basu, Chandranath, *Ananta Muhurta Prachar*, Baishakh, 1295, pp. 11-17.
16. Basu, Chandranath, *Duiti Hindu Patni, Prachar*, Bhadra-Ashwin, 1295, pp. 212-20.
17. Basu, Chandranath, Tridhara, First issue 1297, pp. 1-9 and pp. 33-44.
18. Basu, Chandranath, *Ananta Muhurta, Prachar*, Baishakh, 1295, pp. 16-17.
19. *Ibid.*, p. 17.
20. Basu, Chandranath, *Duiti Hindu Patni, Prachar*, Bhadra-Ashwin, 1295, pp. 217-18.
21. Basu, Narendranath, *Tulonay Samalochana—Bishabriksha and Krishnakanter Uil - Kundanandini and Rohini, Sahitya Kalpadruma*, 3rd year, 8th edition, 1299, p. 223.
22. Sarkar, Surachhandra, *Krishnakanter Uil Samparke Kayekti Katha, Purahit*-Falgun 1300, pp. 181-87.
23. *Ibid.*, pp. 184-85.

24. *Ibid.*, pp. 185-87.
25. Trivedi, Ramendra Sundar, *Sahitya Katha, Bharati*, Agrahayan, 1302.
26. *Ibid.*, pp. 460-61, (ed.) Sengupta, Subodh Chandra, *Samalochana Sanchayan*, 1st Pub., August 1976, pp. 160-72.
27. Trivedi, Ramendra Sundar, *Charitra Katha*, 1320 B.S., pp. 30-31.
28. Trivedi, Ramendra Sundari, *Sahitya Katha, Bharati*, 1320 B.S., p. 461.
29. *Ibid.*, p. 462.
30. Sengupta, Subodh Chandra, *Samalochana Sanchayan, (Tragedir Nayak)*, 1st Publication, August, 1976, p. 159.
31. Pande, Bireshwar, *Bankim Chandra O Hindur adarsha, Sahitya Parisat Patrika*, 1302.
32. *Ibid.*, p. 307.
33. *Ibid.*, p. 318.
34. Sarkar, Sailendra Nath, *Krishnakanter Uil Anushilon*, Feb. 1899, pp. 87-100.
35. *Ibid.*, pp. 98-99.
36. *Ibid.*, pp. 90-93.
37. *Ibid.*, pp. 99-100.
38. *Ibid.*, pp. 89-94.
39. *Ibid.*, p. 89.
40. Rakshit, Haran Chandra, *Bangashahitya Bankim*, Mazilpur, 24 Parganas 3rd edition, pp. 105-09.
41. *Ibid.*, (First Publication, 1306), p. 109.
42. *Ibid.*, p. 105.
43. Basu, Nitya Krishna, *Sahitya Saboker Diary,* Agrahayan 1310, 14th year, 8th Edition, pp. 464-82.
44. *Ibid.*, p. 481.
45. *Ibid.*
46. Sannyal, Bhabani Gopal, *Aristotler Poetics O Sahitya Totta*, First publication, Shraban, 1395, p. 153.
47. Mukhapadhyay, Golak Behari, *Krishnakanter Uil, Bharati*, Shraban-Bhadra 1314, pp. 379-95.
48. *Ibid.*, p. 379.
49. *Ibid.*, pp. 379-80.
50. *Ibid.*, p. 387.
51. *Ibid.*, p. 384.
52. *Ibid.*, pp. 384-85.
53. *Ibid.*, p. 382.

54. *Ibid.*, p. 388.
55. *Ibid.*, p. 389.
56. *Ibid.*
57. *Ibid.*, p. 380.
58. *Ibid.*, p. 392.
59. *Ibid.*, p. 380.
60. Chakraborty, Lokenath, *Krishnakanter Uil*, *Bangadarshan*, 8th year, 6th issue, Agrahayan, 1315 B.S., pp. 420-29 & 9th year, 9th issue, Poush 1315 B.S., pp. 465-72.
61. Chakraborty, Lokenath, *Bharmar (Krishnakanter Uil), Bangadarshan*, 9th year, 1st issue, Baishakh, 1316 B.S., pp. 23-36.
62. Chakraborty, Lokenath, *Bharmer Prosonga, Bangadarshan*, 9th year, 2nd issue, Jaistha 1316 B.S., pp. 68-83.
63. Chakraborty, Lokenath, *Krishnakanter Uil Somalochana, Bangadarshan*, 8th year, 8th issue, Agrahayan, 1315 B.S., pp. 420-22.
64. *Ibid.*, p. 423.
65. *Ibid.*, pp. 471-72 (Poush 1315 B.S.).
66. *Ibid.*, p. 427 (Agrahayan 1315 B.S.).
67. *Ibid.*, pp. 469-70 (Poush 1315 B.S.).
68. Chakraborty, Lokenath, *Bhramar (Krishnakanter Uil), Bangadarshan*, 9th year, 1st issue, Baishakh, 1316 B.S., p. 23.
69. Suresh Chandra Samajpati, Editor, *Sahitya Patrika* observes—Loknath's Criticism of Bhramar is "Orthodox without specially" (*Masik Sahitya Samalochana*), Sahitya, Baishakh 1316 B.S., p. 61.
70. Samajpati, Suresh Chandra, *Masik Sahitya Samalochana, Sahitya*, Baishakh, 1316 B.S., p. 61.
71. Chakraborty, Lokenath, *Bhramar Prosonga, Bangadarshan*, 9th year, 2nd issue, Jaistha 1316 B.S., p. 78.
72. Basu, Jyotish Chandra, *Bhramar, Janmbhumi*, 18th year, 1st issue, Baishakh, 1317 B.S., pp. 15-23, 18th year, 2nd issue, Jaistha, 1317 B.S., pp. 67-71, 18th year, 4th issue, Shraban, 1317 B.S., pp. 153-55.
73. *Ibid.*, 18th year, 4th issue, Shraban, 1317 B.S., p. 154.
74. Basu, Jitendra Lal, *Bankimchandra, Bangadarshan*, 10th year, 4th issue, Shraban 1317 B.S., pp. 169-80.
75. *Ibid.*, p. 170.
76. Chattopadhyay, Sachis Chandra, *Swargiya Bankimchandra Chattopadhyayr Jibon Charit*, 2nd Ed. 1322 B.S. (First published 1318 B.S.).
77. *Ibid.*, p. 441.
78. *Ibid.*, pp. 527-28.
79. *Ibid.*, p. 581.

80. Ghosal, Sarchhandra, *Krishnakanter Uil, Bharatbarsa*, 1st year, 6th issue, Agrahayan 1320 B.S., pp. 815-21.
81. *Ibid.*, pp. 816-19.
82. *Ibid.*, p. 821.
83. Vedantasastri, Ramsahaya, *Bhramar (Samalochana), Archana*, 11th year, 7th issue, Bhadra, 1321 B.S., pp. 295-301.
84. Vedantasastri, Ramsahaya, *Gobindalal Charitra, Archana*, 15th year, 2nd issue, Chaitra, 1324 B.S., pp. 68-71, Archana, 15th year, 3rd issue, Baishakh, 1325 B.S., pp. 87-94.
85. Vedantasastri, Ramsahaya, *Bankimchandra (Bhramor O Rohini)*, Bankim Chatushpath, 1334 B.S., pp. 1-12.
86. Vedantasastri, Ramsahaya, *Bhramar (Samalochana) Archana*, 11th year, 7th issue, Bhadra, 1321 B.S., pp. 295-96.
87. *Ibid.*, p. 297.
88. Vedantasastri, Ramsahaya, *Gobindalal Charitra, Archana*, 15th year, 2nd issue, Chaitra, 1324 B.S., p. 70.
89. *Ibid.*, p. 71.
90. *Ibid.*, 15th year, 3rd issue, Baishakh, 1325 B.S., p. 93.
91. *Ibid.*, 15th year, 2nd issue, Chaitra, 1324 B.S., p. 71.
92. Vedantasastri, Ramsahaya, *Bankimchandra (Bhramar O Rohini)*, Bankim Chatuspath, 1334 B.S., p. 1.
93. Bondopadhyay, Chandi Charan, *Bangla Sahityer Kromonnoti o Bankim Chandra*, Manasi, 6th year, 2nd part, 3rd issue, Asharh, 1322 B.S., p. 437.
94. *Ibid.*
95. Bandopadhyay, Lalit Kumar, *Bankim Chandrer Akhayikabli, Bharatbarsha*, 3rd year, 1st part, 1st issue, Asharh,1322 B.S., pp. 6-11.
96. Bandopadhyay, Lalit Kumar, *Ma, Bharatbarsha*, 3rd year, 1st part, 2nd issue, Shrabon, 1322 B.S., pp. 264-82.
97. Bandopadhyay, Lalit Kumar, *Dui Bhagini, Bharatbarsha*, 4th year, 1st part, 3rd issue, Bhadra 1323 B.S., pp. 391-407.
98. Bandopadhyay, Lalit Kumar, *Kabya Sudha*, Kartik, 1323.
99. Bandopadhyay, Lalit Kumar, *Sakhi, Cal-Dhaka*, Maimon-Singh, 1328 B.S.
100. Bandopadhyay, Lalit Kumar, *Bankimchandrer Akhyaikabali*, p. 10.
101. Bandopadhyay, Lalit Kumar, Ma, *Dui-Bhagini*, pp. 398-401.
102. *Ibid.*, pp. 281-82.
103. Bandopadhyay, Lalit Kumar, *Dui-Bhagini*, pp. 398-401.
104. Bandopadhyay, Lalit Kumar, *Kabya Sudha*, op. cit., pp. 85-90.
105. Bandopadhyay, Lalit Kumar, *Sakhi*, op. cit., p. 35.

106. Sen, Shashanka Mohan, *Bangabani*, Pt. I & II, Dhaka Elbert Lib. 1915.
107. Sen, Shashanka Mohan, *Manimandir*, C.U. 1928.
108. Sengupta, S.C., *Bangla Somalochana Parichay*, 1st Pub. 1376, pp. 296-97.
109. Sen, Shashanka Mohan, *Bangabani,* op. cit., pp. 67-68.
110. *Ibid.*, p. 68.
111. *Ibid.*, p. 70.
112. *Ibid.*, p. 69.
113. Sen, Shashanka Mohan, *Banimandir*, C.U. 1928, p. 102.
114. *Ibid.*, p. 202.
115. *Ibid.*
116. *Ibid.*, p. 203.
117. *Ibid.*, p. 560.
118. Bondopadhyay, Kalipada, *Pronoya Amulak Sandeha, Sarathi*, Year-1, Issue-X, Chaitra, 1327 B.S., pp. 575-81.
119. *Ibid.*, p. 578.
120. *Ibid.*, p. 579.
121. Duttagupta, Akshay Kumar, *Bankimchandra*, 1327 B.S.
122. Duttagupta, Akshay Kumar, *Bankimchandra*, 2nd edn., Jignsa, Jaishtha, 1362 B.S., p. 193.
123. *Ibid.*, p. 560.
124. *Ibid.*, pp. 195-99.
125. *Ibid.*, pp. 198-99.
126. Akshay Kumar opposed the idea of Sachis Chandra Chattopadhyay to be regarded Bhramar as westernized lady.
127. Duttagupta, Akshay Kumar, *Bankimchandra*, 2nd edition, 1382 B.S., p. 201.
128. Sengupta, Naresh Chandra, *Sahitye Swadhinata, Archana*, Part-XIX, Issue-IX, Kartik, 1329 B.S., pp. 298-304.
129. Sengupta, Naresh Chandra, *Banglar Katha, Bnashari*, year-1, Issue-XII, Asharh 22, 1330 B.S., pp. 5-6.
130. Sengupta, Naresh Chandra, *Sahitye Swadhinata*, p. 200.
131. Sengupta, Naresh Chandra, *Banglar Katha*, p. 6.
132. *Ibid.*, p. 5.
133. Chattopadhyay, Saratchandra, *Adhunik Sahityer Kaifiat*, *Bangabani*, Shraban, 1330 B.S., pp. 681-85.
134. Chattopadhyay, Saratchandra, *Sahitya O Niti*, *Bangabani*, 1331 B.S., Reprinted: *Sarat Sahitya Samagra*, pp. 1975-78.
135. *Sarat Sahitya Samagra (Swadesh O Sahitya)*, op. cit., p. 1977.

136. *Ibid.*
137. Chattopadhyay, Saratchandra, *Adhunik Sahityer Kaifiat, Bangabani,* 2nd year, 1st half, 6th issue, Shraban, 1330, p. 685.
138. Bondopadhyay, Shrikumar, *Bangla Sahityer Upanyaser Dhara,* 5th Edn. 1372 B.S., p. 129.
139. Roy, Hemendra Kumar, *Sekele Bankim*, Yamuna, 13th year, 7th issue, Kartik, 1330 B.S., pp. 387-94.
140. *Ibid.*, p. 393.
141. Samayal, Bhabani Gopal, op. cit., p. 54.
142. Mazumder, Biman Behari, *Bankimchandra Nari Jagaraner Abhas, Sachitra Shaishir,* 2nd year 22nd week, 28th Chaitra, 1331, pp. 720-22.
143. *Ibid.*, p. 721.
144. Singha, Jatindra Mohan, *Arter Anushasan, Manasi O Marmmabani,* 17th year, 1st part, 2nd issue, Chaitra, 1331 B.S., pp. 107-12.
145. *Ibid.*, p. 110.
146. *Ibid.*, p. 111.
147. *Ibid.*
148. *Ibid.*
149. Sengupta, Dr. Satyaprasad, *Pashchatya Sahityer Samalochanar Dhara,* 2nd edition, August 1, 1977, p. 129.
150. Singha, Jatindra Mohan, *Arter Anushasan*, p. 112.
151. Royrakshit, Bhupendra Kishore, *Rohini Charitra, Pratibha*, year 15, Issue-IV, Magh-Chaitra, 1332 B.S., pp. 182-88.
152. *Ibid.*, p. 186.
153. *Bankim Rachanabali, (Krishnakanter Uil),* Part-I, Sahitya Samsad, 5th Publication, Chaitra, 1376 B.S., p. 595.
154. Royrakshit, Dhupendra Kishore, op. cit., p. 188.
155. Bhattacharjee, Adhyapak Manju Gopal, *Arter dik dia Bankimer Kono charitra ki asonggota?, panchapuspa*, Chaitra, 1336, pp. 1695-1701.
156. Bhattacharjee, Adhyapak Manju Gopal, *Art O Bankimchandra, Panchapuspa*, Jaistha, 1337, pp. 281-89.
157. Bhattacharjee Adhyapak Manju Gopal, *Arter dik dia Bankimer knono charitra ki asanggata?* Panohapuspa, Chaitra, 1336, pp. 1695-96.
158. Bhattacharjee, Adhyapak, Manju Gopal, *Art O Bankimchandra, Panchapuspa*, Jaistha, 1337, p. 281.
159. Basu, Amarendra Nath, *Krishnakanter Uiller Pradhan Charitraguli Byartha Hailo Keno?*, Panchapuspa, Baishakh, 1337, pp. 25-33.
160. Basu, Amarendra Nath, op. cit., p. 28.

161. *Ibid.*, p. 32.
162. Debsharma, Balai, *Krishnakanter Uil Biyoganta Kina?*, *Masik Basumati*, Baishakh, 1338, pp. 87-88.
163. Debsharma, Balai, *Bankim Pratiya, Bharater Sadhana*, Falgun, pp. 290-92.
164. Debsharma, Balai, *Krishnakanter Uil Biyoganta Kina?*, *Masik Basumati*, Baishakh, 1338, p. 88.
165. Debsharma, Balai, *Bankim Prativa, Bharater Sadhana*, Falgun, p. 291.
166. Debsharma, Balai, *Krishnakanter Uil Biyoganto Kina? Masik Basumati*, Baishakh, 1338, p. 88.
167. Sengupta, Subodh Chandra, *Bankimchandra* O *Saratchandra, Bichitra*, Magh, 1337, pp. 164-71.
168. *Ibid.*, p. 167.

9
Rajsingha

RABINDRANATH TAGORE (1861-1941)

Rabindranath Tagore, discussed in detail about the fourth edition of novel *Rajsingha* in his essay of the same title,[1] and presented the first literary criticism on the same novel. Rabindranath was a poet of genius and a powerful critic, and he left the stamp of his excellence in his criticism on *Rajsingha*. The essay *Rajsingha* marked the first impressionist[2] trend in Bengali critical literature. Rabindranath beautifully explained the characteristics and varieties of the tempestuous picture of family life and political world. Such a criticism of extra-ordinary intuition was not seen found earlier.

At the very outset of the essay, Tagore mentioned the swiftness of the language of *Rajsingha*. He superbly explained the structural beauty, dominance of historical elements in novel, relationship of personal life with history, and above all, individual's mingling with history.

What should be the readers' expectation in literature? Tagore answered to his question also. He has said: "In literature, we hope to get the truth of life but not the burden of it."[3] Rabindranath enjoyed the beauty treasured up in *Rajsingha* giving the readers a share in it.

There were many a characters and incidents in this novel which were historical and unhistorical. But Bankimchandra had bestowed such a force and impulse in all such incidents that a total chronic impression was created. Praising this technique highly, Tagore said: ..."each chapter (part) of the book (novel) as if seen to the other swift as a fountain."[4] Tagore observed that the heroes of the history portion of this novel were Aurangzeb,

Rajsingha and the Almighty himself, and the heroine of the novel-portion was Zebunnesa. He laid much emphasis upon the unhistorical Zebunnesa episode. Describing the inner mysteries of Zebunnesa in a superb poetic language, Tagore had shown that Zebunnesa, the Emperor's daughter, was not a portrait of penance of an impassioned life:

> ...she was a helpless play thing in the hands of the humour-some all-knowing Almighty. At one side: stormy night saw outbursts of the suppressed agonies of the women who had sacrificed everything. Who will take care of her in the midst of this hum-drum? Surely none but he, who is wide awake in the darkness of the night and is watching and directing silently the course of events, had been looking into this insignificant woman rolling in the dust with fixed eyes.[5]

Important thing that is to be noticed is that neither the glory of history nor the facts of history have been given priority by the critic. To him, what matters is the glory that is present in human nature. In that age of Bankim criticism, Tagore's was a new attitude. Pure literary criticism is a creative work itself—Tagore's criticism of *Rajsingha* is a bright example of this.

SAILENDRA NATH SARKAR

Sailendra Nath Sarkar's critical attitude, as reflected in his critical work *Rajsingha Anushilan,*[6] did not follow the critical track laid down by Tagore. Sailendra Nath termed *Rajsingha* as misnomer.[7] His second point of grievance was that *Rajsingha* was not a historical novel; because historical facts here had not been given novelistic vitality.

According to him Bankim's *Rajsingha* could not be called a novel for the same reason as *Tod's Rajasthan* could not be considered as a work of fiction. His third point of grievance was that this novel was inferior to other novels of Bankimchandra.

If the main point of criticism was to assess the value of creative work, then Sailendra Nath did not fulfill it. Still, a few points in his criticism deserve attention. Analysing the circumstances leading to Chanchal Kumari's attachment to Rajsingha and the nature of love, he said that Chanchal

Kumari's love was not simply that of a youthful amateur, it was the heartiest feminine love for the brave. The way Desdemona (Shakespeare) got inclined towards Othello through listening to his adventures of heroism, so also, listening to the heroic adventures of Rajasingha, Chanchal Kumari's love developed silently. The most memorable part of *Rajsingha* was Mobarak-Zebunnesa love episode. Shailendra Nath has drawn the readers' attention to this point. He has said: "Zebunnesa's love and Mobarak's fate are the most pathetic. Zebunnesa could not understand that she was in love with Mobarak."[8] During the era of Bankim, there was tendency of character criticism. The same is there in the essay in discussion. Chanchal Kumari is insolent, fickle, whole *Rajsingha* is heroic, sound, and religious, Maniklal is tricky, devoted to master, heroic and jocular where Nirmal Kumari is clever and wise—these are the threads of Shailendra Nath's criticism of the characters.

Besides, he tried to show that the hero and heroine Rajsingha and Chanchal Kumari were comparatively less brighter than their respective deputies—Maniklal and Nirmal Kumari.[9]

RAM MOHAN CHAKRABORTY

Ram Mohan's *Rajsingha Upannyas Samalochana*[10] was more advertisement than a critical study. The critic, here was an advertiser. Some points like—Rajsingha's Self-sacrifice to the country, Aurangzeb's hatred for the Hindus, Zebunnesa's voluptuousness, the nefarious picture of the 'Badshahi-Harem'[11] were brought out for public judgement.

Through this advertisement of *Rajsingha*, Ram Mohan made an attempt to analyse the gradual evolution of Bankim Chandra's attitude. He had seen Bankimchandra in the first state of his novel as a poet of beauty, and in the second stage, as a preacher of patriotism. He said:

> In the early stage, Bankim babu's novel is full of poetic beauty and moving grace in chapter and passage just like a young maiden whose physical beauty manifests youthful charm in every limb, and in the second stage, the flower is fully blossomed, and poetry matures into knowledge.[12]

The creator of *Rajsingha* was placed in the second stage by the critic. Because, *Rajsingha's* main tone was: "Let the motherland triumph, Let the motherland triumph."[13] Ram Mohan here searches for the source of creation leaving aside the manifold varieties in it. Herein lays the critic's personality and its literary significance.

SOURINDRA MOHAN GUPTA

Sourindra Mohan Gupta's *Yugmachitra*[14] is the first successful document of the comparative criticism of *Rajsingha*. In this essay, a comparative study between Eponine of Victor Hugo's *Les-Miserable* and Doriya of *Rajsingha* was made. Sourindra Mohan's criticism revealed a searching spirit to trace the development and falling-action of both the characters. He sought to establish his point by showing a consistency between the despair and sorrows of the characters, the inconsistencies at places, and finally evaluating the beauty of the characters arising out of the use of inspired poetic language. Sourindra criticism arises out of the use of inspired poetic language. Sourindra Mohan's skill in presenting the consistency between the events of Dariya's carrier with those of Eponine was beyond question. The vivid picture of Dariya which Sourindra Mohan has drawn, not only reflected his fundamental genius, but also gave new dimension to the character of Dariya. He said:

> Dariya a married woman—deserted, hence, sentimental; her suppressed tears and controlled emotions cannot reflect her sentiment. Her emotions shake the strings of the readers' heart.[15]

Every sentence of this essay bore the mark of the sympathetic effect produced in the mind of the readers by the character of Dariya. The critic said:

> The whole event is warm with their (Dariya & Eponine) sighs, but the sighs are not understood, the whole scene is full of tears, yet there is no dearth of pleasure, for shaken, but sentimental, proud, loving and full of pity yet stern in sarcasm, susceptible to fear and cowardly in nature, yet heroic.[16]

Sourindra Mohan, here, has given us a new light by explicating the characters from the humanist's point of view.

Above all, Sourindra Mohan goes deep the mind of Dariya through introspection and romantic imagination and seeks to explain its nature and thus has made an attempt to understand this wonderful character. But, Sourindra Mohan is not free from romantic exuberance and excesses: "Dariya is a white 'Shephalika' bathed in dew, Eponine is a worm eaten pale 'Jasmine'."[17] Such are the examples. Even if Sourindra Mohan's is a comparative study, he is keen in analysis of the inner mysteries of the character of Dariya.

IMDADAL HAQUE

Imdadal Haque, in his historical study—*Hindu Musalman O Banga Sahitya*[18] brought the charge of communalism against Bankim. According to him, Aurangzeb was a prudent and self-controlled Emperor, never resorted to non-vegetarian food after the attaining youth, yet, Bankim painted him as a devil. Zebunnesa was devoted to religious discourses, poetic discussions and study of the *Koran*. Yet Bankim plunged her into sin. Imdadal believed that Bankim's motive behind the composing of this book was to disgrace the Muslim Community.[19]

BROJENDRA SUNDAR SANNYAL

Bankim was rescued from this change of Muslim-hatred by Brojendra Sundar Sannyal who in his essay Zebunnesa[20] recreated the life of Zebunnesa with historical facts.

SARACHHANDRA GHOSAL

Sarachhandra, in his *Bankimchandrer Rajsingha*[21] elaborately discussed the gulf of differences between *Rajsingha* published in the *Bangadarshan* and the fourth edition of the same. Sarachhandra was believer of Bankim's literary ideals and therefore, be claimed excellence of every addition and alteration.[22] But Sarachhandra did not point out the artistic necessity of this excellence except in the character of Chanchal Kumari. He said that in the *Bangadarshan*, Chanchal Kumari was fickle, but in the Fourth edition, Bankim decorated this fickleness with coyness which had brightened her feminine self.[23]

LALIT KUMAR BANDOPADHYAY

Lalit Kumar Bandopadhyay's criticism of *Rajsingha* could be traced in his (I) *Bankimchandrer Akshyaikabali,*[24] (II) *Ma,*[25] (III) *Shashuri Bou,*[26] and (IV) *Sakhi.*[27]

In the first essay, Lalit Kumar attempted to justify the title; in the second, he searched for motherly virtues in the female characters, in the third, the nature of the relation between mother-in-law and daughter-in-law, and in the fourth, the significance of Nirmal Kumari's friendship was discussed.

Lalit Kumar said that Chanchal Kumari's spirit, heroism and devotion; Nirmal Kumari's friendship, talent of speech, and intelligence; Mobarak—Zebunnesa and Doriya's stories of love etc. in spite of being touching to the heart, were only relating charms and subordinate elements in the book, Rana Rajsingha's 'Kshatriya'—like-nature, his skill in war, and heroic ventures were the main incidents of the book, hence, the title was justified.[28]

According to the critic, motherly virtues developed a little only in the character of Yodhpuri Begum and Tasbirwali of *Rajsingha*. Lalit Kumar thought that the writer had designed Doriya to make contrast of her magnificent love with the voluptuousness of the princes Zebunnesa; and just for artistic purpose, motherly virtues had not been incorporated into these two characters.[29]

Of all the elements of Bankim literature, Nirmal Kumari's friendship appeared to be most attractive to Lalit Kumar. According to him, such a friendship was a rare thing not only in Bankim, but also in the ancient literature.[30]

Lalit Kumar was a renowned professor and an erudite scholar both in English and the ancient Indian Literature; and his erudition has been reflected in his essays. But, in fact, we scarcely come across any evidence of pure literary criticism in this essay of Lalit Kumar. Lalit Kumar has searched for the family pictures in *Rajsingha*, but has not given any indication towards solution of any critical problem in it.

SHASHANKA MOHAN SEN (1872-1928)

Although a historical novel, the main theme of *Rajsingha* was based upon family ideals and conjugal love. Shashanka Mohan Sen interpreted *Rajsingha* in this light in his book *Bangabani.*[31] He characterized the writers of *Rajsingha* as the path-finder of patriotism and conjugal love. According to him, Bankim's patriotic soul searched for solace even in the midst of political crisis all around. He said that in the midst of political strife and war-cry and clashing and cranking of the swords, only event which had left impression in our mind:

> Badshahjadi (Daughter of king) is ignorant of love. In the world of love, what will be the fate of Badshahjadi, what will happen to her in the end ?—This forms the backbone (theme) of the new edition of Rajsingha.[32]

Shashanka Mohan has laid more emphasis upon the high ideals than the artistic skill of this book. His originality and perception follow this ideal.

AKSHAY KUMAR DUTTAGUPTA

The beautiful and excellent criticism of *Rajsingha* after Rabindranath Tagore could be found in Akshay Kumar's *Bankimchandra.*[33]

Akshay Kumar's criticism has been divided into two distinct parts. The first part dealt with the historical judgement of *Rajsingha*'s history based upon historical facts and the second part dealt with an overall evaluation of the fictional aspects of the work.

Emphasizing the historical aspect, he pointed out that historical facts had beautified the novel and heroine laid its importance. He clearly said that in such events like Zebunnesa's tragic tale, Chanchal Kumari's hero-worship and racial vanity, 'decoit' Maniklal's gratitude, Dariya's heart-racking agony, Aurangzeb's partiality towards Nirmal Kumari—the poetic truth was more stable, deep and profound than historical truth. Hence, the novel had been beautified by history.[34]

Akshay Kumar rightly said that like *Chandrashekhar* two separate romances had also been interwoven in *Rajsingha* and by plunging the minor and major characters into the political whirlpool, Bankim attempted to reveal the human tract of each character.

As stated earlier, Rabindranath found 'Aurangzeb', 'Rajsingha' & the 'Almighty' as the protagonists of the history portion; but Akshay Kumar differed with him. According to Akshay Kumar, there was working of fate in Rajsingha, but God's direct hand was nowhere distinctly evident. He believed that the events of the history portion had been set in motion by Aurongzeb's evil designs and diplomatic tricks. He had further said that Aurongzeb was not the real hero of any portion. He said:

> Rajsingha and Chanchal Kumari is the hero and heroine of the first romance, Zebunnesa is the heroine of the second romance which is without a hero. In the first romance, Zebunnesa is the heroine of the second romance which is without a hero. In the first romance, Aurongzeb is a rival of the hero, but not co-hero; and in the second romance, he is the enemy of the heroine's father and her beloved.[35]

Akshay Kumar for the first time had focused Bankim's greatness in delving deep into the inner recesses of human heart in *Rajsingha*. His criticism of *Rajsingha* shows the critic's unprejudiced artistic sense. He pays equal attention both to the artistic and thematic aspects. Above all, maintaining a wise detachment, Akshay Kumar has tried to show that in spite of the limitations[36] of the writer, *Rajsingha* is adorned with pure artistic beauty.

BHUPENDRANATH ROY

Bhupendranath Roy attempted to trace the gradual development of the character of the crazy Dariya of *Rajsingha* in the hands of Ramesh Chandra, Girish Chandra, etc. in his *Dariya Charitrer Kromobikash*.[37]

He tried to establish a psychological basis of Dariya's actions springing from her heart changed by careless and casual cajoling by the indifferent Mobarak. The critic pointed out that the feminine kindness and softness fled from the heart of Dariya when Mobarak instead of self-sacrifice, sought to derive self-satisfaction through a casual gesture of bestowing a little pity on her, and this changed her love with pungency which prompted her to do wrong to Zebunnesa and finally do away with the life of Mobarak.[38]

Bhupendranath's reasoned for Dariya's failure to kill Zebunnesa. He argued that in order to prolong Zebunnesa's endless repentance throughout her life, Dariya did not kill Zebunnesa even if she was in a position to kill her.[39] There are such occasional sparks of literary judgement in the essay.

MANINDRANATH BONDOPADHYAY

The last criticism of *Rajsingha* before Bankim Centenary was Manindranath's *Bankim Prasanga—Rajsingha*.[40] The special feature of this essay was elaborate information about the historical facts. In the advertisement of fourth edition of *Rajsingha*, Bankim had made mention of the historians like Tod, Orm, Manushi, etc. Manindranath. He had collected materials from the historians in reference and supplemented them from the written documents of the travelers like Barnier and Tyavernier etc. He tried to analyse the background of *Rajsingha* with diligence and sincerity; and concluded that Bankimchandra had simplified the most critical chapter of the history of the Rajputs as well as the Hindus for the common readers in this book.

It seems that Manindranath treats *Rajsingha* not as a historical novel, but as a record of history.[41] This study of Manindranath may not have any literary value, but the historical facts, which he has found out through painstaking investigation, has no doubt a special significance.

SUMMING UP

Although small in volume, *Rajsingha* inspired substantial critical evaluations. A trend towards pure literary criticism and progressive attitude is noticed in most of the essays. In most of the critical essays attempts have been made to find out the inner mysteries of human life along with a judicious analysis of artistic beauty of the novel. Controversies centred round whether Bankim was a hater of the Muslim or not. Elaborate discussions were made on the incidents, characters and historical elements, nationalistic motives of Bankim and the working of fate. Amongst characters, Zebunnesa and Dariya were given priority by the critics.

References

1. Tagore, Rabindranath, *Rajsingha, Sadhana*, Chaitra, 1300 B.S., Reprinted, *Adhunik Sahitya,* 1314 B.S.
2. Mukhopadhyay, Arun Kumar, *Bangla Samalochanar Itihas*, Shraban, 1372 B.S., p. 111.
3. Tagore, Rabindranath, *Adhunik Sahitya (Rajasingha*), Kartik, 1365 B.S., p. 93.
4. *Ibid*., p. 97.
5. *Ibid*., p. 99.
6. Sarkar, Sailendranath, *Rajsingha Anushilon, Prayas,* Aug., 1900, pp. 463-77.
7. *Ibid*., p. 463.
8. *Ibid*., p. 475.
9. *Ibid*., pp. 471-74.
10. Chakraborty, Rammohan, *Rajsingha Upannyas Somalochana, Nabaprava*, Chaitra, 1307 B.S., pp. 79-82.
11. *Ibid*., pp. 81-82.
12. *Ibid*., p. 80.
13. *Ibid.*
14. Gupta, Sourindra Mohan, *Somalochani,* 1st year, 7th issue, 1309 B.S., pp. 259-69.
15. *Ibid*., pp. 261-62.
16. *Ibid*., p. 269.
17. *Ibid*., p. 268.
18. Haque, Imdadal, *Hindu Musalman O Bangasahitya, Bharati*, Baishakh, 1310 B.S.
19. *Ibid*., p. 29.
20. Sannyal, Brojendra Sundar, *Zebunnesa, Samalochani*, Issue-X, 1310 B.S.
21. *Ibid*., pp. 309-17.
22. Ghosal, Sarachhandra, *Bankimchandrer Rajsingha, Archana*, Kartik, 1320 B.S.
23. *Ibid*., pp. 309-17.
24. Bandopadhyay, Lalit Kumar, *Bankimchandrer Akshyaikabali*, 1322 B.S.
25. Bandopadhyay, Lalit Kumar, *Ma, Bharatbarsha*, Bhadra, 1328 B.S., pp. 501-22.

26. Bandopadhyay, Lalit Kumar, *Shashuri Bou, Kabyasudha*, Kartik, 1328 B.S.
27. Bandopadhyay, Lalit Kumar, *Sakhi,* Calcutta-Dhaka-Maymensinghe, 1328 B.S.
28. Bandopadhyay, Lalit Kumar, *Bankimchandrer Akshyaikabali*, op. cit., p. 10.
29. Bandopadhyay, Lalit Kumar, *Ma*, op. cit., pp. 501-03.
30. Bandopadhyay, Lalit Kumar, *Sakhi*, op. cit., p. 77.
31. Sen, Shashanka Mohan, *Bangabani*, (1st & 2nd part) Dhaka Elbert Lib., pp. 70-71.
32. *Ibid*., p. 71.
33. Duttagupta, Akshay Kumar, *Bankimchandra*, 1327 B.S.
34. Duttagupta, Akshay Kumar, *Bankimchandra*, 2nd edn. May 1975, p. 205.
35. *Ibid*., p. 208.
36. Bankimchandra had written in the introduction of Rajsingha (4th Edn.) that his aim was the establish the martial of Hindus. (Int., Rajsingha)
37. Roy, Bhupendra Nath, *Deriya Charitrer Kromobikash, Sachitra Shishir*, 29th Magh, 1333 B.S., pp. 338-41, 7th Falgun 1333, pp. 365-67, 14th Falgun, 21st Falgun, 28th Falgun, 1333 B.S., pp. 393-96, 424-26, 449-51.
38. *Ibid*., 29th Magh, 1333 B.S., pp. 338-39.
39. *Ibid*., pp. 340-41.
40. Bondopadhyay, Manindranath, *Bankim Prasanga-Raisingha*, 1339 B.S.
41. *Ibid*., p. 449.

10
Anandamath, Devi Chaudhurani, and *Sitaram*

ANANDAMATH

KALIPRASANNA GHOSH (1843-1910)

The first criticism on *Anandamath* was written anonymously in the periodical 'Sadharani.'[1] Kaliprasanna occupies the place of the first critic of *Anandamath* for his essay on the novel, entitled "Anandamather Mulmantra."[2] Written in the last decade of the nineteenth century when nationalism began to have firm grip over the minds of intellectuals of Bengal, the essay reveals the critic's restlessness regarding the frustrating conditions of Bengal; and, this probably accounts for much of his advices and emotions which determinates the major part of it. The critic's own mental condition is highlighted in the patriotic song Vandemataram, and, hence, comes the emotional outburst. This incantation in *Anandamath* is written to disperse this hypnotic drowsiness, this poetic prayer to the image of the mother is for the eradication of this unnatural indifference, this disease without treatment and the untimely death.[3] He also asserted that portions of this novel were highly poetic and picturesque, it was not a 'Historical novel',[4] it depicted the socio-political conditions of the age, and the main incident of the book was based upon historical truth, there were such incidents like Shanti's half-covered feminine heart and the wilderness of Bhabananda's love for Kalyani, but these were only secondary events of the novel, the primary inner reality of the book was devotion to motherland.[5]

BISHNU CHARAN CHATTOPADHYAY

Bishnu Charan Chattopadhyay's "Anandamath (Somalochana)"[6] was a long criticism of *Anandamath*. The ideology, language, characterization and the description of war—all these points had been given due importance by the critic. He raised various objections such as inconsistency, improbability, unfulfilment and artistic defects in the novel which deserve appreciation, but his initial garrulity regarding Bankim idolatry[7] is painful.

Bishnu Charan critically evaluates the controversial statements of Bankim that occasionally a Bengalee woman is not a helper to the Benglee—that social revolution is in most cases torturous to self, that revolutionaries are suicidal, that the English had rescued Bengal from anarchy[8] and so on and so forth. The critic said that even if there was a little self-torture in the said rejoiced 'Santanas' looting, there was no example of 'Suicidal revolutionaries'. There was no such picture in *Anandamath* that the English had rescued Bengal from anarchy. Above all, Kalyani and Shanti's fight against tremendous odds was an example of surprisingly helping attitude. But he said without hesitation that howsoever helpful Shanti might be, hers was an unnatural character.[9]

The critic thought that wise devotion, dedicated and selfless service and blessed finality were the main themes of *Anandamath*.[10] But he commented with prejudice that too much of this ideal at the close of the book had spoilt the artistic beauty.[11]

Gradual development of human nature and its finality should be the objective of novel, but it is lamentably lacking in *Anandamath*. Rightly he said, "the gardener of this garden is an expert in making wreath with the big blooming flowers, but he fails to help a bud blossoming to appear before the readers with all its varieties."[12] According to the critic, Shanti was an image of strange taste, Stayananda's character was mysterious and magical, Jibananda's game of penance was neither penance nor promise, it was mere cheating, and Bhabananda's fall was meaningless, rejuvenation of Kalyani was an unnatural event.[13] With factual evidence, the critic had shown that the war episode in *Anandamath* was unnatural and funny.[14] The language in this book was also not pleasing to the critic.[15]

He said that despite defects in handling of the plot and characterization, the main attraction of this book lay in its total appeal. *Anandamath* was a bright reflection of the then political history, its special strain being patriotism and its special wealth was the patriotic song, 'Vandemataram.'[16] Bishnu Charan attempted a total evaluation of the book by bringing these points to the notice of the readers.

DEBENDRA BIJOY BASU

Debendra Bijoy Basu, in his "Noveler Shilpa ba Kabittba",[17] had given priority to art in his discussion of the novel. According to him, art is the life in a novel. A novel without art is not a novel at all. Debendra Bijoy thought that *Anandamath* was a fine purposeful novel, but it was lacking in real art.[18]

HEMENDRA PRASAD GHOSH (1876-1963)

Hemendra Prasad Ghosh had discussed *Anandamath* separately in his essay "Bankimchandra-Anandamath"[19] and in reference, he had evaluated *Anandamath* in "Upanyasik Bankimchandra."[20] Even if the essays were written in long time-gap, there was no basic difference in his attitude and critical view. Hemendra Prasad had evaluated it in the light that it was a nationalistic novel—its main objective was to imbibe the Bengalees with the ideals of patriotism.[21] But the critic, with reasonings, had pointed out that Bankim's artistic genius suffered a set-back in this book and it reflected a thoroughly exhausted Bankim.[22] Certain other things had also been pointed out with facts. The critic pointed out some of the marks of the exhausted genius. These are first, the character of Shanti is strange, unnatural, her riding is ludicrous, and that the change of this character from the fifth edition had spoilt her beauty. Secondly, introduction of dramatic moments in order to keep Kalyani out is unnecessary. Thirdly, Bhabanande is not indispensable in the book.[23]

However, the critic pointed out that Shanti's attraction lay in her love appeal, and remarked,—"Shanti's spirit could not have any appeal to us without her love."[24]

GIRIJA PRASANNA ROYCHOWDHURY (1862-1899)

The next criticism of *Anandamath* is Girija Prasanna Roychowdhury's "Bankimchandra (Tritiyabhag)."[25] The critic had mainly discussed the artistic beauty and skill in characterization of the book in relation to the language and incidents, and the characters like Satyananda, Shanti, Bhabananda, Kalyani, Jibananda, Mahendra and Nimai. Analysis of characters with too much of emotion is the main characteristic of this essay.

Analysing the character of Satyananda, the critic said: "I paid my tribute silently to the creator of Satyananda. Mother: When would you give birth of such a son."[26] Such emotions are there in the essay. According to the critic, the creator of *Anandamath* was a great patriot, an inherent devotee of the Aryan Cult. His creations like Satyananda were the images of this cult.

Shanti was the next character to attract Girija Prasanna, because she was a selfless and devoted wife, and an ascetic woman. But the critic was hurt by the writer's words—"Shanti was made considerably tame."[27] According to the critic, the writer's effort to show naturalness in the character of Shanti was a fruitless effort because "When the character becomes appealing almost naturally, why should there be anxiety for naturalness?"[28]

In spite of emotionalism and verbosity, Girija Prasanna anticipates Rabindranath Tagore in his attempt at the artistic evaluation of the plot, character and incidents of the novel ignoring the profound social appeal of the revolutionary work of Bankim.

PRAMATHA NATH SEN

Pramatha Nath Sen attempted at the criticism of *Anandamath* after Girija Prasanna in his essays—"Mrinalini Charitra"[29] and "Bankimchandrer Swadesh Prem",[30] and he also wrote an analytical criticism of Kalyani in his essay of the same title.[31]

In the discussion of *Anandamath* in his first essay (Mrinalini Charitra), the critic observed that Shanti, Kalyani, Jibananda, etc. has been imagined as nurtured by Hindu cult. The critic said—"The Hindu men have to be inspired by the characters like a Ananda and Mahendra, and in the same fashion, Hindu women have to learn self-sacrifice and self-establishment from Kalyani and Shanti."[32] But in the second essay 'Bankimchandrer Swadeshprem', this orthodox Hindu attitude was abandoned. Here, he laid emphasis upon 'Vandemataram' and patriotism as the basis of the novel. He had strongly said that *Anandamath* was a vehement protest against the accusation that nothing could be done by the Bengalees.[33]

Pramatha Nath deserves much credit for his criticism of the character of Kalyani where he has touched not only the features of her nature, but also explained the springs of action in her. He observed that originally Kalyani was intensely domestic, her interests confined to her husband and daughter. She did not desire anything beyond that, not even heaven. With the taking of poison by Sukumari, Kalyani found a relation between God's ordeal and Sukumari's taking of poison—"Apprehending something ominous for her husband she drank the remaining poison regarding it as nectar."[34] While evaluating the character of Kalyani, Pramatha Nath had attempted to highlight the inner vision of the writer. He thought that in the character of Kalyani, Bankim had wanted to show how wifely virtue could be exemplified without directly helping the creed of the husband.[35]

BIRESWAR GOSWAMI

Bireswar Goswami's "Satyananda"[36] is a remarkable contemporary criticism. His discussion is primarily confined to Satyananda.

He has discussed Satyananda as a man having divine power, a saint, dispassionate, unselfish, kind and devoted to God. But side by side, he said—it so happened once in England that the 'Divine Right' of a king was smashed by the anger of the subjects.[37]

Bireswar has further tried to show the philosophical base and ethical implications of the book. The critic explained why the 'Santanas', who were believers in the 'Baishnavite' faith, were engaged in warfare. Unlike the Baishnavites, they did not believe on Ahimsa, rather the aim of their Baishnavism was destruction of the Evil and the rescue of the world. Therefore, they were the worshipers of 'Strength' (Shakti). The followers of Chaitanyadev worship God by 'Bhakti', the Santanas' of *Anandamath* worshipped 'Shakti' in order to destroy the enemies by force. This formed their philosophical base of the organization.[38] The critic went on to say that the 'French Revolution' being inspired by Rousseu's famous book *Le Central Social* indicated a new civilization ensuring eternal good for mankind, *Anandamath* was impregnated with such implications.[39]

Monmoth Nath Bondopadhyay's essay 'Anandamath'[40] is the next detailed critical work of the novel. Even if his power of judgement, the depth and analysis and skill are comparatively loose, his style of expression had to be appreciated.

In his essay, Monmoth Nath classified the novel *Anandamath* into three stages: common fictional stage, ethical or public-teaching stage, and philosophical stage.

The essayist thought that in spite of being primarily ethical, 'Anandamath' was like a common novel in respect of story elements, incidents and characterization. He established an affinity between poetry and novel in the events like description of Shanti's beauty, Bhabananda's reflections on Kalyani, and Mahendra and Kalyani's meeting after the war.

Monmoth Nath's attitude, a literary critic is reflected in such ideas. He has rightly said that the historical events of 'Anandamath', instead of taking us to the royal situation of the historical Kingdom or to the royal place of Rajput of Maharashtrians, takes us to a solitary corner of remote village.[41]

The critic tried to prove with dependable evidences that 'Anandamath' sought to teach the doctrine of patriotism and not sexual love. He thought that the spiritual source of 'Anandamath' lay in *The Geeta* where Lord Krishna teaches Arjuna the ways to achieve 'Moksha'. He said that the central spiritual teaching of the book was that a true preceptor could be had by engagement in work in genuine devotion, and finally the disciple would achieve the real wisdom.[42]

Monmoth Nath's criticism is a step forward in the history of *Anandamath* criticism, because a new venture is made here towards a realistic evaluation of the book.

BIPIN CHANDRA PAL (1858-1932)

After Monmoth Nath, Bipin Chandra Pal attempted at the criticism of *Anandamath* in his different works[43] written at different times. Even though written at different times, there is a consistency in all the writings. The critic's evaluation is based upon sound reasoning and facts.

A believiour of realism in literature, Bipin Chandra tried to establish through his analysis that *Anandamath* failed to satisfy artistic taste and lacked in poetic appeal.[44] Yet he thought that in spite of unbridled passions[45] in some of the scenes, the creed, which the writer had tried to establish in this book, was not artificial, even if occasionally traditional. The critic opined that in this book *Bankimchandra* had tried to establish a synthesis between the European thought and the ancient Indian thought, and thereby to prove the supremacy of the Indian thought.[46]

Bipin Chandra interpreted Bankim's psychology in a way to show that the writer inspired to countrymen towards a higher philosophy of work ('Karmayuga') by synthesizing the indulgence of senses and the restraint of senses.[47] Therefore, Jibananda's penance was arranged because he could not transmute self-enjoyment into self-sacrifice. The cult of sacrifice in this book was not born of the cult of enjoyment and therefore, the critic thought that there was indiscipline amongst the sanyasis.[48]

However, the song 'Anandamath' appeared to be most charming to the critic and he believed that it was the very subsistence of the book. Analysing the song both philosophically and spiritually, Bipin Chandra concluded that the image of mother shown in *Anandamath* was not imaginary, it was real portrait.[49]

Bipin Chandra's criticism shows his originality of understanding and expression. Himself a patriot his criticism is favoured with nationalistic sentiment.

PRAFULLA KUMAR SARKAR (1884-1944)

Prafulla Kumar Sarkar discussed *Anandamath* in his essay "Samaj Sanskare Bankimchandra."[50] He concentrated himself to the characters of Kalyani and Shanti, who hold out the glorious future of Bengalee Hindus. Prafulla Kumar viewed these two characters as idealistic sketches of Hindu womanhood. He said that the Hindu woman Shanti proved herself to be an ideal partner of Jibananda in his crusade. Their love transcended the worldly limitations and elevated to the level of eternity.[51] In his work, traditional critical trend is evident.

He studied *Anandamath* in his three different essays—"Bankimchandrer Akshyaikabali,"[52] "Ma"[53] and "Kabyasudha."[54] The critic dealt with the title in the first essay, in the second essay he discussed the mother images of the different female characters, and in the third he treated the character of Nimai.

Lalit Kumar analysed that even if the situations like the conjugal love of Jibananda and Shanti, and motherly affection of Kalyani were intense, the focal point of *Anandamath* was patriotism. The images in the temple *Anandamath* signified this patriotism; hence, the title was justified.[55]

In the analysis of Kalyani and Nimai, their sweet motherly ideals were highlighted. He said, a deep religious sense being mixed up with devotion to husband and affection for children. Kalyani did not hesitate to take poison. He further said that in the character of Shanti, the writer had tried to exemplify the spiritual conjugal love, therefore, her motherliness had been neglected.[56] According to Lalit Kumar, Nimai was a developed version of Shyama Sundari of *Kapalkundala*. The selfishness in Shyama Sundari was rectified in Nimai.

Lalit Kumar's critical works show originality in respect of treatment of the subject, but his criticism is more descriptive than analytical.

PANCHKARI BONDOPADHYAY (1863-1923)

Panchkari Bondopadhyay left a spiritual and straight forward say on *Anandamath* in his essay "Bankimchandrer Troyee."[58] He did not hesitate to point out the artistic defects. He boldly said that the 'Anushilan Tatta' which Bankim had tried to show in this book was imported from Europe. The 'individual and communal culture' of the German Scholar Fichte had been given a local colour for the understanding of the bengalees.[59] The critic was very much conscious of the traits of Bengalee culture, so, he was not ready to accept the Sannyasis' of *Anandamath* as Bengalee-Sannyasis, and here, he thought *Anandamath* to be an expression of the 'Utopian' ideals like the works of the Lake-Poets. 'Sannyasi' in theory but expert in looting, the critic fails to understand them.[60] The critic firmly believed that the ideal laid down upon the Sannyasis by Bankim was purely European, because Sannyasis with wife rarely found in India.[61] And he further said that by forming the group of Sannyasis with wives, Bankim had fallen in trouble and Shanti's excess and Bhabananda's attraction for Kalyani, etc. had become strange.

Probably, Bankim wanted to show in this book that attraction for home had to be abandoned at the altar of service to the society. But that well-designed intention of the writer had not been approved by the critic. So, he remarked rather sarcastically—"Bankimchandra has composed an excellent poem upon those excellent Sannyasis. There are in this book, the beauty of the Baishnaba, the spirit of the 'Tantrik', and the fine air of modern English idealism. The story has become laudatory due to this combination, but the conclusion is not clear."[62] Then, wherein lies the success of *Anandamath*. The critic remarked still more sarcastically—"The glory of *Anandamath* is not in its characterization or painting, but in the rhyme 'Vandemataram' and in presentation of the image of mother."[63] This solitary remark of the critic sufficiently exposes the book.

SHASHANKA MOHAN SEN (1872-1928)

Shashanka Mohan Sen tried to explain in 'Bangabani'[64] the gradual evolution of the inner visions of Bankim's mind, and, side by side, he also commented on the artistic quality of the novel, *Anandamath*.

Shashanka Mohan tried to show that the writer had followed the Indian ideals of 'Sang-Sannyas' by relating conjugal love with love for country and had established that patriotism which had its basis upon Nishkham Karma, and finally, he had established conjugal love in the temple of religion."[65] He clearly said that Bankim in matters of art had abandoned the European suspicion and laxity in conjugal love and initiated a sublime ideal of love in this book. But Shashanka Mohan is unhesitatingly critical about the artistic achievement and vitality of the book in comparison with the earlier works.[66]

RABINDRANATH TAGORE

Before Rabindranath Tagore, all the critics of the first two decades of the present century, who tried to evaluate *Anandamath,* were carried away by the emotional, social and religious appeal of this revolutionary work of Bankim, and failed to make an artistic appraisal, the only exception being Girija Prasanna Roy Chowdhury, who might be regarded as the precursor of Rabindranath on artistic evaluation of *Anandamath*. Himself a great literary genius, Rabindranath was not at all influenced by the contemporary trend of literary criticism rather revolutionaries Bengali literary criticism by his own contributions. It is needless to say that criticism of pure literary type could only be expected from this master mind.

Being conscious of the tremendous social impact of *Anandamath,* and its evaluation in the same light, Rabindranath did well to level his criticism of *Anandamath* as 'literary criticism',[67] to be distinguished from contemporary social and religious evaluations of the novel. Rabindranath found fault with the characterization as well as the plot construction and structure of the book. He said that the characters of *Anandamath* were all sham unlike the characters of other novels, e.g., Nagendranath, Krishnakanta, Bhramar and Gobindalal which were adorned with depth, vitality and forcefulness of personality. He raised the question: "The idea which has directed and centralized the varieties of human nature towards as revolution,—where has Bankim Babu shown that their natural different opinions, rise of fresh spirits in them have been mono-directed being in the turmoil of great ideal?"[68] According to Rabindranath, the whole of it was an 'unreal phantasmagoria'.[69] He thought if Bankim was successful in the creation of individual characters, he was equally a failure in the creation of characters in a group.[70] He further thought that against the historical background in which these characters had been imagined, Bankim had not indicated how, by and by, characters abandoning the worldly ties assembled on a common platform imbibed with the same ideal thought torture, tyranny and unfruitful attempts.[71]

The above views of Rabindranath published in 'Manasi O Marmabani' were sharply commented by the 'Bharati'. The periodical doubted whether Tagore's opinion about *Anandamath* remained unchanged even after Swadeshi Movement since this editor considered *Anandamath* to be as glorious as a 'Bhagawat'of patriotism and not as a novel.[72]

In fact, Tagore's opinion of *Anandamath* had been never changed. He had never approved this book as a pure literary piece. To him, it was not important from literary standpoint whether Bhabananda, Satyananda and others had ushered a new era of patriotic fervor, the important point was that whether with these characters a definite literary idealism was established or not.[73] However, Rabindranath was happy with the presentation of interactions in the character of Shanti.[74]

Rabindranath's critical approach is a landmark in the modern criticism of *Anandamath,* because his is a purely literary approach. Specially, the well-determined conclusion which he has drawn makes, on the one hand, his strong originality, and on the other hand, it inspires the critics to take a fresh look at *Anandamath.*

KIRAN SHANKAR ROY

Kiran Shankar Roy's critical essay *Anandamath*[75] was an elaborate criticism of novel. Kiran Shankar discussed the artistic defects, inconsistency of characters, and faulty selection of subject matter along with the structural defects of the book.

He also raised the point that *Anandamath* was not from the free foreign influence of the unbridled sentimental passions of nineteenth century.[76]

Discussing the artistic failure of the novel, the critic pointed out that the characters were imaginary, not real, that the spirit of revolt although pronounced in the scene of famine was not maintained till the end, that the background of lawlessness and tyranny against which the 'Santana' rose in revolt was absent and that war narratives were marked by jocularity and fun.[77]

Kiran Shankar found improbability both in male and female characters. As there was a pretention of supernatural power in the character of Satyananda,[78] so also Shanti was nothing more than a burden in this book.[79] But the critic expressed his satisfaction on the portrait of Mahendra. He said that Bankim's negligence for Mahendra was responsible for the manifestation of Mahendra as a character of flesh and blood, "Too much care would have made Mahendra and exceptionally heroic man or an exceptionally great man, but that would have been equally improbable."[80]

AKSHAY KUMAR DASGUPTA

Akshay Kumar's criticism of *Anandamath* in his book *Bankimchandra*[81] was thoughtful and intelligent. He was dependent upon the evaluation of the story element, characters, the writer's inspiration and ideology.

The most noticeable thing about Akshay Kumar is that he built up his own criticism of *Anandamath* taking into account the past tradition of Bankim's criticism around the novel, sometimes accepting or approving one or two views and at other times rejecting some of them. This sense of tradition in criticism was first set by Akshay Kumar.

Indeed, his review of the past critics prepared his mind to from his own outlook. He, naturally, fell into the artistic tradition began by Girija Prasanna and matured by Rabindranath. He opined that Bankim attempted to establish ideal by creating beauty in conformity to art, but his attempt to combine together past, present and future art had become defective. He said: "The ideal of the 'Santanas' is of the future, their weakness is of the present or of all times, and the background is of the historical past."[82] According to him, Shanti is not a woman of past or present; she is the right partner of future countrymen with the spirit of sacrifice.[83]

Akshay Kumar clearly said that the plot of *Anandamath* was not designed in conformity to the claim of Bankim in the advertisement of the book.[84] According to Akshay Kumar, Mahendra was fine and natural amongst the Santanas,[85] Satyananda was a shadowy unsubstantial creation, Jibananda and Bhabananda even it infatuating and weak, were strong in patriotism.[86] The critic's remarks were based upon facts and reasonings.

Regarding plot construction the critic pointed out that the plot began with the description of a terrific famine, but its impact vanished after a few chapters, the struggle in the background of the establishment of *Anandamath* was absent, which had weakened the book.[87]

Akshay Kumar's critical approach is characterised by clarity of thought, impartiality and fair judgement which mark him out as a critic of pure literary school.

CHITTARANJAN DAS (1870-1925)

Chittaranjan Das, in his essay 'Bankimchandra',[88] said that there might be in *Anandamath* the 'positivism' of Comte, the daring nation idea of Europe, sannyas of 'Middle Age', 'English romanticism', and even, there might be the inherent flows of art, but there was the Bengalee—the Bengalee who could identify himself as Indian through application[89] (*Anushilon*).

ARABINDA GHOSH

Arabinda Ghosh evaluated the inward inspiration and the idea arising out of this inspiration of the creator 'Vandemataram' in his essay 'Vandemataram Mantra'.[90] He said that in the *Anandamath,* Bankim had proclaimed a power through an allegory. This power is not physical strength alone, it is a moral force. Ascetic spirit, self-sacrifice at the altar of national liberation, unity, a religious fervor in patriotism, such moral points had been expressed through Vandemataram.[91] This searching spirit and philosophical approach of Arabinda Ghosh introduce a new approach to *Anandamath.*

NIBARAN CHANDRA DASGUPTA

Nibaran Chandra Dasgupta gave a line by line analysis of 'Vandemataram' in his essay 'Bankimer Matrirup'.[92] He laid much emphasis upon the duty of the government or kind. 'Vandemataram' showed what should be the duty of the king towards the subjects, he should see the welfare of the kingdom, it was the inner significance of 'Sukhadang Baradang Mataram'.[93]

Nibaran Chandra's is a fundamental approach and it throws a new light of 'Vandemataram'.

OTHER CRITICS ON *ANANDAMATH*

With the rapid spread of the nationalistic sentiment all over the country, the patriotic song 'Vandemataram' of *Anandamath* gained in tremendous popularity and it was chanted with great enthusiasm everywhere. The twenties and thirties saw the country raising the slogan of 'Vandemataram'. This enthusiasm with the Bankim song incorporated in a book dealing with a Hindu revolt was looked upon by the Muslims with much suspicion and hatred.[94] In came the Muslim protest, and this provoked many Hindu critics to raise their pens in defence of 'Vandemataram'.

On the eve of Bankim Centenary, a strong movement precipitated; and strong resistance came against the proposal of making 'Vandemataram' the national anthem.[95] At that time, a group of critics took meticulous care to glorify 'Vandemataram' and proposed to make it the national anthem. Those critics did not concentrate themselves only on dry logic and facts, their criticisms were provocative from the literary standpoint also. To name a few of such essays—Sarala Bala Sarkar's 'Yatiyatar Mahasangeet-vandemataram'.[96] Kshitish Chandra Dasgupta's 'Vandemataram-Deshaprem O Pritipurna Bandana Gan'.[97] Ashok Nath Shastri's 'Yatiyajibane Vandemataram',[98] Bankim Chandra Sen's Vandemataram[99] and 'Vandemataramer Shakti'.[100]

Sarala Bala opined that 'Vandemataram' was full of patriotic adoration.[101] Kshitish Chandra Strongly emphasized that 'Vandemataram' was not a war-cry against any community; it was a song of adoration for the motherland.[102] Ashoknath also had the same opinion.[103] Bankim Chandra Sen said that it was an allegorical representation of the inner truth of India. The glorious image of the mother in this song had immensely inspired the 'sanatans' of *Anandamath*.[104] The inner strain of all those essays was patriotism. All the critics were of the opinion that 'Vandemataram' should be judged as the fullest expression of patriotism.

DEVI CHAUDHURANI

THAKURDAS MUKHAPADHYAY (1258-1310)

Thakurdas Mukhapadhyay's *Devi Chaudhurani*[105] is the first criticism of the novel. In this essay, the critic's main points of discussion are the inspiration behind the novelist, the idealism and philosophy and characterization of *Devi Chaudhurani.*

The critic is conscious of the two principal trends of literary criticism—ancient and modern; and in his own standard he falls into modern school, since the ancient school is characterised by understanding through judgement[106] which is absent in him.

The purpose of literature, according to him, is to purify the mind;[107] and in his opinion Bankim followed this principle in his novel *Devi Chaudhurani.* Evaluating the novel from idealistic and philosophical point of view the critic remarked that, as in *Anandamath,* so in *Devi Chaudhurani*, Bankim handled the story to preach his own religious opinion. Indeed, the main purpose of Bankim was to uphold the desireless state of meditation. Thakurdas took pains to explain this point by referring to "Arya Shastra", and opined that 'Nishkam Karma' (desireless work) was the very basis of *Devi Chaudhurani.*[108]

In fact, Thakurdas regarded *Devi Chaudhurani* as a conclusion of *Anandamath* in so far as idealism and philosophy of Bankim was concerned. He pointed out that the basis of *Anandamath* was first patriotism and then knowledge, while in *Devi Chaudhurani* both these ideals were made primary. The main ground of his contention was that *Devi Chaudhurani* was a combination of Shanti and Kalyani. From that he logically concluded that *Devi Chaudhurani* was superior to *Anandamath.*

Turning to characters we find that he examined *Devi Chaudhurani* and Brojeswar as expression of ideals embodied in the novel. According to him Prafulla was an epitome of Nishkam Karma. This is the rare quality which sustained Prafulla who was a citadel of beauty and a rare example of devoted wife. However, the modernity of the critic is revealed in his enjoyment of the characterization when he shows himself attracted to Prafulla for her coyness; and he remarks that there was coyness behind every action of Prafulla.

Thakurdas criticism strikes a modern note, but he is not free from the flow of the age. Emotional Thakurdas has made a comparative study of Prafulla and Kundanandini, and said: "Kunda is coy, simple, and a pre-matured bud.... Whereas Prafulla is a full-blossomed lotus, the world delights in her flavor."[109] Thakurdas as the first critic of *Devi Chaudhurani* deserves special attention. His ideological and philosophical interpretation of the novel and characters is also unorthodox, and the modern psychological treatment of characters shall have to wait.

DEBENDRA BIJOY BASU

Debendra Bijoy Basu discussed the artistic features of *Devi Chaudhurani* in his essay entitled *Noveler Shilpo ba Kabitwa.*[110] According to Debendra Bijoy, art, which is the soul[111] of novel has been distorted in *Devi Chaudhurani*, because of too much emphasis upon ethic and aim. His grievance was that the writer had mixed art with artificiality and thereby spoilt the artistic beauty.[112]

JNYANENDRA LAL ROY

Jnyanendra Lal Roy came next as a critic of *Devi Chaudhurani* in his *Probandha Lahari.*[113] He discussed many inconsistences in this book. He termed it sometimes as a scripture, sometimes as an allegory. He observed that in the allegory of Prafulla, Bankim's religious ideals and his thoughts about worldly life had been expressed. And, therefore, Jnyanendralal had devoted himself whole-heartedly to the study of scriptural elements in this book.

According to him, *Devi Chaudhurani* is a religious scripture because Prafulla is the living image of 'Dharma Tattba' and 'Anushilan Tattba'. The teaching of Nishkam Karma which Bankim had pointed out in the "Dharma Tattba" had been reflected in the life of Prafulla. That which was spiritual in "Dharma Tattba" had become physical in Prafulla. He divided human passions into four parts—Bodily (Shaririki). Concerning knowledge (Jnyananjani), concerning action (Karjyakarani) and concerning mind (Chittarajani). Human aim is to exult, develop, and balance those passions. Bankimchandra had told of these passions in Dharma Tattba. The present critic believed that the same teaching could be found in *Devi Chaudhurani* also.[114]

Jnyanendra Lal's explanation of the allegory in *Devi Chaudhurani* is inconsistent and painstaking. He said: "Bhabani Pathak is intelligence and strength, *Devi Chaudhurani*—conscience and wisdom, and the dacoits are those passions like greed, jealously, etc."[115]

Unlike Thakurdas Mukhopadhyay Jnyanendra Lal considered Brojeswar as a hateful man who agreed to lash his helpless innocent wife with a broom-stick by the order of his father. This was not the mark of a devoted son, but it marked his cowardice and meanness. Towards the close of the essay, Jnyanendra Lal had seen Prafulla as a common woman and Brojeswar an object of hatred.

Although, Jnyanendra Lal considered it as a religious scripture, he found some defects in it from the artistic point of view. He found some of the situations effective, obscure and? Unfulfilled.[116] And it is here that the criticism is free from the old barriers.

HEMENDRA PRASAD GHOSE (1876-1963)

Hemendra Prasad's criticism of *Devi Chaudhurani* is found in his *Bankimchandra,*"[117] *Upanyasik Bankimchandra*[118] and *Rishi Bankimchandra.*[119] Hemendra Prasad emphasized the ethical side of *Devi Chaudhurani* in these essays. His discussion was not primarily based upon literary art, to him, the writer was a teacher of "Nishkam Karma" and an organizer of a nation.[120] According to Hemendra Prasad, while the dedication in *Anandamath* was 'Sakam' in *Devi Chaudhurani*, it was 'Nishkam', and the teaching and preaching of this 'Nishkam Karma' was the aim of *Devi Chaudhurani.*[121]

Although, Hemendra Prasad found the book ethically significant, some of the situations like Prafulla's wrestling with man, winning the senses through decoity, and entry into family life were beyond the limit of probability. About Brojeswar, the critic remarks: "Brojeswar is a shadow beside Devi. He is as if a creation of a modern angry writer."[122]

HIRENDRANATH DUTTA (1868-1942)

Hirendranath Dutta's criticism of *Devi Chaudhurani* appeared under the title *Profullmukhi.*[123] As the tile indicates the primary aim of the critic is to make an analysis of the heroine of the novel. The critic fulfilled his task quite satisfactorily and gave a new turn to the criticism of *Devi Chaudhurani.*

The scope of theme being limited, the critic could make a searching probe into one of the most widely discussed heroines of Bankim faction. His analysis falls into two part is: (i) inconsistences of Prafulla and (ii) mysteries of Prafulla's last life.

First the critic drew attention to the inconsistencies in the character of Prafulla. He posed the following questions: (a) Bankimchandra wanted to represent Prafulla as an image of 'Nishkam Dharma'. But had Prafulla made expression of this in her words and actions? If so, then why had Prafulla entered into family life discarding 'Sannyas'? Does it indicate the integrity of her 'Nishkam Dharma'? (b) Supposing that the fundamental aim of writing *Devi Chaudhurani* is to create an ideal woman in family, then why has the writer made this attempt with the help of a few words only without resorting to such varieties of incidents?[124]

'Sannyas' is not appropriate to a housewife, if the writer's aim is to highlight this principle along with presentation of the ineffectiveness of the life of Devi, then why the chapter presenting Prafulla as a queen is presented so brightly?

Besides, the thinking mind of Hirendranath went deep into explaining the tough mysteries of Prafulla's last life. According to the critic, from Prafulla's meeting with Brojeswar towards the end of her 'Sannyas', the rest part of the book was "poetically superb".[125] Because in this part, Prafulla's human side was so vividly exposed that "Devi's ten years of modification comes into nothingness."[126]

Hirendranath's criticism strikes novelty. Prafullamukhi is a new gem in the chain of *Devi Chaudhurani* criticism which is impartial and free from prejudice.

GIRIJA PRASANNA ROYCHOWDHURY (1862-99)

Girija Prasanna's criticism of *Devi Chaudhurani* is found in his essay *Devi Chaudhurani-charitra-Bishlesion-Bakhya-Somalochana*[127] under *Bankimchandra (Part-III)*. Even if Girija Prasanna's criticism was written and published after the death of Bankimchandra, his work showed the trends of Bankim-criticism in Bankim's lifetime. Emotion and excess of idolatry are marked in this essay.

Explaining the last part of Prafulla's 'Sannyas life'. Girija Prasanna had said:

> ...as the blooming flower remains clammy with rain-water in rainy season, which drop with a little tossing so also Devi's eyes were clammy with tears.[128]

Girija Prasanna's presentation of the characters with frequent quotations, and use of the style of Bankim's diction show the trend of criticism during Bankim's lifetime.

Preaching of the Hindu ethic and ideals, according to Girija Prasanna, was the chief objective of the writer. He believed that these ideals, have been well-exemplified in the portrayal of the character of Prafulla. Influenced by these ideals, he remarked about Brojeswar's devotion to his father: "...such devotion to father is an example to the modern youth."[129]

Girija Prasanna as a Bankim critic could not approve of Hirendranath's evaluation of Prafulla; and he wrote a detailed essay entitled *Prafullamukhi (Pratibad)*[130] contradicting Hirendranath's arguments.

In the above-mentioned reactionary essay, Girija Prasanna tried to solve the question posed by Hirendranath and also tried to give consistent analysis of the inconsistencies in question. In this attempt, Girija Prasanna very skillfully analysed the inner significance of the character of Prafulla. It could be said that this essay of Girija Prasanna is superior to his previous one so far as the analysis of the character is concerned.

According to Girija Prasanna, Prafulla's life can be divided into two parts which are well-designed; in the first part, Prafulla fails to achieve success as an ascetic because it is not her duty to practice asceticism; and, therefore, she has to return to family life, which forms the second part of her life. Regarding the charming first part of Prafulla's life Girija Prasanna remarkes that a true poet brings out the subtle aim of life from the inner recesses of mind and presents it in wider perspective.[131] Girija Prasanna thinks that Prafulla is not the image of 'Nishkam Dharma', she is the image of Nishkam domestic life and the novel had dealt with the nature of Nishkam domestic life. Therefore, the writer has dropped the plan of prolonging this 'Nishkam Dharma' in the Chapter II to avoid unnecessary volume of the book.

It is already mentioned that Girija Prasanna is a believer of Bankim's literary ideals. So, an impartial judgement from him is a vain effort. Nevertheless, Girija Prasanna has a distinct perception of the character of Prafulla in conformity to the writer's aim and he has given it a clear expression.

PRAMATHA NATH SEN

Bankim criticism after Bankim's death also continued to be preoccupied with the Hindu creed, this is evident in Pramatha Nath Sen's critical work *Mrinalini Charitra*.[132] According to him, Prafulla, in spite of being a devoted follower of "Nishkam Dharma" is not an ideal Hindu woman, because none of the successors of Sita and Sabitri is expected to wrestle with her male counterparts.[133] The main aim of this essay is explication of adherence to Hindu Cult from literary point of view.

LALIT KUMAR BANDOPADHYAY (1275-1336)

Although, in *Devi Chaudhurani* can be found "the expression of conflict and compromise between devotion to father and love to wife,"[134] Prafulla's 'devi' image in her 'Sannyas' life is the main aim of the book. Therefore, the title of the book is justified. This is, in brief, Lalit Kumar's say in his chapters on *Devi Chaudhurani* under *Bankim Chandrer Akhyaikabali*.[135]

In the essay entitled *Ma*,[136] Lalit Kumar searched for the motherly image of the female characters in this boo.[137] The critic concentrated himself in finding out the motherly image of Prafulla's mother and Brojeswar's mother. Lalit Kumar said that Prafulla's mother set an example of sacrifice at the cost of her self-respect for the happiness of her daughter, and here the love of a Bengalee mother was vividly pictured.[138]

Like Prafulla's mother, Lalit Kumar thought, Brojeswar's mother was also a perfect motherly portrait. According to him, display of kindness towards the shelter less daughter-in-law, mother's anxiety to hear the death news of Brojeswar, acceptance of the new bride—all these were examples of Bengalee family ideals.[139] In the eye of Lalit Kumar, Sagar was an incomplete motherly portrait and Nayanbou was an 'ugly realistic one'.[140]

Lalit Kumar further discussed about this book in his essay *Shasuri Bou.*[141] It needs no mention that to ascertain the relation between mother-in-law and daughter-in-law is the main thing of this discussion. Quoting profusely from the book, Lalit Kumar tried to establish that Prafulla was an ideal daughter-in-law while Brojeswar's mother was an ideal mother-in-law.[142]

According to Lalit Kumar, Diba and Nisha of *Devi Chaudhurani* form a classic example of 'Sakhi', and Lalit Kumar evaluated it in his *Sakhi.*[143] Lalit Kumar went to the extent to say that Diba and Nisha were as good as Sriradhika's Sakhies of the Baishnab Literature and Shakuntala's couple of sakhies Anusuya and Priyanbada.[144] Their contribution to the shaping of heroine's spiritual life had also been pointed out by Lalit Kumar.[145]

Another feature of Lalit Kumar's essay was to find out the nature of family pictures. Here Lalit Kumar seems to be more a surveyor than a critic. There is more information in his essays than analysis. But there was no critic prior to Lalit Kumar to handle the arduous task with so much of seriousness and sincerity. And herein lies to speciality of Lalit Kumar.

CHANDICHARAN BONDOPADHYAY (1858-1916)

Chandicharan Bondopadhyay in his essay *Bangla Sahityer Kromonnoti O Bankimchandra,*[146] searched for the ideals of Hindu woman in Prafulla and Sagar. According to the critic, Sagar's feeling of pity for her co-sister (syapatni) Prafulla and her willingness to leave her husband to Prafulla's bed-room—were rare examples to be found with Hindu woman only. Besides, the ideals of sacrifice were possible only by a Hindu woman, Chandicharan found in Prafulla's giving up of the leadership of the gang of decoits, and her subsequent service to Brojeswar and others of his family,[147] a reflection of ideal Hindu woman house.

PANCHKARI BONDOPADHYAY (1863-1923)

Panchkari Bondopadhyay's *Bankimchandrar Troyee*[148] was an ideal contemporary criticism of *Devi Chaudhurani*. Panchkari showed a new trend where theory mingled with beauty. Here he tried to evaluate Bankim's social thought along with the novelty of his ideas in organizing the Bengali Society. Side by side, he had pointed out the artistic defects of the novel and the incorporation of western ideal[149] in it.

The critic had high appraisal for this great attempt of the writer of *Devi Chaudhurani*, because attempts had been made here to train men through practice. But this was not clearly perceptible in the novel, because of the assertion of attraction towards family life. The critic did not find any reason why Prafulla had been made so great while she had only to wash dishes in Brojeswar's house. Of course, he had praised the poetic ability of the writer to create the background of Prafulla's return to home. He said: "Giving one night's pleasure to Prafulla with her husband, the poet has pricked a thorn in the way of her greatness."[150] To Panchkari, Prafulla was full of abstraction, and the novelist failed to maintain consistency between Prafulla's 'Sannyas' life and her transformation to family life again.[151]

According to Panchkari, the novelist occasionally sacrificed art in order to bring home to the readers his didactic ideals, and, in this connection, the critic referred to the duality in Bankim revealed in his adherence to amatory sentiment and his temptation of domesticity, for which he introduced the return of Prafulla home even after he so many lesons.[152]

It appears that Panchkari is a blood critic with a strong artistic sense, but too much philosophical tendency in his essay has overpowered his pure literary evaluations.

BIJOYRATNA MAZUMDER

Bijoyratna Mazumder searched for humour in *Devi Chaudhurani* in his essay *Bankimchandrer Upanyase Hasyaras*.[153]

In order to create humour in *Devi Chaudhurani*, Bankimchandra did not create any conventional character of a 'fool' (Bidushak), he created humour through the usual characters in the novel. Bijoyratna attempted to assess the credit of the writer in this respect. He observed Bankim's attempts to create natural, fine and new type of humour through such characters as Brahma Thakurani, Gobrar Ma, Sagar and Nayan Bou. He pointed out that centering round the temptation of taking 'Sandesh' and the subsequent discussion between Sagar and Nayan Bou Bankim had produced a humour of superb merit.[154] Bijoyratna is the first critic to look at the book from this view point.

SHASHANKA MOHAN SEN (1872-1928)

The trend, pattern and tone so Shashanka Mohan's criticism of *Devi Chaudhurani*[155] are almost like those of Panchkari Bondopadhyay. But Shashanka Mohan went a step further to give a more comprehensive criticism of *Devi Chaudhurani*.[156]

Shashanka Mohan's observations were mainly based upon the following points—He categorically pointed out that the writer of *Devi Chaudhurani* had felt the necessity of 'Nishkam Dharma' in the family life of Bengalee Hindus that Devi was the 'Nishkam' decoit of patriotism, that Prafulla was the housewife in accordance with 'Nishkam' ideals and that Brojeswar was a devoted son in accordance with the Indian family ideals. Shashanka Mohan said:

> The selfless love of *Anandamath* has been neglected in *Devi Chaudhurani* through strife and conflicts of passions like jealousy, etc. and *Devi Chaudhurani* is written with this intention.[157]

The critic further said that the return of Devi to the domestic life neither championed nor condemned any ideal. It was an indication of Bankim's regards for the 'Song-sannyas'.

Towards the last part of life Bankimchandra's literary genius was on the path of decline and he resorted to preaching, Novels like *Devi Chaudhurani* are the evidence. Shashanka Mohan had drawn our attention to this decadence in Bankim's art, referring to which he said: "The use of the verses of the *Geeta* in the exchanges of Prafulla and Nisha has interfered the realm of art."[158]

Shashanka Mohan opined that Bankim had struck a happy blend of the good and the beautiful in *Devi Chaudhurani*, and drew the reader's attention to the great truth in the novel by pointing out that *Devi Chaudhurani* in the midst of renunciation and penance had cherished in the heart of hearts the secret desire to meet her husband and return home. The critic successfully brought out the fact that it was the natural Prafulla behind the artificial *Devi Chaudhurani* who draws our sympathy and pity.[159] The humorous element, especially a female heart which is there under the grade of an artificial asceticism delights us. By discovering this vital truth, Shashanka Mohan imparted a new life to the novel.

BIPIN CHANDRA PAL (1858-1932)

Bipin Chandra Pal's assessment of *Devi Chaudhurani* is spread over four different essays[160] written in intervals. Surprisingly enough, these are strikingly similar in ideas and technique.

In evaluating *Devi Chaudhurani*, Bipin Chandra was carried by the conviction that devotion to God[161] lay at the root of Bankim's patriotism, and that the principal aim of Bankim in writing the novel was the strike a synthesis among different ideals. Guided by this ideas he remarked that Bankim wanted to evolve a work ethos in *Devi Chaudhurani* through synthesis of Hindu ideals and European religion of practice,[162] worldliness and of the worldliness, epicureanism and restraint,[163] and thus to rise to the level of universalism. While paying tribute to Bankim in this respect Bipin Chandra commented that from the point of fine arts, Bankim's artistic genius suffered a setback in this book.[164]

Although Bipin Chandra's remarks are thought provoking, these need explanations for proper appreciation.

AKSHAY KUMAR DUTTAGUPTA

Akshay Kumar's criticism of *Devi Chaudhurani* is found in his complete work *Bankimchandra*.[165] The reality in the book attracted the critic more. That the Bengalee women ware not confined exclusively within the four walls and that some of them had masculine spirit and gesture—this was the fact working in the mind of Bankimchandra while writing *Devi Chaudhurani*. But Bankim could not accept an Bengalee woman resorting the dacoity, therefore, "He had given a new colour to her decoity and accepting her manliness as an example of 'Anushilon Dharma' establishes a new truth in feminine ideals."[166] Akshay Kumar has evaluated *Devi Chaudhurani* in this light.

Akshay Kumar clearly said that there was no inconsistency between the reality and imagination in *Devi Chaudhurani*, the story of *Devi Chaudhurani* was based upon the elements already existing in the Bengalee family life. According to him, all the characters—Haraballav and his wife, Sagar Bou, Nayan Bou were created in conformity with these ideals.[167]

Delving deep into the inner truth of the character of Prafulla, Akshay Kumar pointed out that the character of Prafulla was not only rooted in the past and present but also hinted at the future. The novelist had vested her with the philosophy of desireless work that she had become an idol for the future generations. However, the critic did not agree that the character of Prafulla was an artistic achievement of Bankim.[168]

JOGINDRA NATH SAMADDAR

Jogindra Nath's *Sadalap-Devi Chaudhurani*[169] was not a critical essay. Quoting exclusively and freely from the novel itself, Jogindra Nath made an attempt to consider the extent of devotion to husband in the character of Prafulla, a Hindu wife, and devotion to father in the character of Brojeswar.

KSHITINDRANATH THAKUR (1869-1937)

Kshitindranath in his book *Art o Sahitya*[170] had discussed how far *Devi Chaudhurani* has fulfilled the claim of art. Kshitindranath claimed that the imitation of reality leading to a happy ending to be the soul of art, and from this attitude, he has discussed *Devi Chaudhurani*. According to him, Prafulla's mother, Brahmthakurani, Sagar Bou and the landscape described in the book were based upon reality. He said that according to the Indian ideals—all women were mothers, in the character of Prafulla, Bankim had made an attempt to exemplify this universal motherhood and thus, maintained the dignity of art.[171] But he could not wink in the kissing scene in the house of Sagar, which he believed bordered on obscenity, and this spoilt the art.[172]

Kshitindranath's assessment of *Devi Chaudhurani* shows that even in the beginning of twenties, some critics, at least, tried to carry on the classical tradition against the strong current of western culture.

ROMESH BASU

The last Bankim pre-centenary critic of *Devi Chaudhurani* is Romesh Basu. Romesh Basu tried to throw light upon the factual side of *Devi Chaudhurani* in his *Bankim Sahitye Manabatar Adarsha*.[173]

With a thorough command over Bankim literature Ramesh Basu viewed the novel *Devi Chaudhurani* as a manifestation of the ideals expounded in *Dharmatatta* and *Krishna Charitra*. In fact, he considered *Devi Chaudhurani* as a philosophical novel, and remarked that manifestation of *Devi Chaudhurani* in the character of Prafulla demonstrated how 'Swadharmabad', 'Karmabad' and 'Karmasannyas' of the *Geeta* can be materialized in practical life.[174]

SITARAM

GIRIJA PRASANNA ROYCHOWDHURY (1862-1899)

The first and foremost critic of Bankim's last novel *Sitaram* was Girija Prasanna Roychowdhury. Girija Prasanna, in his *Bankimchandra—Tritiya Bhag (Sitaram)*,[175] explained and analysed the different characters of *Sitraram* on the basis of ethics, ideals and facts. According to Girija Prasanna, the implications of the verses of the *Geeta* (62-68 from Ch. II & 1-9 from Ch. III) cited by Bankim, had been incorporated in the action of Sitaram and Jayanti. He said that Shree was the ideal of Hindu wife. And the ideals of 'Karmayoga' of the *Geeta* had been demonstrated in her character. According to Girija Prasanna, Jayanti was a criminal in the eye of God, because "Exposure of body is a matter of shame and hence, observed—

Jayanti forgot this simple things and decided abandon this shame—thus she proved herself guilty to God."[176] Nevertheless, the critic thought that Jayanti's crime, her sin, pride and her excellent character have been rightly depicted in this book, he said: "Jayanti is everywhere complete, everywhere fully blooming, everywhere bright."[177] But he felt emotional when he explained: "Alas mother, when shall I find you again in this country, my mother."[178]

Girija Prasanna displayed the traditional trend when he said: "In the book, I have seen Roma's death. This death is at the same time Sitaram's punishment."[179] In the same vein he remarked: "That which is called poetic beauty by the critics, it is not that it has not been reflected in Gangaram, yet, we do not feel analyzing this sinner's character."[180]

The critic has analysed the characters form spiritual point of view and has judged how far Bankim is successful in delineating his characters artistically demonstrating the ideals he upheld.

GIRISH CHANDRA LAHIRI

Girish Chandra, in his essay, *Aitihasik Tathyer Parinam*[181] discussed the historical elements in Sitaram and said: "Sitaram's finality is obscure. It remains an imaginary story of the villagers."[182] Girish Chandra's second point of grievance was that the writer had wanted to safeguard the weakness of the Bengalees against patriotic zeal and heroism. But, by preaching the 'Nishkam Dharma' of the *Bhagawat Geeta,* he had spoilt the beauty of the novel.[183]

Girish Chandra has primarily hinted at the weaknesses which distracts from the artistic beauty of the novel. But he did not discuss them elaborately. However, his findings are bound to be illuminating to future critics.

SURESH CHANDRA SEN

Communalism was not a new charge against Bankim's literature. Suresh Chandra Sen in his *Kabyakatha,*[184] defended the writer of Sitaram against this charge, and pointed out that Bankimchandra had rather tried to establish mutual understanding between the Hindus and Muslims in Sitaram.

Chandsha Fakir was the example of it. According to him: "This Chandsha was a combination of both the communities, he was a beautiful image of 'Nishkam Dharma' and bore impartial attitude to all."[185]

PRAFULLA KUMAR SARKAR (1884-1944)

Prafulla Kumar Sarkar's *Nitishikshay. Bankimchandra*[186] was the next critical study where *Sitaram* had been included in discussion. This discussion showed the critical trends and mentality prevailing during Bankim's lifetime. In fact, the critic found the writer as a social preacher. After a thorough study of *Sitaram* Prafulla Kumar came to the conclusion that Sitaram was a man of blue-blood, man of character, religious, patriotic, but his character was mainly drawn in order to show the evil effect of lustiviousness.[187] To give a spiritual as well as allegorical explanation of how Bankim Chandra made use of the principles of the Goethe in *Sitaram*. Kalidas searched for these principles in the title of each chapter with the character and the story and its development. The essayist made use of the allegory in the following manner: "Sitaram—sentiment-soul, Gangaram—mind, Chandrachur—conscience and intelligence, Jayanti—Devotion, Shree—philosophical 'sattbagun' (the first of the three vital natures), Bhusan—Body, Shyampur—Heart."[189]

Throwing light into the 'Bhaktiyoga', the critic has said that Bhakti (Devotion) is superior to knowledge and therefore, Jayanti is more beautiful than Shree. Philosophical 'sattbagun' follows the way of devotion, so, Shree has followed Jayanti.[190] From top to bottom, the essay shows such allegorical interpretation.

Bankim has breathed life into the dry history infusing the principles of the *Geeta*, and the critic's main concern is to see how the principles achieve fulfillment. Discussing this difficult path of the critic, Kalidas takes much pain to interpret what is self-evident. This shows the dangers of a critic in evaluating a literary work on the touchstone of religious doctrines.

LALIT KUMAR BANDOPADHYAY (1275-1336)

Lalit Kumar Bandopadhyay, in his discussion about Sitaram, laid emphasis upon the finding of motherliness in the female characters in his essay *Ma*.[191] Although, he searched for it according to the ideals of Hindu motherhood, he showed subtlety in explaining it through the actions of the characters. He clearly said that although incidents and situations were opposed to the fullest development of motherhood in the character of Shree, it found fullest expression towards the end thorough her anxiety for the children of Nanda and Rama.[192] According to the critic: Nanda was the brightest example of Hindu motherhood in this book. He further marked in this character a vivid influence of Fullara of Kabi-Kankan.[193] (Mukundaram Chakraborty).

PANCHKARI BONDOPADHYAY (1863-1923)

Panchkari Bondopadhyay's essay *Bankimchandrer Troyee*[194] reflects the critic's ability for pure criticism. According to Panchkari, Shree was an enigma in this novel. He sternly said: "Shree cannot be told an allegory, her character is not been represented in that light. She is not an 'abstraction' even, because 'abstraction' cannot be represented in this way."[195]

Bankimchandra had considered this novel as a media of expression of ethic and ideals. Panchkari's criticism followed this direction, but he said defiantly that the lustiviousness of Gangaram and Roma was unworthy of this novel, this episode did not help expressing the ethical principles and ethical decisions: "Gangaram's love and Sitaram's licentiousness for Shree do not suit as allegory, but these two incidents form the soul of the novel, the story is built upon these two stories."[196]

His belief in 'Shiba-tattba' ethics was voiced: "why should such a sincere devotee fall a victim to lasciviousness?"[197] This question about Sitaram shows his affinity with his contemporaries. However, Panchkari's criticism bears marks maturity to a great extent than his contemporaries.

AKSHAY KUMAR DUTTAGUPTA

In the Bankim pre-centenary period, Akshay Kumar has left the impression of wise and creative criticism in his book *Bankimchandra*.[198] He is the first critic towards a complete evaluation. Akshay Kumar focused the writer's genius aim of the composition, basis of characterization and their inner significance, artistic flows, the historical background of the book, etc. in the small canvas of the book. His critical style and approach were more or less modern. His opinion has straightforward, free, reserved and based upon judicious argument.

Discussing the artistic flows of the character of Sitaram, Akshay Kumar clearly said that the way in which Bankimchandra adorned Sitaram in the beginning with ethical significance and then gradually pushed him towards hell by snatching away severely his ethical strength and glory, which was a little sensational, a little melodramatic in accordance with the ancient romantic ideals.[199]

The critic's treatment of Sitaram's character is realistic and very much penetrating. He pointed out that Sitaram's fall was demoniac not human, and that there was much scope for endowing more human qualities and complexities in Sitaram. The critic added further, in Sitaram's character one missed very much the struggle of a magnanimous character, and the contract between the great passion and the great mind.[200]

According to Akshay Kumar, artistically Shree was not perfect, she was just a dull shadow of Jayanti, in her character, and there was nothing of the sharpness of intelligence, depth of enthusiasm, sincerity of devotion which was there in the character of Jayanti. Criticising Roma, Akshay Kumar said that from the artistic point of view, Roma and Bhramar where of the same nature, and as there was a mingling of love and sentiment in Bhramar, so also, in Roma, there was a mingling of love for husband, affection for children, and cowardice. According to the critic, "Roma is the Bengalee woman intensified as Bhramar."[201] Towards the end of his discussion, Akshay Kumar remarked, "Bankim's writing of Sitaram would not be fruitless if the politically ambitious Hindus are inspired by it."[202] The whole critical treatise is bright with straightforward statements and detached critical views. It is a superb addition to *Sitaram* criticism both from the artistic and philosophical point of view.

RAMSAHAYA VEDANTASASTRI

Ramsahaya's essay *Sitaramer Shree*[203] shows the trend of Bankim criticism during his period. Summing up of the novel, he says that Bankim's diction, a search for the character development, emotionalism, etc. are evident.

According to the critic the character of Shree is all along obscure.[204] But without trying to delve into the character and untie the knots of obscurity he fell into emotional outburst. "Come Shree, come in that image, image as a minister, as dauntless goddess Durga in danger, in battle on the back of lion. You will come; you shall have to come one day."[205]

ADHYAPAK MANJUGOPAL BHATTACHARJEE

In his essay *Art O Bankimchandra,* Manjugopal found the writer of *Sitaram* as a socially conscious artist. According to him, Bankimchandra felt the necessity of sanctity in family life and when this sanctity was polluted, life became intolerable; *Sitaram* was the clear instance of it. Manjugopal evaluated *Sitaram* in this light. According to him, Shree was more responsible for the fall of Sitaram than Sitaram himself.[206] The unnatural arrangement of Shree being Sitaram's wife, Sitaram had no right over her, was the cause of Sitaram's fall.[207] Further, he believed that the character of Sitaram could not be judged from the angles of ideals and ethics. Because he was neither a God nor a saint, the usual nature of ordinary human beings was reflected in his character.[208]

SUBODH CHANDRA SENGUPTA

Subodh Chandra Sengupta referred to Bankim's novel *Sitaram* in his *Bankimchandra O Sarat Chandra*.[209] Making a comparative estimate of the art of Bankimchandra and Sarat Chandra, Subodh Chandra said that in Sarat Chandra, there is the weakness of diverting hearts, while in Bankim's novel, there is the development of regulated indomitable force of human hearts.[210] For examples, he cited Bankim's Shree and Saratchandra's Shorashi. According to him, both were deserted, but even if saintly, there were differences in degrees. There was no mental conflict in the life of Shree, no conflict is there between her voluptuousness and sufferings: "She has subjugated her heart easily and without any effort. And she had tried hard towards an uprising for Hindu Kingdom with her disciplined strength. She could do so, because there was no conflict in her."[211] But, in Shorashi, there was a conflict between a woman in the domestic life and a saint.

Subodh Chandra, in this short discussion, has left the impression of his fair critical judgement and argumentative skill. There are marks of modern critical trend in his essay.

SUMMING UP

Criticism of *Anandamath, Devi Chaudhurani* and *Sitaram* became one sided and partial because Bankim wanted to preach Neo-Hinduism and nationalism through these novels. The main points of discussion were religious orthodoxy, communalism, Hindu social ideals and Bankim's mental awareness. The artistic evaluations of these novels became secondary. Most of the critics evaluated *Anandamath* as a nationalistic document, and, except for a few critics none gave any attention to trace the marks of artistic decay of the great genius in the novel. As regards *Devi Chaudhurani* and *Sitaram*, the spiritual and religious bases of these novels were discussed. Few attempts were made for artistic evaluation. The character of Prafulla in *Devi Chaudhurani* created controversy.

References

1. *Bankim Parichay* (Jiban Katha), C.U. 1938.
2. Ghosh, Kaliprasanna, *Anandamather Mulmantra*, *Bandhab*, 7th year, 1st Issue, 1289 B.S., pp. 14-16.
3. *Ibid.*, p. 16.
4. Bankimchandra himself has written that he will be highly obliged in *Anandamath* is not considered as a historical novel. (Advertisement of *Devi Chaudhurani*, 1884).
5. Ghosh, Kaliprasanna, op. cit., pp. 14-15.
6. Chattopadhyay, Bishnu Charan, *Anandamath* (Somalochana), Nabyabharat, 1st part, 9th issue, Magh, 1290 B.S., pp. 393-408.
7. *Ibid.*, pp. 393-94.
8. *Anandamath* (The first-time advertisement) B.S.P., 1st century, Asharh, 1345 B.S., p. 3.
9. Chattopadhyay, Bishnucharan, op. cit., pp. 398-99.
10. *Ibid.*, pp. 400-01.
11. *Ibid.*, p. 401.
12. *Ibid.*, p. 403.
13. *Ibid.*, pp. 403-04.

14. *Ibid.*, pp. 404-05.
15. *Ibid.*, p. 406.
16. *Ibid.*, pp. 405-06.
17. Basu, Debendra Bijoy, *Noveler Shilpa ba Kabittba*, Nabyabharat, Magh, 1290, Reprinted, Bondopadhyay, Dr. Shrikumar & Paul, Dr. Prafulla Chandra (Ed.) *Somalochana Sahitya*, 5th Edition, Poush, 1379 B.S., pp. 37-50.
18. Bondopadhyay, Dr. Shrikumar & Paul, Dr. Prafulla Chandra (Ed.), *Somalochana Sahitya*, 5th Edition, Paush, 1379 B.S., p. 49.
19. Ghosh, Hemendra Prasad, *Bankimchandra-Anandamath*, Dasi, 5th part, 6th Issue, June 1896, pp. 316-25.
20. Ghosh, Hemendra Prasad, *Upanyasik Bankimchandra*, Sahitya, Kartik, 1315 B.S., pp. 354-63.
21. *Ibid.*, p. 357.
22. Ghosh, Hemendra Prasad, *Bankimchandra-Anandamath*, pp. 316-17.
23. *Ibid.*, pp. 317-23.
24. *Ibid.*, p. 320.
25. Roychowdhury, Girija Prasanna, *Bankimchandra* (Tritiyabhag), 1897.
26. *Ibid.*, p. 9.
27. *Anandamath,* Advertisement of the fifth time B.S.P., 3rd Print, Bhadra, 1364 B.S., p. 4.
28. Roychowdhury, Girija Prasanna, *Bankimchandra* (Tritiyabhag), 1879, p. 47.
29. Sen, Pramatha Nath, *Mrinalinir Charitra*, Bharati, Bhadra-Agrahayan, 1312 B.S., pp. 764-69.
30. Sen, Pramatha Nath, *Bankimchandrer Swadesh Prem, Sahitya*, 17th year, 9th Issue, Poush, 1313 B.S., pp. 513-36.
31. Sen, Pramatha Nath, Kalyani, *Sahitya*, 17th year, 10th & 11th issue, Magh & Falgun, 1313 B.S., pp. (Magh) 612-24 & (Falgun) 674-79.
32. Sen, Pramatha Nath, *Mrinalinir Charitra*, p. 781.
33. Sen, Pramatha Nath, Bankimchandrer Swadesh Prem, p. 624.
34. Sen, Pramatha Nath, Kalyani, p. 624.
35. *Ibid.*, p. 679.
36. Goswami, Bireswar, *Satyananda, Sahitya*, 18th year, 8th Issue & 9th, Agrahayan & Poush, 1314 B.S., pp. (Agra.) 472-84 & (Poush) 528-32.
37. *Ibid.*, (Agrahayan), p. 479.
38. *Ibid.*, p. 475.

39. *Ibid.*, p. 476.
40. Bondopadhyay, Monmoth Nath, *Anandamath*, Bangadarshan, (Nabaparijya), 8th year, 1st Issue, Baishakh, 1315 B.S., pp. 8-15.
41. *Ibid.*, p. 8.
42. *Ibid.*, p. 16.
43. (a) Pal, Bipin Chandra, *Vandemataram*, (1) Dharma, 1st year, 19th Issue, Monday, Poush, 1316 B.S., pp. 5-8.

    (b) Pal, Bipin Chandra, *Vandemataram*, (2) Dharma, 1st year, 22nd Issue, 18th Magh, 1316 B.S., pp. 5-7.

    (c) Pal, Bipin Chandra, *Vandemataram,* (3) Dharma, 1st year, 23rd Issue, Monday, 25th Magh, 1316 B.S., pp. 6-8.

    (d) Pal, Bipin Chandra, *Shirshak-Dharma Niti O Art,* Narayan, 2nd pt., 5th Issue, Ashwin, 1322 B.S., pp. 1179-81.

    (e) Pal, Bipin Chandra, *Shirshak-Dharma O Art*, Narayan, 2nd year, 1st part, 1st issue, Agrahyan, 1322 B.S., pp. 17-19.

    (f) Pal, Bipin Chandra, *Banglar nabajuger Katha (Ekadash Katha) Bankim Sahitya, Bangabani*, 2nd year, 1st half, 1st issue, Falgun, 1329 B.S., pp. 90-98.

    (g) Pal, Bipin Chandra, *Banglar Nabajuger Katha (Dwadash Katha) Bankimchandrer Dharma Bakhya,* Bangabani, 2nd year, 1st half, 2nd issue, Chaitra, 1329 B.S., pp. 225-35.

    (h) Pal, Bipin Chandra, *Nabajuger Bangla Sahitye Bankimchandra, Nabyabharat*, 24th part, 5th Issue, Bhadra, 1330 B.S., pp. 235-49.
44. Pal, Bipin Chandra, *Shirshak Dharma O Art*, p. 18.
45. *Ibid.*, p. 1181.
46. *Ibid.*, p. 18.
47. Pal, Bipin Chandra, *Banglar Nabajuger Katha (Swdashs Katha),* p. 95.
48. Pal, Bipin Chandra, *Banglar Nabajuger Katha (Swdashs Katha),* p. 226.
49. Pal, Bipin Chandra, *Vandemataram* (3), pp. 6-7.
50. Sarkar, Prafulla Kumar, *Samal Sanskare Bankimchandra*, Bangadarshan, (Nabaparjay) 1317 B.S., Reprinted, Chattapadhyay, Nekul (Ed.), Prafulla Kumar Sarkar, *Probondha Sangraha*, July 1969, pp. 9-29.
51. Chattopadhyay, Nakul (Ed.) Prafulla Kumar Sarkar, *Probondha Sangraha*, July 1969, pp. 19-22.
52. Bandopadhyay, Lalit Kumar, *Bankimchandrer Akshyaikbali, Bharatbarsha*, Asharh, 1322 B.S., pp. 6-11.
53. Bandopadhyay, Lalit Kumar, *Ma, Bharatbarsha*, 3rd year, 1st part, 3rd Issue, Bhadra, 1322 B.S., pp. 501-22.
54. Bandopadhyay, Lalit Kumar, *Kabyasudha,* Kartik, 1322 B.S.

55. Bandopadhyay, Lalit Kumar, *Bankimchandrer Akshyaikabali*, Asharh, 1322 B.S., p. 11.
56. Bandopadhyay, Lalit Kumar, *Ma*, pp. 505-09.
57. Bandopadhyay, Lalit Kumar, *Kabyasudha*, pp. 22-25.
58. Bandopadhyay, Panchkari, *Bankimchandrer Troyee, Narayan,* Baishakh, 1322 B.S., pp. 530-44.
59. *Ibid.*, p. 536.
60. *Ibid.*, p. 537.
61. *Ibid.*
62. *Ibid.*, p. 538.
63. *Ibid.*, p. 539.
64. Sen, Shashanka Mohan, *Bangabani,* (1st & 2nd part), Dhaka Albert Library, 1915.
65. *Ibid.*, 2nd part, p. 72.
66. *Ibid.*, 2nd part, pp. 71-72.
67. Bankimchandra, Viswa-Bharati, 1977, p. 96.
68. *Manasi O Marmabani*, Falgun 1323, Reprinted, *Bankimchandra,* Viswa-Bharati, 1977, p. 95. This periodical published Tagore's views on *'Anandamath'* which has a historical significance. In 1291 B.S. Rabindranath Tagore and Chandranath Bose had exchanged letters regarding their views on Anandamath (Tagore's letters are no longer traceable). Thirty-two years after Bipin Bihari Gupta tried to revive this old issue and sought Rabindranath's opinion in this context, which was published in *'Manasi O Marmabani'* (Falgun, 1323).
69. *Ibid.*, p. 95.
70. *Ibid.*
71. *Ibid.*, p. 96.
72. *Maskabari O Montabya*, *Bharati,* 40th year, 12th Issue, Chaitra, 1323, p. 1277. The *'Bharati'*, one of the most distinguished periodicals of Calcutta made comments on Rabindranath's views on *Anandamath* published in *'Manasi O Marmabani'* (Falgun, 1323, Reprinted, *Bankimchandra*, Viswa-Bharati, 1977, pp. 95-96). These comments were made under the caption '*Maskabari O Mantabya'* with reproductions from the original. However, Rabindranath did not involve himself any more in the controversy.
73. Tagore, Rabindranath, *Sahityer Pathe (Sahityer Rup),* Baishakh, 1335 B.S., Reprinted, *Bankimchandra,* Viswa-Bharati, 1977, p. 100.
74. Tagore, Rabindranath, *Panchabhut (Naranari*), Chaitra, 1299 B.S., Reprinted *Bankimchandra,* Viswa-Bharati, 1977, p. 88.
75. Roy, Kiran Shankar, *Anandamath,* Sebujpatra, 6th year, 7th issue, Kartik, 1326 B.S., pp. 403-23.
76. *Ibid.*, pp. 403-07.

77. *Ibid.*, pp. 406-12.
78. *Ibid.*, p. 416.
79. *Ibid.*, p. 421.
80. *Ibid.*, p. 420.
81. Duttagupta, Akshay Kumar, Bankimchandra, 1327 B.S.
82. Duttagupta, Akshay Kumar, Bankimchandra, 2nd Edition, Jignasa, May 1975, p. 222.
83. *Ibid.*
84. *Ibid.*, p. 221.
85. *Ibid.*, p. 224.
86. *Ibid.*, p. 225.
87. *Ibid.*, pp. 226-27.
88. Das, Chittaranjan, *Bankimchandra*, Mahila, 13th Asharh, 1331.
89. *Ibid.*, pp. 222-23.
90. Ghosh, Arabinda, *Bandemataram Mantra*, Desh, 4th year, Issue 48th, October 23, 1937, pp. 782-83.
91. *Ibid.*, p. 783.
92. Dasgupta, Nibaran Chandra, "*Bankimer matrirun*", Desh, 4th year, Issue 48, October 23, 1937, pp. 787-90.
93. *Ibid.*, p. 789.
94. (a) Brojendra Nath Bondopadhyay and Sajani Kanta Das have written that the decedent Muslims have marked communualism and started movement. (Anandamath, B.S.P., 3rd Print, Bhadra, 1364 B.S. (Edtl.)

    (b) Maulavi Md. K. Chand cited examples from *Anandamath* to show Bankim's hatred for Islam. (Sahitye Hindu Musalmaner Miloner Antaray, Archana, Shrabon, 1324 B.S., p. 222).
95. Maulana Akram Khan opposing this song raised a proposal in Muslim League, but the Maulana himself recited *Bandemataram* with Surendranath in Swadeshi Age. (Dasgupta, Kshitish Chandra, Bandemataram, Desh, 4th year, 49th issue, Saturday, 30th Oct. 1937, p. 876.)
96. Sarkar, Sarala Bala, *Yatiyatar Mahasangest-Bandemataram*, Desh, 4th year, 49th Issue, Saturday, October 30th, 1937, pp. 447-48.
97. Dasgupta, Kshitish Chandra, *Bandemataram-Deshaprem O Pritipurna bandana Gan,* Desh 4th year, 49th Issue, Saturday, October 30th, 1937, pp. 575-76.
98. Shastri, Ashoknath, *Jatiya Jibane Bandemataram*, Desh, 4th year, 39th Issue, Saturday, October 30th, 1937, pp. 881-82.
99. Sen, Bankim Chandra, *Bandemataram*, Desh, 4th year, 50th issue, Saturday, November 6th, 1937, p. 915.

100. Sen, Bankim Chandra, *Bandemataramer Shakti*, Desh, 4th year, 51st issue, November 13th, 1937, pp. 983-84.
101. Sarkar, Saralabala, op. cit., p. 848.
102. Dasgupta, Kshitish Chandra, op. cit., pp. 875-76.
103. Shastri, Ashoknath, op. cit., pp. 881-82.
104. Sen, Bankim Chandra, *Bandematramer Shakti*, p. 984.
105. Mukhopadhyay, Thakurdas, *Devi Chaudhurani*, Pakshik Somalochana, 1st part, 2nd Paksha, 10th issue, Asharh, 1291 B.S., pp. 294-317.
106. Mukhopadhyay, T.D., *Samalochana Sahitya*, Pakshik Somalochak, 1291, Reprinted, *Samalochana Sahitya*, edited by Dr. Srikumar Bondopadhyay & Dr. Prafulla Chandra Paul, 5th Ed. Poush, 1379, p. 7.
107. Mukhopadhyay, Thakurdas, *Devi Chaudhurani*, p. 297.
108. *Ibid.*, p. 302.
109. *Ibid.*, p. 308.
110. Basu, Debendra Bijoy, *Noveler Shilpo ba kahitya*, *Nabyabharat*, 1292 B.S., Reprinted *Samalochana Sahitya*, pp. 37-50.
111. Somalochana Sahitya, p. 46.
112. *Ibid.*, p. 49.
113. Roy, Jnyanendra Lal, *Probandha Lahari,* (Bankimbabur *Devi Chaudhurani*) 1303 B.S.
114. *Ibid.*, p. 70.
115. *Ibid.*, p. 71.
116. *Ibid.*, p. 67.
117. Ghose, Hemendra Prasad, *Bankimchandra*, Dasi, 1st part, 11th issue, November, 1896, pp. 565-77.
118. Ghose, Hemendra Prasad, *Upanyassik Bankimchandra*, Sahitya, Kartik, 1315 B.S., pp. 354-63.
119. Ghose, H.P., *Hrishi Bankimchandra*, Narayan, Baishakh, 1322, pp. 563-71.
120. *Ibid.*, p. 565.
121. Ghose, H.P., *Upanyasik Bankimchandra*, p. 357.
122. Ghose, Hemendra Prasad, Bankimchandra, p. 521.
123. Dutta, Hirendranath, *Prafullamukhi*, Bharati, Falgun, 1304, p. 580-89.
124. *Ibid.*, p. 582.
125. *Ibid.*, p. 587.
126. *Ibid.*, p. 588.

127. Roychowdhury, Girija Prasanna, *Devi Chaudhurani-Charitra-Bishlesion-Bakhya-Somalochana, Bankimchandra pt.-III*, 1897, pp. 1-50.
128. *Ibid.*, pp. 11-12.
129. *Ibid.*, p. 38.
130. Roychowdhury, Girija Prasanna, *Prafullamukhi (Pratibad)*, *Nabyabharat,* Part-XVI, Issue-V, Bhadra, 1305 B.S., pp. 267-73.
131. *Ibid.*
132. Sen, Pramatha Nath, *Mrinalini Charitra, Bharati*, Bhadra-Agrahayan, 1312 B.S., pp. 764-89.
133. *Ibid.*, pp. 781-82.
134. Bandopadhyay, Lalit Kumar, *Bankimchandrer Akhyaikabali*, *Bharatbarsha*, Asharh, 1322 B.S., p. 10.
135. *Ibid.*, pp. 6-11.
136. Bandopadhyay, Lalit Kumar, *Ma, Bharatbarsha*, Bhadra, 1322, pp. 501-22.
137. *Ibid.*, pp. 509-13.
138. *Ibid.*, pp. 509-10.
139. *Ibid.*, pp. 510-11.
140. *Ibid.*, p. 512.
141. Bandopadhyay, Lalit Kumar, *Kabya Sudha (Shasuri Bou),* Kartik, 1323 B.S., pp. 79-101.
142. *Ibid.*, pp. 93-101.
143. Bandopadhyay, Lalit Kumar, *Sakhi,* Calcutta-Dhaka-Moymonsingh, 1326.
144. *Ibid.*, p. 117.
145. *Ibid.*, p. 122.
146. Bondopadhyay, Chandicharan, *Bangla Sahityer Kromonnoti O Bankimchandra, Manasi,* Kartik, 1321 B.S., pp. 417-39.
147. *Ibid.*, p. 435.
148. Bandopadhyay, Panchkari, *Bankimchandrar Troyee, Narayan*, 1322 B.S., p. 530.
149. This *Anushilon Tattba* is a pure European thing, Bankimchandra has derived it from the German scholar fiction and this training of unity and integrity has been given a Bengali colour by Bankimchandra for the teaching of the Bangalees. (Bandopadhyay, Panchkari, *Bankimchandrer Troyee*, 1322 B.S., p. 536)
150. Bandopadhyay, Panchkari, op. cit., p. 539.
151. *Ibid.*, p. 541.
152. *Ibid.*, p. 540.

153. Mazumder, Bijoy Ratna, *Bankimchandrer Upanyase Hasyaras,* Mormobani, Bhadra 16, 1322 B.S., pp. 125-29.
154. *Ibid.*, p. 128.
155. Sen, Shashanka Mohan, *Bangabani*, (Part-I & II), Dhaka Albert Library, 1915.
156. *Ibid.*, Part-II, pp. 76-80.
157. *Ibid.*, p. 76.
158. *Ibid.*, p. 80.
159. *Ibid.*, p. 77.
160. (a) Pal, Bipin Chandra, *Shirshak Dharma O Art, Narayan*, 2nd year, 1st part, 1st issue, Ashwin, 1323 B.S., pp. 18-19.
   (b) Pal, Bipin Chandra, *Banglar Nabayoger Katha (Ekadash Katha), Bangabani,* 2nd year, 1st part, 1st issue, Falgun, 1329 B.S., pp. 90-98.
   (c) Pal, Bipin Chandra, *Banglar Nabayuger Katha (Dwadash Katha), Bangabani*, 2nd year, 1st part, 2nd issue, Chaitra, 1329 B.S., pp. 225-35.
   (d) Pal, Bipin Chandra, *Nabayoger Bangla Sahitye Bankimchandra, Nabyabharat*, 24th part, 5th issue, Bhadra,1330 B.S., pp. 235-49.
161. Pal, Bipin Chandra, *Nabayoger Bangla Sahitye Bankimchandra, Nabyabharat,* 24th part, p. 242.
162. Pal, Bipin Chandra, *Shirshak Dharma O Art,* p. 18.
163. Pal, Bipin Chandra, *Banglar Nabayoger Katha (Ekadash Katha),* p. 96.
164. Pal, Bipin Chandra, *Shirshak Dharma O Art,* p. 18.
165. Duttagupta, Akshay Kumar, *Bankimchandra,* 1327 B.S.
166. Duttagupta, Akshay Kumar, *Bankimchandra*, 2nd Edn. May 1975, p. 232.
167. *Ibid.*, pp. 234-35.
168. *Ibid.*, p. 241.
169. Samaddar, Yogendra Nath, *Sadalap-Davichowdhurini, Sahitya*, Ashwin, 1328 B.S., pp. 413-21.
170. Thakur, Kshitindra Nath, *Art O Sahitya*, 8th Magh, 1329 B.S.
171. *Ibid.*, p. 98.
172. *Ibid.*, p. 99.
173. Basu, Romesh, *Bankim Sahitye Manabatar Adarsha*, *Sabujpatra*, Shraban-Bhadra, 1334 B.S., pp. 631-73.
174. *Ibid.*, pp. 665-66.
175. Roychowdhury, Girija Prasanna, Bankimchandra-Tritiya Bhag (Sitaram), 1897.

176. *Ibid.*, p. 83.
177. *Ibid.*, p. 84.
178. *Ibid.*
179. *Ibid.*, p. 94.
180. *Ibid.*
181. Lahiri, Girish Chandra, *Aitihasik Tathyer Parinam*, *Pradip,* Poush, 1306 B.S., pp. 25-29.
182. *Ibid.*, p. 27.
183. *Ibid.*, p. 28.
184. Sen, Suresh Chandra, *Kabyakatha (Bankimchandra O Musalman Samproday),* 1909.
185. *Ibid.*, p. 56.
186. Sarkar, Prafulla Kumar, *Nitishikshay Bankimchandra*, Bangadarshan, 1318, Reprinted, Prafulla Kumar Sarkar, *Probondha Sangraha*, Edited by Nakul Chattopadhyay, Shraban, 1376 B.S., pp. 43-50.
187. *Ibid.*, pp. 43-44.
188. Mallik, Adhyapak Kalidas, *Bankimchandrer Sitaram*, *Bharatbarsha*, 2nd year, 2nd part, 5th issue, Baishakh, 1322, pp. 831-41.
189. *Ibid.*, p. 833.
190. *Ibid.*, p. 834.
191. Bandopadhyay, Lalit Kumar, *Bharatbarsha*, Bhadra, 1322, pp. 501-22.
192. *Ibid.*, p. 515.
193. *Ibid.*, pp. 515-17.
194. Bondopadhyay, Panchkari, *Bankimchandrer Troyee, Narayan*, 1322 B.S., pp. 530-44.
195. *Ibid.*, p. 542.
196. *Ibid.*, p. 543.
197. *Ibid.*, p. 542.
198. Duttagupta, Akshay Kumar, *Bankimchandra*, 1327 B.S.
199. Duttagupta, Akshay Kumar, *Bankimchandra,* 2nd Edn. May 1975, p. 239.
200. *Ibid.*
201. *Ibid.*, p. 241.
202. *Ibid.*, p. 245.
203. Vedantasastri, Ramsahaya, *Sitaram Shree, Archana*, 26th part, 7th issue, Bhadra, 1336 B.S., pp. 243-46.
204. *Ibid.*, p. 243.
205. *Ibid.*, p. 245.

206. Bhattacharjee, Adhyapak, Manjugopal, *Art O Bankimchandra, Panchapushpa*, Jaistha, 1337 B.S., pp. 281-89.
207. *Ibid.*, p. 289.
208. *Ibid.*
209. Sengupta, Subodh Chandra, "*Bankimchandra O Saratchandra*", *Bichitra*, Magh, 1337 B.S., pp. 164-71.
210. *Ibid.*, p. 170.
211. *Ibid.*, p. 171.

11
Miscellaneous Essays of Bankimchandra

(A) LOKA RAHASYA

SHRIKRISHNA DAS

Immediately after the publication of *Lokarahasya* in book form, Shrikrishna Das, the editor of *Jnyannkur*, wrote a criticism of the book with the headline *Prabandha Granther Sankshipta Samalochana.*[1] It was the first critical work on Lok Rahasya.[2] Shrikrishna Das had divided the essays of Lok Rahasya into two groups—*Spastha Rahasya* (Broad Humour) and *Sanket Rahasya* (Quiet Humour).[3] According to the critic the skillful use of quite humour in places of such essays like *Byaqhracharjyabrihallangul*, *Engrejistrotra O Subarnagola* was unsurpassable[4] in Bengali literature and "cows are not husbands because cows have a little freedom,"[5] of *Dwampatya Chanda Bidhir Ainer* had been noted as an example of *broad humour.*[6] Besides, the critic had much appreciation for Bankim's use of irony and sarcasm.[7]

SURESH CHANDRA KABIRATNA

Suresh Chandra Kabiratna in his essay *Banga Sahitye Bankimer Prabhab*[8] had clearly highlighted *Loka Rahasya.* The flow of humour in the book charmed him. But he remarked that the irony used in the book was unsurmountable.[9]

(B) BIGNAN RAHASYA

Bignan Rahasya was published in book form in 19th April 1875 and the first criticism of it before Bankim Centenary was written by Shrikrishna Das with headline *Prapta Granther*

Samalochana—Bignan Rahasya.[10] At the very outset of the essay he highly appreciated Bankim's genius, his diligence and perseverance. According to the critic it was a precious gem of Bengali language—its language was sweet—its tone was charming. He closed his discussion with the line that fact is more beautiful than fiction and it would be evident to every reader of the book.[11]

(C) KAMALAKANTA

PANCHKARI GHOSE

Panchkari Ghose's essay entitled *Kamalakanta*[12] is the first detailed critical work on *Kamalakanta*. On the footnote of the essay Panchkari has written that this essay is not a criticism of *Kamalakanta*. It is an attempt to highlight the beauty of *Kamalakanti* following Dodd's Beauties of Shakespeare.[13] Even if it is the main feature of the essay, the essayist has cited prolific examples to show the 'moderate'[14] and 'socialist' ideas of Bankim. As for example, in the essay entitled *Biral* (The Cat)[15] Panchkari has searched for those socialist ideals through the queries of the cat.[16]

The adoration of mothers which found its flutiest expression in the 'Bandemataram' of *Anandamath* had its first successful expression in Kamalakanta. Panchkari found it in the inner significance of *Amar Durgotsab.*[17] Panchkari's concluding remark was that even if all other works of Bankim were destroyed Bankim would live by *Kamalkanter Daptar* only.[18]

BATUKNATH BHATTACHARJEE

Batuknath Bhattacharjee's observations on *Kamalakanta* in his essay *Bankim Pratibha*[19] is a contemporary criticism marked by clarity and fineness.

Analysing *Kamalakanta*, Batuknath pointed out that Bankimchandra had searched for idealistic pattern in *Kamalakanta*. He has tried to enliven our later feeling of the truth that man is man under all circumstances. In fact, it is Batuknath who first pointed out that Bankim's love for humanity is vividly reflected in the midst of the sarcasm and humour in this book. And it is because of this genuine love for humanity that *Kamalakanta* has become so sweet and so moving. He has said: "Kamalakanta is apparently indifferent, but his mind is full of ideas—full to the brain like the river of Bengal. His irony is free from grudge—his humour free from force—there is fan without stigma."[20]

Form the idealistic point of view *Kamalakanta* stands alone and alone in the Bengali literature. Of this Batuknath remarked—"This idealism—this attempt to leave this dreary world for that dome of joy like a bird—is the speciality of this Daptar."[21]

AKSHAY KUMAR DUTTAGUPTA

Before the Bankim centenary thoughtful and scholastic assessment was made on *Kamalakanta* by Akshay Kumar Duttagupta in his book *Bankimchandra*.[22] The critic has briefly touched upon not only the different aspects of the book but also the different facts of Bankim's personality. He upheld the extraordinary qualities of Bankim as a poet, philosopher, social preacher, and patriot. He has categorically stated that in it *Kamalkanta* there is no poetic sentiment, no pomp of a philosopher, no austerity of a social teacher, no insensitiveness of a politician and no obstinacy of a patriot. Here humour is mixed with pity, strange with truth, simplicity with pangs, diction with perception, emotion with realism and irony with broadness.[23] According to him *Kamalakanta* is the glory of *Bangadarshan*[24] for its sweetness of language, charm of ideas, simple and reserved humour and genuine patriotism.

MURALIDHAR GANGOPADHYAY

Murlidhar Gangopadhyay has written criticism of Kamalkanta in his essay *Prabandhe Bankim Partibha*.[25] He has discussed *Kamalakanta* in the light that Bankimchandra was not a 'misanthrope'[26] rather by virtue of his extraordinary genius he could show massive 'selfish side'[27] of human nature. Muralidhar remarked that as Saratchandra lashed the social lapses in *Pallismaj*, so also, Bankim lashed the selfish, 'Bottle-friends' and 'time-servers'.[28]

Besides, Muralidhar has found out that Bankim had social political and psychological awareness in his work *Basanter Kokil*.

He has further pointed out by citing examples that ideologically *Basanter Kokil* belongs to the group of Wordsworth's *Skylark*.[29]

SURESH CHANDRA KABIRATNA

Suresh Chandra's *Bangasahitye Bankimchandrer Prabhab*[30] is a more matured work than that of Muralidhar. This essay is marked by forceful language and clarity of discussion. According to him, humour in *Kamalakanta* is mixed with poetry and patriotism. This is the keynote of Suresh Chandra's evaluation. He remarked, *Kamalakanter Daptar* is as invaluable an asset[31] in the Bengali literature as Carlyle's *Sartor Resartus* and *Heroes and Heroworship are*, in the English literature. Suresh Chandra believes that *Kamalakanter Daptar*, even if written after Dequincy's '*Opium Eater*', Bankim's originality is nowhere lessened. Where Dequincy had told the tales of sorrows and happiness, Bankim through the autobiography of the Opium Eater has represented philosophy and patriotism.[32]

(D) SAMYA

HEMENDRA PRASAD GHOSE (1876-1963)

The many faced genius of Bankim also found expression in his treatment of socialism in his '*Samya*', obviously under the impact of the Western philosophers especially J.S. Mill which he himself admitted, and subsequently confirmed by Shrish Chandra Das. However, Bankim's own ideas about socialism also changed and no further edition of the book published by him. It appears that in Bankim's days no critic was attracted to the contents of '*Samya*', i.e., socialism, and none wielded his pen to evaluate it. However, the first critic in the post-Bankim period who tried to throw some light on Bankim's '*Samya*' was Hemendra Prasad Ghose who discussed '*Samya*' in his book *Bankimchandra*. In his short discussion, the critic said that a human being must enjoy certain equal rights, and he appreciated Bankimchandra, saying that he had wielded his pen against the existing social discrepancies between king and the subjects, Zamindar and Rayats, master-servant, woman and man, etc. in his '*Samya*'.[33] Needless to say that Hemendra Prasad mainly tried to uphold Bankim's views without delving deep into the arguments of Bankim's social criticism. Two more critics after him also made attempts at evaluating this work of Bankim, but none of them could equal him in critical estimation.

(E) KRISHNA CHARITRA

RABINDRANATH TAGORE (1861-1941)

Rabindranath Tagore discussed *"Krishna Charitra"* in details before Bankim Centenary.[34] Rabindranath termed the period of turning point of Bengali society.[35] Here, he felt 'an independent spirit of genius'[36]—the spirit which was dependable force to the dispirited cowards[37] and he thought that Bankim in this book hoisted the flag of free human intelligence.[38] He further said—"According to us Krishna is not the hero of *Krishna Charitra*, free wisdom, instinct is the supreme hero. Firstly, Bankim has wanted to say that dull pursuit of Shastra or convention will not be the motto of our worship. We will worship carefully following the supreme ideal of our mind. Then he shows that which is Shastra is not always believable, that which is believable is the Shastra. And this is the spiritual strength of *Krishna Charitra* and this had made *Krishna Charitra* magnanimous."[39] So, much of Tagore's appreciation of Krishna Charitra is seen above.

Then he states his points of disagreement with Bankim. He said that according to us in the present book Bankim has mostly finished the work of destruction, but he has not given much attention to the constructive side.[40] He complained that the way in which ideals are to be set up in literature, Bankim does not follow this.[41] He further complained—"The quarrel which was unnecessarily brought in by Bankim in this book are painful to us."[42]

His next point of disagreement was that in *Krishna Charitra* Bankim had expressed his impatience towards the people of opposing creed as well as the Europeans, raised too much of unnecessary arguments and polluted the subject matter by raising unwanted social issues. Therefore, Tagore thought:

> The beauty, gravity and liberal attitude have not been maintained in the book's gravity and liberal attitude

> have not been maintained in the book's language, idea and style which has spoiled the brightness of the ideal character.[43]

The point to be noticed is that even if Tagore ruthlessly criticized Bankim of *Krishna Charitra*, he had appreciated him for his avoidance of blind and unintelligible pursuit of 'Shastra'. He said that from the very beginning Bankim has kept his sword open in a fighting attitude, therefore, he found no scope for representing the complete picture of his Krishna, but he must not be blamed for this. We learn at least the difference between the conventional Krishna and the natural one.[44]

Rabindranath dealt *Krishna Charitra* as a whole weighting the pros and cons of Bankim's arguments and evaluating them from literary and artistic point of view, which is a turning point of Bankim criticism.

MADHUSUDHAN SARKAR

In his essay *Nrisinghabatar Bankimchandra*,[45] Madhusudan Sarkar has attempted at an appraisal of Bankim's *Krishna Charitra*, but as the title indicates, the essay borders on satire. His attention was how to discredit Bankim. He saw Bankim as a protagonist of class-hatred, and pointed that his *Krishna Charitra* was an expression of the wrapped sceptic principle, and that in Bankim's 'Krishna' the character of the Buddha had been idolized.[46] In Madhusudan's hands literary criticism declined from the height to which Rabindranath had raised.

KALINATH DUTTA

Kalinath Dutta's criticism of *Krishna Charitra*, in his article '*Bankimchandra*'[47] revealed his conservative outlook. Of course, he appreciated Bankim for his intelligence and sense of judgement revealed in *Krishna Charitra*. But he could not approve of the Bankim's interpretation of the character of Krishna from idealistic point of view as it lacked in divine love and renunciation which forms the basis of traditional character of Krishna.[48] Obviously, this is what has pained the critic's orthodox mind.

SHRIMAT UTTAMANANDA SWAMI

Uttamananda Swami discussed *Krishna Charitra* in detail in his essay "*Bankimchandra.*"[49] Factual analysis is the basis of his criticism.

Uttamananda tried to prove with sufficient citations and factual explanation that *Krishna Charitra* was not a piece of devotional writing. But he had praised Bankim's erudition. Religious explanation was said to be a thing beyond the jurisdiction of Bankim. He said that Shrikrishna of *Krishna Charitra* was physically handicapped and almost inanimate; his body was full of injuries. The allegorical explanation of 'Raslila' in the book, Uttamananda thought to be completely opposite to those of Shridhar Swami and Sankardev.[50] He strongly asserted that his Droupadi explanation was ornamental but not ideological, novelty was there but no reality, decision was there but no assimilation.[51] Uttamananda Swami was not a critic, he was a religious preacher, so it was natural that his opinions on *Krishna Charitra* would be adverse.

SURENDRANATH BHATTACHARJEE

Surendranath Bhattacharjee wrote his essay "*Radhakrishna Tattba*"[52] as a protest against Bankim's *Krishna Charitra*. The book is divided into four parts. Surendranath could not approve Bankim's arguments and explanations in *Krishna Charitra*. He said that Bankim's 'Krishna' could be an idol to those young men who had westernized culture and were devoid of devotion. But to the devotees of 'Bhakti Yoga', to the stern ascetic of 'Gnyanayoga', to the all-abandoned 'Bairagi' he could not be an object of worship, because Bankim's 'Krishna' was devoid of Godliness. According to Surendranath, Bankim had tried to establish Shrikrishna as a human being, which actually he was not, he was a God. His further complaint was that in this attempt Bankim had insulted the 'Shastra' also. He regretted that Bankim failed to understand the reality of this incarnation—Krishna and therefore had given an adverse explanation.[53]

It needs be mentioned here that Surendranath through his protest against *Krishna Charitra* of Bankim has given his own opinion about Krishna.

HARAN CHANDRA RAKSIT

Haran Chandra's observations on *Krishna Charitra* in his '*Bangashitye Bankim*' are almost similar to those of Uttamananda Swami.[54] He observed that *Krishna Charitra* is valueless to the devotees for absence of devotion in it. He said with annoyance that Bankim by explaining *Krishna Charitra* in his own way has left space for skepticism in Krishna's Godliness. But nevertheless, Haran Chandra appreciated Bankim's erudition and searching spirit.[55]

BIPIN CHANDRA PAL (1858-1932)

Bipin Chandra discussed *Krishna Charitra* in two separate essays—*Shirshak Dharma o Art*[56] and *Banglar Nabajuger Katha*[57] (*Dwadash Katha*). Bipin Chandra was a believer of both rationalism and materialism. His criticism bears the stamp of it. He remarked—that Bankimchandra by co-ordinating the modern idea and ideology of worship with those of the ancient, had made an attempt by which he universalized the Hindu worship and the Hindu creed through the creation of the Krishna, who is not only a shadow of the ancient but also a symbol of superman of the modern expectism.[58] He further said that Bankimchandra by making *Krishna Charitra* an image of European humanism co-ordinated Indian worship with the modern universal human nature enunciated by '*Comte*'. He fulfilled the task initiated by Raja Rammohan[59] and tried to establish in '*Ecce Homo*' in the 19th century. Bankim thus presented Krishna following the same liberal attitude.[60] Bipin Chandra's criticism is a bold step towards the evaluation of *Krishna Charitra*.

AKSHAY KUMAR DUTTAGUPTA

Gourdas Babaji did not regard Krishna as an allegorical figure, he found Krishna in the world of action amongst all men.[61] This exceptional idea was followed by Akshay Kumar while discussing *Krishna Charitra* in his book "*Bankimchandra*".[62] In his opinion, Bankim's *Krishna Charitra* is nothing but an explanation and analysis of Gourdas Babaji's words, that Bankim believed Krishna to be an incarnation of God. According to him, Bankim following "Ecce Homo's" presented Krishna as a human being by his own erudition, subtlety, and perseverance.[63]

RAMESH BASU

Ramesh Basu, in his essay "*Bnakim Sahitye Manabatar Adarsha*"[64] wrote a brief criticism of *Krishna Charitra*. He complained that Bankim by presenting Krishna as an ideal man had deepened human prejudice towards God. But he admitted that Bankim by sound reasoning had eradicated the impression arising in the mind of man by the name Krishna. But he said without any hesitation that Bankim in his attempt to preach religion and humanism through Krishna had broken the string of reasoning. "When should Krishna be worshiped" By this question his Krishna could not earn homage in human society because religion, and humanism are in conflict.[65] The critic's subtle sense observation is also evident in such remarks: "Representing Krishna as a human being outwardly and himself believing him as a God—which is not very much like a devotee, it is by a strong mental force."[66]

(F) BIBIDHA PRABANDHA

KAILASH CHANDRA SINGHA

Kailash Chandra's *"Bangalar Kalanka (Pratibad)"*[67] is the first critical work on *'Bibidha Prabandha'*. He objected to some of the historical facts inserted in the essay *'Bangalar Kalanka'* as not true and attempted towards some new historical facts.[68]

SHRIMAT UTTAMANANDA SWAMI

Uttamananda Swami in his essay *Bankimchandra*[69] wrote a brief criticism of *Uttarcharita*. He said that only those portions of *Uttarcharita* which reflected Bhababhuti were beautiful, but wherever the writer attempts originality he was in dilema. Bankim's remarks that no heroic spirit is there in Bhababhuti's Ramchandra seemed to be childish to Uttamananda. According to him, as the great Ravana bewailed the death of Birbahu, Ramchandra's bewailing for Sita reminds one of that.[70]

RAKHALDAS BONDOPADHYAY (1866-1930)

Rakhaldas Bondopadhyay's "*Aitihasik Gabeshanayay Bankimchandra*"[71] was a historical approach to the historical essays of *Bibidha Prabandha*. It is in a sense an appreciation to

Bankim's curious probing genius. He laid much emphasis upon three essays—*Bharat Kalanka*, *Bangalar Kalanka* and *Bangalir Utpatti*. He praised the scientific approach of Bankim in the first two essays. According to him, no writers still today could dare to say that the Muslims could not capture India as easily as they did Syria and Parasya. Rakhaldas had pointed out with appreciation that the Age in which no believable edition of "Tabakat-E-Nasiri" was printed, no translation of 'Babharti' was printed, even in that Age the question Bankim raised about Muslims invasion arouses surprise.[72]

The essay *Bangalir Utpatti* have been termed by Rakhaldas as the second great spirit by pointing out that the people of Bengal were not descended from pure Aryans, there were so many people having non-Aryan blood.[73]

HARAPRASAD SHASTRI (1853-1931)

Haraprasad's Shastri's '*Bankimbabu o Uttar Charita*'[74] is the first critical work on Bankim's *Uttarcharita*. In this essay Haraprasad discussed much about Bhababhuti than about Bankim. In his criticism of Bankim he had pointed out Bankim's sincerity and the initiation of western style by him. He said that Bankimchandra for the first time had started *Uttarcharita* criticism heartily and it was he who had discussed the traditional rhetorical style for the new European style.[75] For example, he could accept Bankim' interpretation of Bhababhuti's wailing for the sacrifice of Sita as cowardly gesture and a reflection of new love, which detracts the fame of Bhababhuti. Moreover, he thought Ramchandra's wailing was only natural against the circumstances which displayed his inhuman spirit and inhuman courage.[76]

BATUKNATH BHATTACHARJEE

Batuknath Bhattacharjee comes next as the critic of *Bibidha Prabandha* in his "*Bankim Pratibha*".[77] Batuknath draws our attention towards Bankim's right spirit, argumentative skill, analytic genius and comparative criticism. He remarked that Bankim-genius had very skillfully touched the points in readers' mind. According to Batuknath, the opinion expressed by him in his criticism of *Uttarcharita*, the subtle analytic skill he had shown in his comparative study of *Shakuntala-Miranda O Desdemona,* the valuable points he had raised in deciding the pattern of *Geetikabya*, and discussions on both the poets in *Vidyapati O Joydev* were all pleasing.[78]

(G) DHARMATATTBA

PURNA CHANDRA BASU

Purna Chandra Basu's essays—"*Dharma Sambandhe Bankim Babur Abhimat*"[79] and "*Manushyattba*"[80] are the first criticism on *Dharmatattba*. His discussions are against Bankim's spiritual explanation of *Dharmatattba*. In the first essay Purna Chandra discussed Bankim's opinions; at the same time he tried to establish his opinion. For example, Purna Chandra said,—No man finds satiety of all passions and religion is not the only means of happiness. Happiness does not depend upon religion; it depends upon habit and education.[81]

His approach to the next essay '*Manushyattba*' is of the same nature. Purna Chandra thought that Bankimchandra tried to propagate religion of humanity following Comte—which might be applicable in England but never in a country where thirty-three crores of Gods and Goddess are worshiped. He ironically remarked that Bankimbabu's religion and argument were good for nothing, and his directive that the ideals of human life are the steps towards human-progress was not the last word about progress.[82]

THAKURDAS MUKHAPADHYAY (1258-1310)

Thakurdas Mukhapadhyay has given a rather good criticism of Bankim's religious explanation in his book "*Sahitya Mangal*"[83] in the contemporary Age. Co-ordination is the key-word with the western direct science today, and it is the very basis of Bankim's religious analyses. Thakurdas's discussion is fundamentally based upon this idea. He strongly said that Bankim religious interpretation even though related to *Shastra* was nonetheless scientific.[84] According to him as Tindall in England had presented a scientific explanation of the *Shastra* of the Aryans Saints, his 'Equilibrium' and 'Repose' being novel even though archaic, Bankim's dialogues in '*Guru-Shishya-*

Sambad' in the same way a timely explanation of the Aryan Shastra.[85] He clearly said that Bankimchandra had given a straight way explanation of Equilibrium mentioned by Tindall.[86] Thakurdas also had appreciated Bankim's style of presentation of fact. He said happily that Bankim style of representation of the things archaic in a new light is extra-ordinary.[87]

DEVIPRASANNA ROYCHOWDHURY

Deviprasanna Roychowdhury is another contemporary critic of Bankim's *Dharmatattba*. Deviprasanna in his '*Bankimchandra O Brahmadharma*'[88] said that the religion was like the religion of the Brahmas.

BIPIN CHANDRA PAL

Bipin Chandra Pal has given a substantial criticism of Bankim's *Dharmatattba and Anushilan Tattba* in his *Banglar Nabajuger Katha (Dwadash Katha)*.[89] Bipin Chandra by virtue of his subtle analytical skill and sharp power of judgement has tried to show that co-ordination was the main basis of Bankim's explanation of Dharma. Contemporary social consciousness was the basis of these essays. He cleverly explained that it was in the critical times when the western religious thought were fast-influencing the Indians and the stern traditional thoughts in India were troubling a section. At this critical juncture the 'Brahma Samaj' was struggling to establish its own ideology and Bankimchandra was trying to preach a new liberal religion by co-ordination all those cross-currents of European and oriental religious thoughts under the changing circumstances.[90] Bipin Chandra said that the *Anushilan Dharma* which Bankimchandra propagated was an attempt of co-ordination between the Dharma of the *Geeta* and the religion propagated by Comte in Europe.[91]

AKSHAY KUMAR DUTTAGUPTA

Akshay Kumar Duttagupta in his book *Bankimchandra*[92] has discussed about Bankim's religious ideology before Bankim Centenary. A lot of things such as Bankim's pen-fight with Mr. Hasty regarding Hindu religion, and a comparative study of their ideologies, Bankim's similarities and dissimilarities with Shashadhar Tarkachuramani on the point of religion, western influence in Bankim had been dealt with by Akshay Kumar.[93] Akshay Kumar also has laid stress upon Bankim's power of co-ordination as it was done by Bipin Chandra. He said that Bankim realized the Hindus devotion to God and the *Nishkam Karmatattba* of the *Geeta* as the supreme ideology and he judged the two things in the light of European thoughts before presenting his *Anushilan Tattba* coordinating the western and oriental ideals. He formed an opinion of his own substantiated with the opinions of Mill and Comte. Akshay Kumar further said the Bankim had made a mean between *Dharm Tattba* and *Karmatattba* which reflected the western perfectionism and the Bhakti propagated by Bankim, which was a function of the intellect.[94]

RAMESH BASU

Ramesh Basu is another critic of *Dharmatattba* before Bankim Centenary. He also like his predecessors has laid emphasis upon Bankim's power of co-ordination and the western influence in him in his *Bankim Sahitye Manabatar Adarsha*.[95] He said that Bankimchandra had analysed the ancient 'Vaishnaba' and 'Shakta' ideals in the perspective of modern ideals and in that respect, he was much influenced by Shelly's *Nature Religion*.[96] He also said that the new inspiration under western influence in modern India, which Bankimchandra had assimilated had culminated to victory of humanity.[97]

GOPAL HALDAR

The next criticism on *Dharmatattba* and *Anushilan* has been discussed in *'Bankimchandra'*[98] of Gopal Haldar. According to the critic Bankim's *Anushilan Dharma* is a Neo-Religion. Because the Indian religion is here free from the shackle of customs. Gopal Haldar said that the truth Bankim had found out was wider than Matthew Arnold's *'Doctrine of Culture'*—Sweetness and light,[99] wider than the liberalism of 'unity' of Kant, and 'Greatest Good of the Greatest Kumber,[100] of those great men like Mill, was only a part of it. The critic further said that Shelley's remark—'Substance of religion is culture'[101] was deep-rooted in the mind of Bankim and it was evident in *Dharmatattba*. He remarked that the ideas of those foreigners had occupied a great bulk of Bankim's *Anushilan* with which no resemblance were there of our tradition. He clearly said that 'Ecce Homo' and 'Natural Religion' were so sharply echoing in *Dharmatattba* that the familiar ways of Hindu Religion were not found there.[102] Despite all those western influences, the critic agreed that co-ordination is the basis of Bankim. He said that Bankim's patriotism was searching for a National entity; he wanted to give a national identity of the foreign ideals and natural religion. Thus, Bankim has materialised Shelley's humanism. The last three[103] equations of *Anushilan* were the proof of it.

Bipin Chandra Pal and Akshay Kumar Duttagupta, etc. had mentioned of western influence and co-ordination in Bankim but the specialty with Gopal Haldar was that he had established his opinions by appropriate quotations. The simplicity and the style of presentation deserve appreciation.

(H) SHRIMADVAGVADGEETA

DEVIPRASANNA ROYCHOWDHURY

It is Deviprasanna Roychowdhury who for the first time tried to highlight the excellence of Bankim's '*Shrimadvagvadgeeta*' in his essay '*Pratibhar Abatar Bankimchandra*'[104] which was published just after Bankim's death. No other critic before him tried to evaluate this philosophical work of Bankim. He pointed out the high thoughts of Bankim revealed in his *Shrimadvagvadgeeta*, and commented that the interpretation was on original creation of Bankim. According to him, Bankim's interpretation mingled the 'Dialecticism' of Comte and the 'Mayabad' of Barkely and Shankaracharya. He though Bankim's *Shrimadvagvadgeeta* to be a combination of the *Geeta*, the *Bhagvat*, the *Veda*, the *Purana, History, Philosophy, Yoga, Karma, Maya, Kaya, the criticism of Shrimadvagvadgeeta*.[105]

SUMMING UP

All the essays included in this chapter are factual. Some fundamental differences are there in between the critics of the Age of Bankim and that of the Post-Bankim period. The discussions held during the Age of Bankim are all introductory.

But the post-Bankim period, discussions are combination of facts, arguments and psychology. But the critics of all the ages have agreed in one point that Bankim was a great essayist.

References

1. Das, Shrikrishna, *Prapta Granther Sankshipta Samalochana* (Loka Rahasya), Jnyankur, Falgun, 1281 B.S., pp. 186-89.
2. *Ibid.*, p. 187.
3. *Ibid.*
4. *Ibid.*, p. 188.
5. *Bankim Rachanabali*, (Part-II), Sahitya Samsad, Ashwin, 1371 B.S., p. 15.
6. Das, Shrikrishna, *Prapta Granther Sankshipta Samalochana*, p. 189.
7. *Ibid.*
8. Kabiratna, Sureshchandra, *Banga Sahitye Bankimer Prabhab*, Masik Basumati, Bhadra, 1338 B.S., pp. 863-72.
9. *Ibid.*, p. 870.
10. Das, Shrikrishna, *Prapta Granther Sankshipta Samalochana, Bignan Rahasya, Jnyanankur*, 1282 B.S., pp. 863-72.
11. *Ibid.*, p. 327.
12. Ghose, Panchkari, *Kamalakanta*, *Nabyabharat*, Ashwin 1316 B.S.
13. *Ibid.*, (F.N.) p. 333.
14. *Ibid.*, p. 335.
15. *Ibid.*
16. *Ibid.*
17. *Ibid.*, p. 337.
18. *Ibid.*, p. 338.
19. Bhattacharjee, Batuknath, *Bankim Pratibha, Bharatbarshe*, 4th year, Part II, Issue II, Magh, 1323 B.S., pp. 238-39.
20. *Ibid.*, p. 238.
21. Bhattacharjee, Batuknath, *Bankim Pratibha*, *Ibid.*, pp. 238-39.
22. Duttagupta, Akshay Kumar, *Bankimchandra*, 1327 B.S.
23. Duttagupta, Akshay Kumar, *Bankimchandra*, May, 1975, pp. 134-35.
24. *Ibid.*, p. 134.
25. Gangopadhyay, Muralidhar, *Prabandhe Bankim Pratibha*, Sahitya Bhadra, 1329 B.S., pp. 420-23.
26. Gangopadhyay, Muralidhar, op. cit., p. 421.
27. *Ibid.*
28. *Ibid.*, p. 422.

29. *Ibid.*, p. 421.
30. Kabiratna, Suresh Chandra, *Bangasahitye Bankimchandrer Prabhab.* pp. 863-72.
31. *Ibid.*, pp. 863-64.
32. *Ibid.*, p. 864.
33. Ghose, Hemendra Prasad, *Bankimchandra*, 1315 B.S.
34. Togore, R.N., *Krishna Charitra, Sadhana*, Magh-Falgun, 1301 B.S.
35. *Adhunik Sahitya*, Viswa-Bharati, 1365 B.S. p. 68.
36. Tagore, Rabindranath, *Krishna Charitra*, p. 68.
37. *Ibid.*
38. *Ibid.*
39. *Ibid.*, p. 69.
40. *Ibid.*, p. 68.
41. *Ibid.*, p. 83.
42. *Ibid.*, p. 85.
43. *Ibid.*, p. 68.
44. Tagore, Rabindranath, op. cit., p. 83.
45. Sarkar, Madhusudan, *Nrisinqhabatar Bankimchandra, Nabyabharat*, Part-XIII, Issue IX, Poush, 1302 B.S., pp. 449-54.
46. *Ibid.*, p. 454.
47. Dutta, Kalinath, *Bankimchandra, Pradip*, Shraban, 1306 B.S. pp. 206-65.
48. Dutta, Kalinath, op. cit., pp. 264-65.
49. Swami, Shrimat Uttamananda, *Bankimchandra, Nabaprabha*, Chaitra, 1308.
50. *Ibid.*, p. 77.
51. *Ibid.*, p. 82.
52. Bhattacharjee, Surendranath, *Radhakrishna Tattba*. 1313 B.S.
53. Bhattacharjee, Surendranath, op. cit., pp. 9-12.
54. Rakshit, Haran Chandra, *Bangasahitye Bankim*, 3rd End., Poush, 1317 BS.
55. *Ibid.*, p. 242.
56. Pal, Bipin Chandra, *Shirshak Dharma O Art*, Narayan, Agrahayan, 1322.
57. Pal, Bipin Chandra, *Banglar Nadajuger Katha* (Dwadash Katha). Bangabani, Chaitra, 1329 B.S., pp. 225-35
58. Pal, Bipin Chandra, *Shirshat Dharma O Art*, pp. 18-19.
59. Pal, Bipin Chandra, *Banglar Nabajuger Katha*, p. 235.
60. Pal, Bipin Chandra, *Shirshak Dharma O Art*, p. 19.

61. *Bankim Rachanabali*, (Part II), (*Gourdas Babajir Bhikshar Jhuli*). *Sahitya Samsad*, Ashwin, 1371 B.S., p. 270.
62. Duttagupta, Akshay Kumar, *Bankimchandra*, 1327 B.S.
63. Duttagupta, Akshay Kumar, *Bankimchandra*, 2nd edition, May, 1975. pp. 266-67.
64. Basu, Ramesh, *Bankim Sahitye Manabatar Adarsha*, Sabuj Patra, 10th year, Shraban & Bhadra, 1334 B.S., pp. 631-73.
65. Basu, Ramesh, op. cit., p. 671.
66. *Ibid.*, p. 670.
67. Singha, Kailash Chandra, *Bangalar Kalanka (Pratibad)*, *Nabyadharat*, Part II, Issue V, Bhadra, 1291 B.S., pp. 229-26.
68. *Ibid.*, pp. 219-26.
69. Swami, Shrimat Uttamananda, *Nabaprabha*, Part II, Issue II, Chaitra, 1308 B.S., pp. 75-91. '*Bankimchandra*'.
70. Swami, Shrimat Uttamananda, *Bankimchandra*, pp. 87-88.
71. Bondopadhyay, Rakhaldas, *Aitihasik Gabeshanayay Bankimcandra*, Narayan, Baishakh, 1322 B.S., pp. 597-606.
72. *Ibid.*, pp. 597-98.
73. *Ibid.*, pp. 604-05.
74. Shastri, Haraprasad, *Bankimbabu o Uttarcharita, Narayan*, Baishakh, 1322 B.S., pp. 609-20.
75. Shastri, Haraprasad, *Bankimbabu Uttarcharita*, p. 610.
76. *Ibid.*, p. 616.
77. Bhattacharjee, Batuknath, *Bankim Pratibha*, Bharatbarsha, Poush, 1323 B.S., pp. 124-27.
78. *Ibid.*, p. 126.
79. Basu, Purna Chandra, *Dharma Sambandhe Bankimbabur Abhimat. Aryadarshan*, Bhadra, 1291 B.S., pp. 218-23.
80. Basu, Purna Chandra, *Manushyattba*. Aryadarsha, Ashwin, 1291 B.S.
81. Basu, Purna Chandra, *Dharma Sambandhe Bankimbabur Abhimat*, pp. 221-22.
82. Basu, Purna Chandra, *Manushyattba*, pp. 265-71.
83. Mukhapadhyay, Thakurdas, *Sahitya Mangal*, 1295 B.S.
84. *Ibid.*, p. 17.
85. *Ibid.*, p. 3.
86. *Ibid.*, p. 4.
87. Mukhapadhyay, Thakurdas, op. cit., pp. 4-5.
88. Roychowdhury, Deviprasanna, *Bankimchandra O Brahmadharma. Nabyabharat*, Part VII, Issue VII, Kartik, 1296 B.S., pp. 376-83.

89. Pal, Bipin Chandra, *Banglar Nabajuger Katha (Dwadash Katha) Bangabai*, Chaitra, 1329 B.S., pp. 225-35.
90. *Ibid.*, p. 229.
91. *Ibid.*, pp. 231-32.
92. Duttagupta, Akshay Kumar, *Bankimchandra*, 1327 B.S. Rx
93. Duttagupta, Akshay Kumar, *Bankimchandra*, 2nd edn., May 1975, pp. 246-68.
94. *Ibid.*, pp. 253-57.
95. Basu, Ramesh, *Banga Sahitye Manabatar Adarha*, *Subuj Patra*, Shraban & Bhadra, 1334 B.S., pp. 631-73.
96. *Ibid.*, pp. 651-54.
97. *Ibid.*, pp. 671-73.
98. Haldar, Gopal, *Bankimchandra*, Prabashi, Vol. XIII, Part II, Issue II, Agrahayan, 1335 B.S., pp. 200-07.
99. *Dharmatattba*, Chapter I.
100. Haldar, Gopal, *Bankimchandra*, p. 202.
101. *Ibid.*
102. *Ibid.*
103. *Dharmatattba*, (Conclusion).
104. Roychowdhury, Deviprasanna, *Pratibhar Abatar Bankimchandra, Nabhabharat*, Baishakh, 1301 B.S.
105. *Ibid.*, pp. 44-45.

12
Conclusion

In this investigation a comprehensive study has been made of the literary criticism on the works of Bankimchandra Chattopadhyay who has been acclaimed by the posterity as 'Sahitya-Samrat' (Emperor of Literature) of Bengali literature for his invaluable contribution to the writing of novels and essays. Bankimchandra entered the literary scene of Bengal when Bengal Renaissance had already brought tremendous changes in the social and cultural life of Bengal, and revitalized literature, fertilizing it with Western ideas in multi-dimensional aspects. Bankimchandra recreated the Bengali language and made it a fit vehicle for newer ideas. He found the standards of literary judgement and principles of literary criticism, both Eastern and Western in burgeoning stages, and set new critical patterns for posterity. As a matter of fact, Bankim was deeply imbibed in the thoughts and ideas of nineteenth Century England, and under this Western influence he gave a fresh lease of life to literary criticism, in Bengal. Bankim thus not only set up the solid foundation of Bengali criticism, but also heralded a new beginning of modern literary criticism.

Bankim criticism therefore forms the most vital portion of Bengali literary criticism, and in the year of Bankim Centenary, it reached its zenith. But up to the year preceding the Centenary Year much of the archetype of later Bankim criticism was formulated.

Bankim criticism began in the year 1865, and more than seven hundred criticisms appeared during the period under study i.e., upto the year 1937. In fact, the works of Bankim drew the attention of the intellectuals of Bengal, and they felt the urge to express their own opinions in print. As a result, we have a host of critics spreading over a period of nearly seventy-three years. The young and the old, the progressive and the conservative, the journalist and the editor, the politician and the religious leader, the social leader and the teacher, the poet and the prose writer—all exercised their intellect to assess the value of Bankim literature. It is, therefore, self-evident that Bankim literature gave an impetus to literary criticism which has in its turn built up the tradition of critical literature in Bengal.

The study of these seventy-three years of Bankim criticism reveals some special features. First, good criticism did not appear immediately after the publication of the works of Bankim. Secondly, the tone of criticism and the outlook of the critics differed from novel to novel, and essay to essay. This was because of the fact that different problems were posed by different novels and essays. *Kapalkundala* being a fine work of fiction, its criticism appeared to be excellent compared to other works. Again the type and nature of the novel have also influenced numerous critics. Social novels such as *Bishabriksha, Krishnakanter Uil*, etc. posed social questions and the critics raised and discussed those social problems in their criticisms, while spiritual or ethical discussions predominated the criticism of *Devi Chaudhurani* and *Sitaram* which were more ethical than social in nature. It needs be mentioned here that social novels were most widely discussed, and amongst the social novels *Bishabriksha* claims the first place as regards the range of discussion. In the closing year of the pre-Centenary era, *Anandamath* was looked upon with renewed interest against the background of revolutionary Bengal in which the question of 'National Anthem' was ardently discussed. Great emphasis was laid on 'Bandemataram' as it provided the key to unlock the mysteries embodied in *Anandamath*, in view of which the criticism of *Anandamath* was bound to be sentimental and emotional. Thirdly, the shorter novels such as *Indira, Yugolangurio* etc. attracted fewer brilliant critics, probably because of their comparative lack of attractions and novelistic appeal. Fourthly, compared to novels, Bankim's essays attracted lesser number of critics although Bankim contributed in substantial measure to the growth and development of Bengali essay. The reason for comparative neglect of Bankim's essays might be because of its stiffness of treatment and philosophical discussions.

The Bankim criticism for seventy-three years can be divided into five phases for correct appraisal. The period from 1865 to the publication of *Bangadarshan* forms the first phase of Bankim criticism. This synchronises with the brief period of anonymous criticism published in different periodicals of the day. These anonymous criticisms although not strictly literary criticisms paved the way to the growth Bankim criticism by pressing the reader for literary evaluation of Bankim's works.

After the publication of *Bangadarshan* began the second phase of Bankim criticism. It was through *Bangadarshan* that *Bishabriksha*, *Chandrasekhar*, *Krishnakanter Uil* were published. Their publication created much interest in the contemporary literary and social circle, as critics began to discuss the social questions and problems raised in these novels. A host of critics appeared on the scene, a good many upheld the ideals of Bankim while some began to emit venom against Bankim. The greatest contribution of this period of conflicting schools of critics is the enunciation of literary principles. Many of the contemporaries began to defame Bankim. Detractors voiced that Bankim's works had demolished the structure of Hindu ideals and that Bankim was an enemy of society. But the detractors held the scene for a brief period only, and had to retreat finally from the multi-dimensional personality of Bankim and his extraordinary genius. It was then that his followers dominated the literary scene for a longer period.

The period from 1885 till Bankim's demise forms the third phase of Bankim criticism. This period is characterised by changes in Bankim outlook and application of newer principles to evaluate Bankim works. During this period Bankim upheld the ideals of Neo-Hinduism and patriotism through his novels *Anandamath, Devi Chaudhurani* and *Sitaram*. Influenced by the Neo-Hindu ideals and the message of the novels, the critics' discussion during the period centred round religious ideals, racial antagonism and search for fountain heads of ancient classics which were again guided by socio-religious principles.

However, a few critical works such as *Bankimchandra* (Part I & II).[1] *Kundanandini O Suryamukhi*[2], *Banglar Upanyas Lekha,*[3] *Suryamukhi O Kundanandini,*[4] *Kapalkundala O Miranda*[5] etc, rose above the spirit of the Age and set new patterns of criticism by initiating comparative and psychological method of criticism based upon Western value judgement.

The most distinguishing feature of the Bankim Age is that although most of the critics were well versed in western principles, they did not follow these principles blindly. There were some critics who were simultaneously influenced by Western and Eastern value judgements. Some of these critics laid the foundation of classical criticism in Bengali by giving prominence to ancient heritage, adherence to value standards and restraint. However, the exceptional essays such as *Mrinmoyee*[6] *Upanyas Sambandhe Koyekti Katha*[7], *Upanyase Charitra Chitra,*[8] *Noveler Shilpa Ba Kabittba,*[9] etc. do not reveal predominance of classical tendencies. Another characteristic of the period is that most of the criticism are fragmentary in nature. It was only Girija Prasanna Roychowdhury who wrote comprehensive criticism on Bankim literature, amongst which *Monorama*[10] stands out as a supreme example of critical skill in character analysis. Debendra Bijoy Basu laid the foundation of the principle of the art for art's sake.[11]

The first two decades after Bankim's death forms the fourth phase of Bankim criticism. It is a mixed age in which various contradictory or opposing and new ideals and principles from diverse stand points entered the field of criticism. First, there is the profound impact of Bankim's death, and it generated much of eulogist writings. Many of these were intensely emotional and of little literary value. Secondly, the impact of the nationalistic movement coloured the vision of the critics. Thirdly, extensive application of western principle led to the maturity of criticism, and fourthly, the continuation of the past tradition was at its declining phase. Last, but not the least, the entry of Rabindranath into the field of Bankim criticism marks the beginning of a new era in Bankim criticism. The principles enunciated by him opened the doors of pure literary criticism, and his assessment of Bankim and some of his works laid down the standards to be achieved by other critics. It is Tagore who showed that a work of fiction is a work of art and that it has a form, it has a message, it has an appeal, and it must satisfy the literary tastes and temperaments by the manifestations of romance, realism and imaginative treatment of nature and man.

During the first decade of the present century, the tone and temper of Bankim criticism underwent remarkable change under the impact of 'Swadeshi Movement'. Indeed, Bankim and his works were seen in a new light in the context of national resurgence.[12] The critics could not ignore the tremendous impact of Bankim personality behind the upsurge of nationalism. Although a lot of critics viewed his works as an instrument of social reform; a few at least could leave the impression of dispassionate criticism.[13]

The last phase of Bankim criticism, i.e., the last two decades before the Centenary Year forms the matured stage of Bankim criticism. The twenties and thirties were characterised by realism and scientific temper under the impact of the First World War. However, the rapid spread of the spirit of nationalism and nationalistic movement infused emotionalism in critical writings. In this context, Bankim and his works increased in popularity, and due to the profound and widespread influence of the novels of Bankim such as *Durgeshnandini, Kapalkundala, and Bishabriksha, Krishnakanter Uil, Anandamath*, etc. made its impact on the social and cultural life of Bengal. The attempts of critical evaluation were many and various. A host of critics during the period opened new frontiers of literary criticism by attempting at romantic recreation of characters from imaginative point of view.

The last phase of maturity is indeed a period characterised by freedom from conservatism narrowness, blind faith, orthodoxy and ethical bias and it ushered in the era of liberality, progression, creativity and impartiality. The period is also characterised by multiplicity of critical writings with differing tastes and diversity of treatment and interpretation.

A host of distinguished critics contributed to the growth of this healthy and creative trend in Bankim criticism. Liberalism,[14] appropriate application of the literary principles,[15] analysis of the evolutionary process in Bankim works,[16] the raising of the question of art in Bankim works,[17] comparative study of the Bankimchandra and Rabindranath[18] and Bankimchandra and Saratchandra[19] were attempts the evaluation of Bankim's genius.[20] Of course, tendencies of Bankim age did not altogether die away, and reappeared although in a subdued tone in the writing of few critice.[21]

During this long period (1865-1937) of Bankim criticism, few however, attempted to evaluate to mind and art of Bankimchandra as a whole.[22] Most of the critics failed to take into consideration that behind the works of Bankim, there was Bankim, and behind Bankim there was the society, and that society was in a flux, and this accounted for a large volume of fragmentary criticisms on the works of Bankim on piece meal basis. It needs be mentioned here that Bankim was caught up in the social and religious revival of the last part with the introduction of Shalbalini's expiation, Kunda's suicide, the quick disappearance of Rohini from the novel, Gobindalal's rejuvenation etc. through which he sought to glorify a wife's devotion to husband and ancient principles of Hindu cult. Again, it needs be noted that the prevailing tone of romantic idealism in the contemporary western novel also profoundly influenced Bankim. In between the two influences Bankim practiced and propagated the ideals which were not against the principles of life.[23] Bankim's occasional neglect of novel as art-form, his lack of realism and his involvement in social and religious question needs to be viewed in this light, and he should not be blamed for that. Few critics could take such an all-comprehensive view of Bankim's works.

It is through the development of Bankim criticism that the most important types of criticism began to take in definite character in Bengali literature. The classical criticism was introduced by Ramgati Nayaratna, Narendranath Basu, Ramsahaya Vedantasastri, etc. while historical criticism was attempted by Jogesh Chandra Basu, Bipin Chandra Pal, Prafulla Kumar Sarkar etc. The credit of laying the foundation of aesthetic criticism goes to Panchkari Ghose, Gopal Chandra

Bhattacharjee, and Makhanlal Mukhopadhyay etc. Scholastic criticism is predominant in the writings of Lalit Kumar Bandopadhyay, Golak Bihari Mukhopadhyay, Saratchandra Ghosh, Dwijendralal Bhaduri, Jatindra Mohan Singha etc. Psychological approach characterises the criticism of Hemendra Prasad Basu, Hemendra Prasad Ghose, Balai Debsharma etc.

The most striking feature of Bankim criticism during the period under study is the spectacular growth and development of pure literary criticism. It had a good beginning in the hands of eminent critics like Debendra Bijoy Basu, Loknath Chakraborty, Chandrasekhar Mukhopadhyay, Akshay Kumar Sarkar, Girija Prasanna Roychowdhury. Later on, it reached maturity in the hands of Rabindranath Tagore, Hemendra Prasad Ghose. Akshay Kumar Duttagupta Lalit Kumar Bandopadhyay, Bhabesh Chandra Bondopadhyay. In the closing years of the pre-Centenary period Mohitlal Mazumder and Subodh Chandra Sengupta showed signs of immense possibilities of pure criticism in the post-Bankim period.

Although the methods of criticism mentioned above were taking shape during the period under study, no definite school of criticism emerged, in view of which no critic could be grouped under a partial school. Although a particular method of criticism predominated in a writings of a particular critic, most of the critics followed a combination of various methods. Of course, it is an indication of the formative stage of Bankim criticism.

Just as Bankimchandra raised the standard of Bengali literature to the level of Western literature by introducing historical, pseudo-historical, romantic and realistic elements, so also his works inspired volumes of criticisms which were at the initial stages handicapped by the limitation of the age, but finally, Bankim criticism could overcome the psychological inhibitions of the critics through a process of evolution, and thus reached the desired heights in the closing years of the pre-Centenary era.

References

1. Roychowdhury, Girija Prasanna, *Bankimchandra* (Part I & II, 1293, (Part I), 1297 B.S. (Part II)

2. Thakur, Balendra Nath, *Kundanandini O Suryamukhi*, 1958 B.S.
3. Bondopadhyay, Haridas, *Banglar Upanyas Lekhak*, 1295 & 1296 B.S.
4. Thakur, Sudhindra Nath, *Suryamukhi O Kundanandini*, 1298 B.S.
5. Thakur, Sudhindra Nath, *Kapalkundala O Miranda*, 1298 B.S.
6. Mukhapadhyay, Chandrasekhar, *Mrinmoyee*, 1281 B.S.
7. Basu, Debendra Bijoy, *Upanyas Sambandhe Koeti Katha*, 1291 B.S.
8. Basu, Debendra Bijoy, *Upanyaser Charitra Chitra*, 1291 B.S.
9. Basu, Debendra Bijoy, *Noveler Shilpa Ba Kabittba*, 1292 B.S.
10. Roychowdhury, Girija Prasanna, *Monorama*, 1295 B.S.
11. Basu, Debendra Bijoy, *Naveler Shilpa Ba Kabitaba*, 1292 B.S.
12. (a) Sen, Pramatha Nath, *Bankimchandrer Swadesh Prem*, Sahitya, Poush, 1313 B.S., pp. 512-36.
    (b) Trivedi, Ramendra Sundar, *Bankimchandra,* Bangadarshan, Baishakh, 1313 B.S., pp. 20-37.
    (c) Basu, Mankumari, *Bankimchandra Swadeshpriti*, Bharat Mahila, Agrahayan, 1313 B.S. pp. 120-24.
    (d) Pal, Bipin Chandra, Bandemataram, Dharma, Magh 11, 25, 1316 B.S. pp. 5-8.
13. (a) Dutta, Rameshchandra, *Bankimchandra Chattopadhyay*, Nabyabharat, Baishakh, 1301 B.S.
    (b) Dutta, R.C., *Bankimchandra O Adhunik Bangiya Sahiya*, SPP., 1301.
    (c) Sarkar, Shailendra Nath, *Bishabriksha Anushilon*, Prayas, 1899.
    (d) Sarkar, S.N., *Krishnakanter Uil Anushilon*, Prayas, 1899.
    (e) Gupta, Sourindra Mohan, *Yuqmachitra, Somalochanan*, 1309 B.S.
14. (a) Bondopadhyay, Lalit Kumar, *Kabyaudha*, 1323 B.S.
    (b) Bondopadhyay, Lalit Kumar, *Kapalkundala Tattba*, 1322 B.S.
    (c) Bondopadhyay, Lalit Kumar, *Premer Katha*, 1327 B.S.
15. Duttagupta, Akshay Kumar, *Bankimchandra*, 1327 B.S.
16. Sen, Shashanka Mohan, *Bangabani*, 1915.
17. Chattopadhyay, Saratchandra, *Sahitya O Niti*, Poush, 1331 B.S.
18. (a) Bhattacharjee, Gopal Chandra, *Bankimchandra O Rabindranath*, Poush, 1330 B.S.
    (b) Roy, Shibaprasad, *Bankimchandra O Rabindranath*, Magh, 1330 B.S.
19. Sengupta, Subodh Chandra, *Bankimchandra O Saratchandra*, Magh, 1337 B.S.

20. (a) Tagore, Rabindranath, *Bankimchandra*, 1301 B.S.
(b) Mazumder, Mohitlal, *Adhunik Bangla Sahitya*, 1336 B.S.
21. Vedantasastri, Ramsahayay, *Bankimchitra*, 1334 B.S.
22. (a) Tagore, Rabindranath, *Rajsingha,* 1300 B.S.
(b) Tagore, Rabindranath, *Bankimchandra,* 1301 B.S.
(c) Sarkar, Madhusudan, *Nrisingabatar Bankimchandra*, Nabyabharat, 1302.
(d) Rakshit, Haran Chandra, *Bangasahitye Bankim*, 1306 B.S.
(e) Basu, Jitendralal, *Bankimchandra*, Bangadarshan, 1317 B.S.
(f) Bondopadhyay, Chandicharan, *Bangla Sahityer Cramaunnati O Bankimchandra,* Manasi, 1321 B.S.
(g) Sen, Shashanka Mohan, *Bangabani*, 1915.
(h) Duttagupta, Akshay Kumar, *Bankimchandra*, 1327 B.S.
(i) Haldar, Gopal, *Bankimchandra,* Pravasi, 1335 B.S.
23. Bondopadhyay, Dr. Asit Kumar, *Adhunik Bangla Sahityer Sankshipta Itibrittba,* 12th edition, Asharh, 1392 B.S., p. 138.

Bibliography

(A) BENGALI

Al Ajad, Allauddin, *Shilper Sadhana*, 4th edition, Aug. 1974.

Bengal, Yogesh Chandra (ed.), *Bankim Rachanabali* (Upanyas Khanda), Sahitya Samsad, 5th print, Chaitra, 1376 B.S.

Bengal, Yogesh Chandra (ed.), *Bankim Rachanabali* (Part-II), Sahitya Samsad, 3rd Print, Ashwin, 1371 B.S.

Basu, Chandra Nath, *Tridhara*, 1st Edition, 1297 B.S.

——. *Jibankosh*, 1894.

Basu, Nagendra Nath, *Biswakosh* (Part-XVII), 1313 B.S.

Basu, Purnachandra, *Falashruti*, 1314 B.S.

——. *Kabya-Sundari*, Shraban, 1287 B.S.

——. *Sahitya Chinta*, 1303 B.S.

Basu, Rajnarayan, *Bangla Bhasha O Sahitya Bisayak Baktrita*, 1935 Sambat.

Basu, Shankari Prasad, *Vivekananda O Samakalin Bharatbarsha* (Part-I), 3rd print, July, 1979.

——. *Vivekananda O Samakalin Bharatbarsha*, (Part-II), 3rd Print, Aug., 26, 1981.

Basu, Yogesh Chandra, *Bankimchandrer Smriti Chinha* (Kapalkundaler Parikalpanar Kshetra), Knathi-Midnapur, Falgun 1, 1332 B.S.

Bhaja, Haranath, *Suroloke Banger Parichay* (Part-I) 2nd Edition, 1882.

Bhattacharjee, Amitra Sudan, *Bankimchandra O Bangadarshan*, Asharh, 1378 B.S.

——. Bankim Sahitya, April, 1978.

Bhattacharjee, Ashutosh, *Bangla Sahityer Itihas* (Part-II), 3rd edition, 1971.

Bhattacharjee, Ashutosh, *Bankim Upanyaser Shesh Parba*, 1st edn. Ashwin, 1388 B.S.

Bhattacharjee, Bishnupada, *Sahitya Minangsa*, Viswa-Bharati, Shraban, 1355 B.S.

Bhattacharjee, Debendranath, *Bankimchandra*, 1324 B.S.

Bhattacharjee, Debipada, *Upanyaser Katha* (Parba I), 2nd edition, October, 1982.

Bhattacharjee, Dr. Prabhat Kumar, *Bangla Natake Swadeshikatar Prabhab* (1801-1914), 1st Publication, Dolpurnima, 1385 B.S.

Bhattacharjee, Gurudas, *Sahityer Katha*, 1st publication, September, 1959.

Bhattacharjee, Sadhan Kumar, *Shilpatattba Parichay*, June, 1968.

Bhattacharjee, Surendra Mohan, *Radhakrishna Tattba*, 1313 B.S.

Bishi, Pramatha Nath, *Banglar Manisha O Bangla Sahitya* (Part-I), Jagnasa, 1984.

Bishi, Pramatha Nath & Dutta, Bijot Kumar (Ed), *Sahitya Samput*, Viswa-Bharati, 1965.

Biswas, Adhyapak Purnachandra & Mukhapadhyay, Sachindra Nath, *Bangla Bhasha O Sahityer Sankshipta Sar*, 1332 B.S.

Bondopadhyay, Asit Kumar, *Adhunik Bengla Sahityer Sampurna Itibritta.*

——. *Bangla Sahityer Sampurna Itibritta*, 3rd edition, Agrahayan, 1378 B.S.

——. *Samalochanar Katha*, 3rd Print, January, 1971.

Bondopadhyay, Bhabesh Chandra, *Kapalkundala Charitra Samalochana*, Chaitra, 1320 B.S.

Bondopadhyay, Brojendra Nath, *Bangla Samayik Sahitya* (1818-1867) Viswa-Bharati, 1964.

——. *Sahitya Sadhak Charit Mala* (Part-II) B.S.P., 5th Edition, Shraban, 1362 B.S.

——. *Samayik Patra Sampadane Banganari*, Falgun, 1357 B.S.

Bandopadhyay, Brojendra Nath & Das, Sajani Kanta (ed.), *Bibidha* (Bankimchandra Chattopadhyay), B.S.P., 3rd Edn., Bhadra, 1370 B.S.

——. *Balendra Granthabali*, B.S.P. 3rd edn. Sharaban, 1372 B.S.

Bandopadhyay, Charuchandra, *Khrishtiya Unabingsha Shatabdir Banga Sahitye Hasyaras*, Falgun, 1342 B.S.

Bandopadhay, Dr. Shrikumar & Pal, Dr. Prafulla Kumar, *Samalochana Sahitya*, 5th Edition, Poush, 1379 B.S.

Bandopadhyay, Jayanta, *Samalochanar Ruprekha*, Bankim Praba, 1st Publication, August, 1986.

Bandopadhyay, Lalit Kumar, *Kapalkundala Tattba*, 2nd Edn., 1325 B.S.

——. *Kabya Sudha*, 1323 B.S.

——. *Premer Katha*, Jaistha, 1327 B.S.

——. *Sadhu Bhasha Banam Chalit Bhasha*, Magh, 1319 B.S.

——. *Sakhi*, 1328 B.S.

Bondopadhyay, Manoranjan (Pub), *Taraknath Granthabali* (Part-III), 1326 B.S.

Bondopadhyay, Shrikumar, *Banga Sahitye Upanyaser Dhara*, 5th Edition, 1372 B.S.

Bondopadhyay, Tarashankar, *Sahityer Satya* (Amar Jibane Kapal Kundala Bankimer Matripuja).

Bondopadhyay, Yogeshwar, *Bangiya Sahitya Sammilani: Karjyabibarani O Pathita Prabandha* (Bangla Sukumar Sahitya), Year 11, 1315 B.S.

Bankim Parichay, Calcutta University, 1938.

Chakraborty, Radharaman & Mukhapadhyay, Satyakinkar, *Chandrashekhar Tattba*, Baishakh, Purnima, 1339 B.S.

Chattopadhyay, Bankimchandra, *Anandamath*, Bankim Centenary, Edition, B.S.P., 3rd Print, Bhadra, 1364 B.S.

——. *Bishabriksha*, Bankim Centenary Edition, B.S.P., 4th Print, Asharh, 1367.

——. *Chandrasekhar*, Bankim Centenary Edn., B.S.P., 4th Edition, Jaishtha, 1366 B.S.

——. *Devi Chaudhurani*, Bankim Centenary Edition, 5th Edition, jaishtha, 1367 B.S.

——. *Durgeshanandini*, Bankim Centenary Edition, 3rd Print, Chaitra, 1370 B.S.

——. *Indira*, Bankim Centenary Edition, B.S.P., Poush, 1347 B.S.

——. *Kapalkundala*, Bankim Centenary Edn., B.S.P., Asharh, 1345 B.S.

——. *Krishna Charitra*, Bankim Centenary Edition, Shraban, 1348 B.S.

——. *Krishnakanter Uil*, Bankim Centenary Edition, B.S.P., 5th Print, Falgun, 1353 B.S.

——. *Mrinalini*, Bankim Centenary Edition, B.S.P., Poush, 1345 B.S.

——. *Rajani*, Bankim Centenary Edition, 4th Print, B.S.P., Ashwin, 1372 B.S.

——. *Rajsingha*, Bankim Centenary Edn., B.S.P., 3rd Print, Jaishta, 1359 B.S.

——. *Sitaram*, Bankim Centenary Edition, B.S.P., Poush, 1347 B.S.

Chattopadhyay, Bimal Bhusan, *Sahitya Tattber Ruprekha*, Shraban, 1379 B.S.

Chattopadhyay, Haran Chandra, *Bankimchandra*, Falugn, 1338 B.S.

Chattopadhyay, Mahendranath, *Banga Bhashar Itihas* (Part-I), Jaishtha, 1228 Sambat.

Chattopadhyay, Nakul, *Prafulla Kumar Sarkarer Prabandha Sangraha*, Shraban, 1376 B.S.

Chattopadhyay, Shachish Chandra, *Swargiya Bankimchandra Chattopadhyer Jiban Charit*, 1st Edition, 1318 B.S.

——. *Swargiya Bankimchandra Chattopadhyer Jiban Charit*, 2nd Edition, 1322 B.S.

Chattopadhyay, Sudhakar, *Katha Sahityer Bankimchandra*, 2nd Edition, Magh, 1379 B.S.

Chattopadhyay, Sunit Kumar (Editor), *Haraprasad Rachanabali* (Prathama Sambhar), 1st Publication, Agrahayan, 1366 B.S.

——. *Haraprasad Rachnabali* (Dwitiya Sambhar), 1st Publication, Poush, 1366 B.S.

——. *Bangla Bhasha O Bangla Sahityer Katha*, 1917.

Choudhury, Narayan, *Adhunik Sahityer Mullyayan*, 1st Publication, Bhadra, 1365 B.S.

Choudhury, Pramatha, *Prabandha Sangraha*, Viswa-Sahitya, April, 1974.

Choudhury, Shibdas (ed.), *Sabujpatra Patrika Suchi* 1978.

Das, Debajyoti, *Sahitya Parishad Patrikar Lekhak Suchi* (1301-75 B.S.), B.S.P., Baishakh, 1378 B.S.

Das, Kishori Mohan (Pub), *Banga Sahitye Bankim* (Mrinalinir Samalochana), Writeen by Editor, Rongpur Darpan, 2nd Edition, Rongpur, 1319 B.S.

Das, Shrish Chandra, *Sahitya Sandarshan*, 5th Edition, 1948.

Dasgupta, Prafulla Kumar, *Upanyas Sahitye Bankim*, 2nd Edition, Rahs Purnima, 1378 B.S.

Dasgupta, Shanti Kumar (ed.), *Nabinchandra Rachanabali* (Part-I), 1st Pub., Baishakh, 1381 B.S.

Dasgupta, Shanti Kumar, *Sahitya O Alochana*, Shraban, 1357.

Dasgupta, Shanti Bhushan, *Bangla Sahityer Nabayug*, 6th Edition Asharh, 1372 B.S.

Dasgupta, Shanti Bhushan, *Sahityer Swarup*, 2nd Edition, Magh, 1353 B.S.

Deb, Ashutosh, *Nutun Bangla Abhidhan*, 1351 B.S.

Devi, Sarojini, *Adarsha Jibani*, 1909.

Dutta, Bhabatosh, *Chintanayak Bankimchandra*, 2nd Edition, January, 1973.

Dutta, Hirendra Nath, *Darshanik Bankimchandra*, 1347 B.S.

Duttagupta, Akshay Kumar, Bankimchandra, 1st Publication, Dhaka, Shraban, 20. 1327 B.S.

Duttagupta, Akshay Kumar, *Bankimchandra*, 2nd Edition, May, 1975.

Eey, Ekkadi, *Shishu Bankim* (Part-I), 1919.

Ghosh, Ajit Kumar, *Bangla Sahitye Hasyaraser Dhara*, 2nd Edition, 1968.

Ghosh, Binay (Ed.), *Samayik patre Banglar Samaj Chitra* (Part-I), January, 1962.

Ghosh, Binay (Ed.), *Samayik patre Banglar Samaj Chitra* (Part-IV), 1966.

Ghosh, Hemendra Prasad, *Bankimchandra*, Chaitra 7, 1884 Shakabda.

Goswami, Achyut, *Bangla Upanyaser Dhara*, 2nd Edition, 1375 B.S.

Gupta, Bipin Behari, *Puratan Prasanga*, Shraban 6, 1320 B.S.

——. *Pratibha*, 6th Edition, 1319 B.S.

Gupta, Sushil Kumar, *Unabingsha Shatabdite Banglar Nabajagaran*, 2nd Edition, 1977.

Haque, Abdul, *Sahitya O Swadhinata, Bangla Academi*, Dhaka, May, 1974.

Kabirana, Peary Mohan, *Geetabali*, 2nd Edition, 1293 B.S.

Kabyasisharad, Kaliprasanna (Fakirchand Baul), *Bangiya Samalochak* (Kabya), 1287 B.S.

Kanjilal, Shibendra Nath (Publisher), *Samalochana Sangraha*, 8th Edition, Calcutta University, 1965.

Karim, Rejaul, *Bankimchandra O Musalman Samaj*, May 18, 1944.

Kundu, Ashok, *Bankim Abhidhan* (Panyasa Khanda), 1st Publication, 1976.

——. *Bankim Abhidhan* (Part-II), 1st Pub., Baishakh 25, 1384 B.S.

——. *Bankim Abhidhan* (Part-III), 1st Pub., May 4, 1980.

——. *Bankim Upanyaser Upadhan Bichar*, 1st Publication, Baishakh 1, 1382 B.S.

Lahiri, Dr. Kartik, *Bangla Upanyaser Rupakalpana O Prakriti*, Jaishtha, 1379 B.S.

Mazumder, Kedarnath, *Gadya Sahitya*, 1908.

——. *Bangla Samayik Sahitya* (Part-I), July, 1917.

Mazumder, Mahendranath, *Sahitya O Samaj Athaba Bankimbabur Bishabriksha*, 1303 B.S.

Mazumder, Mohitlal, *Bankim Baran*, 2nd Print, Kartik, 1371 B.S.

Mazumder, Mohitlal, *Sahitya Bichar*, Vidyadoy edition, Ashwin, 1337 B.S.

Mazumder, Mohitlal, *Sahitya Bitan*, 3rd Edn. Bhadra, 1368 B.S.

Mazumder, Ujjal (editor), *Bangla Kabye Pashchatya Prabhab*, 1st Publication, 1375 B.S.

Mishra, Manilal, *Shantiniketan* (Introduction), 1321 B.S.

Mitra, Dr. Arun Kumar, *Amrit Lal Basur Jibani O Sahitya*, 1st Publication, January, 1970.

Mitra, Shib Ratan, *Bangiya Sahitya Sebak*, 1338 B.S.

Mukhapadhyay, Arun Kumar, *Bangla Samalochanar Itihas*, 1st Publication, Shraban, 1372 B.S.

Mukhapadhyay, Harimohan (Editor), *Bangabhashar Lekhak*, Bhadra, 19, 1311 B.S.

Mukhapadhyay, Hemchandra, *Manab-Prakriti* (Swargiya Bankim Chandrer Bishabriksha Abalambane Rachita), Chuchura, Jaishatha, 13, 1328 B.S.

Mukhapadhyay, Prashanta Behar, *Bankim Sahitye Samaj O Sadhana*, 1st Edition, New Delhi, 1967.

Mukhapadhyay, Sukha Ranjan, *Adhunik Bangla Sahityer Itihas*, 3rd Edition, January, 1968.

Mukhapadhy, Tarapada, *Adhunik Bangla Kabya* (Pratham Parba), 5th Edition, Asharh, 1374 B.S.

Mukhapadhyay, Thakurdas, *Sahitya Mangal*, 1295 B.S.

Mukhapadhyay, Upendra Ch., *Charitrabhidhan*, 2nd Edition, Dhaka, 1318 B.S.

Mukhapadhyay, Haribandhu & Dasgupta, Shakti Kumar (ed), *Nabinchandra Rachanabali* (Part-II), Baishakh-1, 1382 B.S.

Nag, Ramendra Narayan, *Unabingsha Shatabdite Bangla.*

Nyayratna, Ramgati, *Bangla Bhasha O Bangala Sahitya Bisayak Proztam*, 2nd Edition, Chuchura, 1894 B.S.

Poddar, Aurobinda, *Bankim Manas*, July 20, 1951.

Rakshit, Haran Chandra, *Bangla Sahitye Bankim*, 3rd edn. 24 Pargana, Poush, 1317 B.S.

——. *Victoriya yuge Bangla Sahitya*, 24 Pargana, Ashwin, 1318 B.S.

Roy, Jnanendralal, *Prabanbha Lahari*, 1303 B.S.

Roy, Kalidas, *Sahitya Prosanga* (Part-I, 1933)

Roy, Mukut Choudhury, *Lipikoushal Baishisthya*, Asharh 1, 1343 B.S.

Roy, Girija Prasanna, Bankim Chandra (Durgesh Nandini), (Bankimchandra Anandamath, Devi Choudhurani, Sitaram), 1857 B.S.

——. (Bankimchandra Krishnakanter Uil O Chandrasekhar), 1293 B.S.

——. Kapalkundala, 1319 B.S.

Roychoudhri, Girija Shankar, *Sri Aurobindo O Bangla Swadeshi Yog*, 1st Edn., Aug., 15 1956.

Sanyal, Bhabani Gopal, *Aristoteler Poetics O Sahitatattba*, 1st Pub. Shraban, 1375 BS.

Sarkar, Ajarchandra, *Bankimchandrer Bhasha*, Calcutta University, Jan. 25, 1949.

Sarkar, Gangacharan, *Banga Sahitya O Bangabhasha Bisoye Baktrita*, Dhaka, 1888.

Sen, Dinesh Chandra, *Gharer Kotha O Juga Sahitya*, Baishakh 1, 1329 B.S.

Sen, Shashanka Mohan, *Bangabani*, Dhaka Albert Library, 1915.

Sen, Sukumar, *Bangla Sahityer Itihas*, Part II, 3rd Edition, 1971.

——. *Sarat Sahitya Sangrha* (Akhanda), Ananda Publishers, Ratha Jatra, 1392 B.S.

Sen, Suresha Chandra, *Kabya Katha*, Bankim Chandra O Musalman Samaj), 1909.

Sengupta, Nandagopal, *Satabdi O Sahitya*, Kartik, 1348 B.S.

Sengupta, Dr. Pradyut, *Banglar Samajik Jiban O Natya Sahitya*, 1st Pub., Kojari Lakshmi Purnima, 1383 B.S.

Sengupta, Dr. Satyaprosad, *Pachytya Somalochanar Dhara*, 1st pub., 1966.

Sengupta, Subodh Chandra, *Somalochana Sanchayan*, 1st pub., Aug. 1976.

——. Bangla Somalochana Parichay, 1st Edition, 1970.

——. Bankimchandra, 2nd Edition, Bhahadra 2, 1392 B.S.

Sengupta, Subodh Chandra, Basu, Anjali, *Samsad Banglali Charitrabhidhan*, 1st pub., May 1976.

Shastri, Shibnath, *Ramtanu Lahri O Tatkalin Banga Samaj*, 1904.

Shome, Surya Kumar, *Kundanandini* (Abhinaba Kabya), Bhabanipur, 1227 B.S.

Singha, Bimal Chandra, *Bankim Konika*, Asharh 13, 1348 B.S.

Singha Roy, Jibendra, *Sahitye Rammohan Theke Rabindra Nath* (Part II), Ashwin, 1368 B.S.

Tagore, Rabindranath, *Adhunik Sahitye*, Viswabharati, Kartik, 1365 B.S.

——. *Banakimchandra*, Viswabharati, 1972.

——. *Sankalan*, Viswabharati, 1973.

——. *Panhaabhut*, Viswabharati, Chaitra, 1373 B.S.

Thakur, Kshitindranath, *Art O Sahitya*, Magh, Sripanchami 1329 B.S.

Trivedi, Ramendra Sundra, *Charita Katha*, 1320 B.S.

Vidyabhusan, Yogendranath, *Samalochana Mala* (Bishabriksha), 1884.

(B) ENGLISH

Abocromdie, Laselles, *Principles of Literary Criticism*, Bombay, 1962.

Basu, Nitish, *Literature and Criticism*, May, 1963.

Bywater, Ingram, *Aristotle on the Art of Poetry*, Great Britain, 1947.

Croce, Endotto, *The Essence of Aesthetic*, London, 1921.

Gardner, Helen, *The Business of Criticism*, Oxford, 1952.

George, A.G., *Critics and Criticism*, Bombay, May, 1969.

Ghose, D.N., *Principles of Literary Criticism*, Wowalior, 1970.

Handy, William J. & Westbrook, Max, *Twentieth Century Criticism: The Major Statements*.

Krieger, Murry, *Theory of Criticism*, London, 1976.

Richards, I.A., *Practical Criticism*, London, 1978.

Sears, Lorenzo, *Principle & Methods of Literary Criticism*, New York & London, 1898.

Wellek, Rene & Warren, Austin, *Theory of Literature*, London: 1955.

——. *Concepts of Criticism*, London, 2nd Print, Jan. 1964.

Wimsalt, William. K.J. & Brooks, Cleanth, *Literary Criticism*, Indian Edition, 1964.